Carol

BRIEF FORMS OF GREGG SHORTHAND

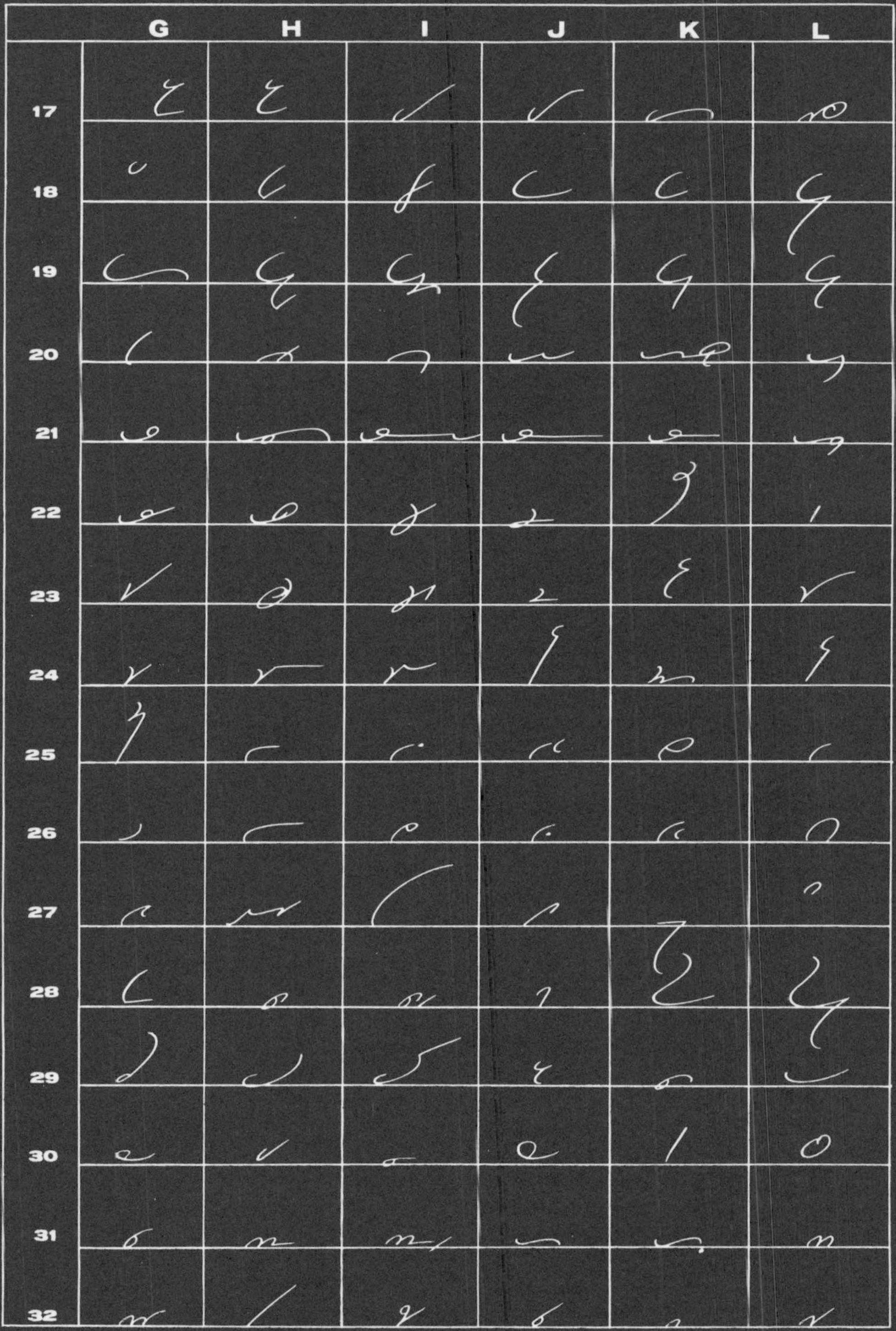

GREGG
SPEED BUILDING
FOR COLLEGES

SIMPLIFIED
SECOND EDITION

GREGG SPEED BUILDING

JOHN R. GREGG

CLYDE I. BLANCHARD
Office Management Consultant, Formerly Professor of Business Education, University of Tulsa

WOODROW W. BALDWIN
Director, School of Business, Simmons College

Shorthand written by CHARLES RADER

FOR COLLEGES

SIMPLIFIED, SECOND EDITION

GREGG PUBLISHING DIVISION
McGraw-Hill Book Company, Inc.
New York Chicago San Francisco Dallas Toronto London

GREGG SPEED BUILDING FOR COLLEGES, SIMPLIFIED, SECOND EDITION

June 1958-RD

Library of Congress Catalog No. 58-6685

Published by GREGG PUBLISHING DIVISION
McGraw-Hill Book Company, Inc.
Printed in the United States of America

Preface

Gregg Speed Building for Colleges, Simplified, Second Edition, is the latest book in the successful Gregg Speed Building series, the first volume of which appeared in 1932.

The authors have retained, with slight modifications, the five-lesson shorthand skill development and transcription cycle that has been a distinctive feature of all editions in the *Gregg Speed Building* series. They have also incorporated many of the suggestions received from college teachers all over the country. The result is a book that will make the teaching of advanced shorthand and transcription in colleges even more effective.

The Second Edition of *Gregg Speed Building for Colleges,* Simplified, is divided into three parts – which are further divided into 16 chapters, each chapter containing five lessons. At the suggestion of many teachers, the number of lessons has been reduced to 80, since that number more nearly meets the requirements of most college courses in advanced shorthand and transcription.

Part I, consisting of Lessons 1 through 5, contains a complete review of all the brief forms of Gregg Shorthand.

Part II, consisting of Lessons 6 through 40, is devoted to departmental dictation and transcription, in which the student works as a stenographer for seven different departments of a business.

Part III, consisting of Lessons 41 through 80, is devoted to vocational dictation and transcription, in which the student works for eight different types of businesses or industries and is given an opportunity to become familiar with the technical vocabularies used in those businesses or industries.

Chapter Openings

Each chapter in Part II opens with two types of improvement drills:

1. Spelling Improvement Drills, in which spelling rules are given, followed by a number of words illustrating the rules.

2. Penmanship Improvement Drills, designed to refine the student's style of writing.

Each chapter in Part III contains a list of the technical words and expressions that apply to the business or industry which is the subject of that chapter. Each term is defined in layman's language, and the shorthand outline for the term is given.

The Cycle

Each chapter, except the first – which is devoted to a complete review of the brief forms of Gregg Shorthand – is organized as a five-lesson speed development and transcription cycle. Each lesson in the cycle has a specific objective.

First Lesson – Building Transcription Skill. This lesson presents a number of the nonshorthand elements of transcription, such as punctuation, typing style, etc. They are called "Transcription English Pointers." The lesson also contains a number of business letters in shorthand that illustrate these Transcription English Pointers.

Second Lesson – Mastering Shorthand Theory. This lesson provides an intensive review, in the form of word lists, of the word beginnings and word endings and the major principles of Gregg Shorthand. Many of the words given in these lists are used in the shorthand practice material included in the lesson in the form of business letters and articles. The articles, entitled "Hints for Success," contain suggestions and information to help the student become a more efficient office worker.

Third Lesson – Building Phrasing Skill. Through helpful analogical drills, this lesson teaches the student to take advantage of the speed values of phrasing. Many of the phrases are used in the business letters in shorthand that follow the phrasing drills.

Fourth Lesson – Progressive Speed Building. The purpose of the Progressive Speed Builders is to force the student to write beyond his present speed. Two types of Progressive Speed Builders are provided:

1. Half-Minute Speed Builder. This consists of letters in type in which the speed of each succeeding half minute is increased.

2. Minute Speed Builder. This consists of letters in type in which the speed of each succeeding minute is increased. The speeds of the Minute Speed Builders are slightly lower than those of the Half-Minute Speed Builders.

Each Progressive Speed Builder is preceded by a shorthand preview, followed by the key, of the more difficult words and phrases in the material to be dictated.

The speed range of both the Half-Minute and the Minute Progressive Speed Builders is increased as the student's shorthand skill develops.

In addition, each fourth lesson contains either business letters or interesting, informative articles in shorthand for the student to read and copy.

Fifth Lesson – Building Sustained Speed. The purpose of this lesson is to help the student develop endurance. It consists of a five-minute take in type, preceded by a shorthand preview. Each fifth lesson also contains material in shorthand for the student to read and copy.

Other Features

1. *Gregg Speed Building for Colleges,* Simplified, Second Edition, was designed and illustrated by a well-known artist. This "new look" helps to create and hold the student's interest as he strives to build his shorthand speed.

2. The word count is given at the end of each shorthand letter and article for the convenience of the student in timing his reading and copying.

3. A chart containing all the brief forms of Gregg Shorthand is given on the inside front cover; a chart of useful phrases is given on the inside back cover.

4. A Student's Transcript, containing a counted key to all the shorthand in the text, is available to the student.

ACKNOWLEDGMENTS:

The authors wish to express their gratitude to the many teachers whose suggestions have been so helpful and to Mr. Charles Rader for the beautiful shorthand notes.

Clyde I. Blanchard
Woodrow W. Baldwin

Contents

Suggestions to Students

The exercises and drills in this text are designed to help you become a stenographer who can take dictation at a high rate of speed and transcribe rapidly and accurately at the typewriter. The extent to which these exercises and drills will contribute to your shorthand growth, however, will depend on how efficiently you practice them. Unless your teacher instructs you otherwise, follow the procedures suggested here for practicing the various drills.

Spelling Improvement Drills

The stenographer who cannot submit transcripts that are free from spelling errors is not long for the business office! Make every effort, therefore, to become a good speller. If there is the slightest doubt in your mind about the spelling of a word, look it up; it is better to be safe than sorry. In practicing the Spelling Improvement Drills, read the spelling rules carefully to be sure you understand them. Then *spell aloud* all the illustrative examples. If a typewriter is available, type the examples two or three times, spelling aloud as you type.

Shorthand Penmanship Drills

The speed with which you transcribe will depend a great deal on how well you can read your notes – and notes that are not written with careful regard to accurate proportion are not easy to read. The penmanship drills are designed to refine your writing style so that you will automatically make your short strokes very short, your long strokes very long, your curves deep and narrow, your straight lines absolutely straight, your circles either very large or very small.

Follow this procedure with each penmanship drill:

1. With the aid of the key if necessary, read the outlines that constitute the drill.

2. Write the first line of the drill, striving for accuracy of outline rather than for speed of execution. Write each form as slowly as necessary (but do not draw) to make an outline in which the proportions are accurate.

3. Write the same line a second time, striving to improve on the forms you wrote first.

4. Follow this same procedure with the remaining lines in the drill.

Transcription English Pointers

As you no doubt realize, your employer will expect you to punctuate correctly and to observe accepted forms of typing style. The Transcription English Pointers are designed to teach you to punctuate correctly and to acquaint you with the conventions of typing style that are accepted by authorities in English.

You will find the following procedure helpful in getting the most out of each Transcription English Pointer:

1. Read the explanation of each pointer to be sure you understand its application.

2. Read the illustrative examples, referring to the type key whenever you cannot read a shorthand outline.

3. Make a shorthand copy of the illustrative examples, inserting the necessary punctuation.

Shorthand Reading and Writing Exercises

Reading and copying shorthand from good models plays an important part in the development of your shorthand speed. Therefore, every lesson will contain some printed shorthand for you to read and copy. In practicing these exercises, follow this suggested procedure:

1. Always read, aloud if possible, each exercise before making a copy of it. This is important!

2. When you cannot immediately read an outline, spell it. If the spelling does not give you the meaning of the outline, refer to the Student's Transcript if one is available to you. If not, write the outline on a slip of paper and find out its meaning in class the next day.

Do not spend more than a few seconds trying to decipher any outline you cannot read.

3. Make a shorthand copy of the exercises, first saying aloud a convenient group of words and then writing it.

Word and Phrase Lists

In the second lesson of each chapter you will find a list of words illustrating a major word-building principle of Gregg Shorthand; in the third lesson, a list of common phrases.

1. Read through each list aloud as rapidly as you can. It should not take you longer than a minute or two to read each list because most of these outlines are already familiar to you. Refer to the key that follows the drill the moment you cannot read an outline.

2. Make a shorthand copy of the list, saying each outline aloud as you write it.

Vocabulary Previews

In the fourth and fifth lessons of each chapter you will find speed builders in type, which will be dictated to you in class. At the head of each speed builder is a shorthand preview. This preview contains the more difficult words and phrases that appear in the speed builder. By practicing these previews beforehand, you will be able to write these speed builders from dictation without difficulty because all the causes of hesitation will have been removed.

Here is the way you should practice the previews:

1. Read the outlines in the preview aloud.

2. Make a shorthand copy of them, saying each word or phrase aloud as you write it.

Speed Builders

Your teacher will no doubt give you specific instructions on how to handle the Progressive Speed Builders in each fourth lesson and the Sustained Speed Builders in each fifth lesson. Your teacher may ask you either to make a shorthand copy of the speed builders or simply to practice the previews, and then to take them in dictation in class the next day.

Technical Word Studies

At the beginning of each chapter in Part III, you will find a Technical Word Study. This Study contains a partial list of expressions frequently used in the business or industry that is the subject of the material in the chapter that you are studying. The definition and shorthand outline are given for each expression.

You cannot, of course, hope to remember all the terms; however, you can develop some familiarity with them if you will:

1. Spell each word aloud.
2. Read the definition.
3. Write the shorthand outline two or three times.
4. Read the outlines you have written.

One Last Suggestion

The personal use of shorthand will do much to increase your dictation speed. If you use only one classroom period and one study period a day to build shorthand speed and then write in longhand everything else that you write the rest of the day, you will be using more longhand than shorthand every day. This makes it difficult for you to keep the longhand out of your mind when you hear words dictated to you. If you will write all your personal memoranda in shorthand, you will soon be *thinking in shorthand;* and you will find that your shorthand speed will be greatly increased.

If you have not already been doing so, substitute your shorthand for longhand wherever possible.

The best of success to you in your quest for shorthand and transcription skill.

PART I Brief-Form Review

Part I contains a complete review of the brief forms of Gregg Shorthand. In the drills and letters of these lessons every brief form, or a derivative of it, appears at least once; many of the brief forms appear several times.

1

Brief Forms and Derivatives

Lesson 1

BRIEF-FORM REVIEW

Derivative Drill

There are 39 brief forms and derivatives in this list. Can you read the entire list in 30 seconds or less?

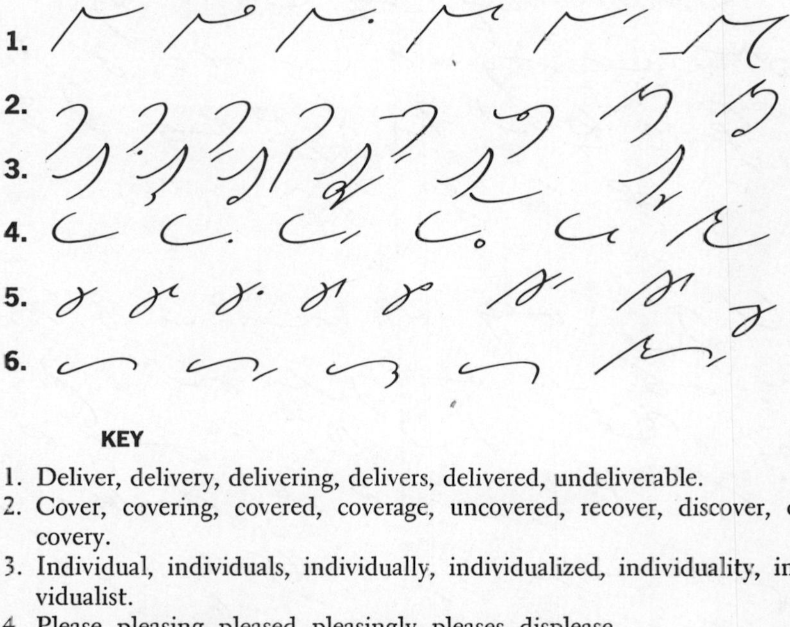

KEY

1. Deliver, delivery, delivering, delivers, delivered, undeliverable.
2. Cover, covering, covered, coverage, uncovered, recover, discover, discovery.
3. Individual, individuals, individually, individualized, individuality, individualist.
4. Please, pleasing, pleased, pleasingly, pleases, displease.
5. Satisfy, satisfies, satisfying, satisfaction, satisfactorily, dissatisfied, dissatisfaction, unsatisfactory.
6. Organize, organized, organizes, organization, disorganized.

Brief-Form Letters

1.

(125)

2.

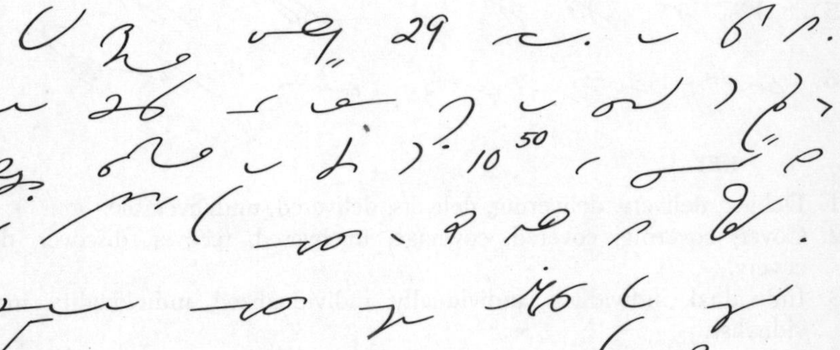

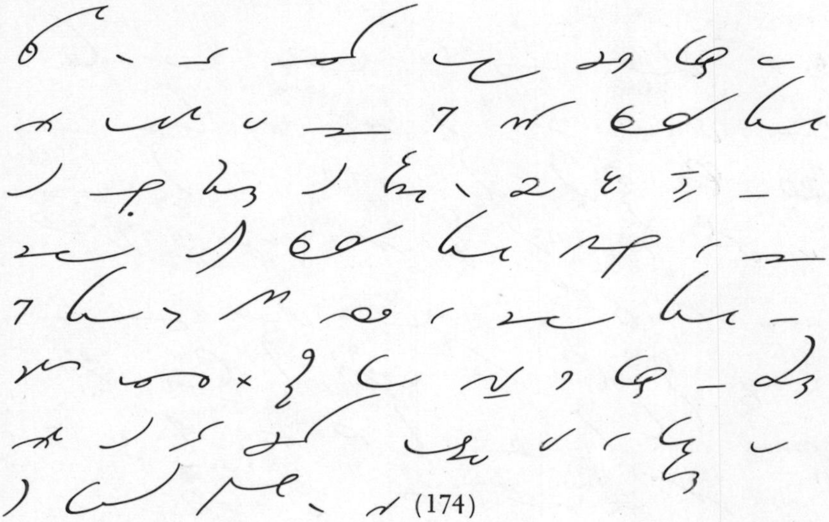

(174)

3.

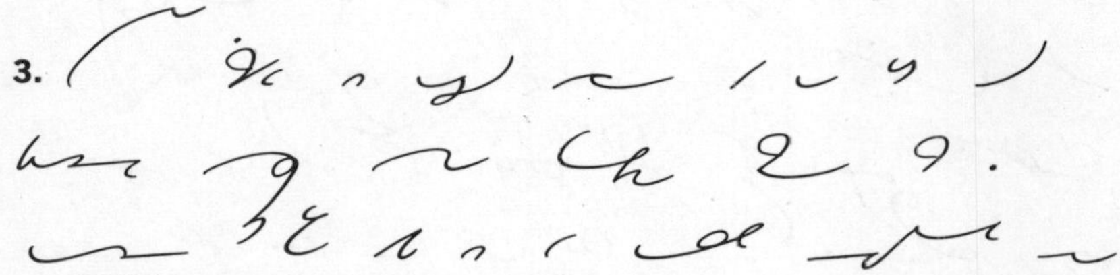

(103)

4.

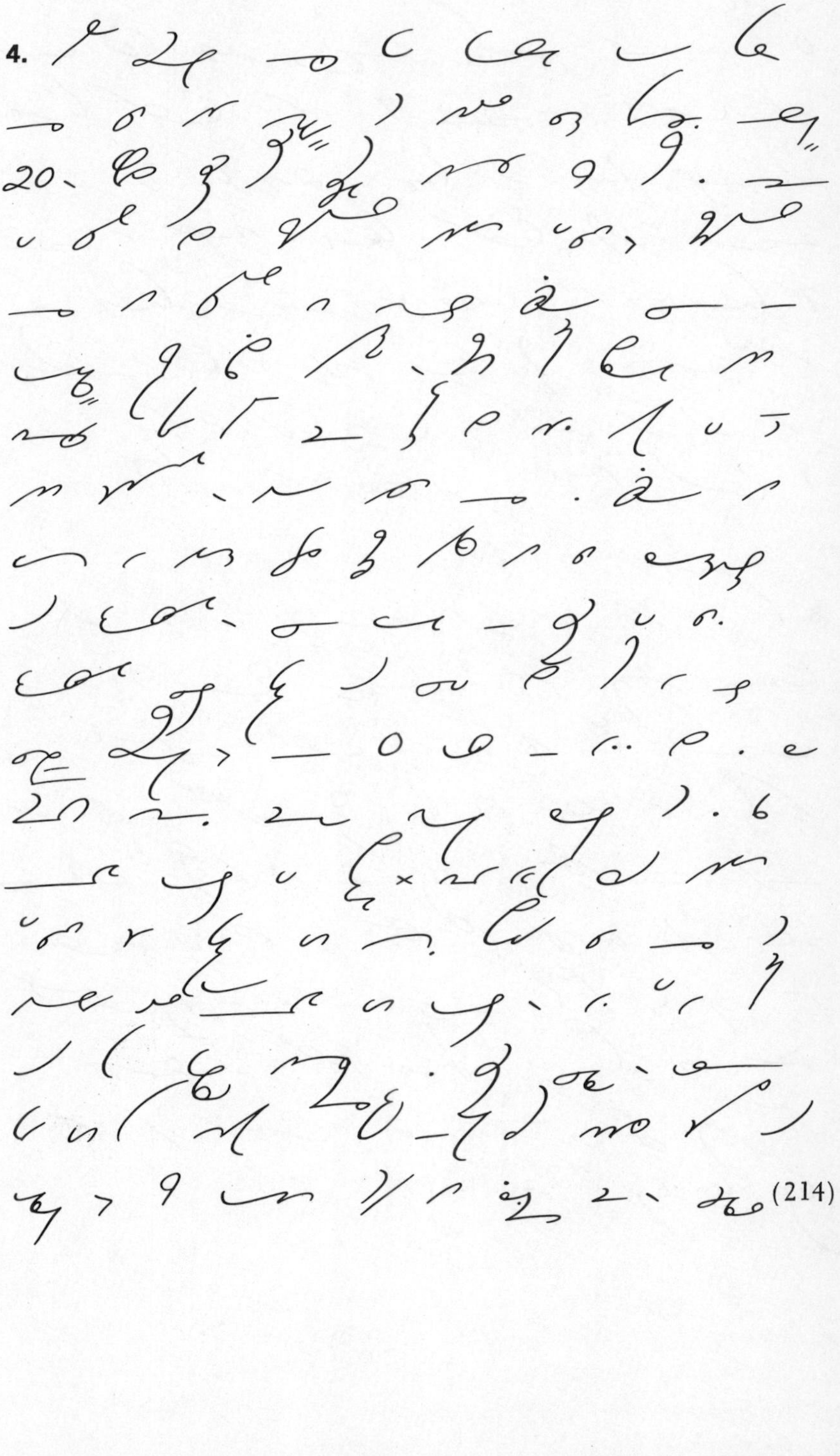

(214)

5.

(138)

6.

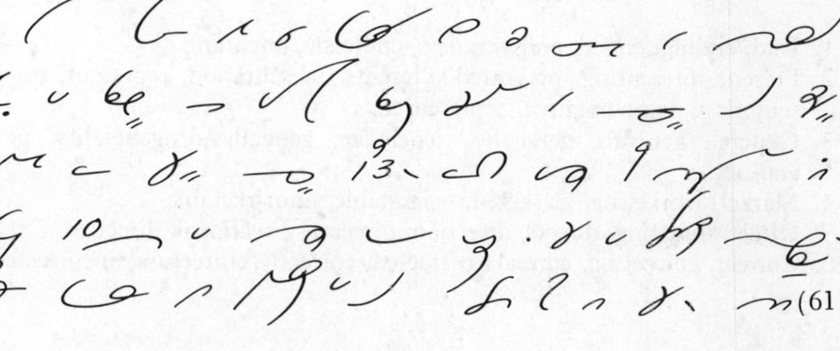

(61)

Lesson 2

BRIEF-FORM REVIEW

Derivative Drill

There are 42 brief forms and derivatives in this list. Can you read the entire list in 30 seconds or less?

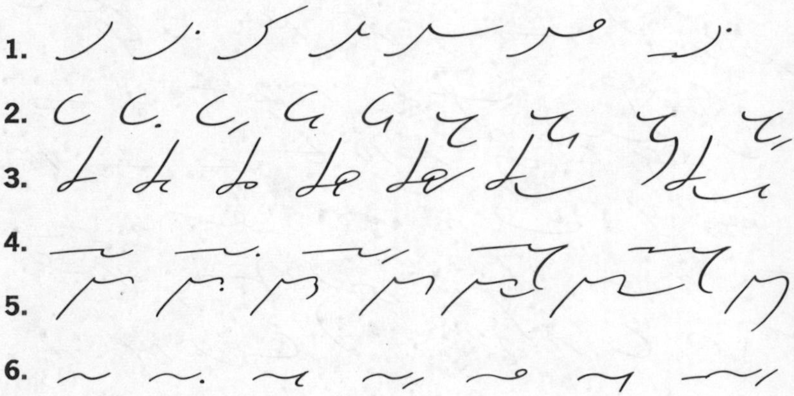

KEY

1. End, ending, ended, ends, endless, endlessly, unending.
2. Present, presenting, presented, presents, presentation, represent, representation, representative, represented.
3. General, generals, generally, generalize, generalized, generality, generalities.
4. Market, marketing, marketed, marketable, unmarketable.
5. Direct, directing, directs, direction, director, directional, directive.
6. Correct, correcting, corrects, corrected, correctly, correction, uncorrected.

Brief-Form Letters

7.

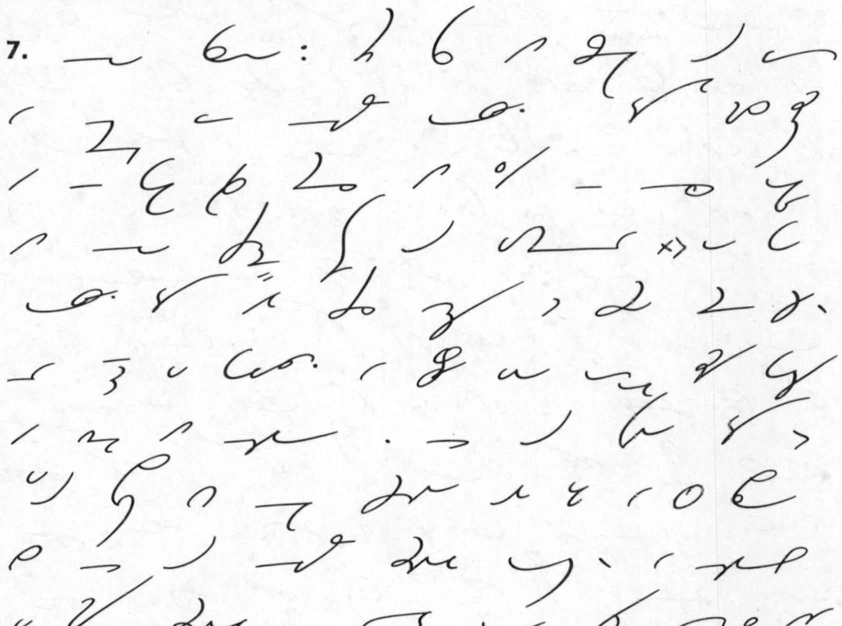

(201)

8. 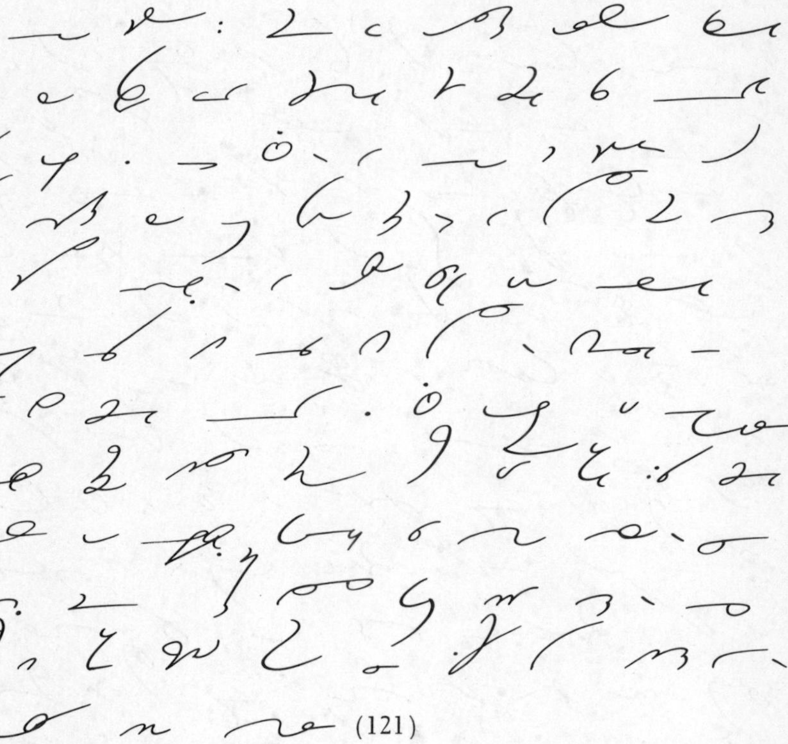

(121)

9. 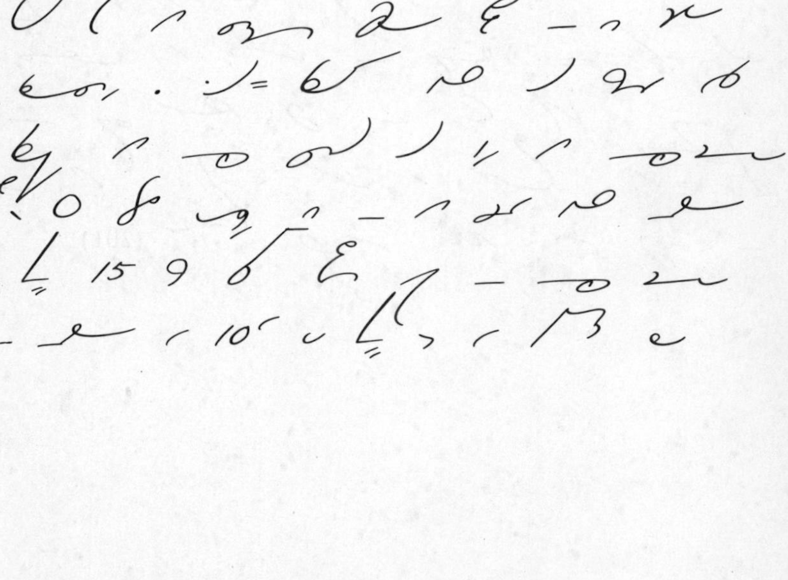

(176)

10.

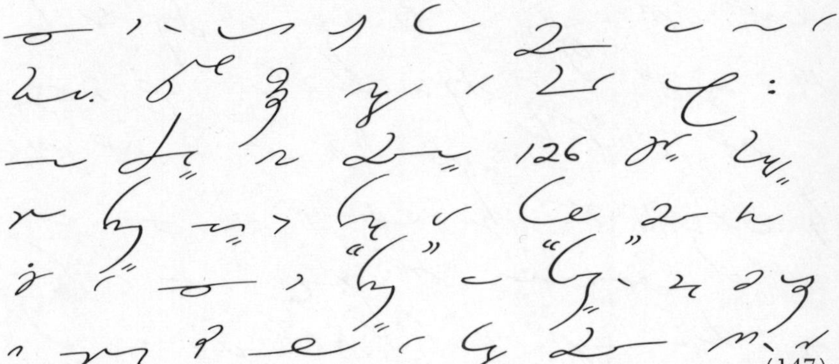

(147)

11.

(118)

Lesson 3

BRIEF-FORM REVIEW

Derivative Drill

There are 42 brief forms and derivatives in this list. Can you read the entire list in 25 seconds or less?

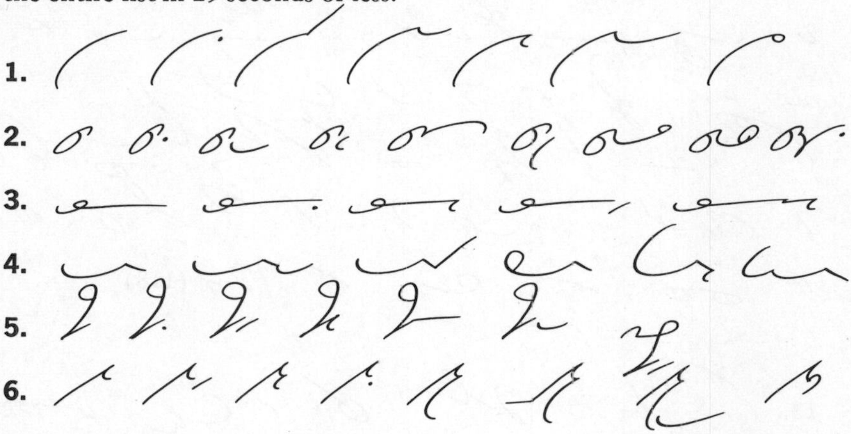

KEY

1. Time, timing, timed, timer, times, timeless, timely.
2. Out, outing, outer, outings, outgo, output, outlet, outright, outstanding.
3. Remember, remembering, remembers, remembered, remembrance.
4. Long, longer, longed, along, belongs, prolong.
5. Advertise, advertising, advertised, advertises, advertisement, advertiser, unadvertised.
6. Desire, desired, desires, desiring, desirable, undesirable, desirability, desirous.

Brief-Form Letters

12. 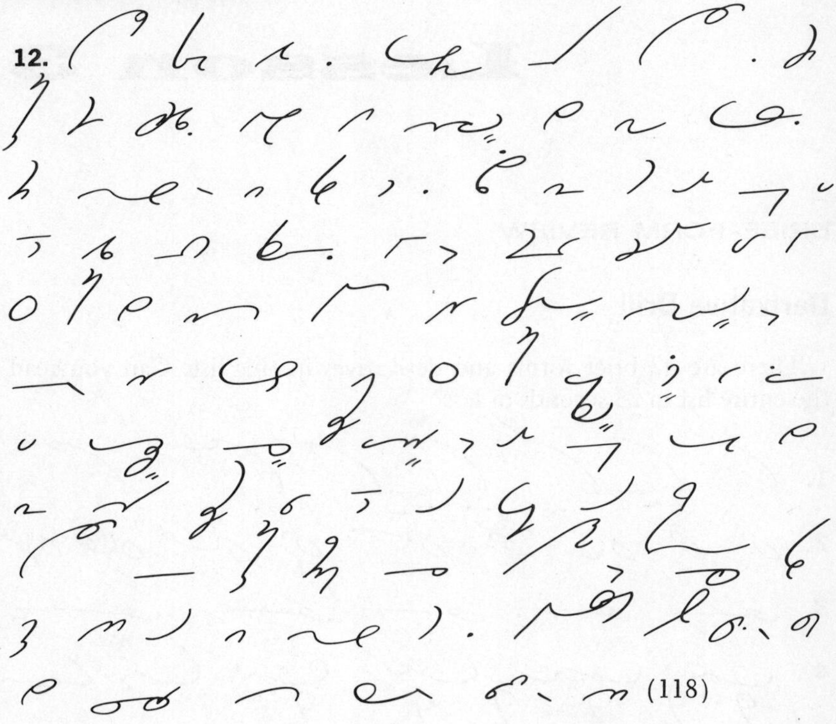 (118)

13. 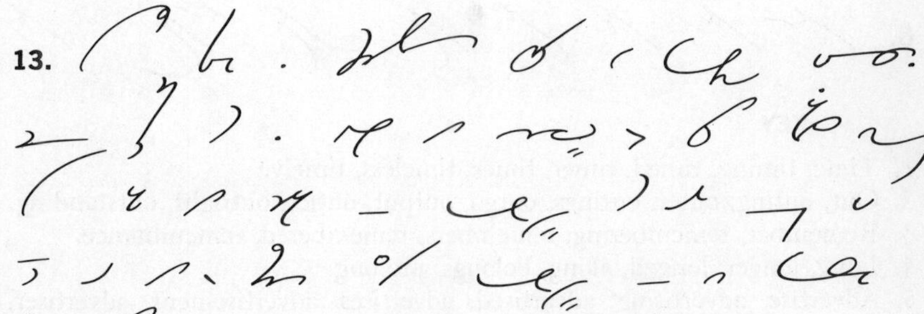

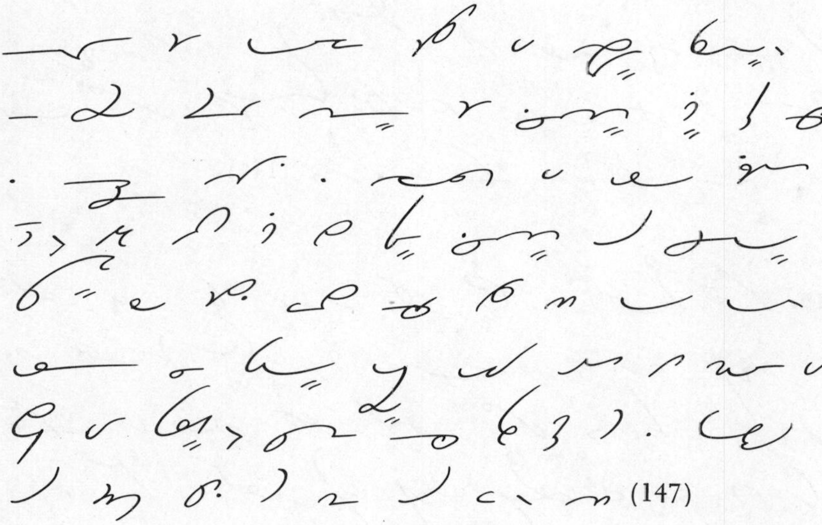

(147)

14.

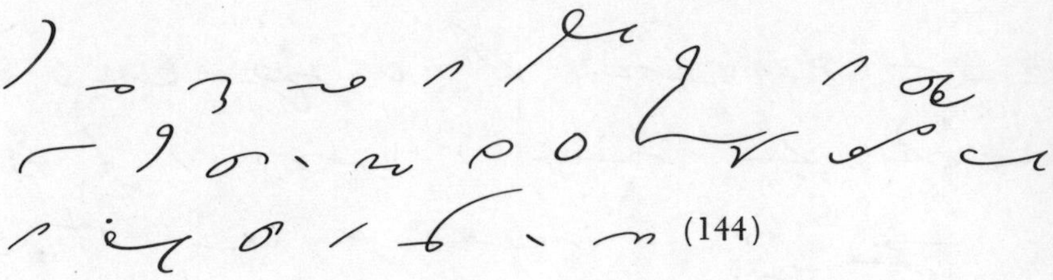

(144)

15.

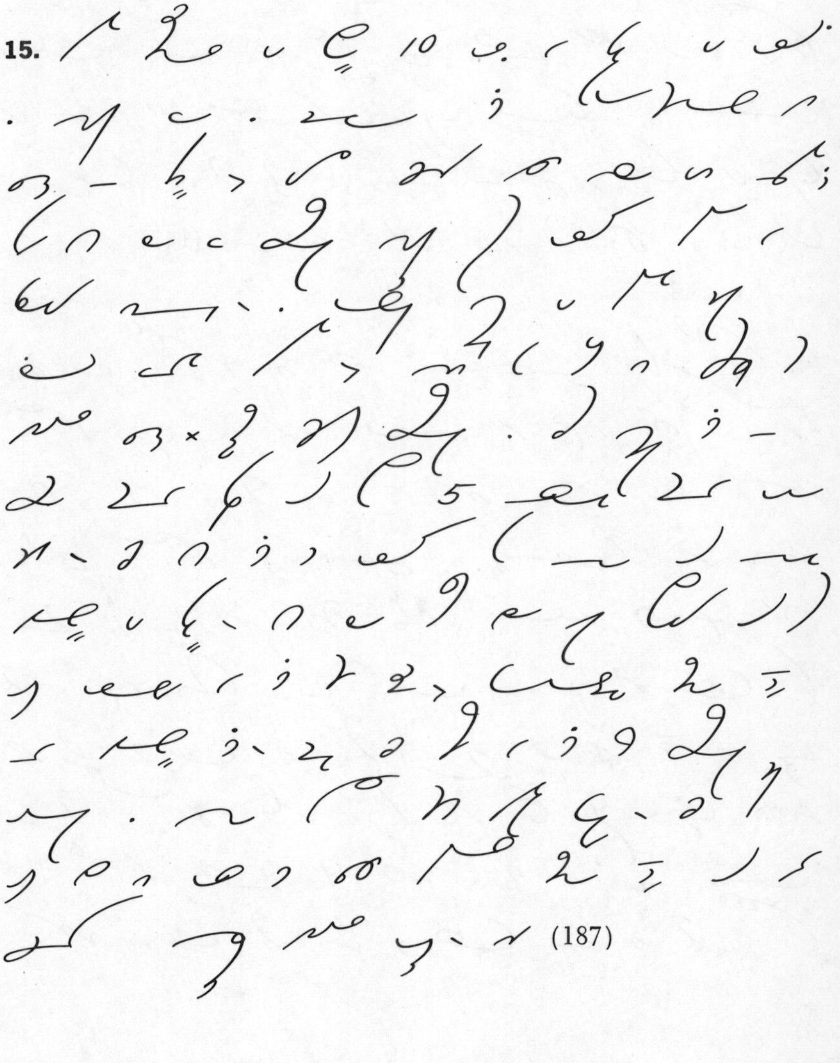

(187)

16.

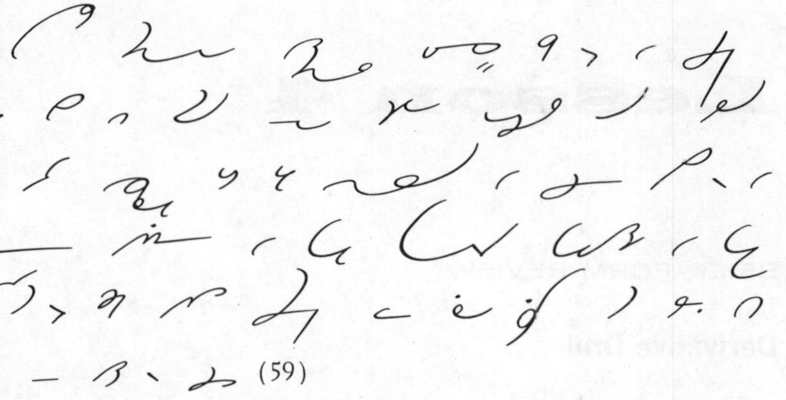

(59)

17.

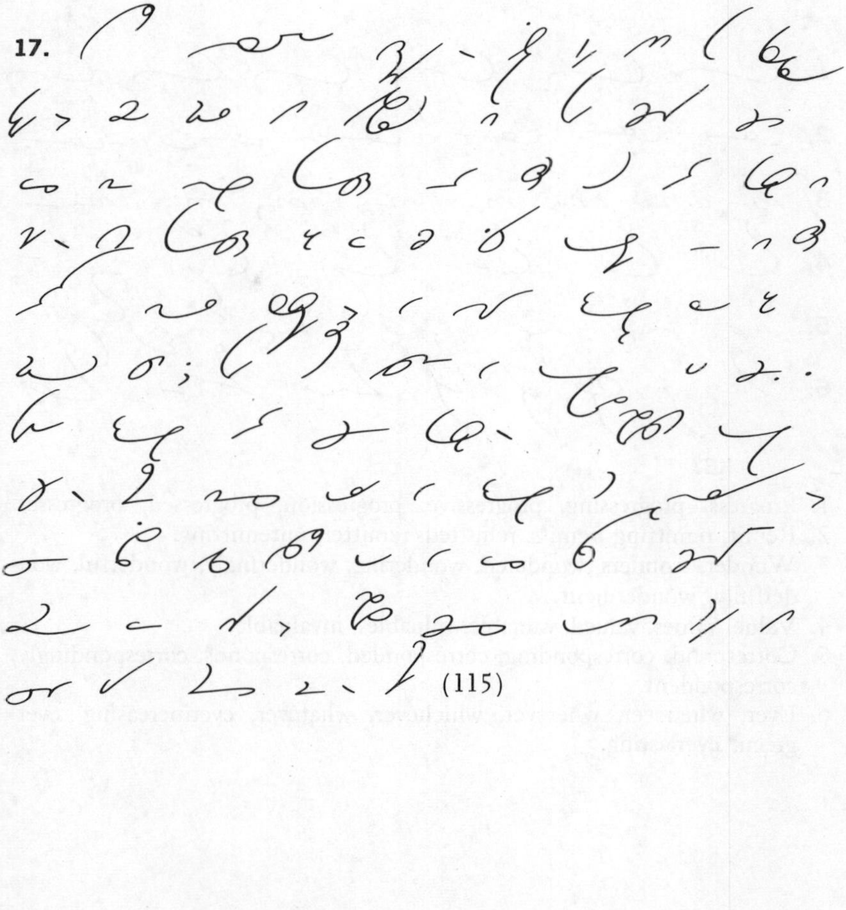

(115)

Lesson 4

BRIEF-FORM REVIEW

Derivative Drill

There are 40 brief forms and derivatives in this list. Can you read the entire list in 25 seconds or less?

1.
2.
3.
4.
5.
6.

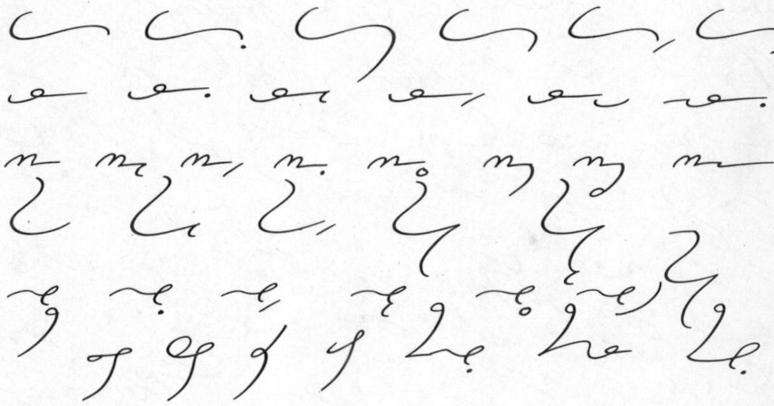

KEY

1. Progress, progressing, progressive, progression, progressed, progresses.
2. Remit, remitting, remits, remitted, remitter, unremitting.
3. Wonder, wonders, wondered, wondering, wonderingly, wonderful, wonderfully, wonderment.
4. Value, values, valued, valuable, valuables, invaluable.
5. Correspond, corresponding, corresponded, corresponds, correspondingly, correspondent.
6. Ever, whenever, wherever, whichever, whatever, everincreasing, evergreen, everlasting.

Brief-Form Letters

18.  (174)

19. 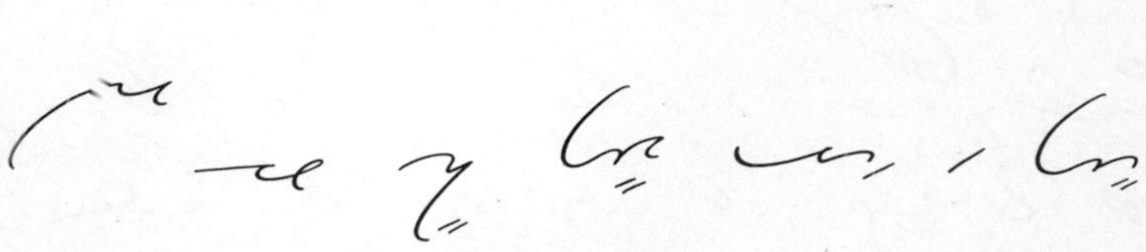

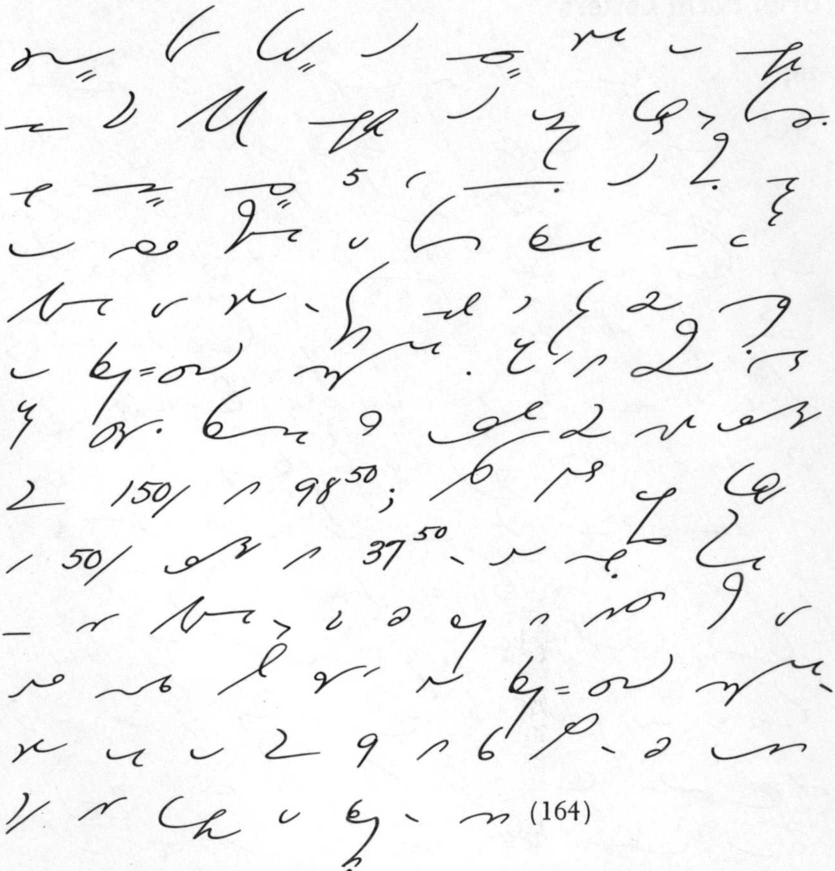

20.

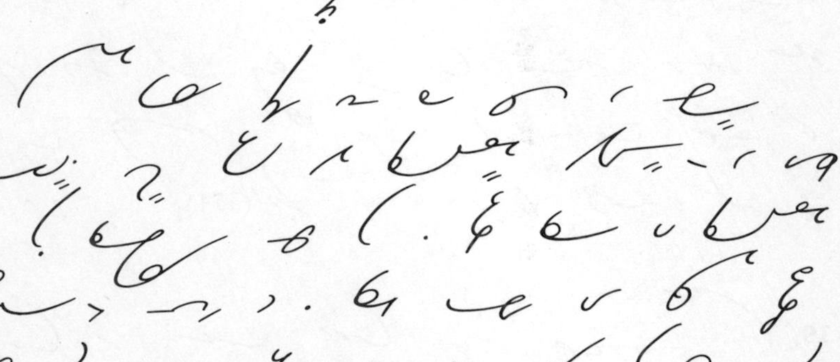

9:30

27

44)

(214)

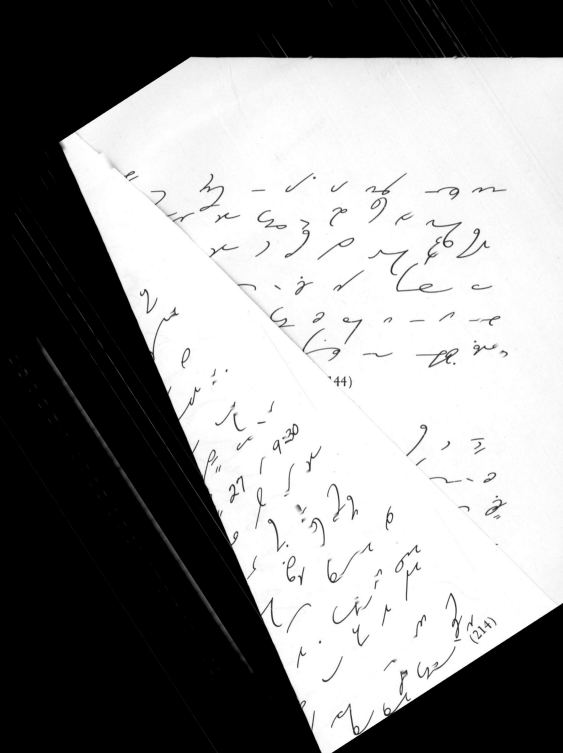

22.

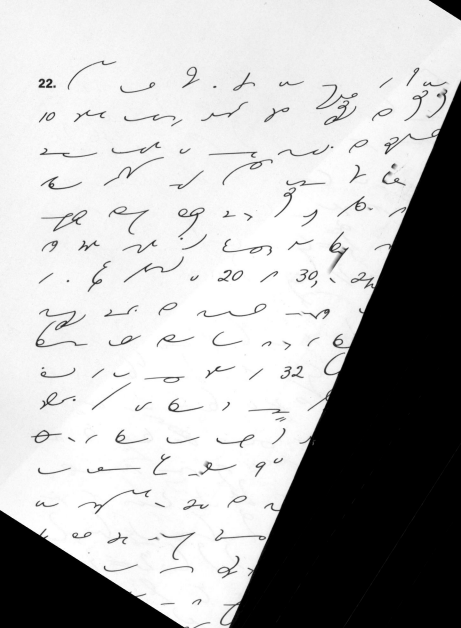

Lesson 5

BRIEF-FORM REVIEW

Derivative Drill

There are 45 brief forms and derivatives in this list. Can you read the entire list in 20 seconds or less?

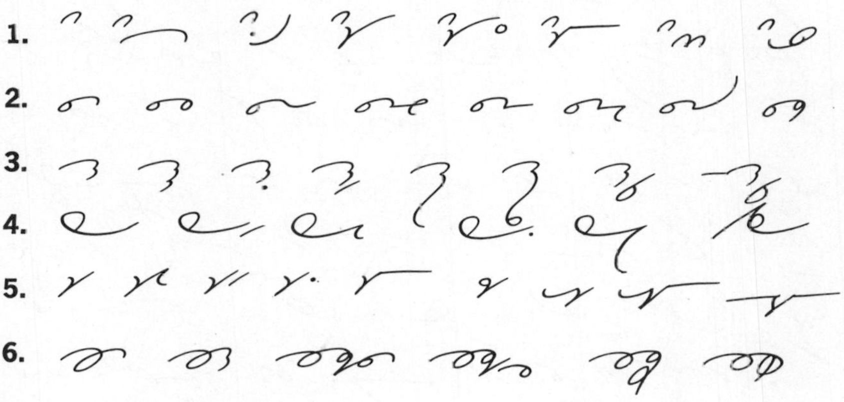

KEY

1. Under, undergo, underhand, understand, understandingly, understatement, underworld, underwrite.
2. Weak, weakly, weaker, weakness, weaken, weakens, weakened, weakest.
3. Consider, considers, considering, considered, considerable, considerably, considerate, inconsiderate.
4. Allow, allowed, allows, allowing, allowable, disallow.
5. State, states, stated, stating, statement, estate, restate, restatement, misstatement.
6. Character, characters, characteristic, characteristically, characterization, characterize.

Brief-Form Letters

23.

(187)

24.

(137)

25.

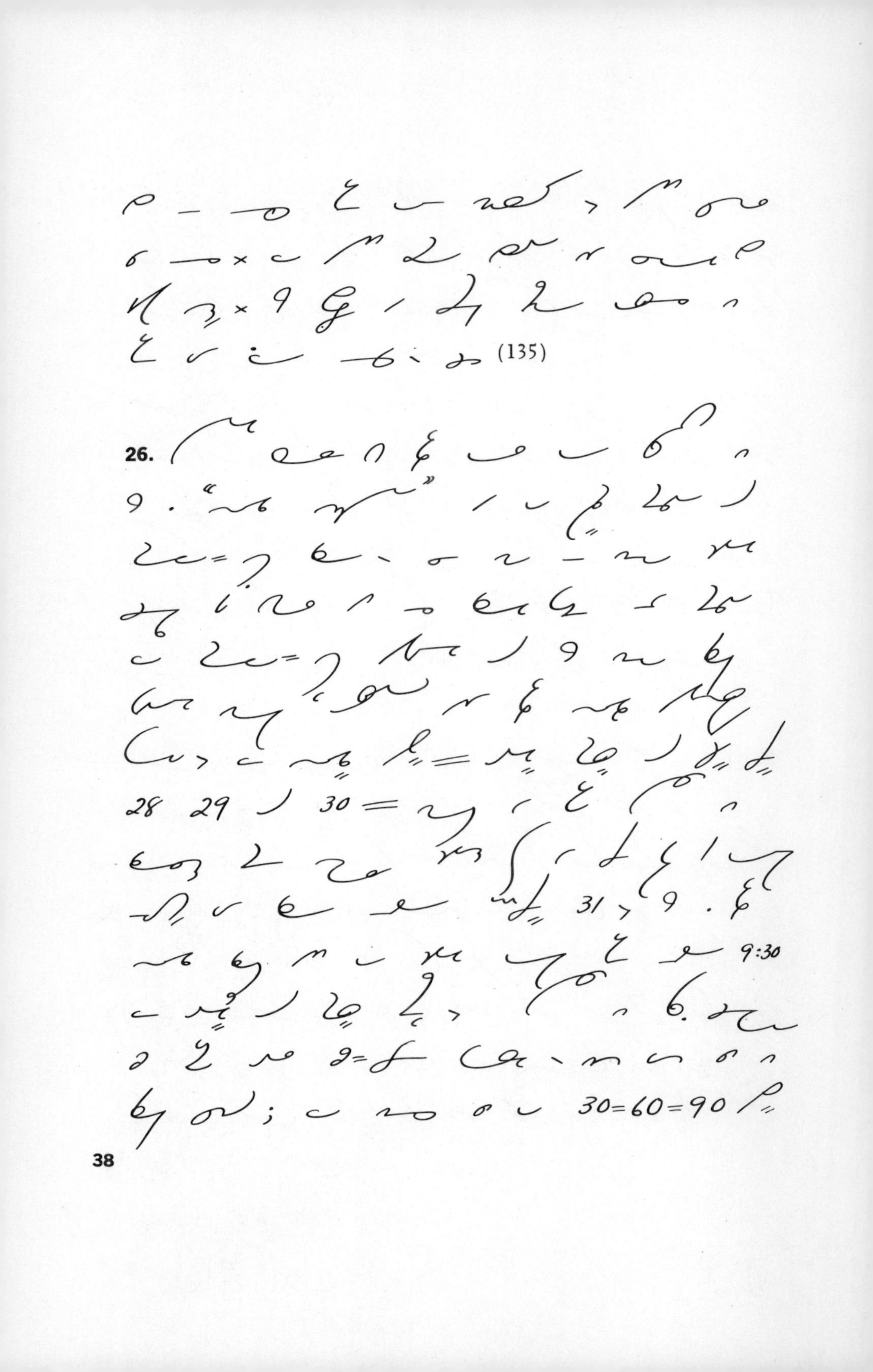

(135)

26.

28 29 30

31

9:30

30=60=90

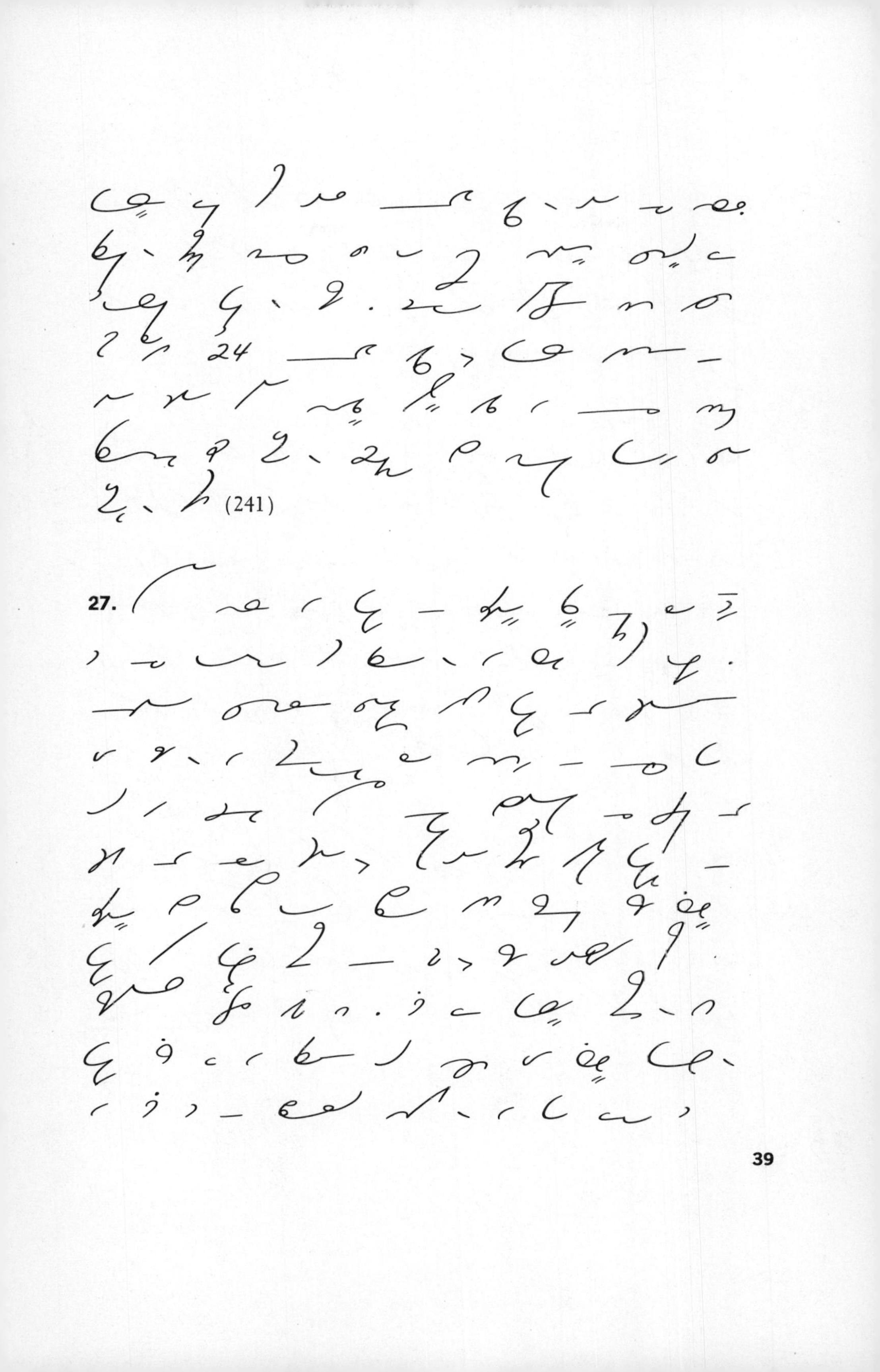

24

(241)

27.

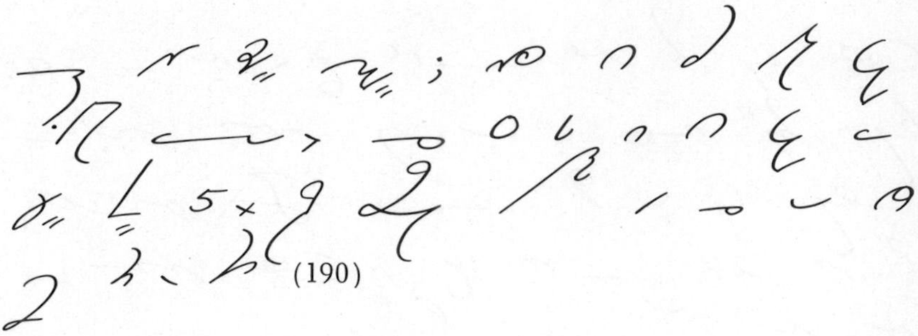

(190)

28.

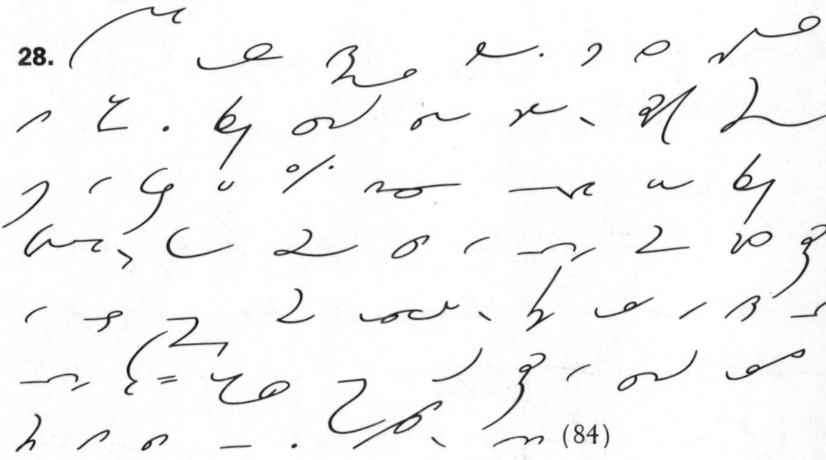

(84)

29.

(55)

PART II Departmental Dictation and Transcription

In Part II you will have an opportunity to "sample" the type of material you would take from dictation and transcribe in seven different departments of an organization:

Chapter	*Department*
2	The Office Service Department
3	The Sales Department
4	The Credit Department
5	The Accounting Department
6	The Purchasing Department
7	The Personnel Department
8	The Manufacturing Department

You will assume that you have been employed as a beginning stenographer by the National Company, 37 South Wabash Avenue, Chicago 3, Illinois. You will be assigned first to the office manager of the company; then periodically you will be transferred to other departments of the company.

A directory of the company's executives follows:

President	William S. Jackson
Vice-President	Richard R. Green
Treasurer	Charles Robertson

Department	*Department Head*
Office Service	John Parker
Sales	Clyde N. McKee
Credit	Ted C. Barnett
Accounting	Henry Wilson
Purchasing	Phillip S. Porter
Personnel	Stanley R. Brown
Manufacturing	James I. Steel

2

The Office Service Department

Spelling and Penmanship Improvement Drills for Chapter 2

SPELLING

In words ending with a silent *e*, the *e* is usually dropped before a suffix that begins with a vowel.

advise, advisory
appraise, appraisal
base, basic
desire, desirous
discipline, disciplinary
enclose, enclosure
ensue, ensuing
force, forcible
guide, guidance
imitate, imitative
measure, measurable
use, usage

Exceptions

advantage, advantageous
dye, dyeing
manage, manageable
mile, mileage
notice, noticeable
outrage, outrageous

PENMANSHIP

1. 

2. 

3. 

4. 

5. 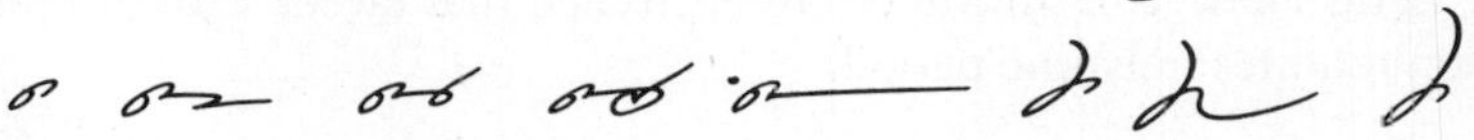

KEY

1. In, more, it, would, when, aim, eat, aid.
2. I, the, and, to, a, you, of, in, we, for, it.
3. Of the, in the, Yours truly, to the, Dear Mr., we are, Dear Sir, for the, Yours very truly, on the.
4. In, more, men, it, would, did, many, today.
5. Use, union, unit, unite, human, few, fuel, view.

Lesson 6

BUILDING TRANSCRIPTION SKILL

Transcription English Pointers

THE USES OF THE PERIOD

1. A sentence that makes a direct statement is followed by a period. Two typewriter spaces follow this period.

We are now ordering our supplies from the Baker Company.

2. A period is used after an abbreviation. Only one space follows this period unless it occurs at the end of a sentence.

Mr. James Wilson has been hired in the Accounting Department.

3. A declarative or an imperative sentence that closes with an abbreviation requires only one period.

Seats go on sale Wednesday at 10 a.m.
The convention will be held in Washington, D. C.

Transcription Speed Builder

30.

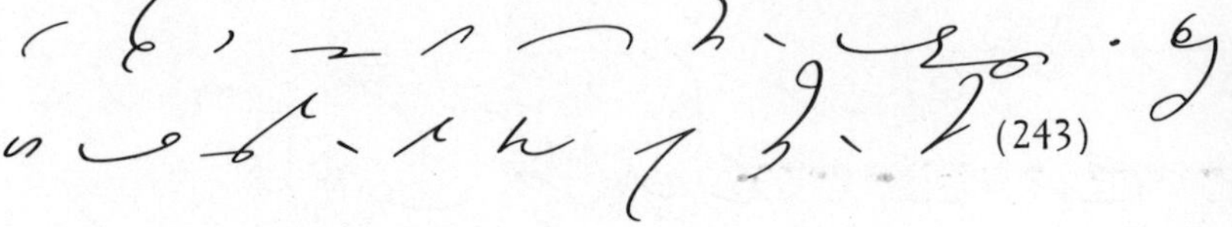

(243)

31.

Commonwealth Products

KNOWN THROUGHOUT THE NATION

Executive Offices . . . . 220 Berkeley Street, BOSTON 17, MASS.

October 6, 19--

Mr. James P. Martin
Stone & Brown
40 West Union Avenue
Clovis, New Mexico

Dear Mr. Martin:

Thank you very much for your order of April 8. We regret that we cannot at the present time accept your order, as we have as many orders as we can possibly fill this season.

We hope, however, to receive an order from you sometime next year, at which time we expect to be able to fill it.

Although we are not able to fill your order, we shall be glad to have you visit our mills whenever you wish. The mills are working night and day, and one of our foremen will show you over them at any time. You will find that we have only the newest type of machinery throughout the mills.

Very truly yours,

Harold L. Carson

KK

Short Letter
Blocked Style
Standard Punctuation

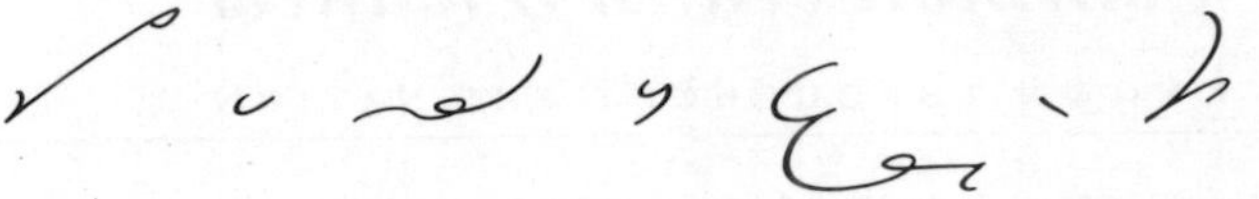
(199)

32. 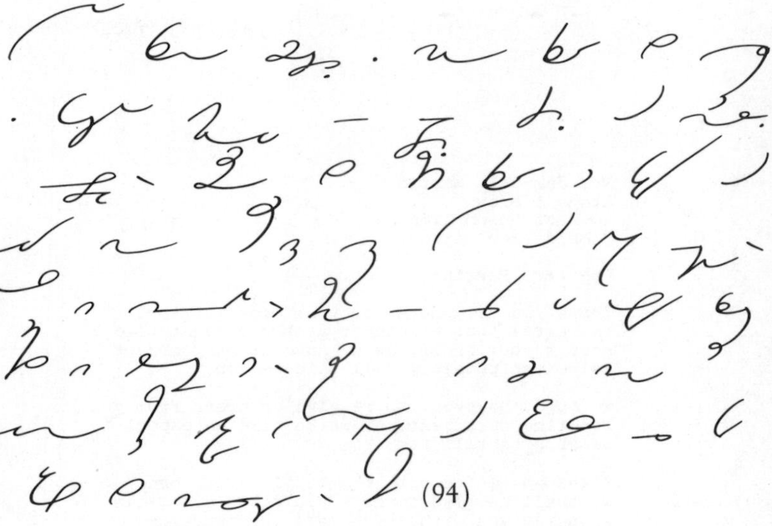
(94)

33. 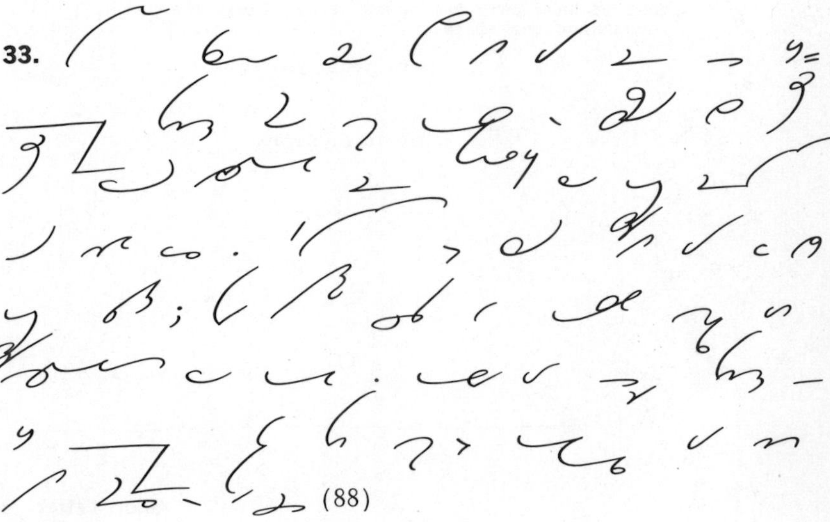
(88)

34. 

(126)

35. 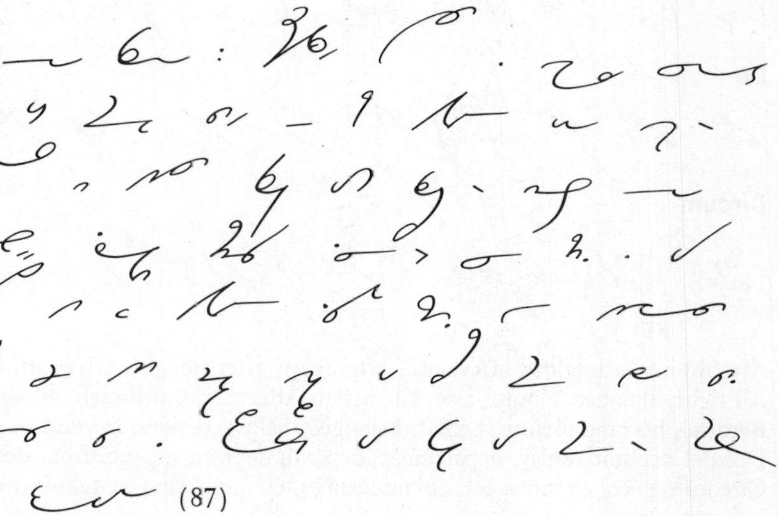

(87)

Lesson 7

MASTERING SHORTHAND THEORY

Word Beginnings

After-

Al-

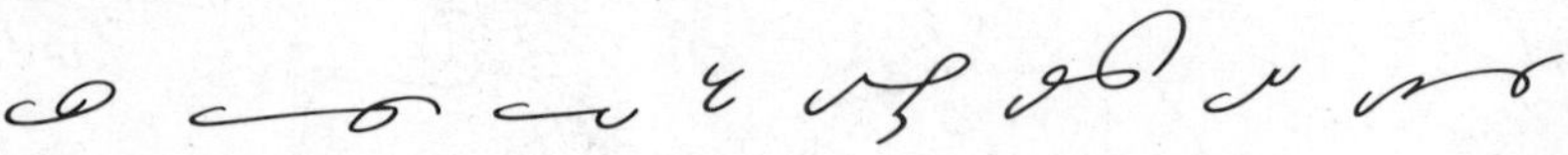

Be-

De-

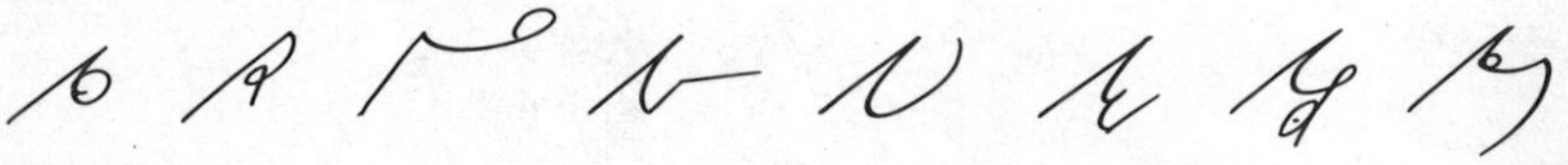

Circum-

KEY

Afterdinner, afterglow, aftermath, afternoon, afterthought, afterward.
All right, almanac, almost, also, alterations, alternative, although, altogether.
Because, become, before, behalf, belonged, below, besides, beyond.
Decide, decision, delay, department, depend, deposit, depreciation, deserve.
Circumference, circumspect, circumstances, circumstantial, circumvent, circumvention.

Reading and Writing Practice

36.

(75)

37.

(53)

38.

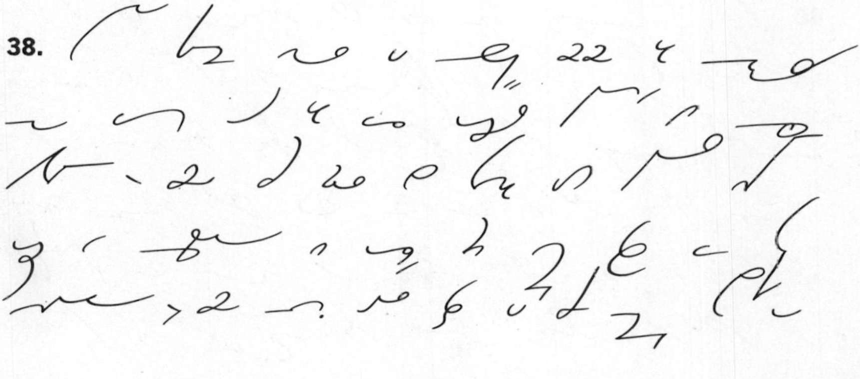

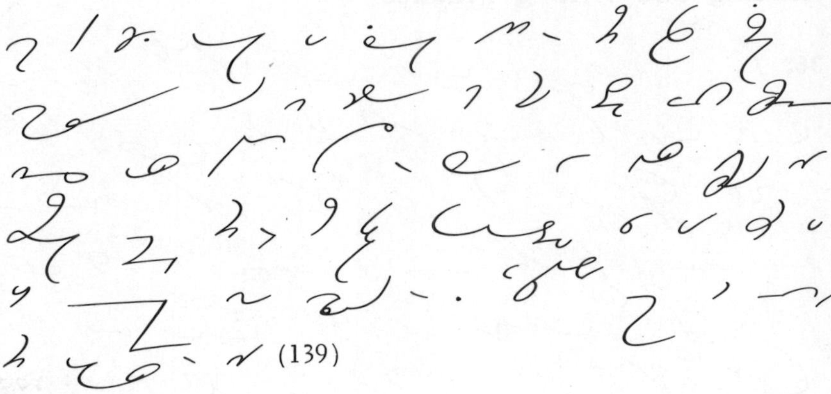

(139)

39. 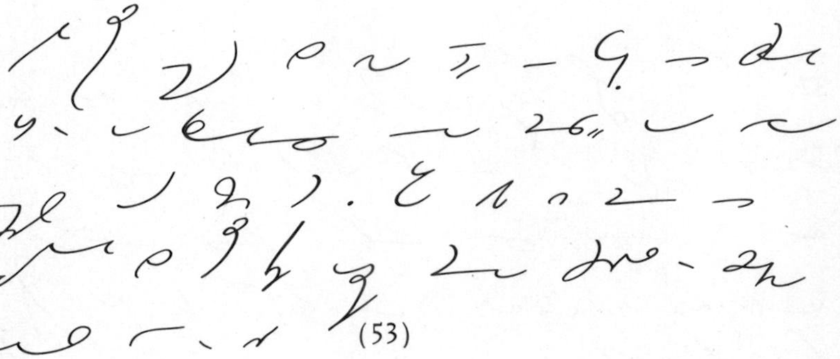

(53)

40. 

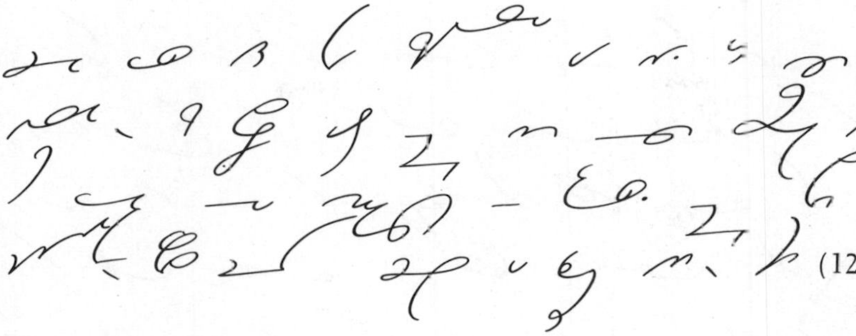

(127)

41. 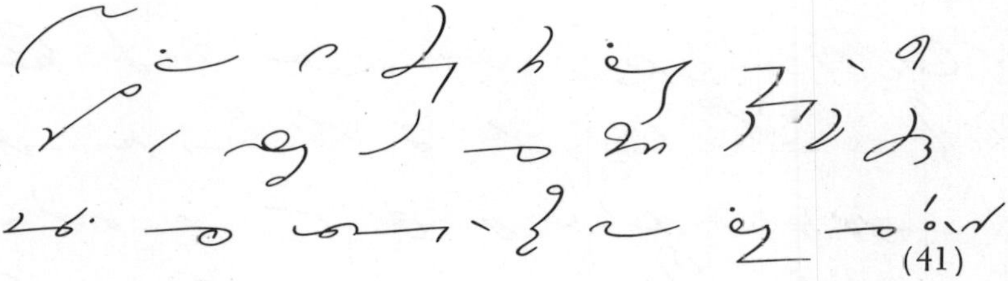

(41)

42. 

(85)

Building Speed Through Reading

43. HINTS FOR SUCCESS

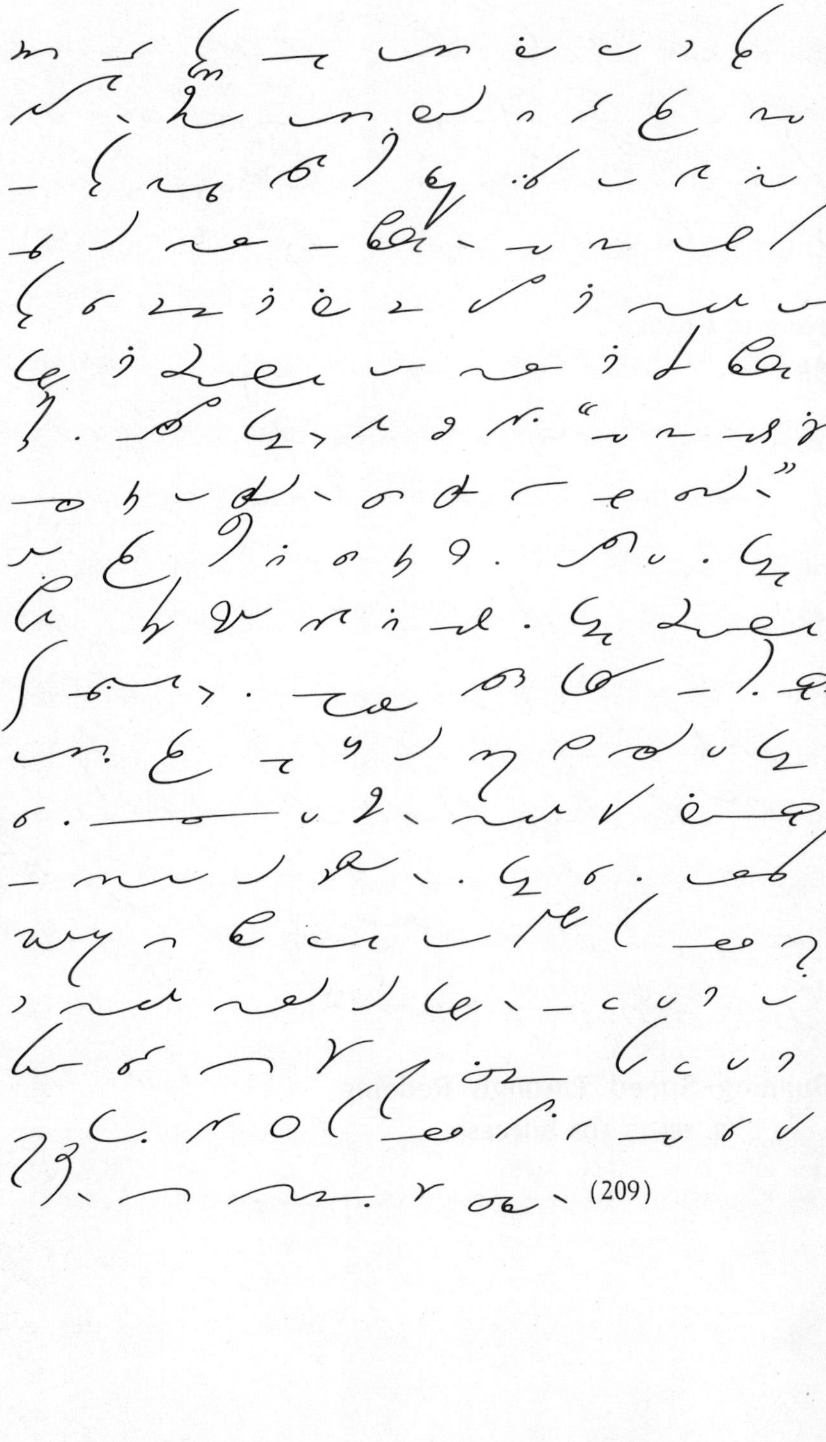

(209)

Lesson 8

BUILDING PHRASING SKILL

Pronoun Phrases

Drill 1

Drill 2

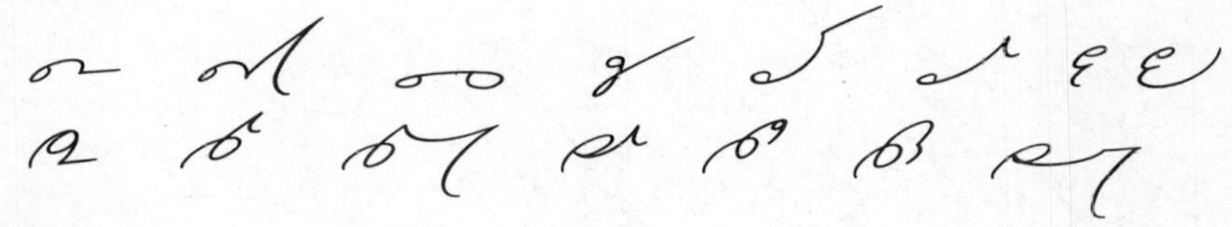

Drill 3

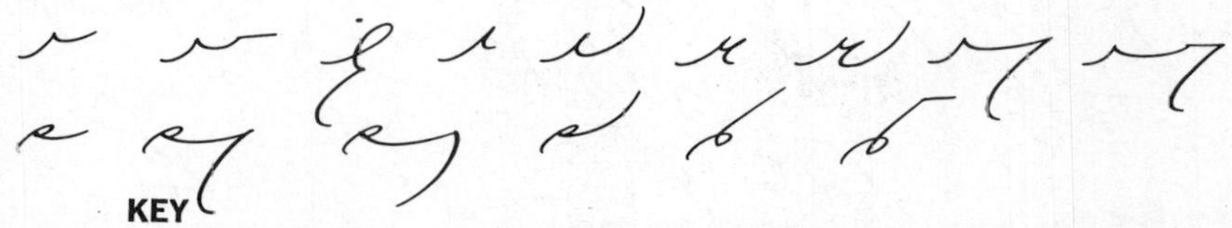

KEY

I am, I am sure, I believe, I cannot understand, I could, I could be, I could have, I need, I realize, I saw, I shall, I shall be glad, I shall have, I shall not be, I shall not have, I think, I understand.

He cannot, he could be, he may, he said, he wanted, he wants, he was, he was not; that is not, that it is, that it will be, that there is, that these, that this is, that will not be.

There are, there are not, there has been, there is, there is not, there was, there was not, there will be, there will not be; they are, they will be, they will have, they want, they would, they would not.

Brief-Form and Phrase Letters

44.

(204)

45.

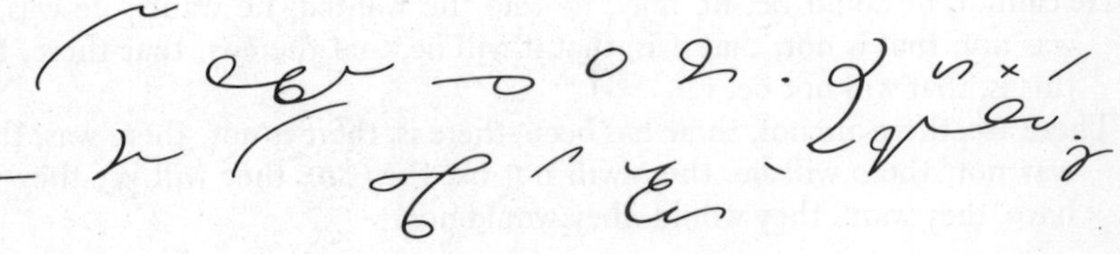

(142)

46.

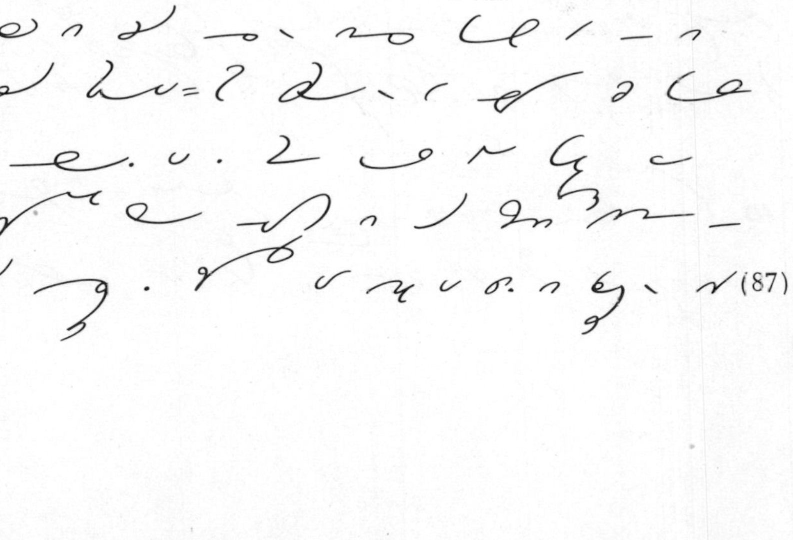

(87)

47.

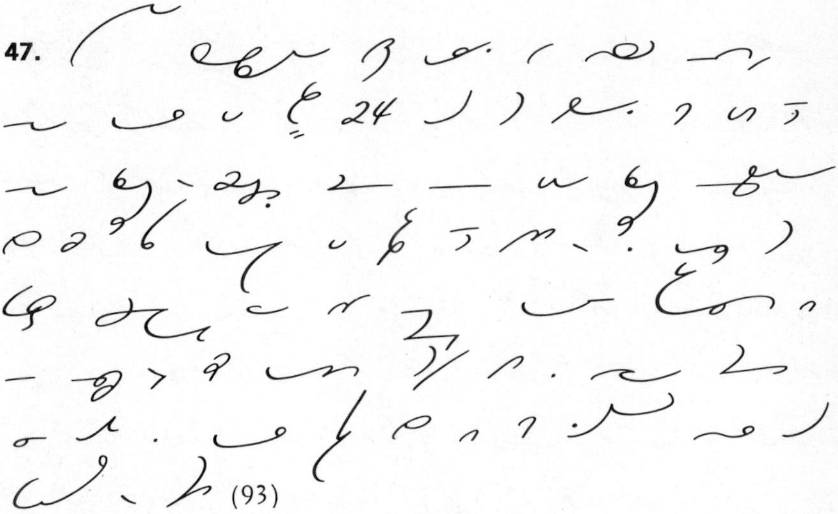

(93)

48.

(82)

49.

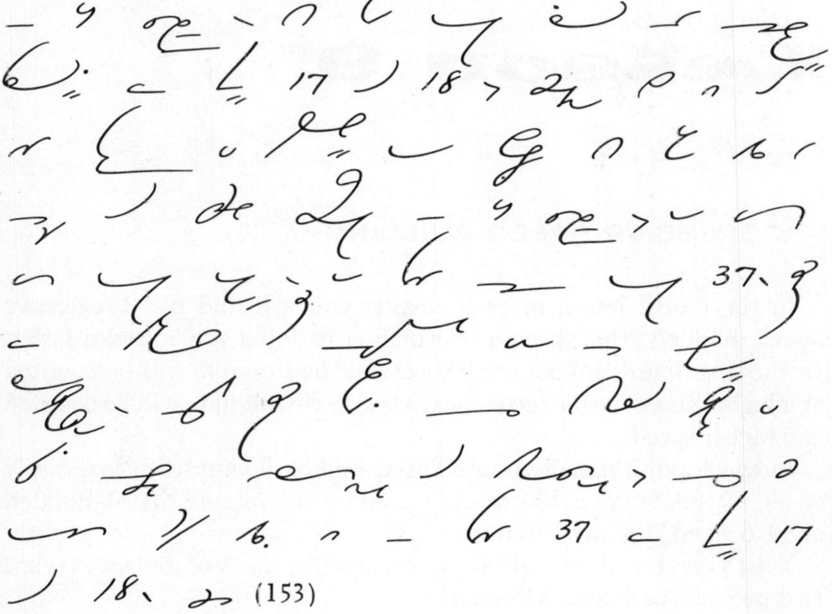

(153)

50.

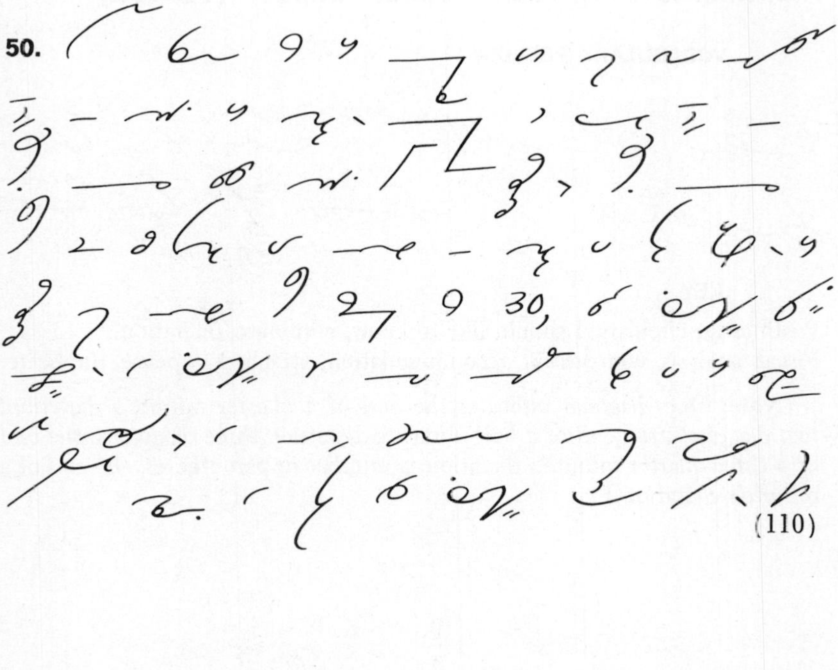

(110)

Lesson 9

PROGRESSIVE SPEED BUILDING

In the fourth lesson of each chapter you will find two Progressive Speed Builders, the purpose of which is to force you to write faster. In the first Speed Builder, each successive *half minute* will be counted at a higher speed; in the second, each succeeding *minute* will be counted at a higher speed.

In this lesson the half-minute Speed Builder is counted progressively at 60, 70, 80, 90, and 100 words a minute; the minute Speed Builder, at 50, 60, and 70 words a minute.

Your first step should always be to practice the Vocabulary Preview that precedes each Speed Builder.

Half-Minute Progressive Speed Builder (60-100)

VOCABULARY PREVIEW

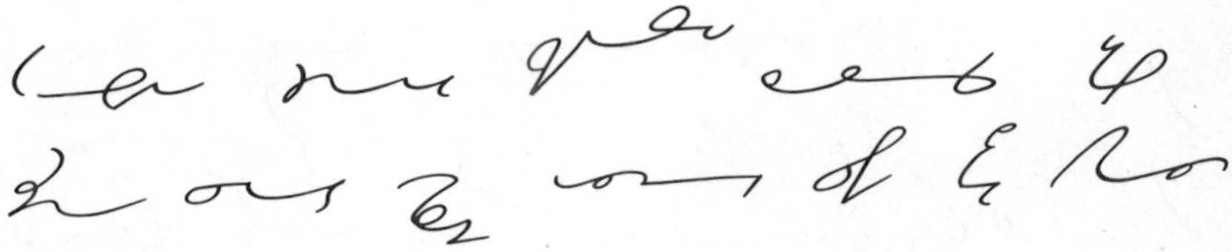

KEY

Postmaster, circulars, I should like to know, eliminate, operation.
Fiscal, analysis, comparison, recommendation, attached, expense, duplicate.

(Note: One diagonal indicates the end of a quarter minute's dictation; two diagonals, the end of a half minute's dictation; three diagonals, the end of a three-quarter minute's dictation; a number in parentheses, the end of a minute's dictation.)

(½ MINUTE AT 60)

51. Memo to Miss Ray. We have received notice from the postmaster that our last mailing/of circulars is being held up because of incorrect use of our mailing permit. //

(½ MINUTE AT 70)

I should like to know what happened, so that we can take the proper steps to eliminate this mistake/ in the future.

Can you and Miss Stone come to my office to discuss this matter at 2 p.m.?//

(½ MINUTE AT 80)

52. Memo to Mr. Steel: Here is my annual report of the operation of our Filing Department. This/report covers the fiscal year just ended and shows a careful and detailed analysis of all our costs.//

(½ MINUTE AT 90)

A comparison of this year's records with those of last year shows that our filing costs have increased 8 per cent. The report carries/a recommendation for changes in office methods that will not only reduce the costs but also speed up our service.//

(½ MINUTE AT 100)

53. Memo to Mr. Parker: Attached is a copy of the new form that should be used for all expense accounts beginning with the June report./

Please note that all expenses are to be given in detail and the bills attached. Please send me your report in duplicate by the first of the month.//

Minute Progressive Speed Builder (50-70)

VOCABULARY PREVIEW

KEY

Happened, pamphlets, to be able, to make, thank you for your letter, separate, poster.

(1 MINUTE AT 50)

54. Dear Miss Jones: Last week we sent three pieces of material to your/shop to be printed. The order was marked "Rush," but we have not received the//material as yet. Can you check to see what happened.

It is///important to us that the pamphlets be sent as soon as possible. Yours truly, (1)

(1 MINUTE AT 60)

55. Dear Mrs. Farmer: I am sure that you have received the pamphlets by this time. They were/ mailed to you the same day you wrote us about them. The sales letter is on the presses//now and should be ready for mailing tomorrow.

We don't seem to be able to find///the third piece, however. Could you check to make sure it was sent to us. Sincerely yours, (2)

(1 MINUTE AT 70)

56. Dear Miss Jones: Thank you for your letter explaining about our printing order. The pamphlets are/ already in the mail and were received in time.

The third piece of printing that I mentioned was sent in a//separate package from the other two pieces. It is a poster that is to be printed on///heavy cardboard.

Let me know whether you are still not able to find this piece. Yours very truly, (3)

Reading and Writing Practice

57.

(223)

58.

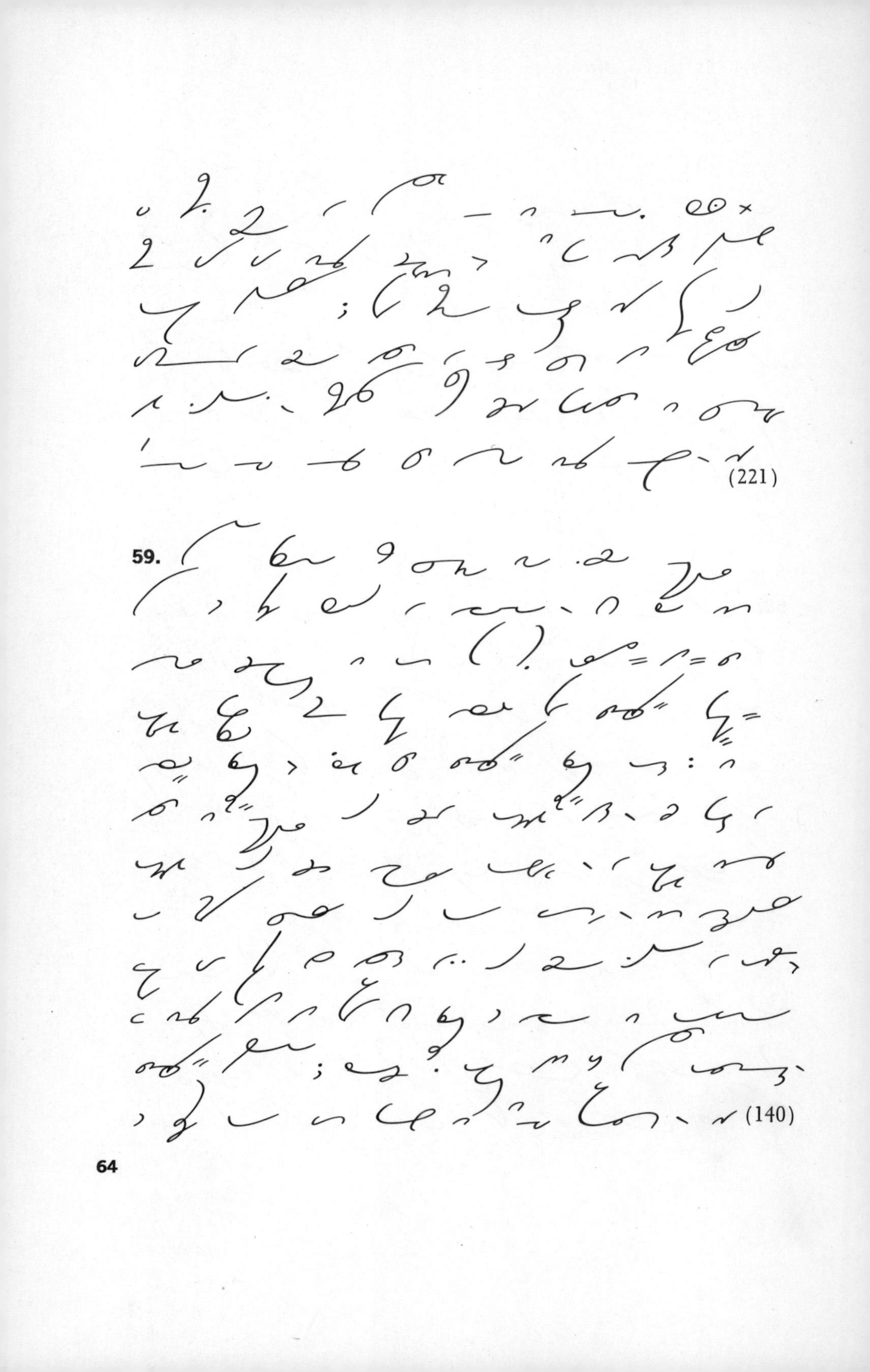

(221)

59.

(140)

Lesson 10

BUILDING SUSTAINED SPEED

Five-Minute Speed Builder

The purpose of the Sustained Speed Builder in the fifth lesson of each chapter is to develop your endurance.

The following correspondence is between Mr. Parker and Mr. Marvin Hall, Director, Efficiency Engineering Company, Evanston 6, Illinois.

VOCABULARY PREVIEW

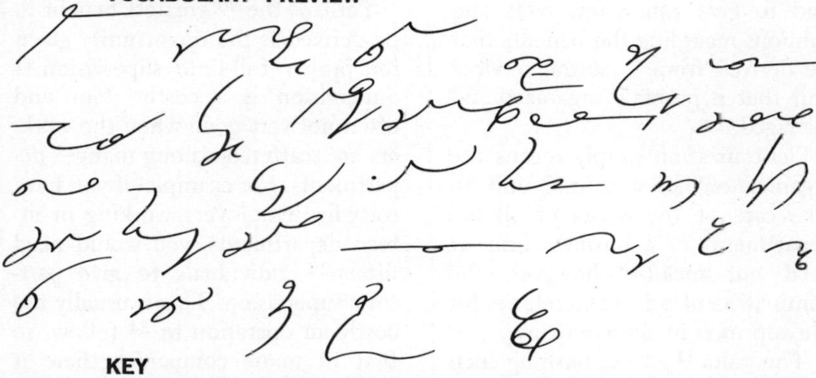

KEY

Determine, stenographers, idle, equipment, established, recommendation.
Employed, benefits, derived, centralization, elimination, secretaries.
Equally, involved, performed, handled, volume, successful, justify.
Factor, centrally, minimum, greatest, opportunity, costly.
Item, scattered, if you have, we shall be glad, preparation.

(Note: Each small raised number represents 20 standard words.)

60. Gentlemen: Our Company would like to determine whether it would be desirable for us to change our[1] correspondence setup. We now have two stenographers in each department. A recent survey, however, has shown[2] that there is a considerable amount of wasted time and idle equipment because of this method.

Will[3] you please supply us, at your usual fee, a report showing the savings that might be made if we changed our[4] procedure and established a central unit or pool, as it is often called. My plan would be to use the information[5] you supply as the basis of a recommendation that you be employed to study our needs and show[6] whatever improvements you think we can make after completing your study. Yours truly,

61. Dear Mr. Parker: We[7] are glad to give you a few facts and opinions regarding the benefits that are derived from a central service[8] unit that is properly organized and managed.

Centralization simply means the organization[9] of a central unit to take care of the needs of all the departments of a business firm. It need not mean,[10] however, the elimination of private secretaries for the top men in the company.

The value[11] of establishing such a unit can easily be shown through a study of the nature of each person's work;[12] of the amount, present and future, of that work; and, equally important, of the flow of the work. The number[13] of employees involved and the location of the space needed should be given consideration also.

The [14] nature of the work that is now being performed in your company should be studied in order to find how much[15] of it could be handled better in a pool. A study should also be made of the volume of work, because a[16] fairly even flow of work is necessary for the successful operation of a central pool. It is[17] generally agreed that a central unit should have at least fifteen employees in order to justify[18] full-time supervision.

Space is a very important factor in making this change. The unit should be centrally[19] located in order that the travel time of each employee be kept at a minimum.

Perhaps the [20] greatest benefit to be derived is the opportunity given for proper full-time supervision.[21] Supervision is a costly item and often not very good when the workers are scattered among many[22] departments. For example, if you have forty-five employees working in fifteen departments, you would need fifteen[23] individuals to give part-time supervision. This is usually too costly an operation to [24] follow, so that in many companies there is little or no supervision.

After you have studied these facts,[25] we shall be glad to present additional information, if you so desire, to aid you in the preparation[26] of your recommendation. Sincerely yours, (529)

Reading and Writing Practice

62.  (73)

63. 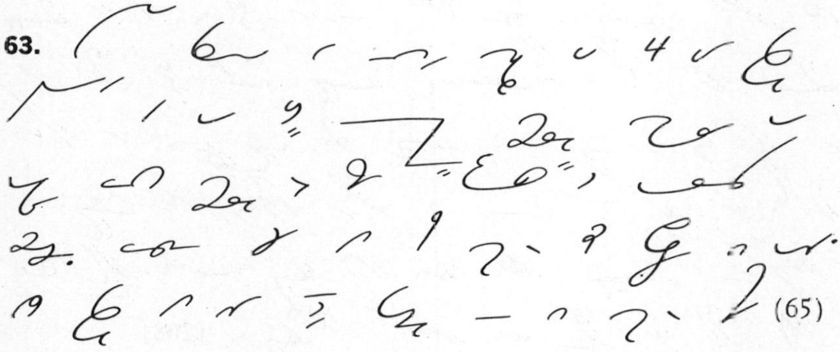 (65)

64. 

(208)

65.

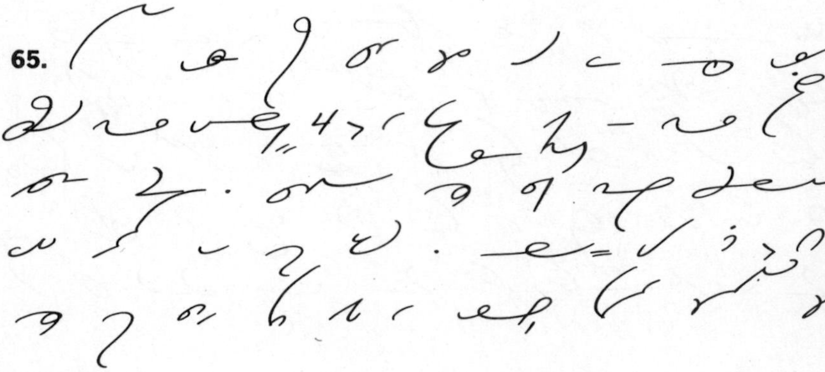

(184)

66.

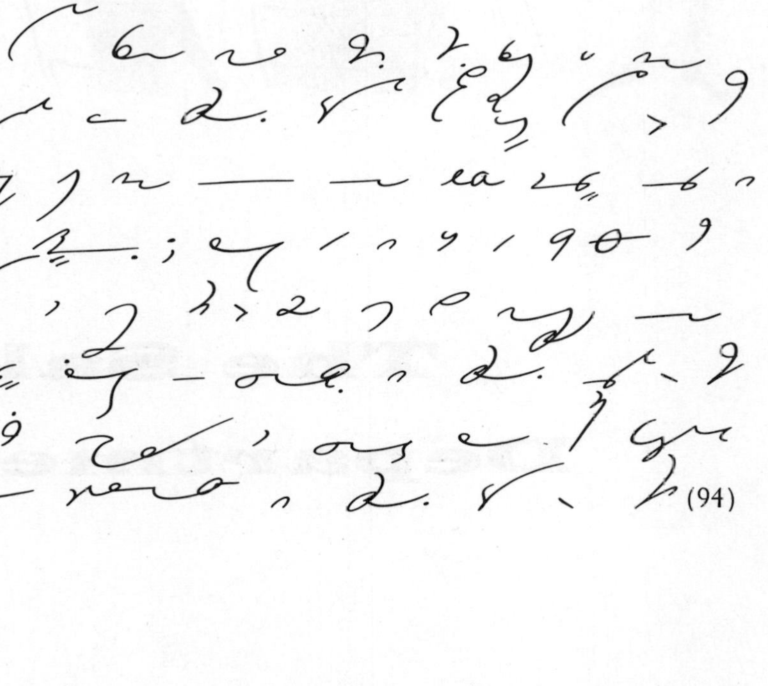

(94)

3

The Sales Department

Spelling and Penmanship Improvement Drills for Chapter 3

SPELLING

When a word ends with a silent e, the e is usually retained before a suffix that begins with a consonant.

apprentice, apprenticeship	like, likely
arrange, arrangement	noise, noiseless
care, careful	refine, refinement
complete, completely	safe, safety
entire, entirely	sincere, sincerely
fate, fateful	state, statement

Exceptions

acknowledge, acknowledgment	judge, judgment
argue, argument	true, truly

PENMANSHIP

1. 

2. 

3. 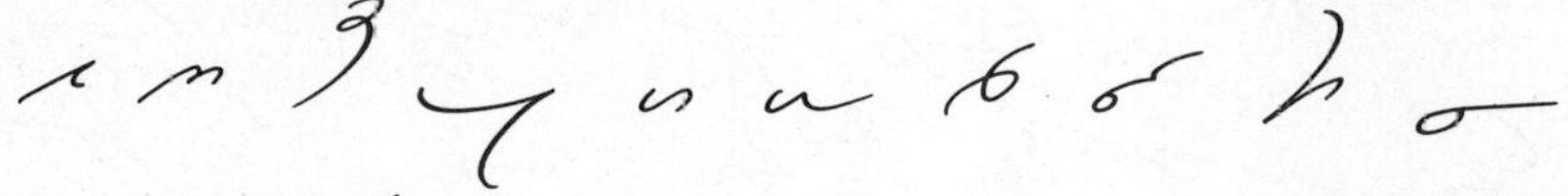

4. 

5. 

KEY

1. Are, will, can, go, were, ail, week, egg.
2. That, is, your, have, will, be, are, not, as.
3. It is, to you, we have, will be, of your, of our, that the, with the, Very truly yours, I am.
4. Of, our, will, you, can, go, of our, letter, you can go.
5. Oil, toy, noise, boy, join, soil, royal, voice.

Lesson 11

BUILDING TRANSCRIPTION SKILL

Transcription English Pointers

THE USES OF THE COLON

Business letters contain many enumerations or listings, as well as explanatory or illustrative statements. The punctuation of these sentence elements depends on the expressions used to introduce the items.

1. When the introductory expressions are:

as follows	this
the following	these

a colon follows the introductory expression.

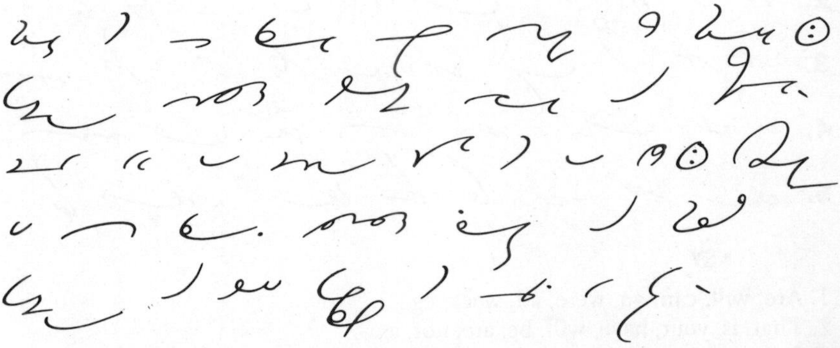

Sources for new sales may be grouped as follows: personal contacts, telephone calls, and advertisements.

Some of the things our school stands for are these: development of good selling techniques, helpful and friendly personality, and thorough preparation for meeting the public.

2. Sometimes the word or phrase that introduces an enumeration or an illustration is merely implied, in which case the colon is used just the same.

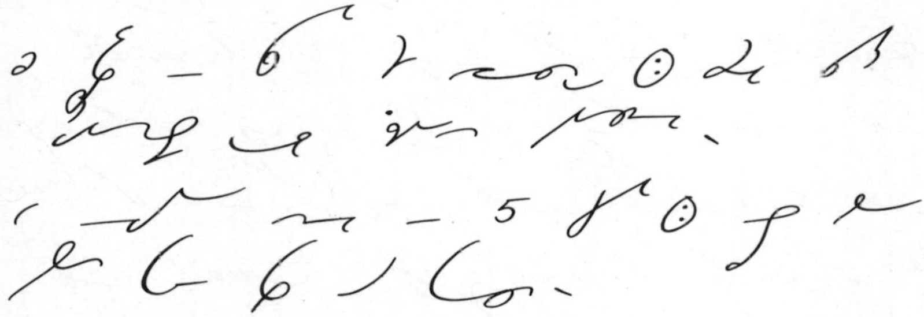

We specialize in items for the collector: first editions, autographed letters, historical documents.

The model comes in five shades: navy, teal, dark brown, beige, and black.

3. Enumerated and illustrative items are often tabulated for convenience in checking and ease of reading.

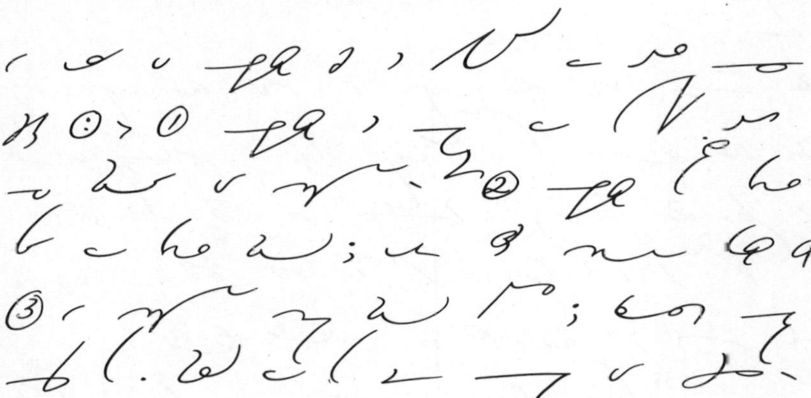

The return of merchandise usually is dependent on three main situations:

1. Merchandise is imperfect or damaged through no fault of the customer.
2. Merchandise has been poorly bought or poorly sold; wrong size, color, price, fashion.
3. The customer cannot be sold directly; selection must be made by a friend or by some members of the family.

Transcription Speed Builder

67.

(95)

68.

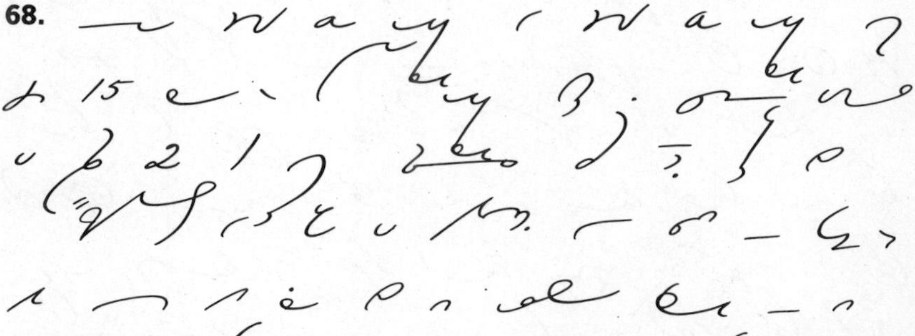

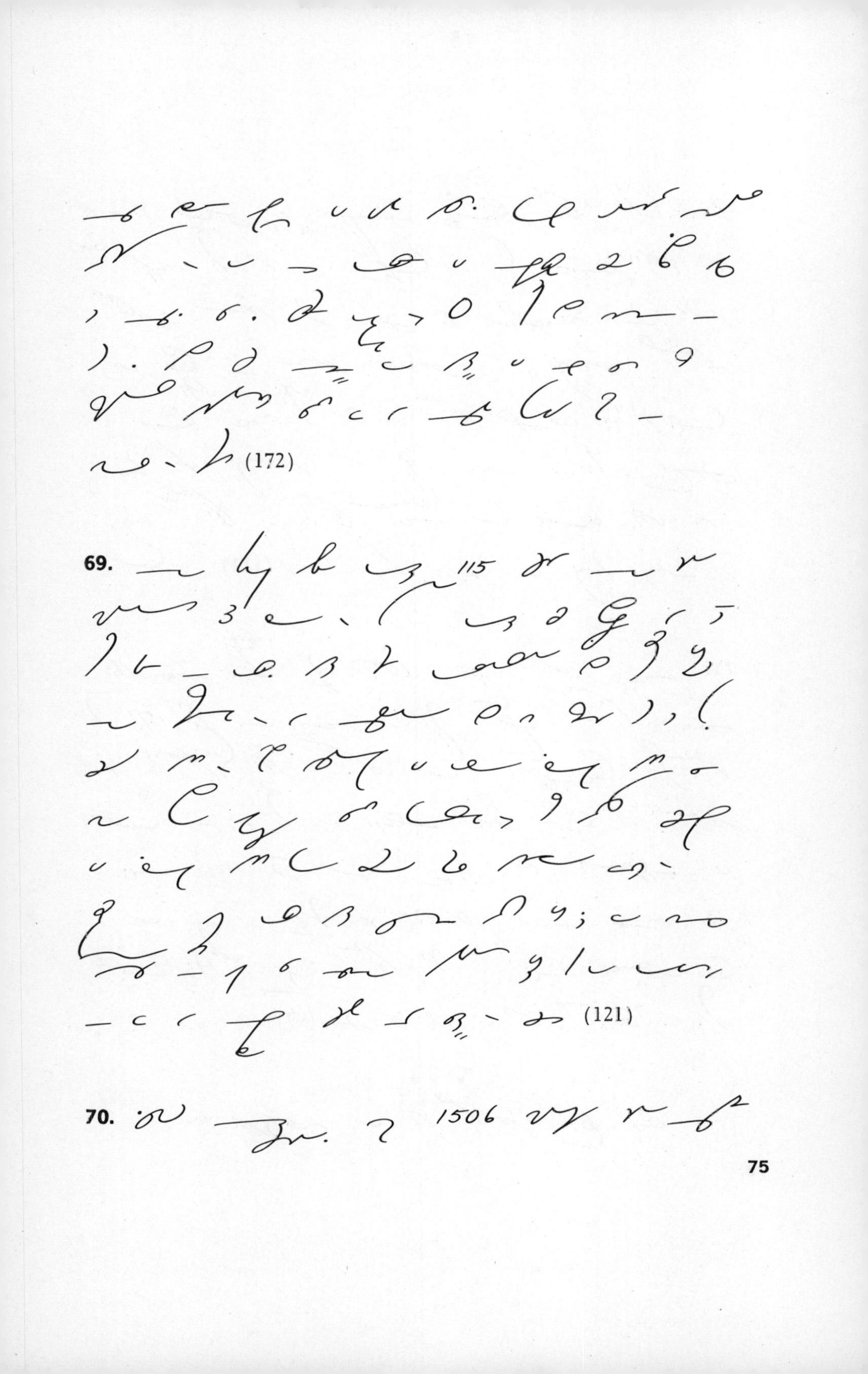

(172)

69. 115

(121)

70. 1506

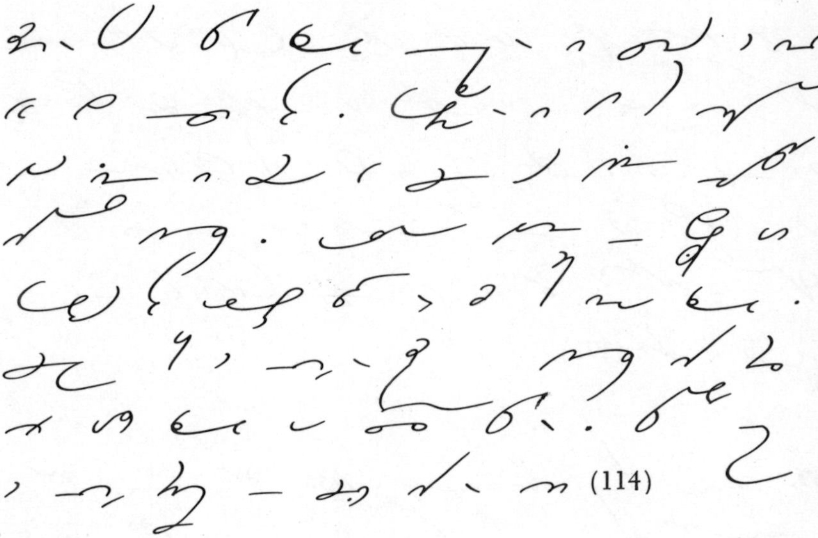

(114)

71.

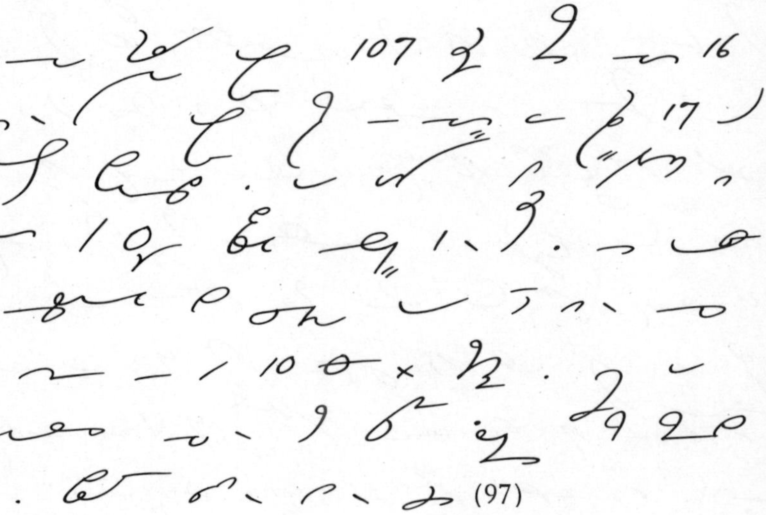

(97)

* * *

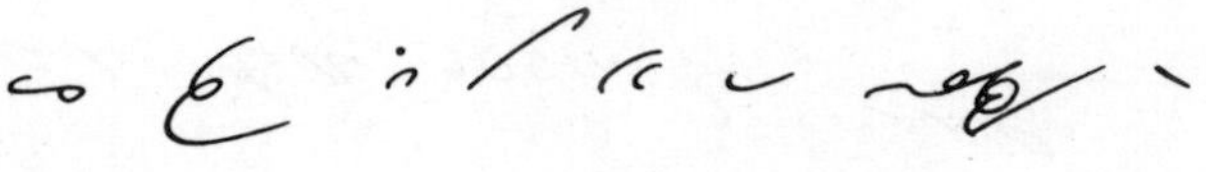

Lesson 12

MASTERING SHORTHAND THEORY

Word Beginnings

Des-, Dis-

Mis-

Electr-, Electric

Em-, Im-

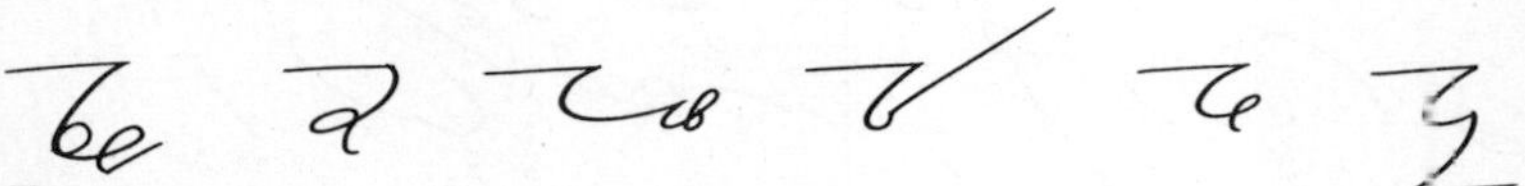

En-

KEY

Describing, description, destinations, destroy, discovered, distant, distribution.

Miscellaneous, misfortune, mislaid, mistake, misunderstand.

Electrical, electrician, electricity, electric brooders, electric iron, electric lights.

Embarrassed, emphasis, employee, imported, impress, improvement.

Encourage, endeavor, enforce, engaged, engineer, engrave, enjoyed.

Reading and Writing Practice

72.

(98)

73.

(128)

74.

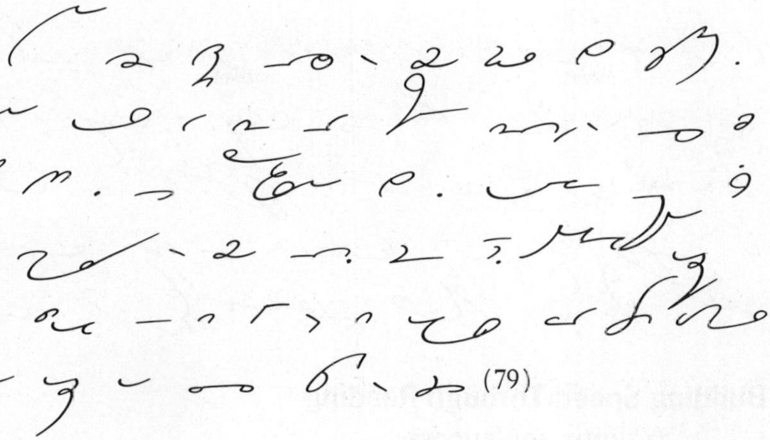

(79)

75.

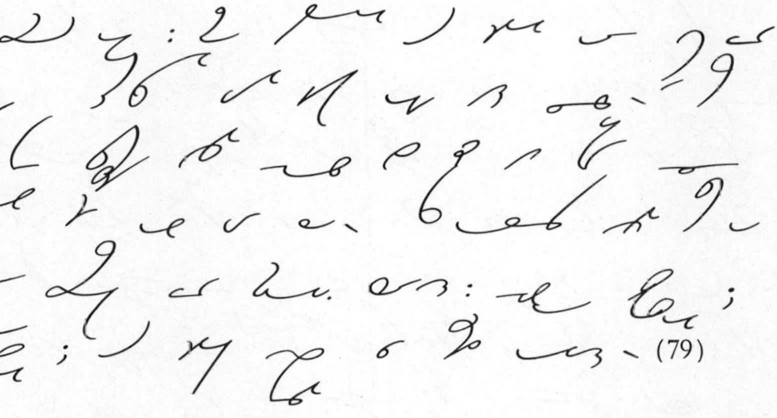

(79)

76.

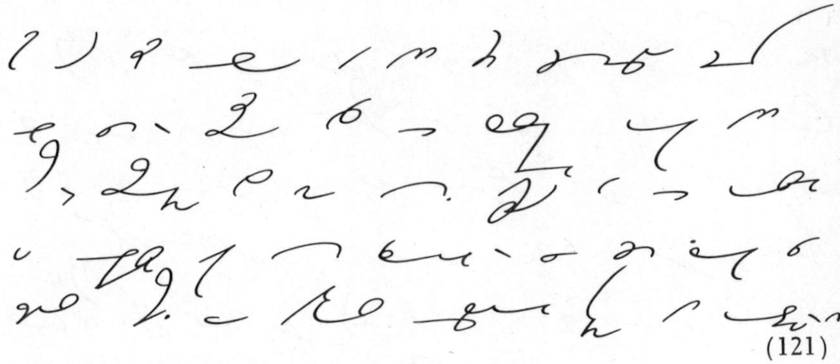

(121)

Building Speed Through Reading

77. HINTS FOR SUCCESS

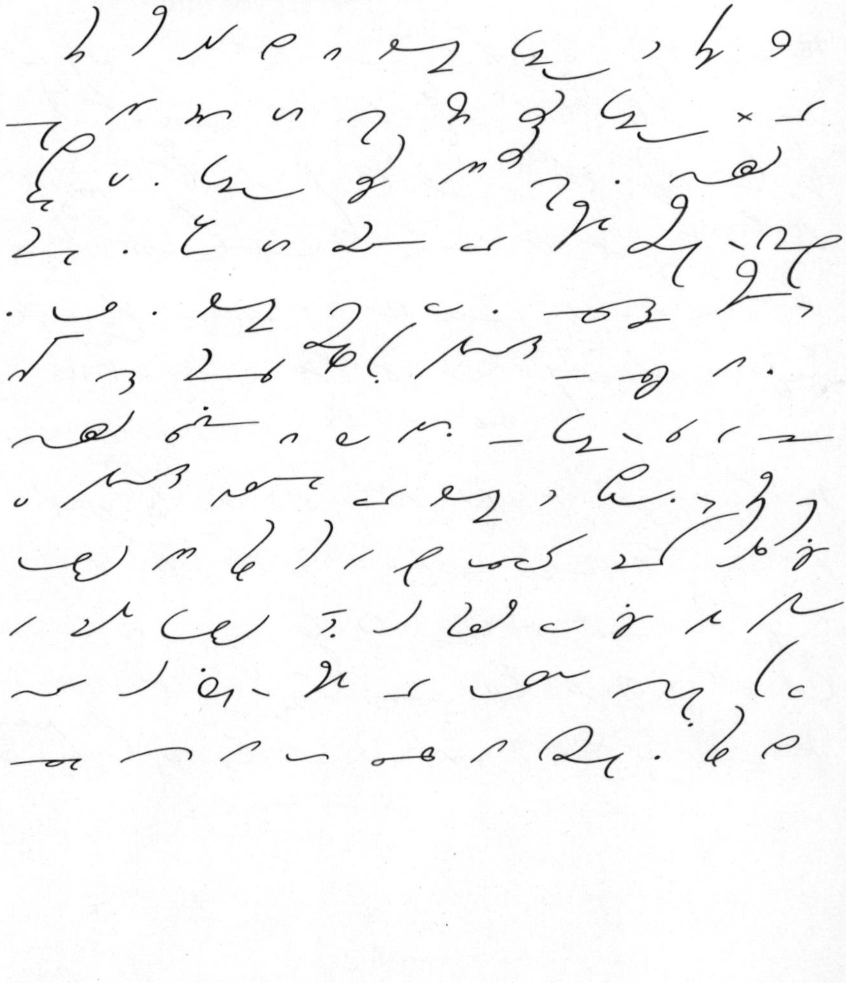

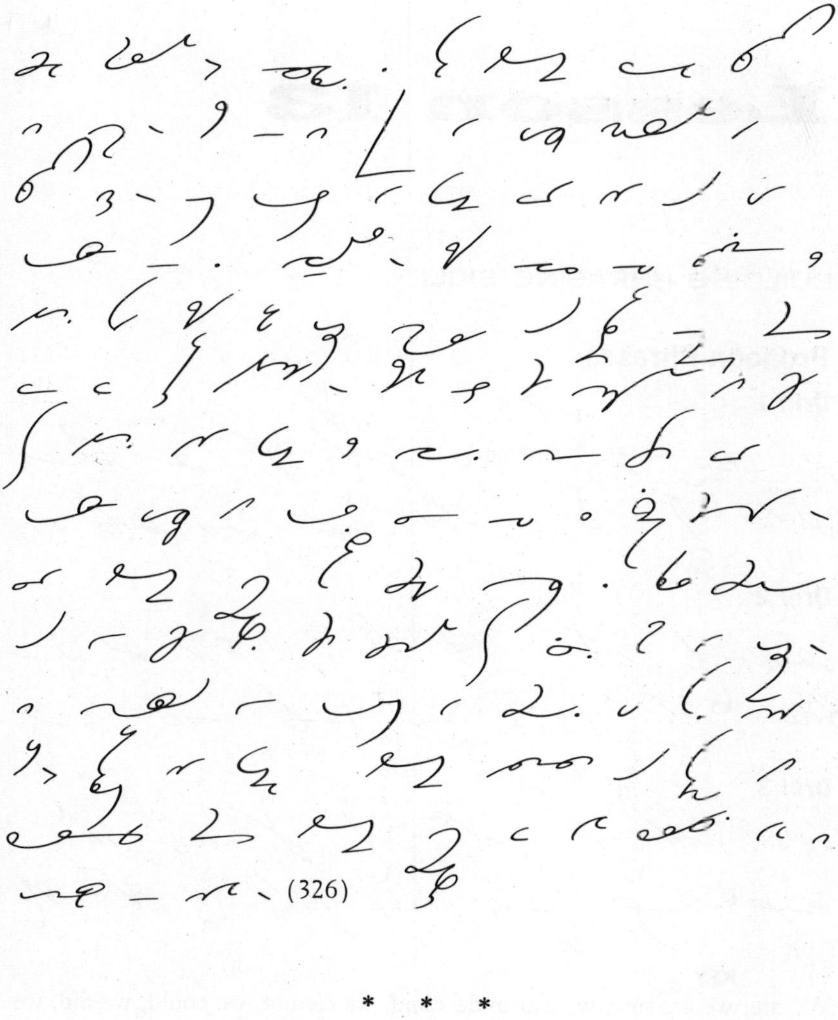

(326)

* * *

Lesson 13

BUILDING PHRASING SKILL

Pronoun Phrases

Drill 1

Drill 2

Drill 3

KEY

We are, we are sure, we can understand, we cannot, we could, we did, we enclose, we feel, we find, we have been able, we have your letter, we hope that, we hope you will, we know, we made.

We must, we shall be able, we should be glad, we should like to have, we understand, we understood, we want, we will; who are, who desire, who have, who is, who know, who made, who make, who will.

You can, you could, you did not, you do not, you have been, you have had, you know, you desire, you may be sure, you may have, you might, you must, you need, you see, you should not, you should be.

Brief-Form and Phrase Letters

78. 

(103)

79. 

(76)

80. 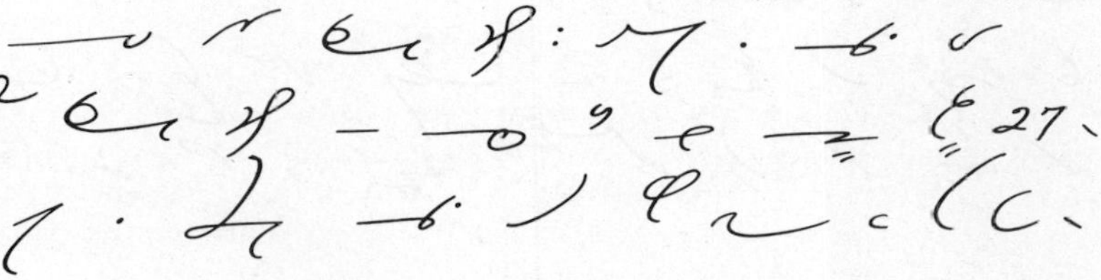

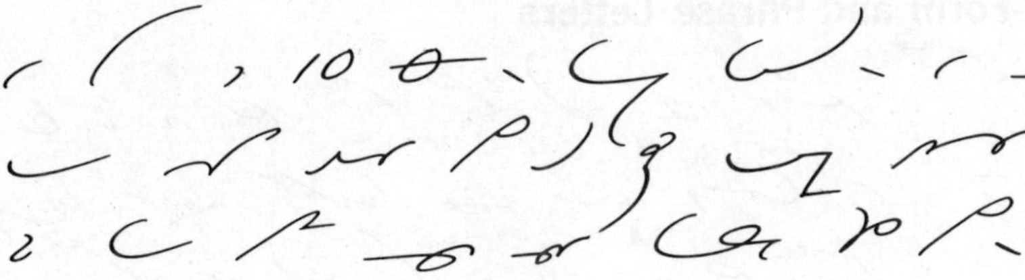

(67)

81. 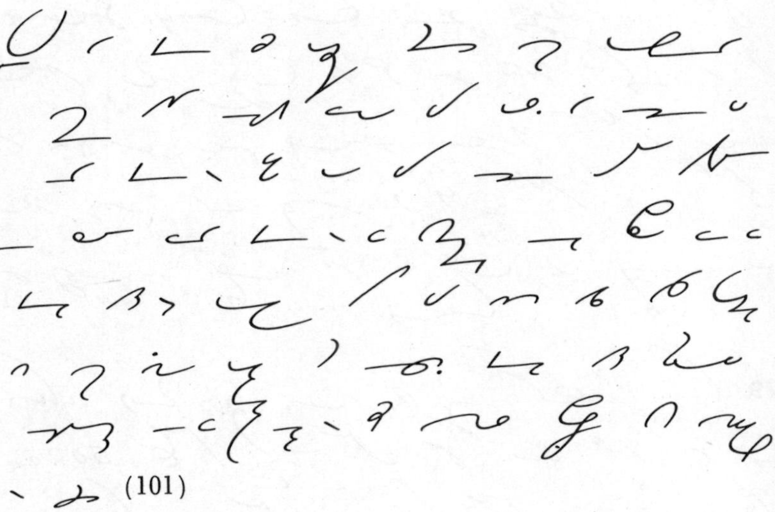

(101)

82. 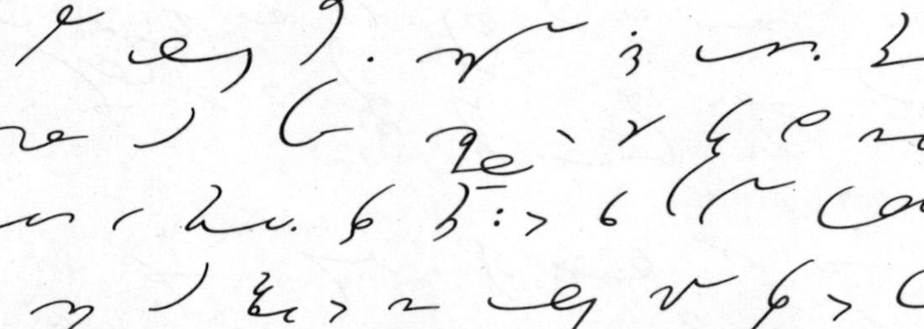

(54)

83. 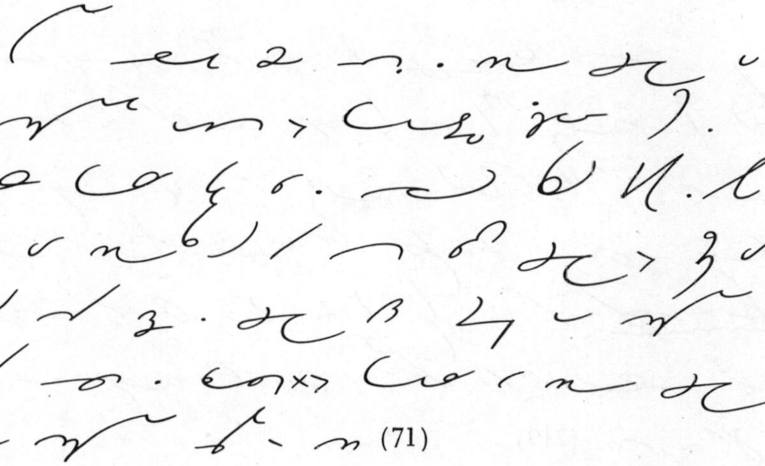

(71)

84. 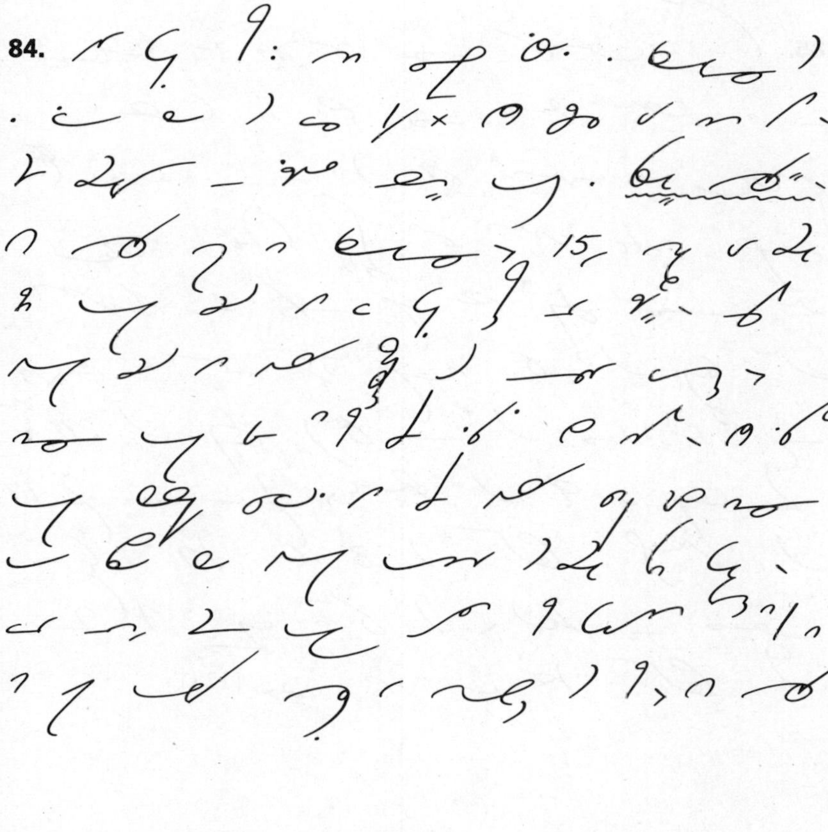

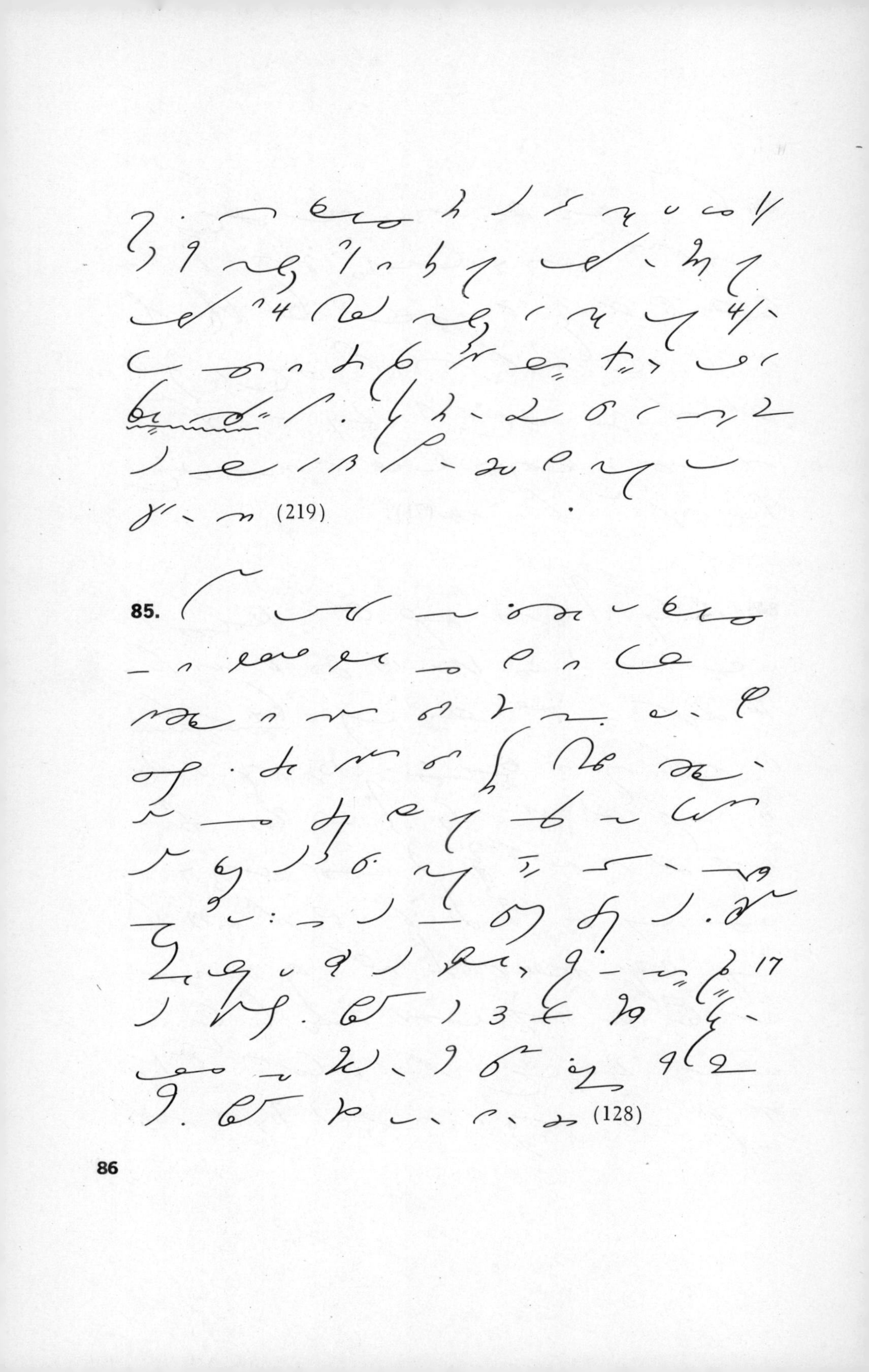

(219)

85.

(128)

Lesson 14

PROGRESSIVE SPEED BUILDING

Half-Minute Progressive Speed Builder (70-110)

VOCABULARY PREVIEW

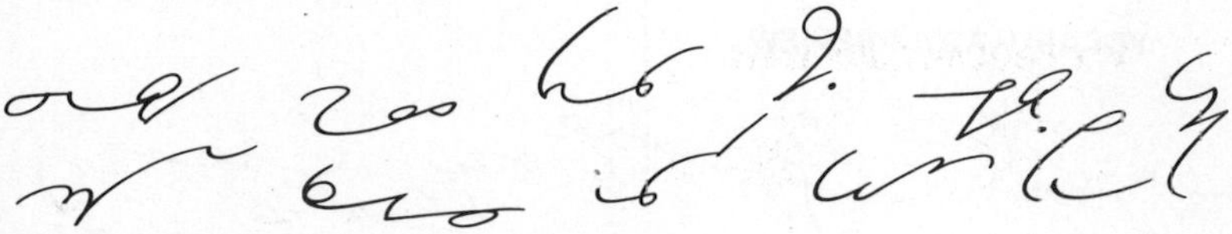

KEY

Analyzed, completely, bulletin, advertising, merchandising, profitable. Customer, salesman, retained, product, ability.

(½ MINUTE AT 70)

86. Dear Jim: The first week of October is over. Did you do your very best? Have you analyzed/your past week's work? If so, were your results satisfactory? Are you completely satisfied with yourself?//

(½ MINUTE AT 80)

This letter is not the usual sales bulletin; it is an appeal to every member/of our staff. We need your help to put October over!

Will you put in a few extra hours each day to help us over the top? Frank//

(½ MINUTE AT 90)

87. Dear Mrs. Young: Thank you for your letter of June 10 containing advertising and merchandising suggestions for our products./ We are returning your suggestions as they do not fit in with our present plans. We appreciate your interest. Yours truly,//

(½ MINUTE AT 100)

88. Bulletin to the Sales Staff: We must build up our repeat sales!

You surely know that repeat sales are the only kind of sales that build a profitable business. / A profit is not made until a sale is made. A sale is not made until a customer sees eye to eye with a salesman. //

(½ MINUTE AT 110)

A customer is not retained until and unless the product is sold and resold. And a repeat sale is not made unless the product is so / satisfactory that the customer just cannot get along without it!

We have that kind of product. You have the necessary sales ability. Go to it! //

Minute Progressive Speed Builder (60-80)

Each of the letters in this assignment is ten words longer than the preceding one. Make an effort to increase your speed by writing each letter in 1 minute.

VOCABULARY PREVIEW

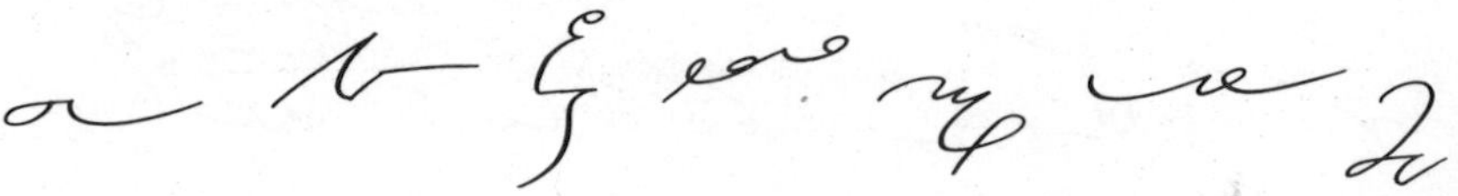

KEY

Annual, department, expensive, territory, co-operation, loyal, convinced.

(1 MINUTE AT 60)

89. Memo to Clyde McKee: In looking over the annual report of the sales / department, I notice that our largest selling costs are involved in the handling of small//accounts. Our largest accounts are the least expensive to handle. With a view to /// increasing our profits, I wonder whether you could not make some changes based on these findings. (1)

(1 MINUTE AT 70)

90. Memo to Our Sales Staff: We must reduce our cost of selling. We find that 58 per cent of / our costs come from calling on very small customers, who are giving us only 12 per cent of our // sales.

An intensive study of your territory is being made, and a new policy will /// be issued by the end of this month. We know that we can count on your complete co-operation. (2)

(1 MINUTE AT 80)

91. Dear Mr. McKee: Of course, I shall be glad to co-operate with the new plan if you think it is the one that / is best for the company as a whole. We have a very loyal following among many small-business men, // however, and I should hate to see them taken out of the territory. I am sure you must have a good reason /// for this policy and I stand ready to be convinced.

I am enclosing my sales report for the past month. Dick (3)

Reading and Writing Practice

92.

(222)

93.

(178)

94. 

(173)

95. 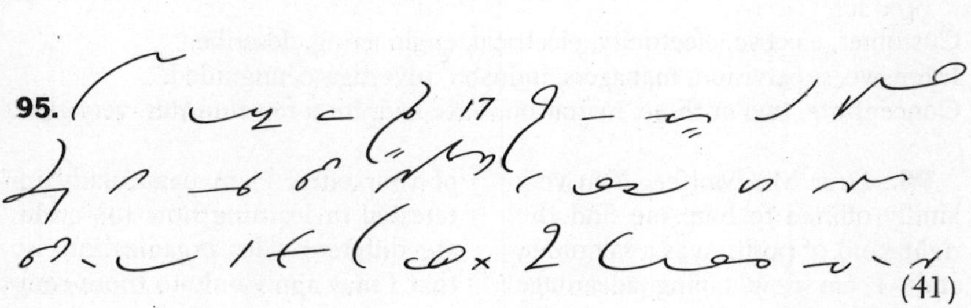

(41)

Lesson 15

BUILDING SUSTAINED SPEED

Five-Minute Speed Builder

The following correspondence is between Mr. McKee and Charles E. Foster, 409 South Phoenix Street, Aurora 6, Illinois.

VOCABULARY PREVIEW

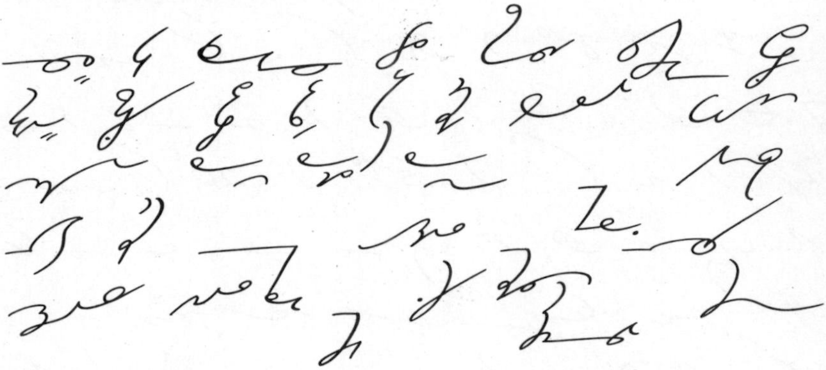

KEY

McKee, position, salesman, particularly, evaluate, advancement, appreciate.
Foster, associated, especially, experienced, objective, sufficient, talents, product.
Customer, electric, electricity, electrical, engineering, describe.
Intensive, supervision, managers, industry, investigate, unguided.
Concentrate, two or three, invitation, have had, for a few minutes, very glad.

96. Dear Mr. McKee: You very kindly offered to help me find the right kind of position as a salesman, and[1] I am now taking advantage of your offer. I am particularly interested in learning how to[2] evaluate different sales organizations so that I may apply only to those companies that offer[3] the best chances for advancement.

I shall appreciate your advice. Sincerely yours,

97. Dear Mr. Foster: I[4] am very glad indeed to give you a few ideas regarding the selection of the right company to become[5] associated with and especially the sales-training program that the company should offer its[6] beginning salesmen.

Companies hiring salesmen follow two general methods: one group builds its salesmen to measure;[7] the second hires only experienced salesmen.

Your objective should be to land a job with a company that[8] will spend sufficient time training you, thus enabling you to make the most of your sales talents.

The selling problems[9] involved, the product, the type of customer, and other important factors determine the kind and the length of[10] training that the beginning salesman should be given.

If you were to sell a product like electric motors, you[11] would need some training in basic electricity. It would help if you had a college degree in electrical[12] engineering. Next, you would have to know the product and all its uses.

It would take a book to describe all[13] the types of training that are offered to salesmen. Some companies offer training courses that run for a year or[14] more. Still others offer short school courses followed by intensive training in the field, under the supervision[15] of field sales managers. A letter to the leading companies in the industry in which you wish to sell will[16] bring you details of the training offered.

The point is, you should think immediately about the training you will[17] receive when you start to find a selling job. Investigate thoroughly and assure yourself that you are going[18] to be really trained—not just left to find your own way, unguided by an experienced hand.

Come in to see me[19] soon, and we will talk over your future in more detail. Cordially yours,

98. Dear Mr. McKee: Thank you very much[20] indeed for your most helpful advice. It will enable me to concentrate my efforts on those companies that[21] come up to the standard you have set.

After I have made two or three contacts, I shall take advantage of your[22] invitation and drop in to talk over my experiences with you. Sincerely yours,

99. Dear Mr. McKee: I[23] have visited five companies and have had most interesting talks with the sales managers of these companies.[24] May I come in next Tuesday afternoon and talk with you for a few minutes? Sincerely yours,

100. Dear Mr. Foster:[25] I shall be glad to see you Tuesday afternoon between three and four. I am interested in hearing what those[26] men told you about their sales-training programs. Cordially yours, (531)

Reading and Writing Practice

101.

(99)

102.

(113)

103.

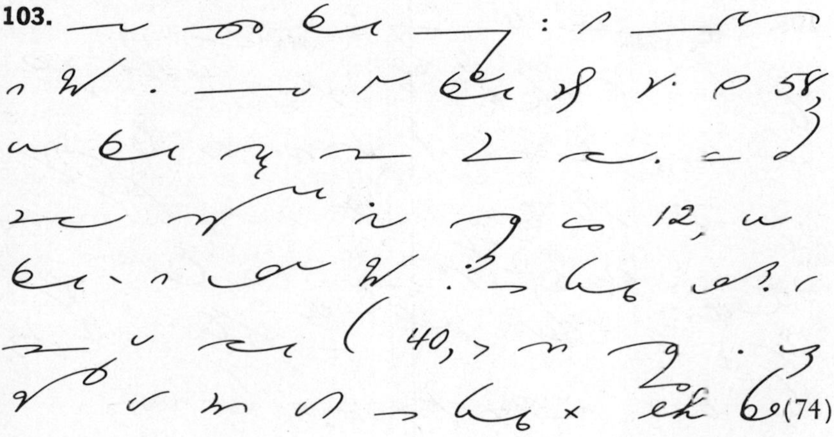

(74)

104.

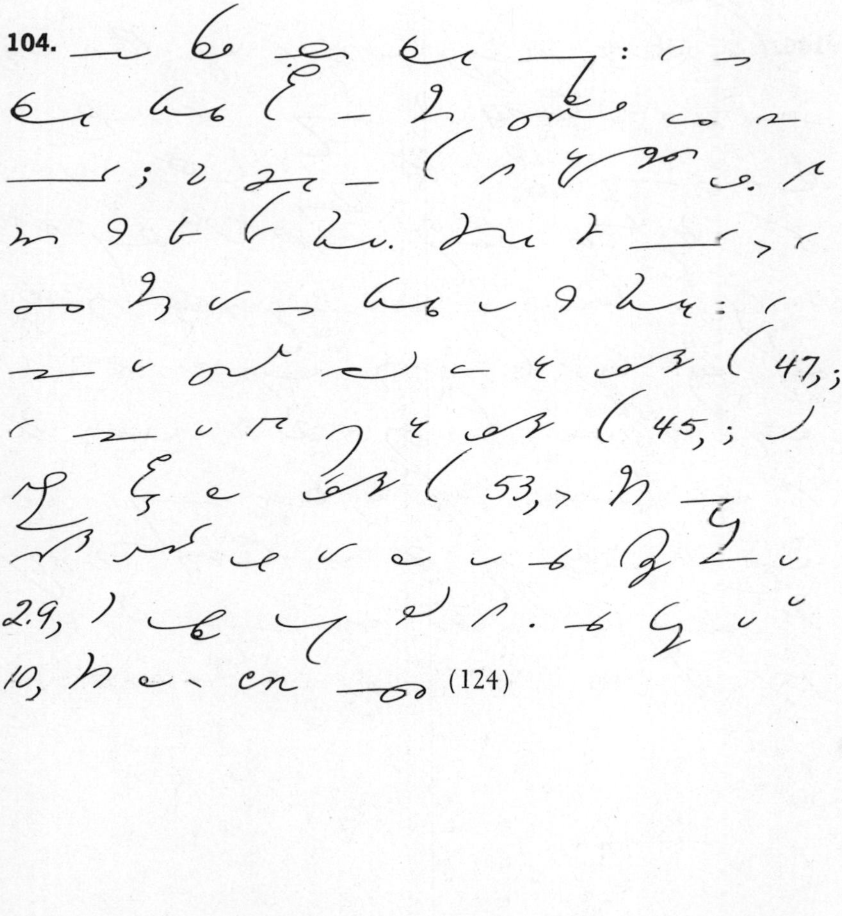

(124)

105.  (80)

106. 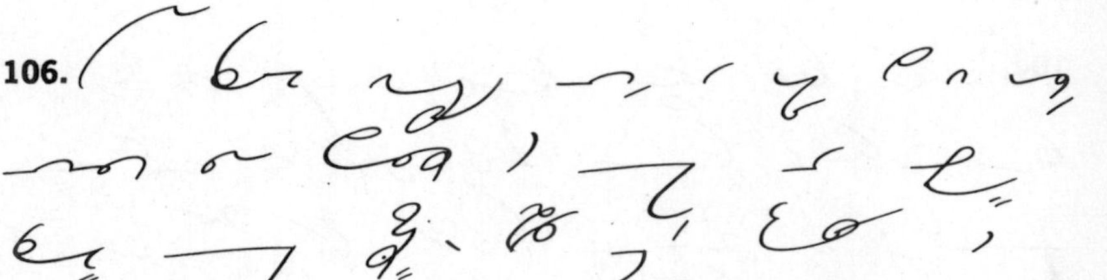 (144)

4

The Credit Department

Spelling and Penmanship Improvement Drills for Chapter 4

SPELLING

When a word of one syllable (or words of more than one syllable that are accented on the last syllable) ends with a single consonant preceded by a single vowel, the consonant is doubled before a suffix that begins with a vowel.

acquit, acquitted
bag, baggage
compel, compelling
equip, equipped
impel, impelled
occur, occurrence
regret, regrettable
remit, remittance
ship, shipped
transfer, transferred

Exceptions

defer, deference
gas, gaseous
infer, inference
prefer, preferable

PENMANSHIP

1.
2.
3.
4.
5.

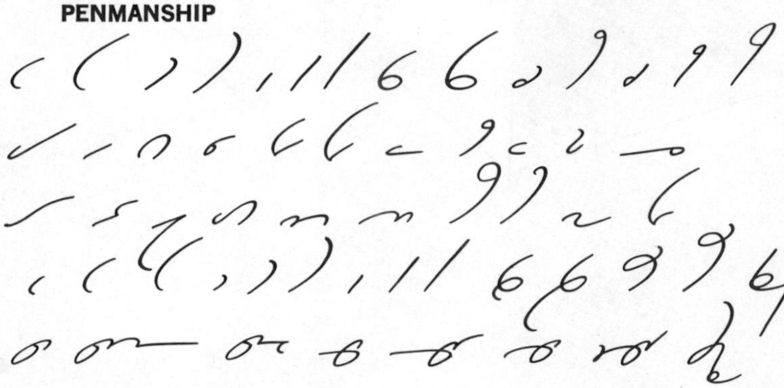

KEY

1. Put, be, for, have, shall, which, j, pay, bay, see, ever, she, each, age.
2. Order, at, this, with, part, but, on, if, all, so, me.
3. And the, at the, to be, of this, you can, Cordially yours, I have, you have, you are, by the.
4. S, put, be, is, for, have, shall, which, j, pass, payable, safe, save, charge.
5. How, outcome, ounce, now, mouth, cow, scout, voucher.

Lesson 16

BUILDING TRANSCRIPTION SKILL

Transcription English Pointers

THE USES OF THE SEMICOLON

1. If the conjunction is omitted between co-ordinate clauses, a semicolon should separate the clauses.

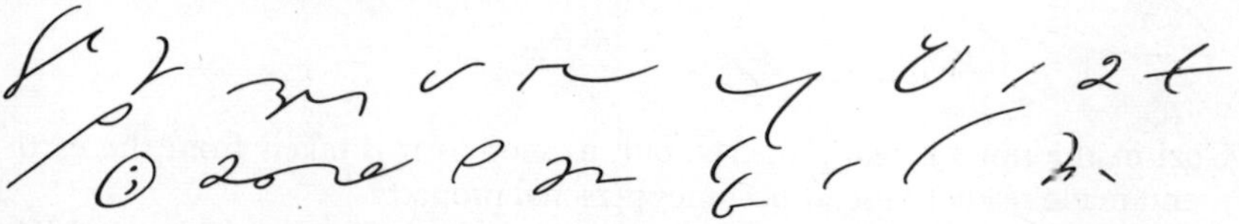

Bids for the construction of the tunnel will be opened at 2 p.m. today; we regret that we cannot postpone the time for you.

2. If the second of two co-ordinate clauses in a sentence is introduced by a transitional word, a semicolon precedes that word. A comma may or may not follow the transitional word, depending on the emphasis intended. The following are examples of such connectives.

accordingly
after all
again
also
as a result
at any rate
at least
besides
consequently
finally
for example
furthermore
hence
however
I feel sure
in addition
in any case
in fact
in other words
in the first place
indeed
likewise
meanwhile
moreover
nevertheless
notwithstanding
on the contrary
on the other hand
otherwise
surely
therefore
thus
yet

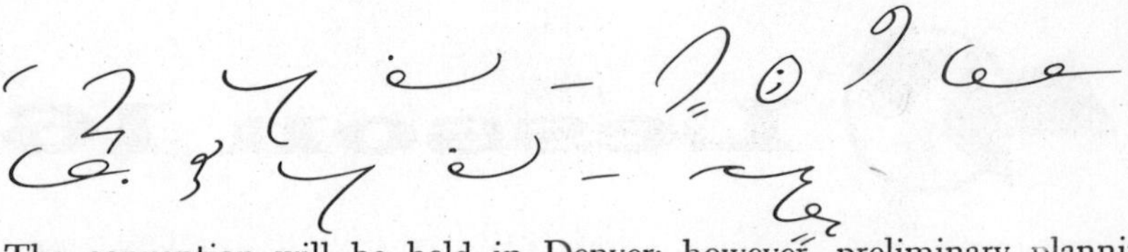

The convention will be held in Denver; however, preliminary planning sessions will be held in Colorado Springs.

3. If one or both of the clauses of a compound sentence contain commas, a semicolon should separate the clauses regardless of the connective used.

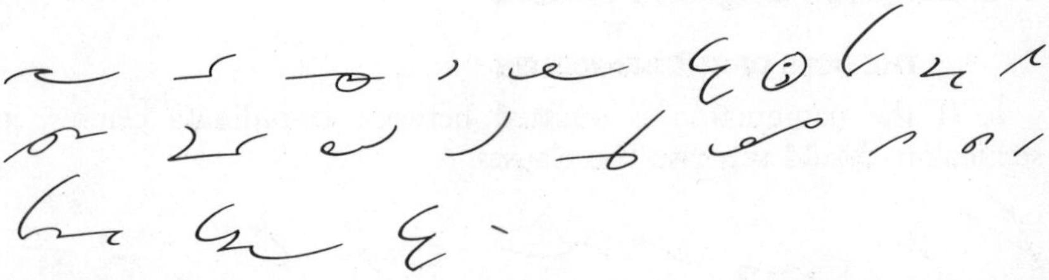

Coal in the mine is real property; but, as soon as it is taken from the earth and made ready to use, it becomes personal property.

(Concluded on page 126)

Transcription Speed Builder

107.

108.

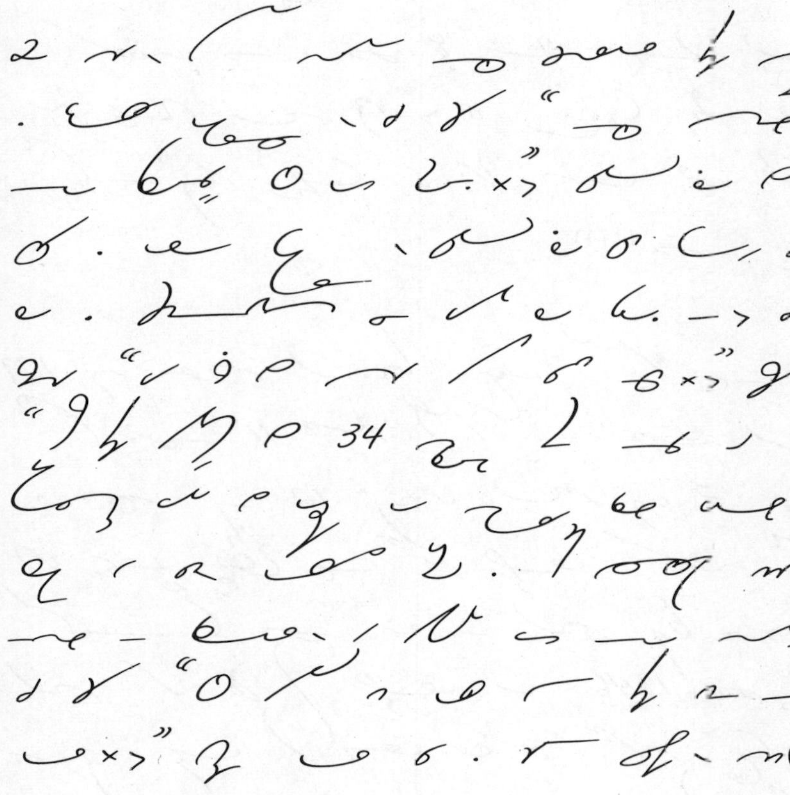

(133)

109.

(114)

110. 129 12 1946 (91)

111. 608 7 28 23 14

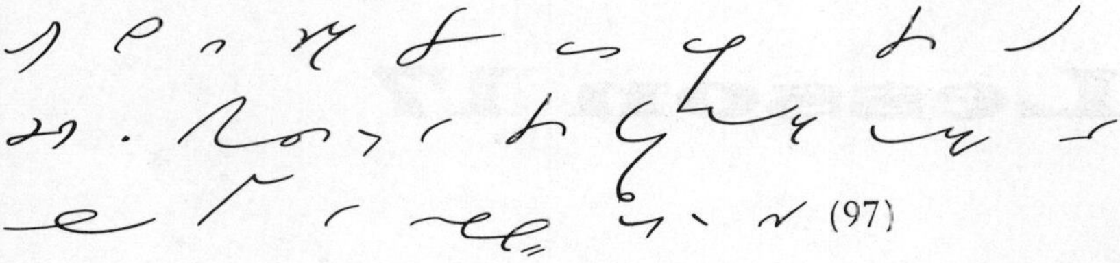

(97)

112.

(91)

113.

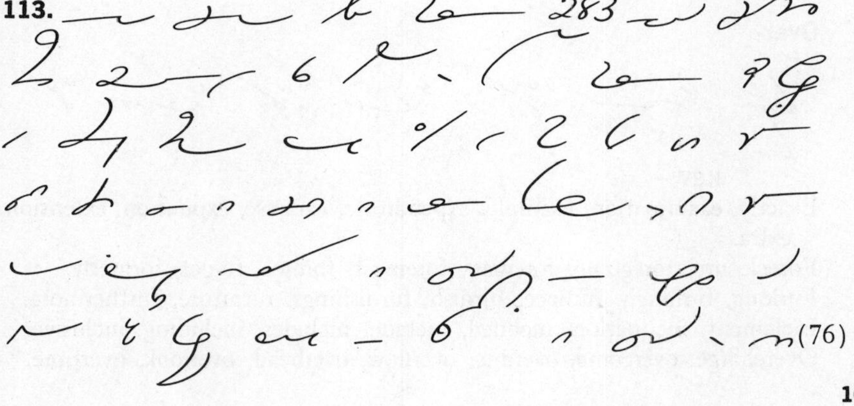

(76)

Lesson 17

MASTERING SHORTHAND THEORY

Word Beginnings

Ex-

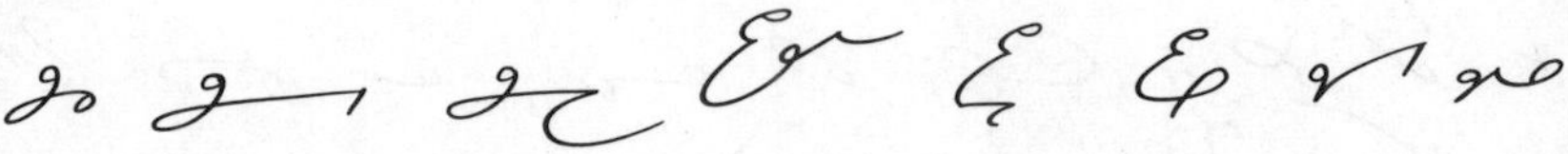

Fore-, For-

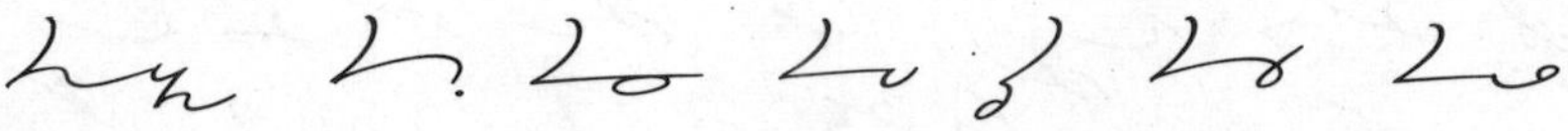

Fur-

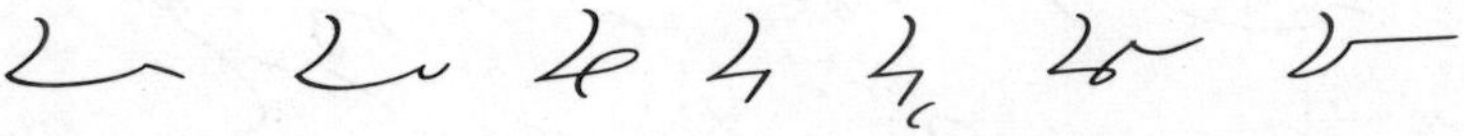

Incl-

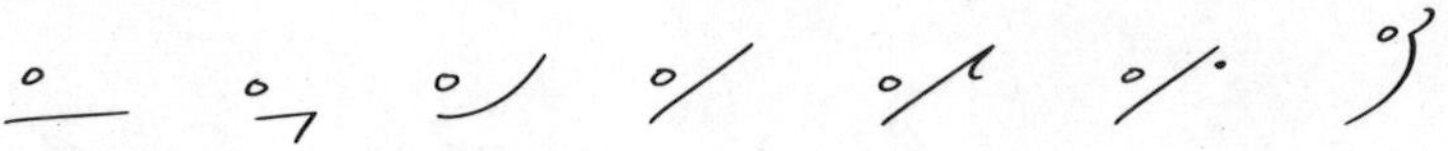

Over-

KEY

Exactly, examination, example, expenditure, expense, expiration, extension, extra.
Foreclosure, foregoing, foreman, foremost, foresee, forget, formerly.
Furlong, furlough, furnace, furnish, furnishings, furniture, furthermore.
Inclement, inclination, inclined, include, includes, including, inclusive.
Overcharge, overcome, overdue, overflow, overhead, overlook, overtime.

Reading and Writing Practice

114.

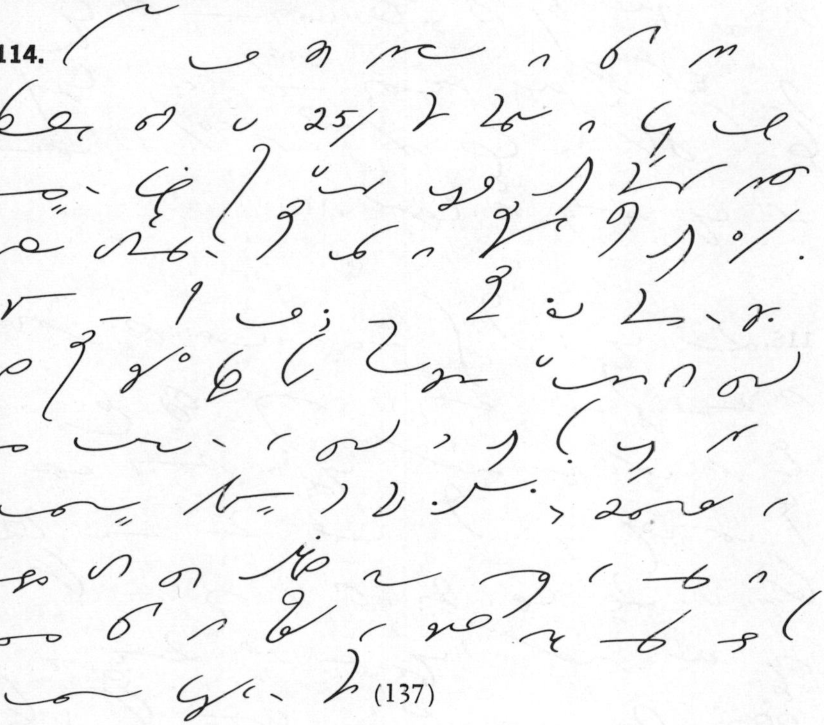

(137)

115.

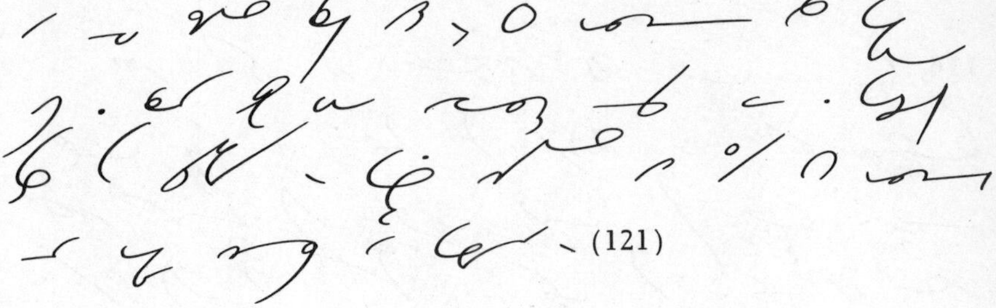

(121)

116.

(129)

117.

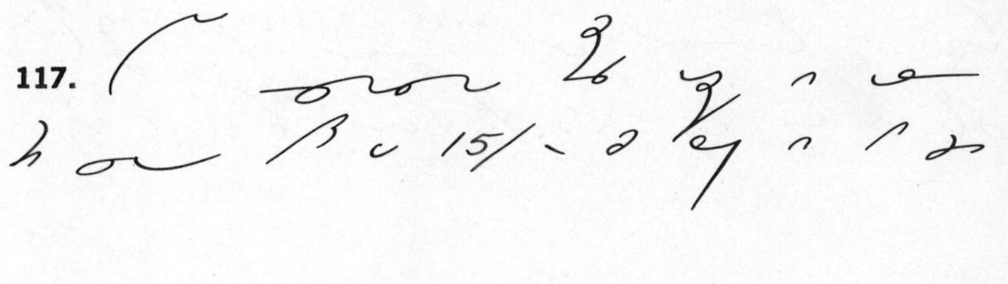

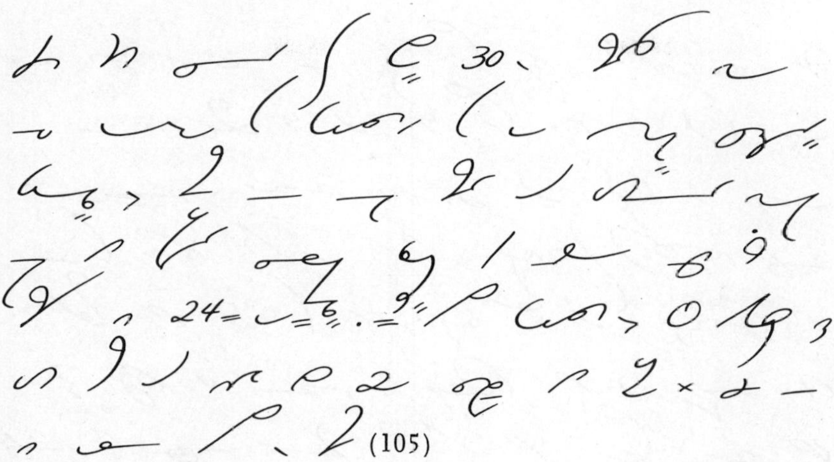

(105)

118. 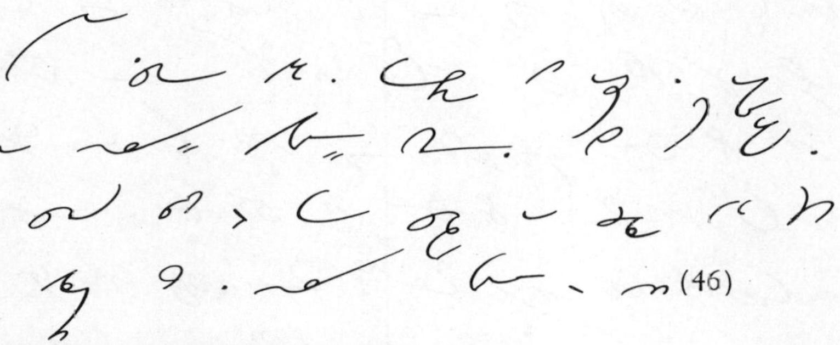

(46)

Building Speed Through Reading

119. HINTS FOR SUCCESS

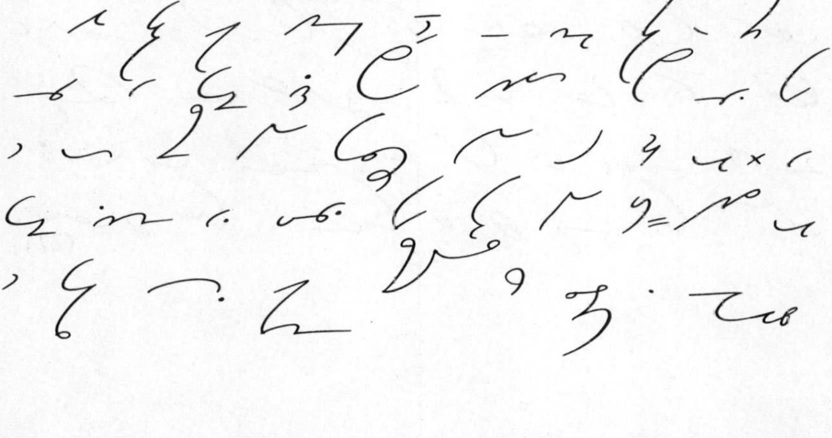

(274)

Lesson 18

BUILDING PHRASING SKILL

Prepositional Phrases

Drill 1

Drill 2

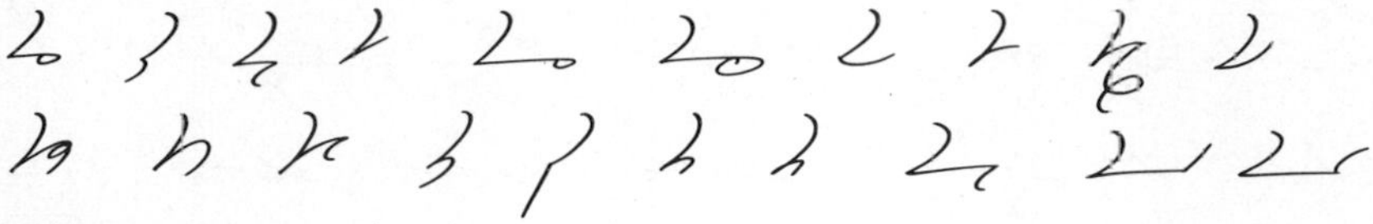

Drill 3

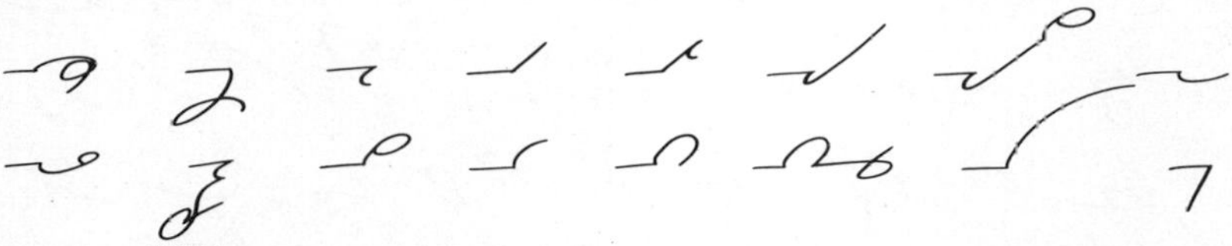

KEY

About it, about that, about the, about them, about these, about this, about you, about which; at all times, at last, at least, at that time, at the; by that time, by the, by this, by this time.

For any, for his, for instance, for it, for me, for my, for our, for the, for the past, for their, for these, for this, for those, for us, for which, for you, for your; from his, from it, from the.

In case, in fact, in his, in it, in its, in order, in order that, in our, in regard, in spite, in that, in the, in this, in this matter, in time, in which.

Brief-Form and Phrase Letters

120.

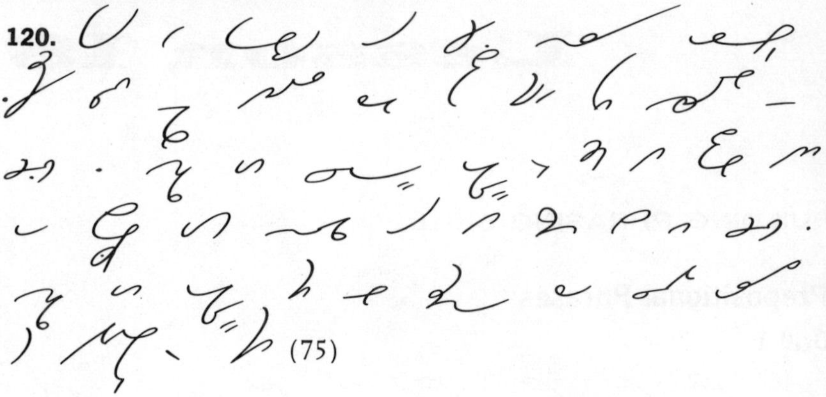

(75)

121.

(102)

122.

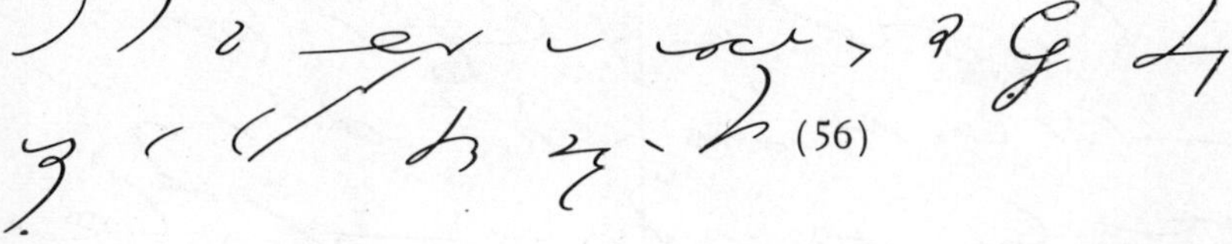

(56)

123.

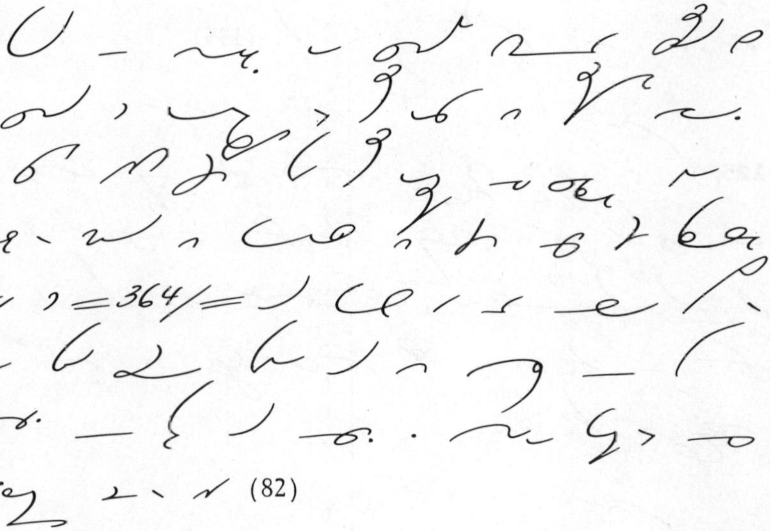

(82)

124.

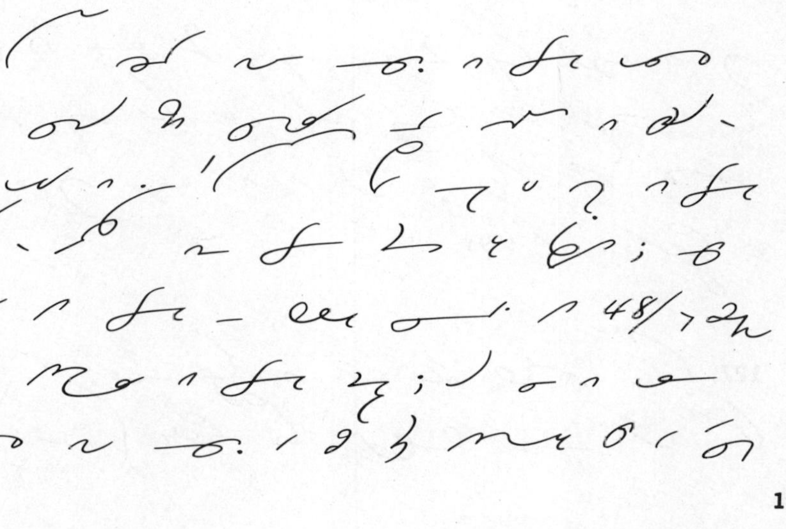

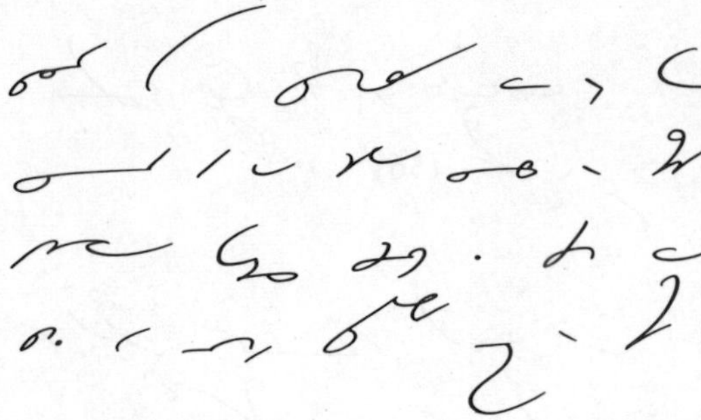

(135)

125.

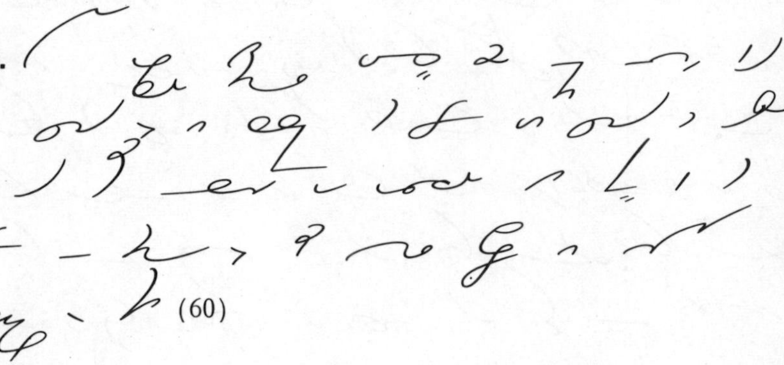

(60)

126.

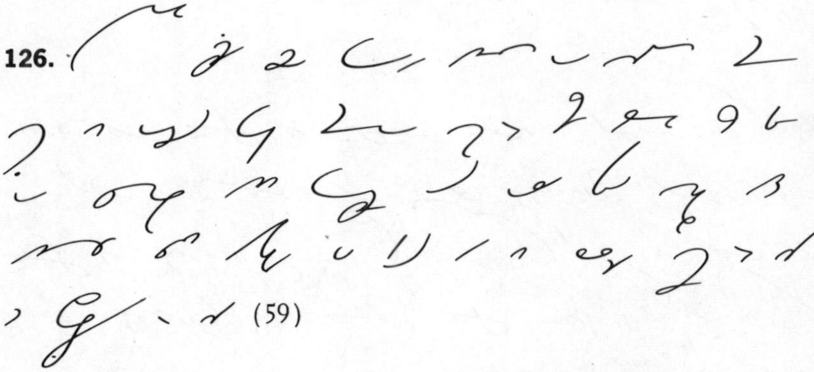

(59)

127.

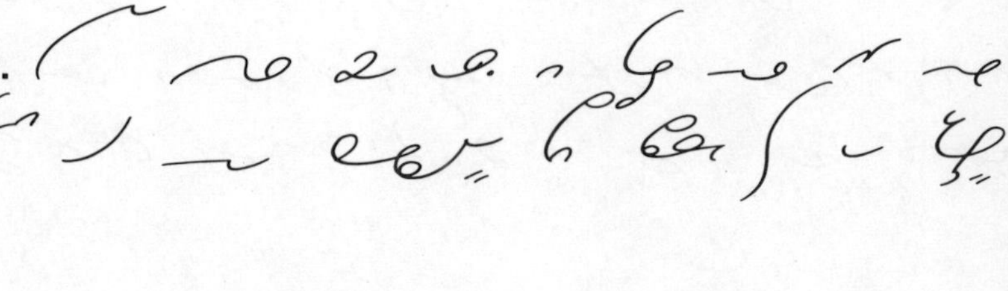

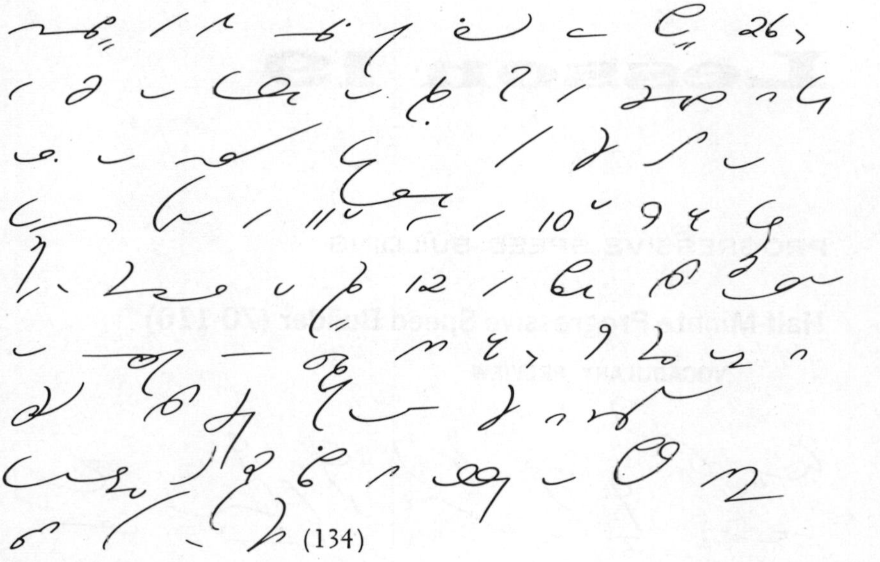

(134)

128.

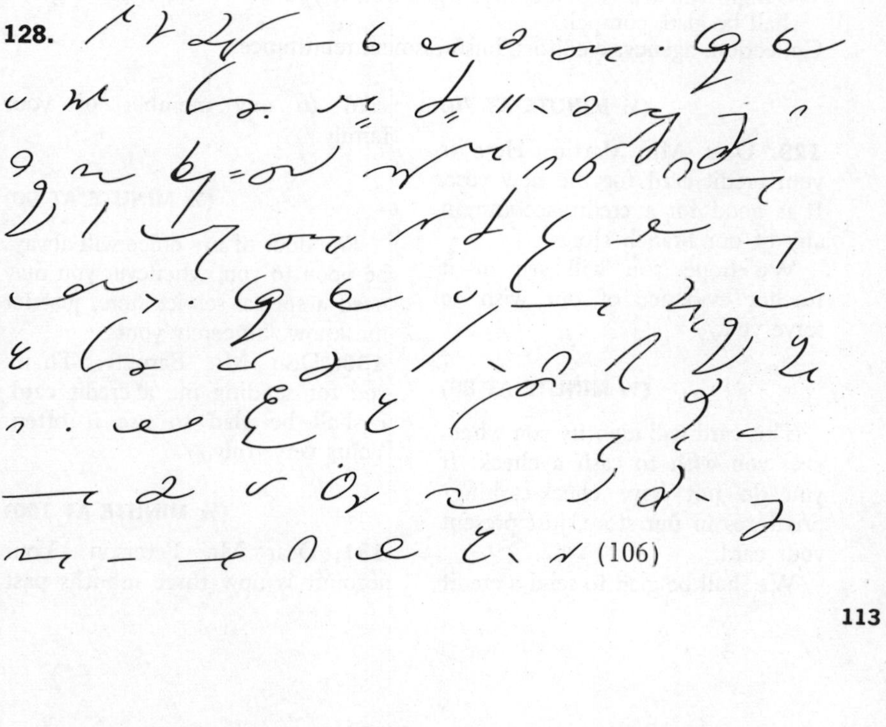

(106)

Lesson 19

PROGRESSIVE SPEED BUILDING

Half-Minute Progressive Speed Builder (70-110)

VOCABULARY PREVIEW

KEY

We hope you will see, identify, whenever, if you do not have, privileges, I shall be glad, compel.
Collection, agency, creditors, businessmen, remittance.

(½ MINUTE AT 70)

129. Dear Mr. Martin: Here is your credit card for the new year. It is good for a credit account/in any of our branch stores.

We hope you will see in it further evidence of our wish to serve you.//

(½ MINUTE AT 80)

This card will identify you whenever you wish to cash a check. If you do not have check-cashing/ privileges in our store, just present your card.

We shall be glad to send a credit card to any member of your family.//

(½ MINUTE AT 90)

The door of my office will always be open to you; whenever you may need a special service here, just let me know./Sincerely yours,

130. Dear Mr. Barnett: Thank you for sending me a credit card. I shall be glad to use it often. Yours very truly,//

(½ MINUTE AT 100)

131. Dear Mr. Peterson: Your account is now three months past due. It looks as if you are going to compel us to place your account with a public/collection agency. Once this step is taken, you will be dealing with a concern whose only interest is to obtain a fee.//

(½ MINUTE AT 110)

If you do not pay this account, we shall be losing dollars and cents; but you will be losing the respect of creditors, the confidence of businessmen,/and the friendship of those who trust you.

We are confident that you do not wish to have this happen. We are, therefore, enclosing a postage-paid envelope for your remittance. Cordially yours,//

Minute Progressive Speed Builder (60-80)

VOCABULARY PREVIEW

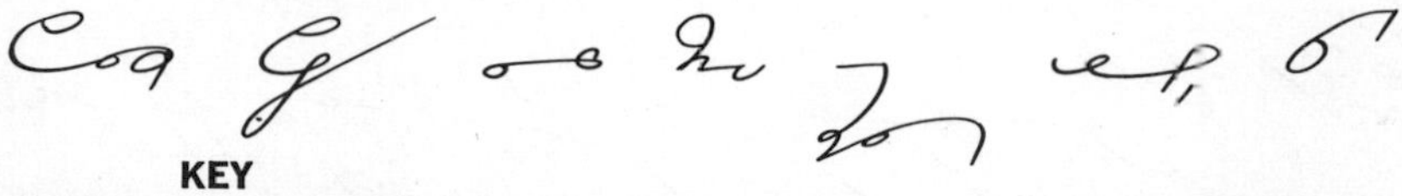

KEY

Application, appreciated, immediately, as you know, investigation, relationship, attention.

(1 MINUTE AT 60)

132. Dear Mr. Farmer: Your application for a credit account with our company/is appreciated. I wish it were possible to send you a credit card//immediately; but, as you know, a routine check is made on all applicants before///a card is issued. This investigation will require two weeks. Sincerely yours, (1)

(1 MINUTE AT 70)

133. Dear Mr. Farmer: We are pleased to notify you that your credit with us has been established/ and your charge account is now open. It is with genuine pleasure that we make our products and// services available to you on a credit basis.

Our bills are mailed on the 10th of the month///and payment is expected before the end of the month. We look forward to serving you. Sincerely yours, (2)

(1 MINUTE AT 80)

134. Dear Mr. Farmer: Thank you for your check in payment of your June account. Your business is appreciated, and/we are looking forward to a long and friendly relationship with you.

I should like to call your attention to//our payment terms. Payment is expected before the end of the month in which your statement is sent; you have been paying/// your statement after this time limit. Your attention to this matter will be appreciated. Yours truly, (3)

Reading and Writing Practice

135.

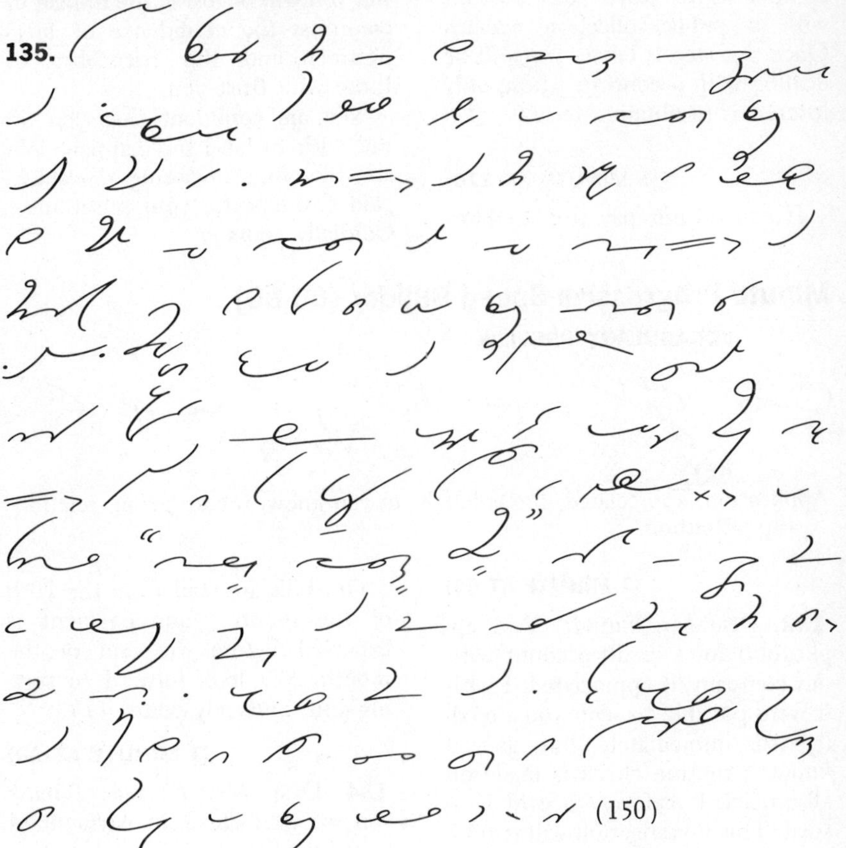

(150)

136.

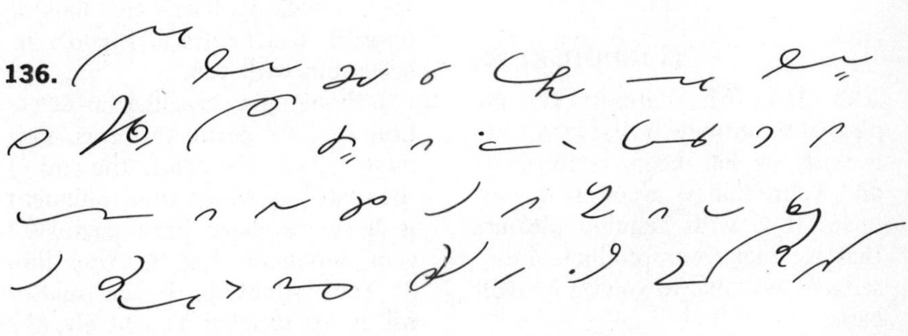

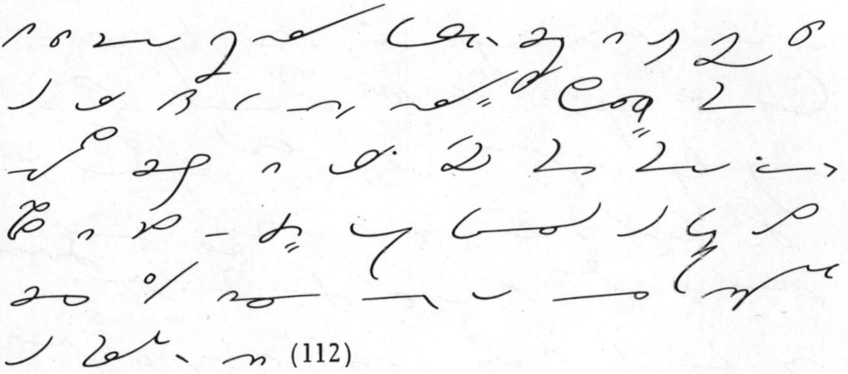

(112)

137.

(87)

138.

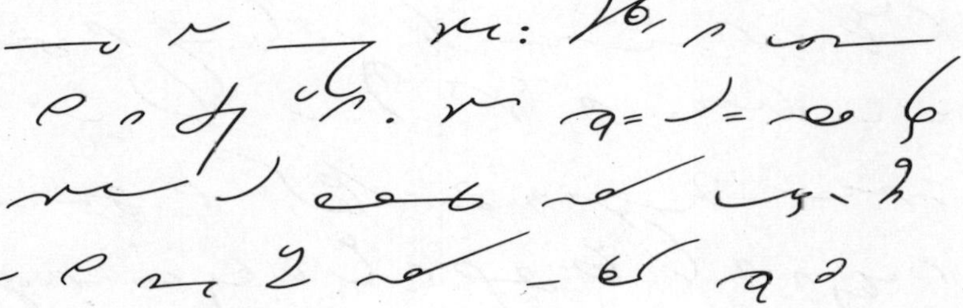

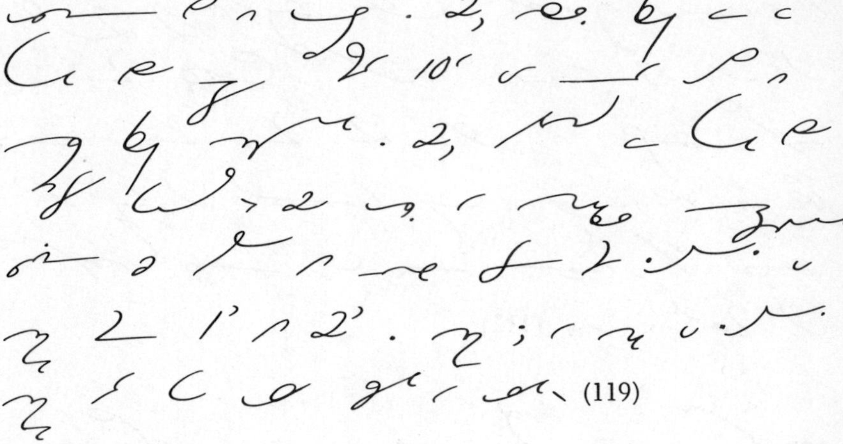

(119)

139.

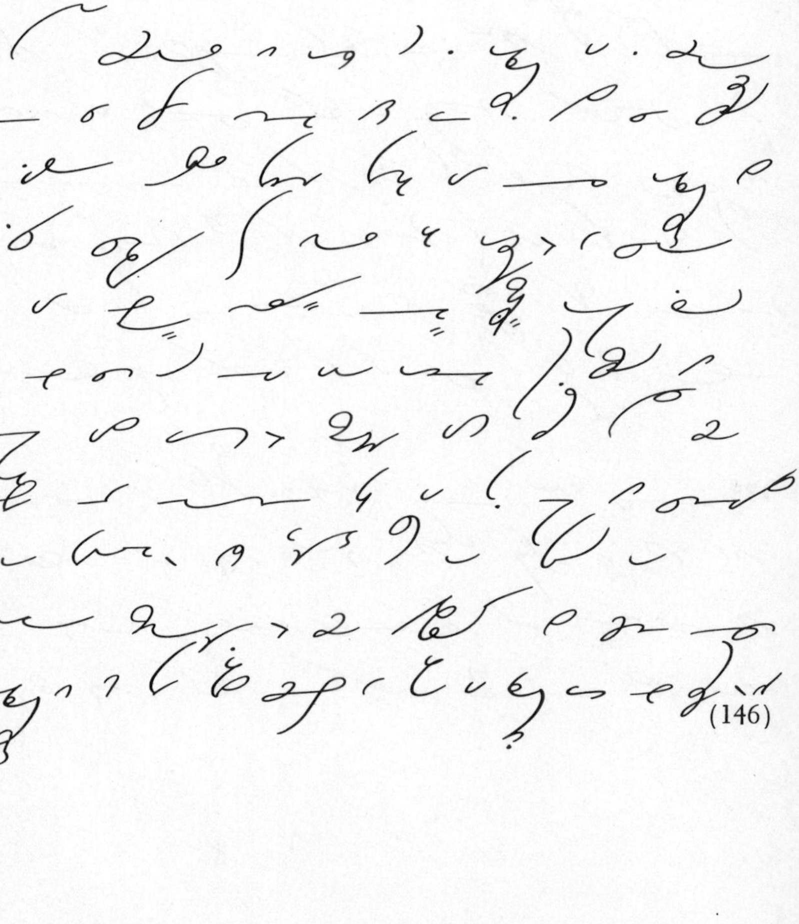

(146)

Lesson 20

BUILDING SUSTAINED SPEED

Five-Minute Speed Builder

The following correspondence is between Mr. Barnett and Charles H. Turner, 215 Iris Street, Evanston 6, Illinois.

VOCABULARY PREVIEW

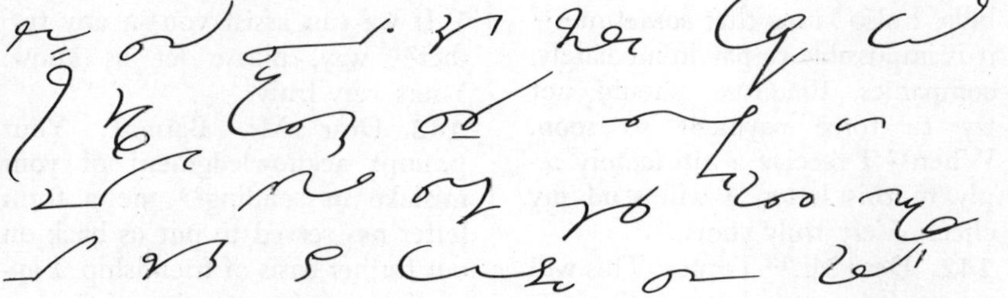

KEY

Turner, account, amounting, substantial, assurance, obliged, promptly.
I have been, for the past, obligations, acquitted, negligence, of course.
Sometimes, to this letter, with reference to the, unfortunate, frequently, co-operate.
Undue, extensions, assist, please let us know, acknowledgment, friendship.

140. Dear Mr. Turner: We find that your account, amounting to $150, has not been paid. As you[1] know, it is difficult to carry out our policy of giving the best service, except through the co-operation[2] of our customers who pay their bills when they become due. Unless we receive a substantial payment, with[3] your assurance of payment of the balance before the end of this month, we shall be obliged to turn your account[4] over to our Legal Department.

Please give this matter your immediate attention. Yours very truly,

141. Dear[5] Mr. Barnett: I have your bill for $150. I also have your letter stating that, unless[6] I pay this bill by the end of this month, you will turn my account over to your legal department. In view of[7] the fact that I have always paid my bills promptly, I can see no reason why you sent me this form letter. As a[8] matter of fact, I have been ill for the past month and unable to take care of my obligations as promptly[9] as usual; circumstances, I think, that leave me acquitted of any negligence.

I realize, of course, that[10] large companies have difficulty in the routine matter of collecting their bills; I also know that sometimes[11] it is impossible to pay immediately; companies, therefore, should not try to force payment so soon. When[12] I receive a satisfactory reply to this letter, I will send my check. Very truly yours,

142. Dear Mr.[13] Turner: This will acknowledge your letter with reference to the letter that you received about your account.

It[14] is unfortunate, under the circumstances, that you received this notice. We know that, frequently, conditions[15] over which our customers have no control prevent them from paying their bills. If we know of these conditions, we are[16] very willing to co-operate, as it is our desire to maintain friendly service in this way.

We assure[17] you that we do not use undue pressure in our collection routine; as a matter of fact, we usually[18] grant longer credit extensions than most of the other firms in our line of business.

A statement, which shows a balance of[19] $150, is enclosed. In view of the conditions presented, we shall be pleased to allow the[20] usual discount if this balance is paid within the next sixty days.

If we can assist you in any further[21] way, please let us know. Yours very truly,

143. Dear Mr. Barnett: Your prompt acknowledgment of your mistake in sending[22] me a form letter has served to put us back on our former basis of friendship. I appreciate your[23] extension of time as well as your offer to grant me the usual discount. You may be sure that my check will reach[24] you within the next sixty days. Sincerely yours, (489)

Reading and Writing Practice

144.

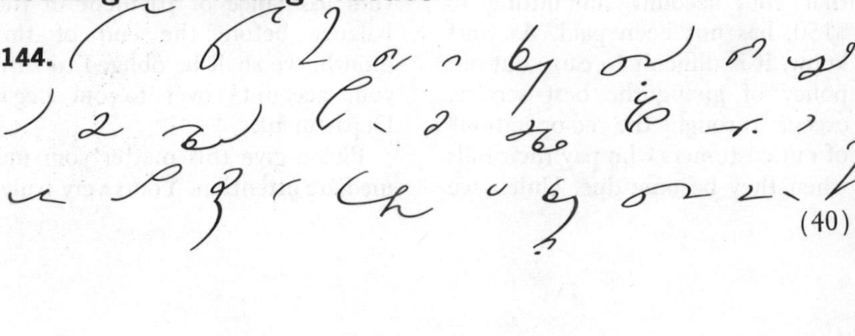

(40)

145.

(94)

146.

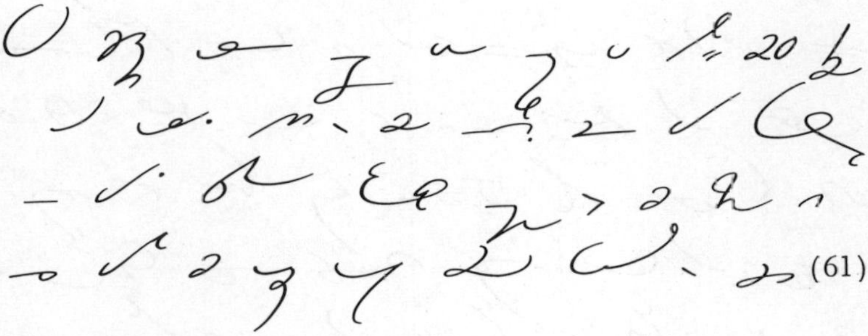

(61)

147.

(46)

148. 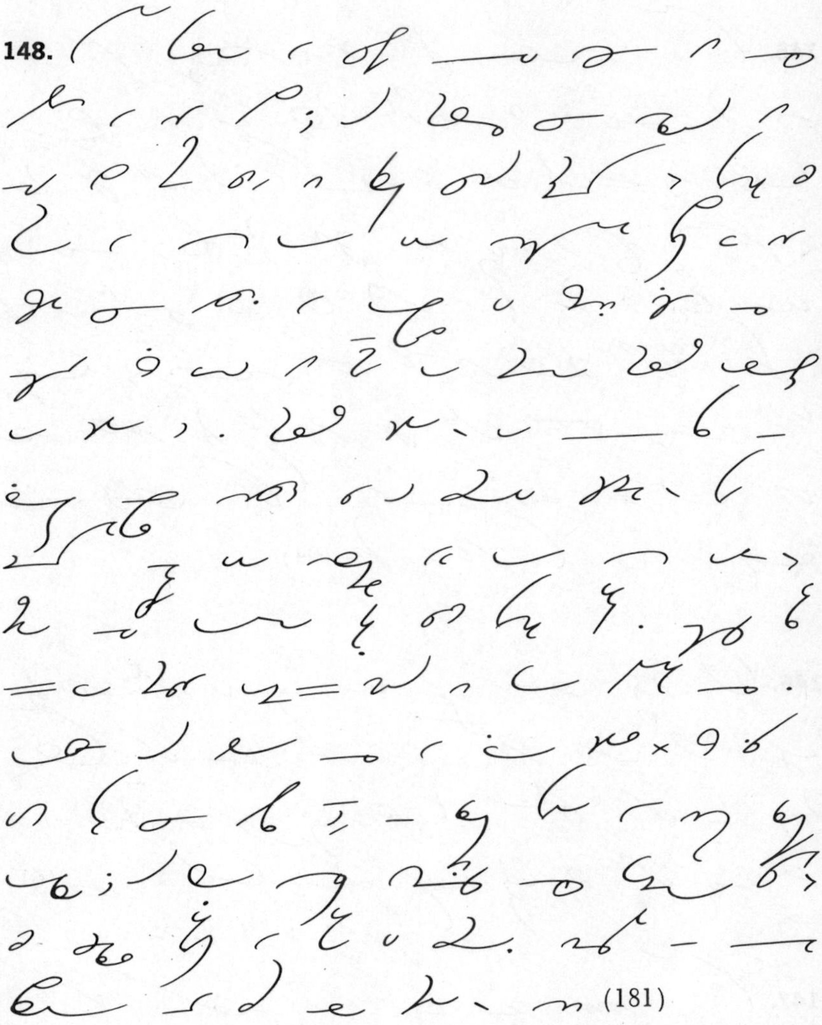

(181)

149. 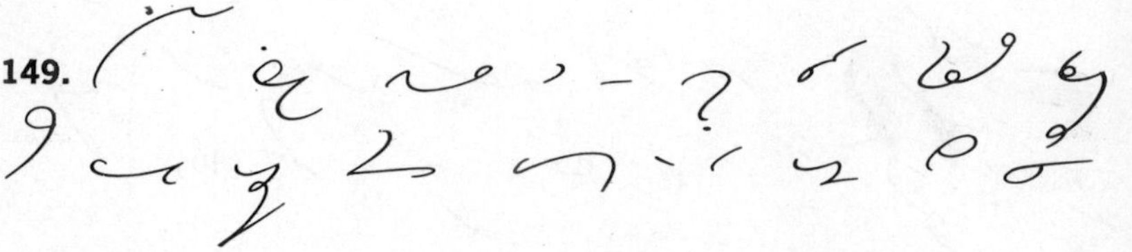

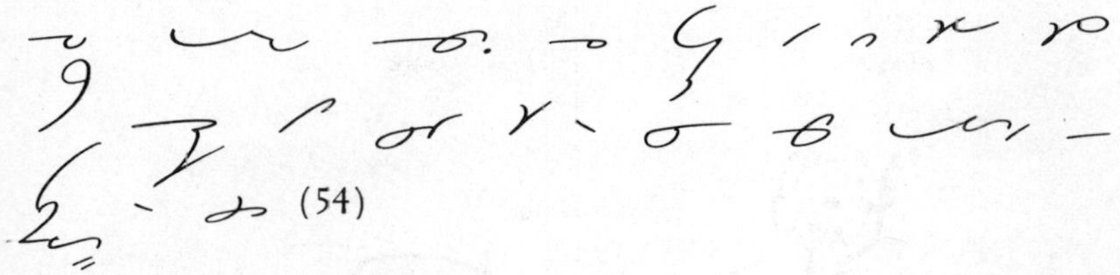 (54)

150. 

(130)

151. 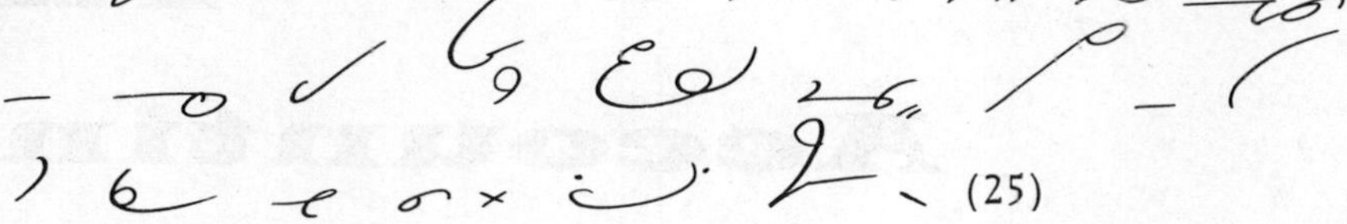 (25)

5 The Accounting Department

Spelling and Penmanship Improvement Drills for Chapter 5

SPELLING

A final consonant is not doubled before a termination beginning with a vowel when:

1. The accent occurs on a syllable other than the last.

benefit, benefited	differ, differing
credit, credited	profit, profited

2. There is more than one consonant at the end of the word.

confirm, confirmation	perform, performance

3. More than one vowel precedes the final consonant.

appear, appearing	need, needy
brief, briefest	obtain, obtaining

PENMANSHIP

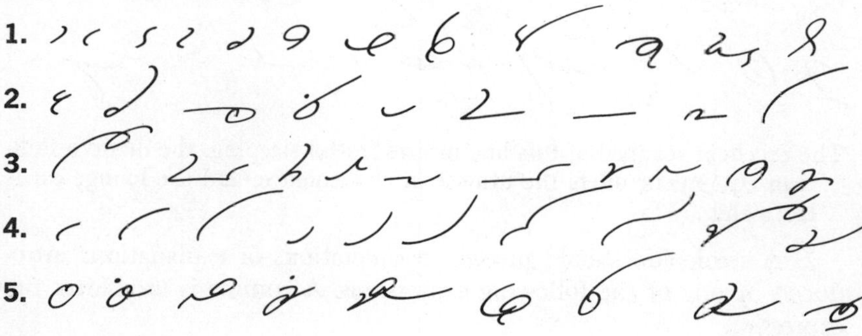

KEY

1. Is, s, says, ses, see, as, raise, pass, system, cases, sources, taxes.
2. Was, very, my, had, our, from, am, one, time.
3. To make, from the, for your, there is, in our, more than, is the, to our, that is, we can.
4. The, ten-den, time, there, and, emd-emt, the time, tenant, estimate, seemed.
5. Why, hire, try, white, style, price, item, file, quiet.

Lesson 21

BUILDING TRANSCRIPTION SKILL

Transcription English Pointers

THE USES OF THE SEMICOLON (CONCLUDED)

A succession of two or more similar words, phrases, or clauses used in the same construction in a sentence is known as a *series*.

1. Long clauses in a series are separated by semicolons.

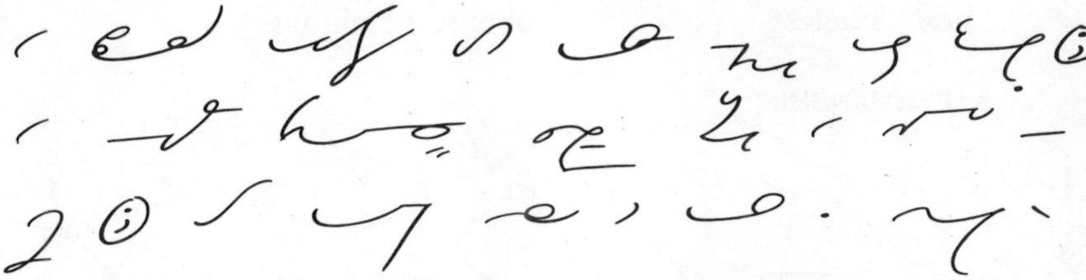

The excellent roadbed of this line insures restful sleeping; the modern Pullman equipment offers the utmost in convenience; and the lounge car is like a club.

2. A semicolon should precede enumerations or explanations introduced by one of the following expressions. A comma is used after the expression.

for example	namely	that is to say
for instance	that is	

We consider our rainwear superior to other popular brands because of three outstanding features; namely, the custom-made appearance, the strength and durability of zipper-plus-snap closings, and their glamorous colors.

We offer many outstanding services; for example, our telephone never sleeps.

Transcription Speed Builder

152.

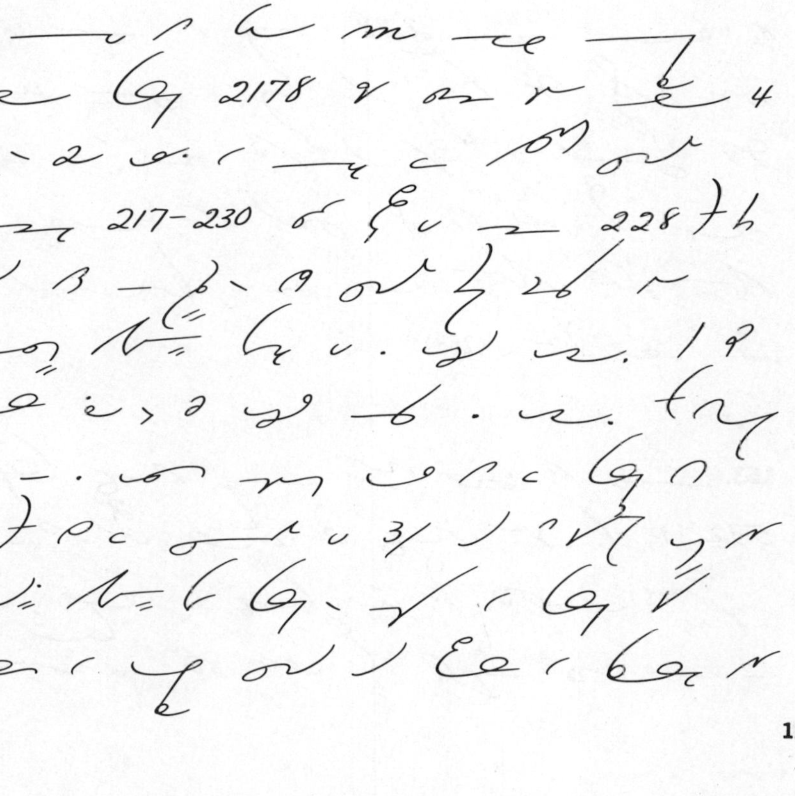

(288)

153.

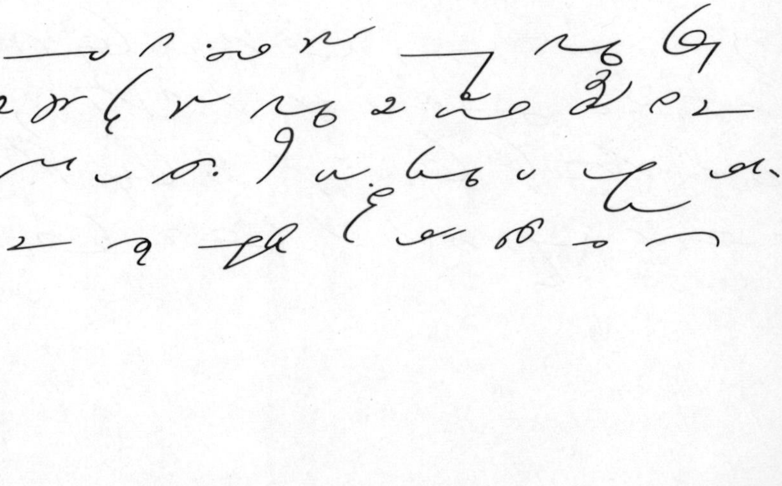

(193)

154.

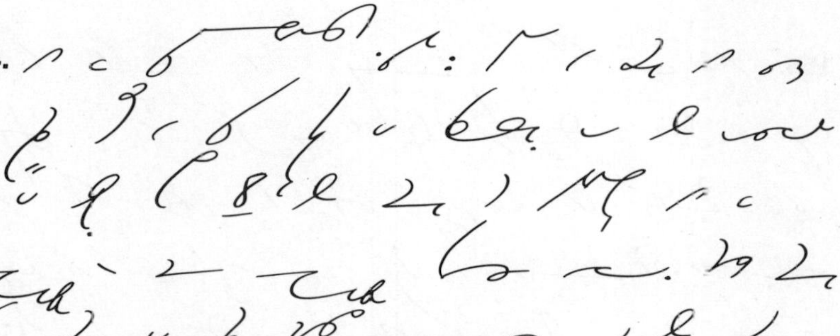

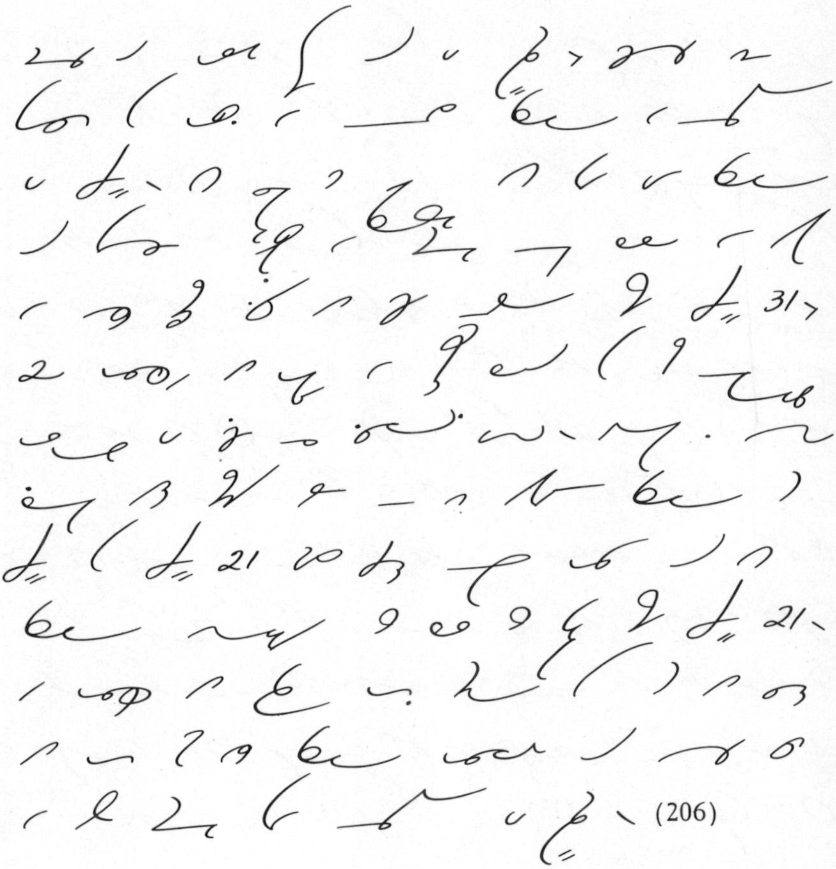

(206)

155.

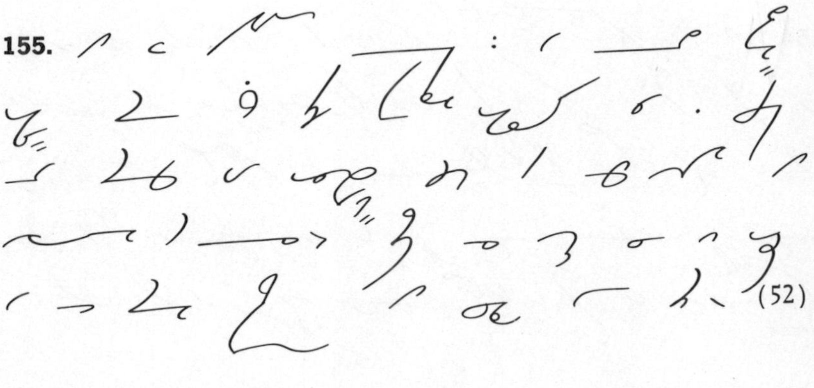

(52)

Lesson 22

MASTERING SHORTHAND THEORY

Word Beginnings

Con-

Post-

Short-

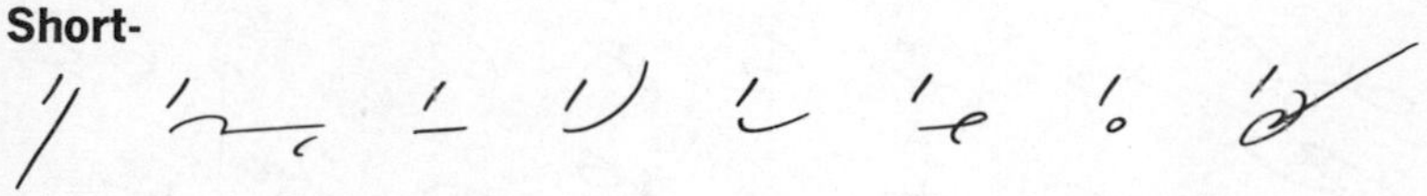

Sub-

Under-

KEY

Concealed, concern, conduct, confer, consistent, contain, control.

Postage, postal, post card, postmarked, postdated, post office, postponing.

Shortage, shortcomings, shorten, shortened, shorter, shortness, shortly, shortsighted.

Submit, subordinate, subscribe, subsequent, subsidiary, substantial, substitute, subway.

Undergo, underline, underneath, underscore, undershirt, understandable.

Reading and Writing Practice

156.

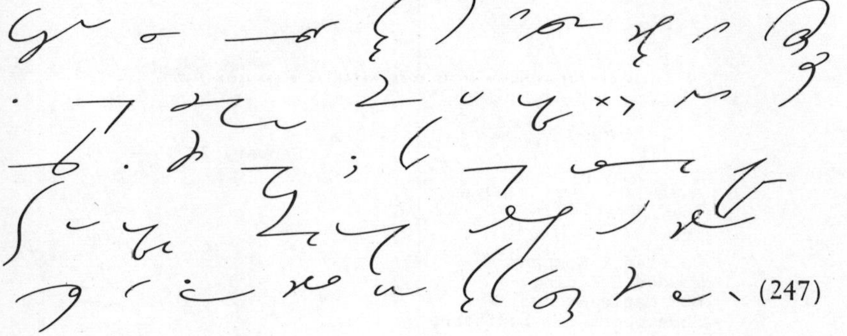

(247)

157.

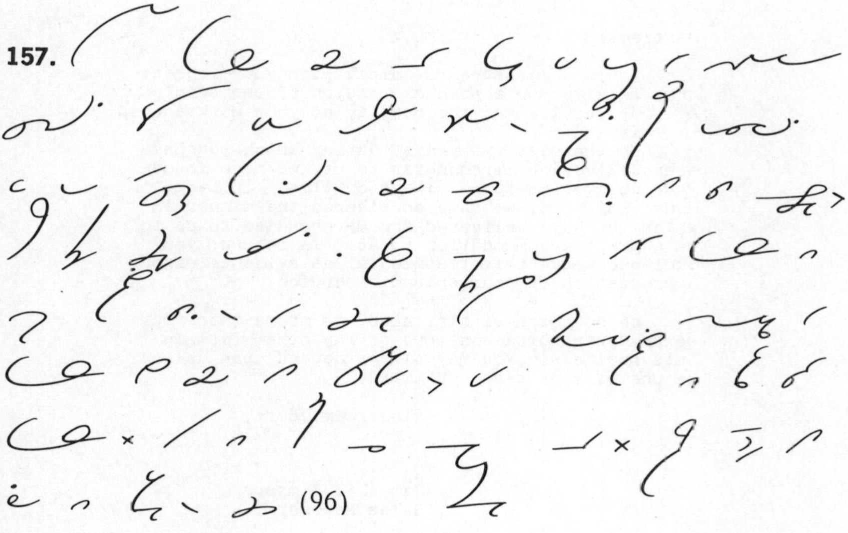

(96)

158.

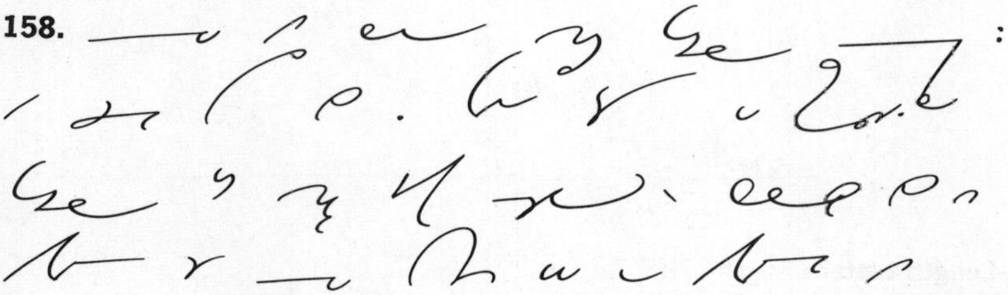

SPLANE & GARDNER, INC.

1238 CAPITOL AVENUE • LITTLE ROCK, ARKANSAS • FRANKLIN 2-4201

January 7, 19--

Holstad & Company
Trades Building
605 Maple Avenue
Shreveport 12, Louisiana

ATTENTION: Mr. Cox

Gentlemen:

It is a pleasure to comply with your request that we give you a true expression of our opinion of your service and the quality of your workmanship.

In the past two years, during which you have been delivering merchandise to us, we have found your deliveries to be always on time. In fact, in many instances, we have considered the manner in which you have delivered the merchandise to us to be a great accommodation to us. In return, you indeed deserve this testimonial as evidence of our appreciation of your splendid service.

We do not hesitate, also, to state that your workmanship surpasses that of any other firm in this business. You may always depend upon us to be one of your best customers.

Sincerely yours,

James A. Simpson
Sales Manager

CK

Average-Length Letter
Semiblocked Style, with Attention Line
Standard Punctuation

(171)

Building Speed Through Reading

159. HINTS FOR SUCCESS

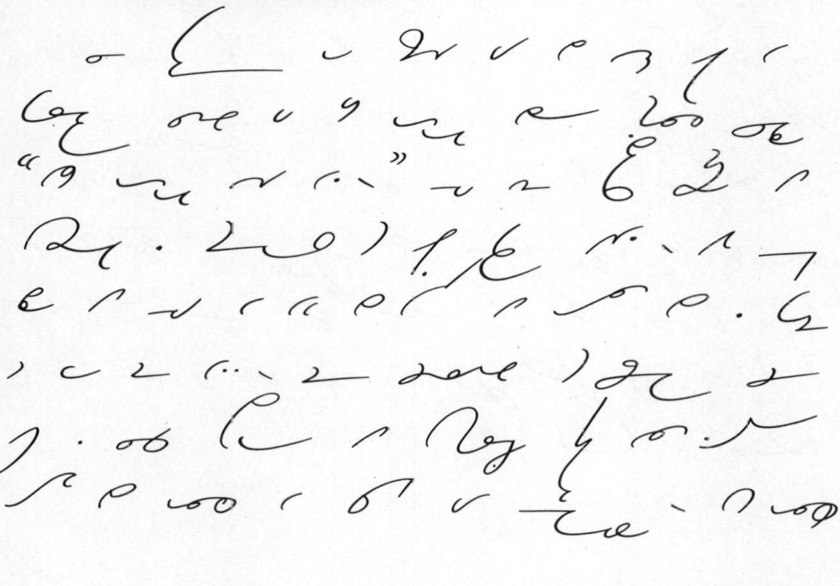

(312)

Lesson 23

BUILDING PHRASING SKILL

Prepositional Phrases

Drill 1

Drill 2

Drill 3

KEY

Of all, of any, of it, of its, of life, of Mr., of our, of ours, of their, of them, of these, of those, of work, of your, on his, on it, on our, on sale.

On that day, on the, on these, on time, on us, on which, on your, to him, to it, to me, to our, to that, to the, to their, to them, to these.

With him, with it, with our, with reference, with such, with that, with the, with the understanding, with them, with these, with this, with those, with us, with which, with which the, with you.

Brief-Form and Phrase Letters

160.

(55)

161.

(76)

162.

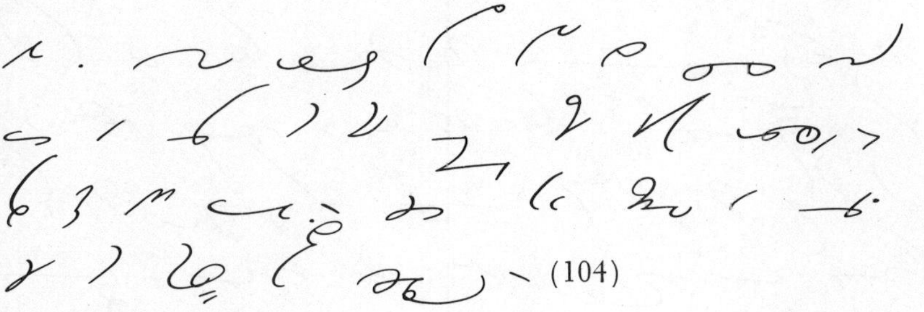

(104)

163.

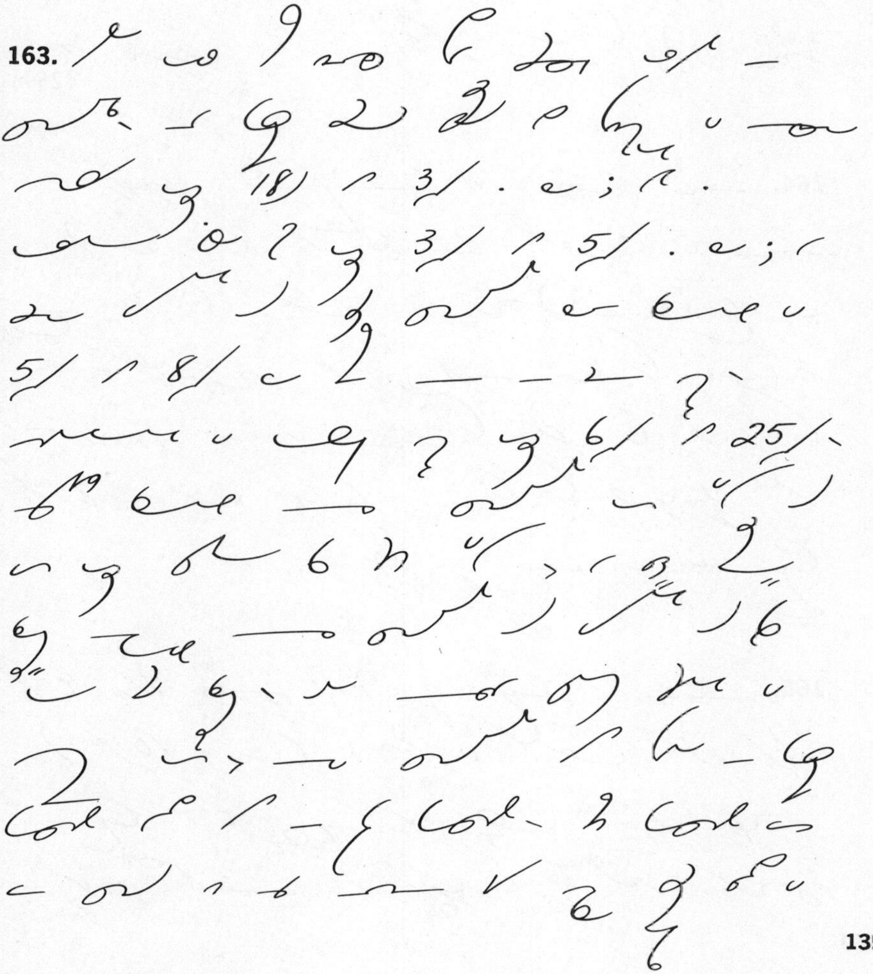

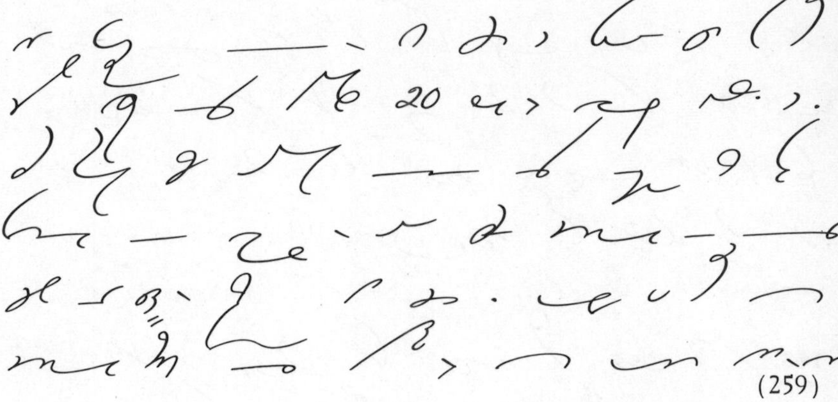

(259)

164.

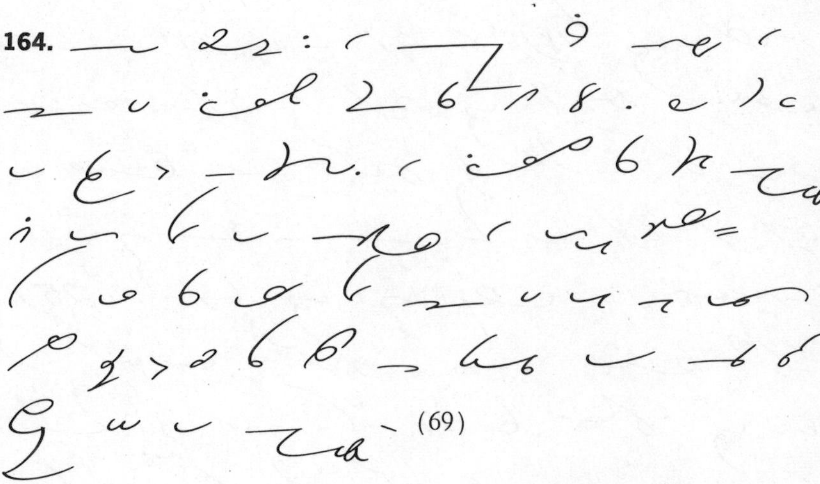

(69)

165.

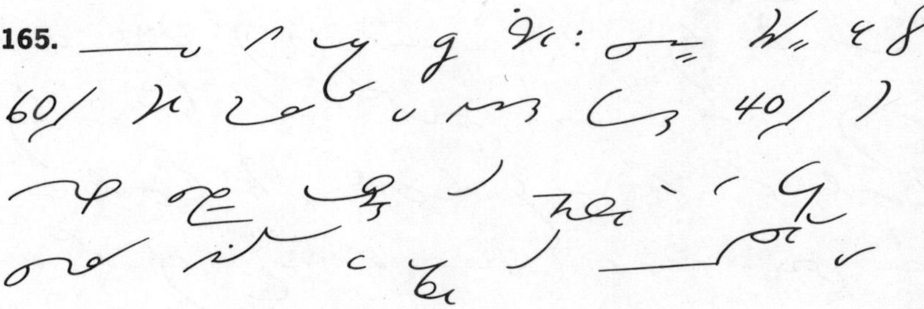

(244)

Lesson 24

PROGRESSIVE SPEED BUILDING

Half-Minute Progressive Speed Builder (80-120)

VOCABULARY PREVIEW

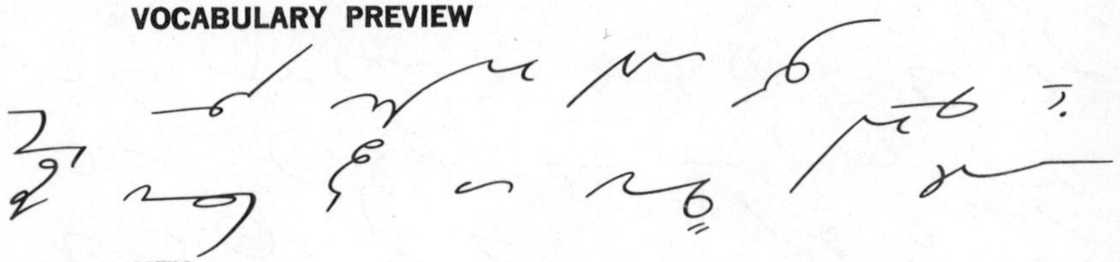

KEY

Information, method, customers, district, at that time, matter, interesting. Efficient, you may not have, exception, of course, Tulsa, debtors, settlement.

(½ MINUTE AT 80)

166. Dear Mr. Edwards: On Friday afternoon, December 6, you were in our office asking for information/regarding the new method of billing that is applied to customers living in your particular district.//

(½ MINUTE AT 90)

I am sorry that I was not here at that time to go over the matter with you, as it is an interesting subject/ and a very efficient way of billing.

You may not have received complete information on this new method of billing.//

(½ MINUTE AT 100)

If you can arrange to drop in at our office any time between eight and five – with the exception of Saturday, of course! – I shall be very/glad to go over this matter with you personally and to discuss any point that you do not understand. Yours very truly,//

(½ MINUTE AT 110)

167. Memo to the Tulsa Branch: Has your branch been able to do anything on the above account since our memo to you on January 27?/

At that time we said that the

debtors claimed to be able to account for the two missing items and that they would be returned to your branch immediately.//

(½ MINUTE AT 120)

It is our suggestion that you check up on this account at this time; and, if it should happen that the debtors are not able to produce the items, make every effort/to get them to make settlement so that we can close our files on this.

Please let us hear from you regarding this very important matter as soon as possible.//

Minute Progressive Speed Builder (70-90)

VOCABULARY PREVIEW

KEY

Breakdown, send you, curtains, with the understanding that, subtracting, with this letter, inquiry.

(1 MINUTE AT 70)

168. Gentlemen: Appearing on my statement from you for this month's purchases is a charge for $7.50/for which I cannot account. Could you give me a breakdown of this purchase, please. If I can//find out which items this charge represents, perhaps I can recall the purchase. The rest of the bill///is all right. I will send you a check when I receive your answer to this letter. Sincerely, (1)

(1 MINUTE AT 80)

169. Dear Mr. Foster: Thank you for writing us regarding your statement and the $7.50 charge you/ could not account for.

This charge is for a set of curtains purchased August 15. According to a note attached//to the bill, these curtains were taken on approval, with the understanding that, if they were not returned within///a week, they were to be charged to your account. I hope that this explanation is satisfactory. Yours truly, (2)

(1 MINUTE AT 90)

170. Gentlemen: I appreciate your writing to me to explain the $7.50 charge on my bill for August./ There has been an error, however, as I did not purchase any curtains. I do not know how the charge got on my account; but//you can, undoubtedly, find where it should go. I am subtracting the $7.50 from the bill and am sending///you a check for $24.50 with this letter.

Thank you for your prompt attention to my inquiry. Sincerely, (3)

Reading and Writing Practice

171.

(94)

172.

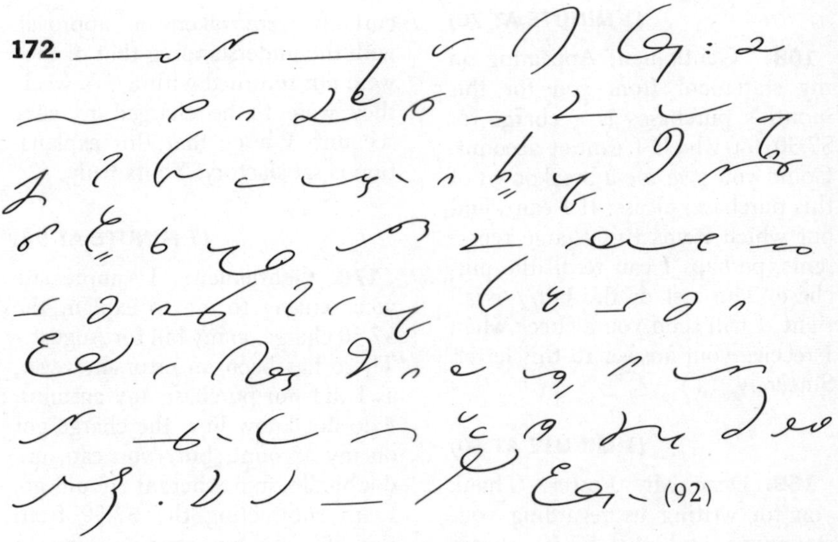

(92)

173.

(307)

174.

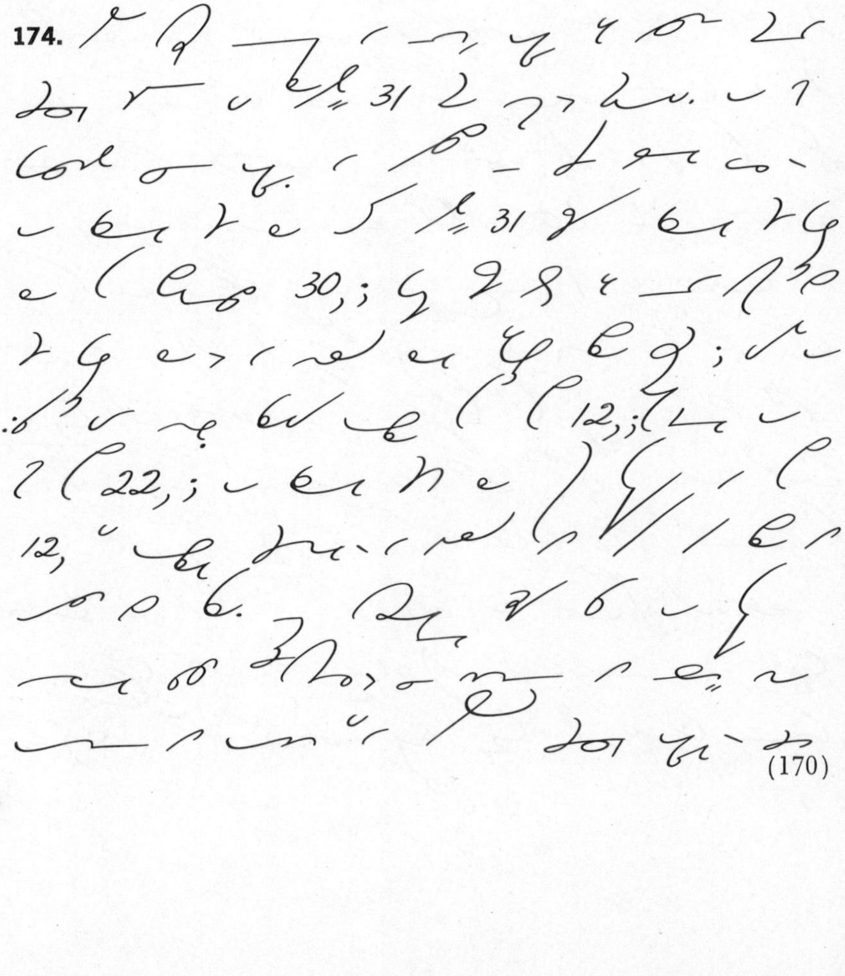

(170)

Lesson 25

BUILDING SUSTAINED SPEED

Five-Minute Speed Builder

The following interoffice correspondence is between Mr. Wilson and Jim Young, Manager, St. Louis Branch, 2173 North Maple Avenue, St. Louis 7, Missouri.

VOCABULARY PREVIEW

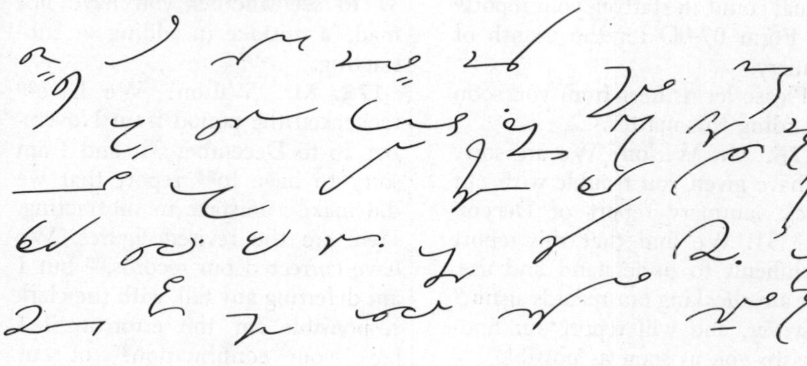

KEY

Young, empty, containers, Summary, submitted, inventory, you must have.
However, represented, actual, please let us, hear from you, trouble, to understand, as soon as possible.
Monthly, will you please, auditor, adjustment, certain, to make, shortages.
Period, according, was not, subtracting, rechecked, we did, deferring, responsible.
Confirmation, expect, in the future, records, customary, quarterly.

175. Mr. Young: We have your letter of March 4, in which you have tried to explain the differences that show up on[1] your January empty container stock, Summary Form 074-D.

On December 31, you[2] submitted a report showing an actual inventory of all empty containers on hand at your branch. You[3] must have kept a copy of this report. There was an error, however. The figures did not check with the inventory[4] that you were carrying on Form 520, but we thought that the report represented an actual[5] count. That is what we were after at the time. Why, then, did you not use this actual count in starting your report[6] on Form 074-D for the month of January?

Please let us hear from you soon regarding this matter.[7]

176. Mr. Wilson: We are sorry to have given you trouble with our stock summary report of December[8] 31. We find that this report is difficult to understand and use. We are checking our records again,[9] however, and will report our findings to you as soon as possible.

177. Mr. Young: There is nothing difficult[10] to understand about this monthly report. You say that the losses shown are for an eleven-month period.[11] Will you please tell us how you figure this out. In November, the traveling auditor made an adjustment on[12] your stock record Form 520, adding certain small differences to your book inventory in order to[13] make the book inventory the same as the actual count. That leaves anything before November 26[14] out of the report.

Now, if you had such large shortages between November 26 and January[15] 31, how did they happen? The greater portion of the difference can be traced to the period beginning[16] November 26 and ending December 31. On December 31, according to your own[17] statement, your actual inventory was not nearly so high as the figures with which you began Form 074-D[18] for the month of January.

Please check over this period from November 26 to December[19] 31 to see whether you have not made a mistake in adding or subtracting.

178. Mr. Wilson: We have[20] rechecked the period from November 26 to December 31, and I am sorry to have to[21] report that we did make a mistake in subtracting. Here are the revised figures. We have corrected our records,[22] but I am deferring any talk with the clerk responsible for the error until I have your confirmation[23] of our figures.

We are sorry to have caused you all this trouble.

179. Mr. Young: Your reports are now in order,[24] and we shall expect your book inventory in the future to check with your stock records after our traveling[25] auditor has made the customary quarterly adjustments. (512)

Reading and Writing Practice

180.

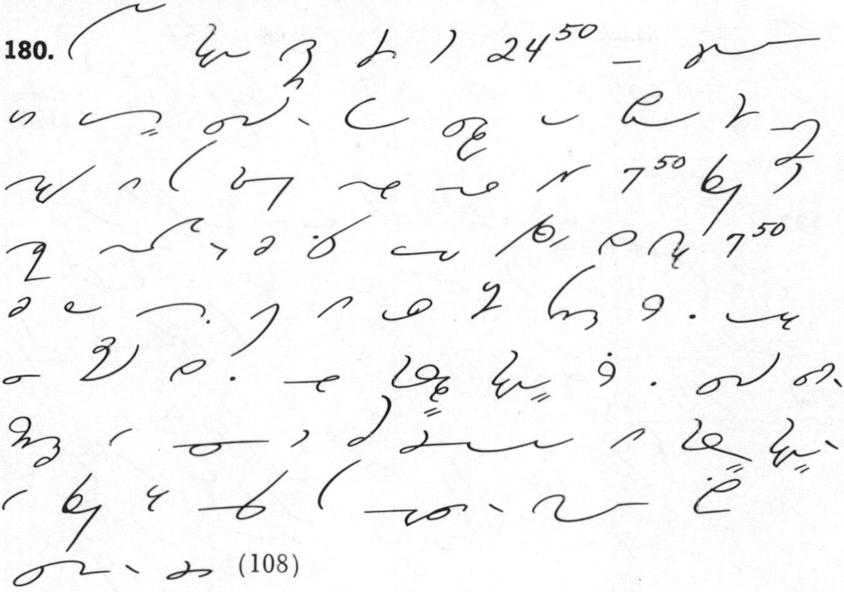

(108)

181.

(123)

182.

(204)

183.

(78)

184.

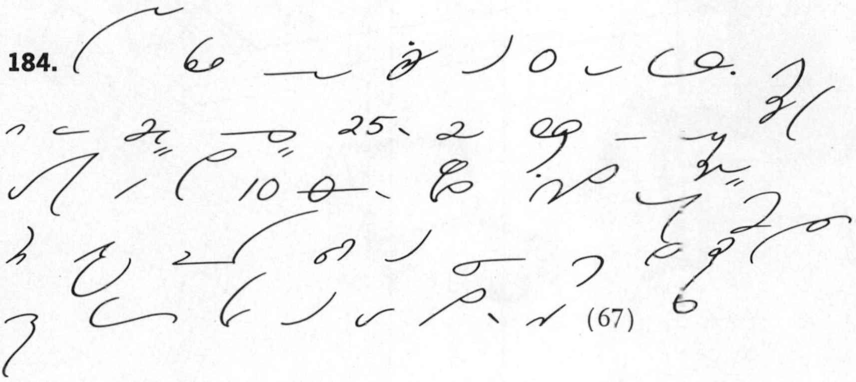

(67)

185.

(62)

6

The Purchasing Department

Spelling and Penmanship Improvement Drills for Chapter 6

SPELLING

When a word ends in *y* preceded by a consonant, the *y* is usually changed to *i* before a suffix that does not begin with *i*.

accompany, accompanying
beauty, beautiful
commodity, commodities
copy, copying
duty, dutiful
envy, enviable
heavy, heavier
likely, likelihood
modify, modifies
notify, notification
ordinary, ordinarily
plenty, plentiful
ratify, ratification
timely, timeliness

Exceptions

secretary, secretaryship
shy, shyness

PENMANSHIP

KEY

1. The, there, they, that, this, those, these, for the, though, although, thought, health.
2. Received, get, please, do, been, letter, can, would, she, when.
3. In this, to have, to your, to get, for you, so that, of course, on your, they are, there are.
4. War, correct, glad, of your, work, milk.
5. Appliance, trial, diet, science, prior, violation.

Lesson 26

BUILDING TRANSCRIPTION SKILL

Transcription English Pointers

THE USES OF THE COMMA

1. When the last member of a *series* of three or more items, whether words, phrases, or clauses, is preceded by *and, or,* or *nor,* a comma is placed before the conjunction as well as between the other items.

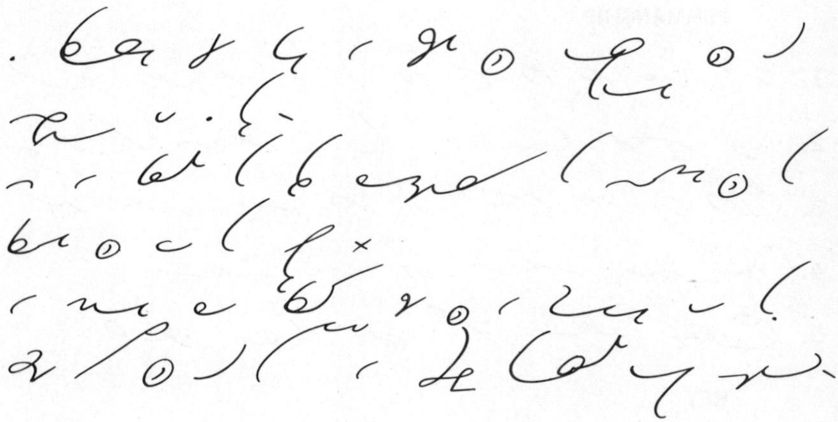

A balance sheet presents the assets, liabilities, and capital of a business.
Can the points be best illustrated by cartoons, by charts, or by tables?
The walls were painted yesterday, the floors are being waxed today, and tomorrow the venetian blinds will be installed.

2. When two or more adjectives modify a noun, a comma should separate the adjectives if each adjective modifies the noun alone.

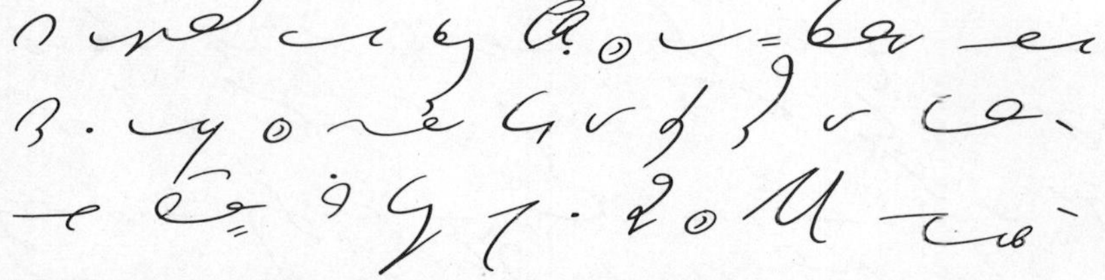

This restaurant always serves appetizing, well-balanced meals.
This is a logical, clear presentation of the chief advantages of the plan.
Miss Allen has proved to be an efficient, dependable employee.

> *Note:* If the word *and* can be inserted between the adjectives, use the comma.

If, however, the first adjective modifies the idea of the combination of the noun and the second adjective, no comma should be used.

An alert young man stood behind the counter.
A new key-driven calculator has been installed in our office.
Observe all previous instructions in typing this particular timed drill.

(Continued on page 183)

Transcription Speed Builder

186.

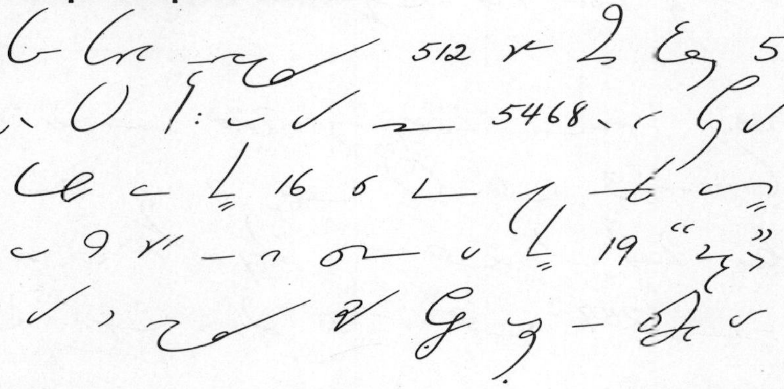

(158)

187.

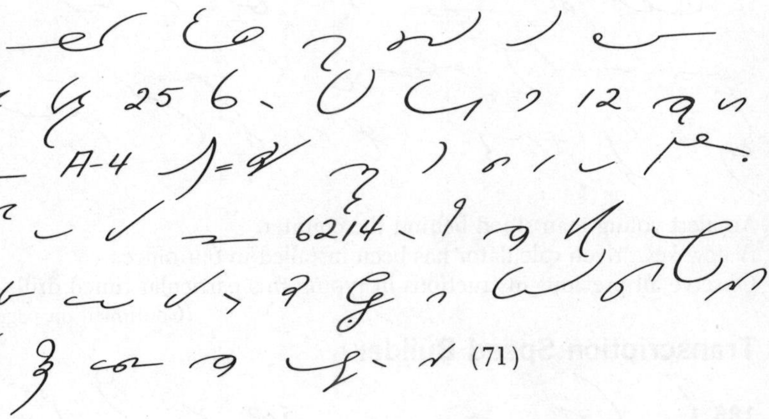

(71)

188.

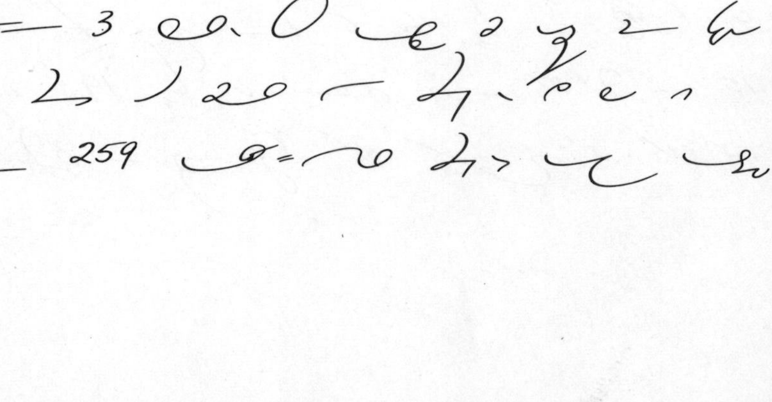

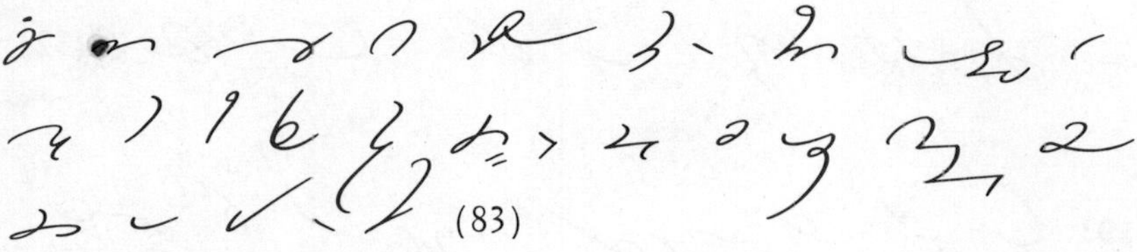

(83)

189.

(161)

190.

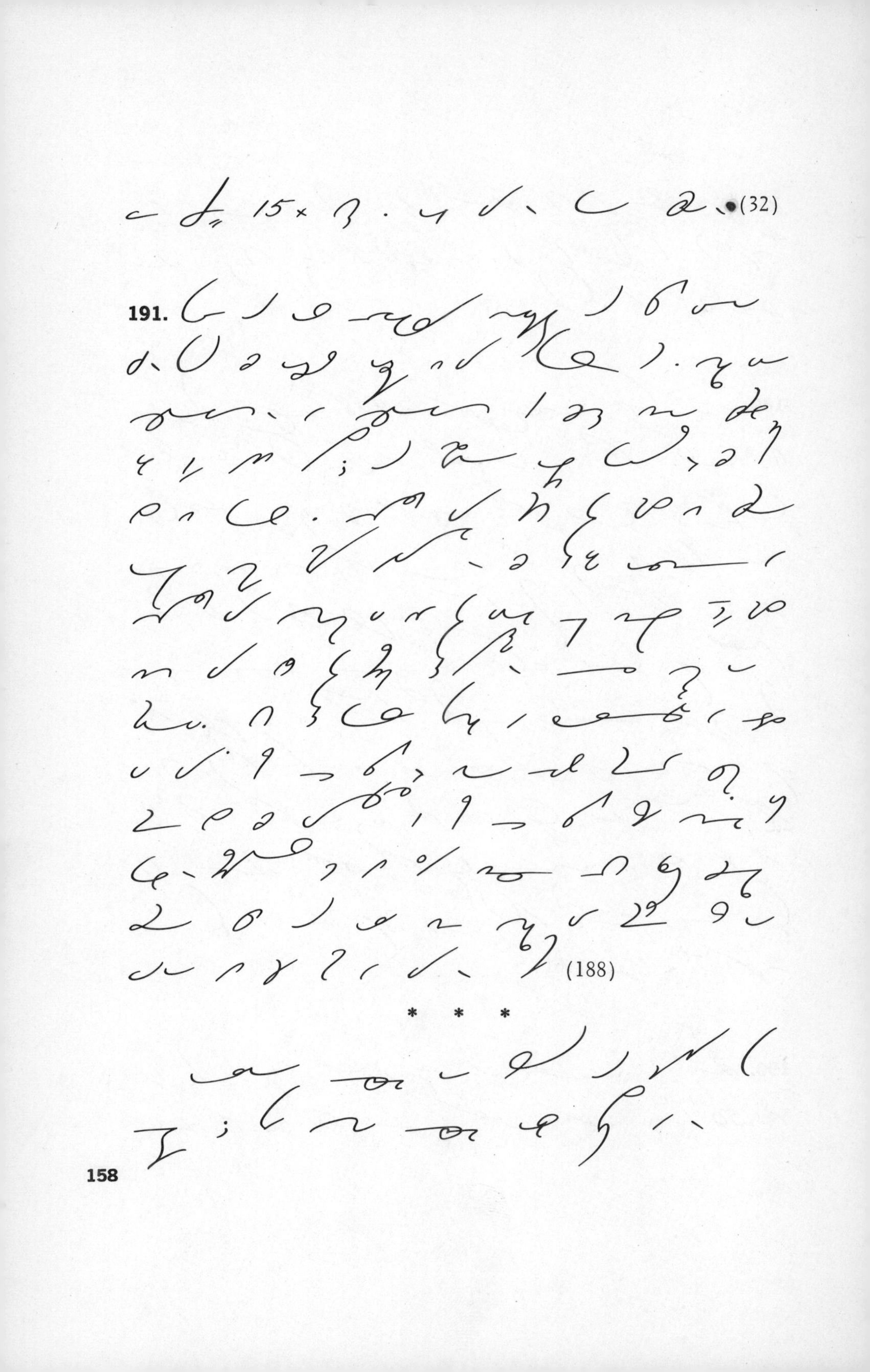

15 (32)

191. (188)

* * *

Lesson 27

MASTERING SHORTHAND THEORY

Word Endings

-ally

-ily

-ly

-ble

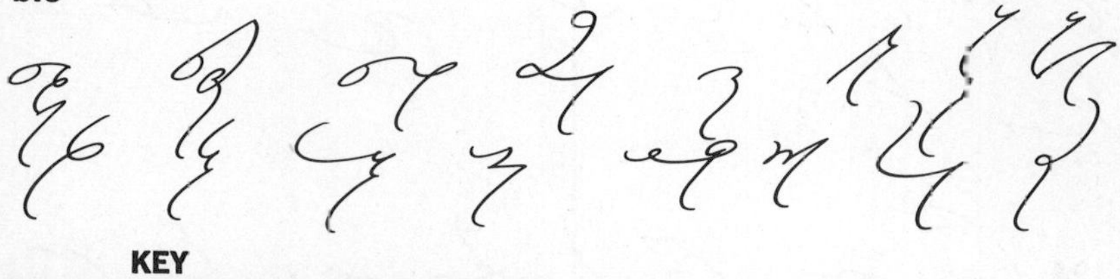

KEY

Especially, essentially, finally, legally, naturally, normally, totally.
Busily, easily, families, heartily, heavily, primarily, readily, temporarily.
Amply, carefully, certainly, consequently, correctly, costly, daily, definitely, early, directly, entirely, exactly, fairly, greatly, highly, only.
Acceptable, advisable, agreeable, available, considerable, desirable, objectionable, obtainable, payable, possible, plausible, reasonable, reliable, suitable, valuable, visible.

Reading and Writing Practice

192.

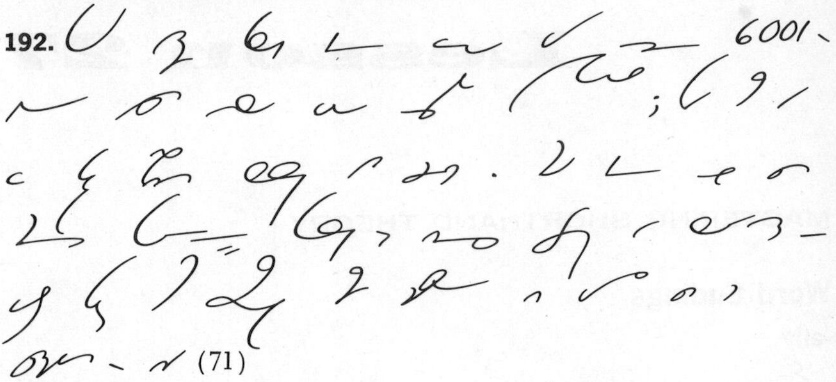

(71)

193.

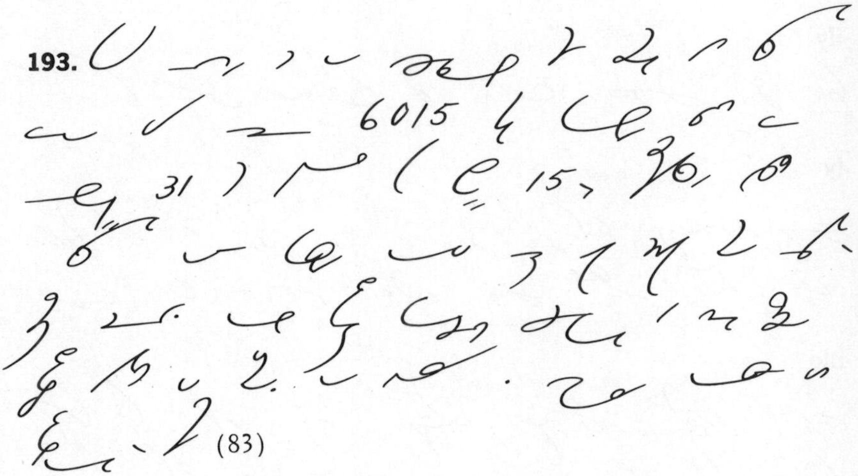

(83)

194.

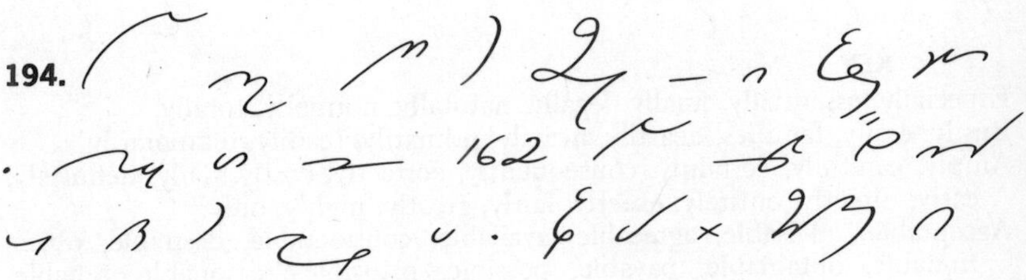

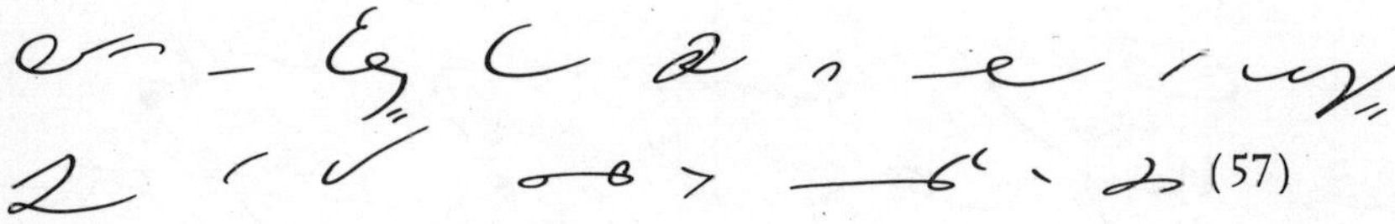

(57)

195.

(99)

196.

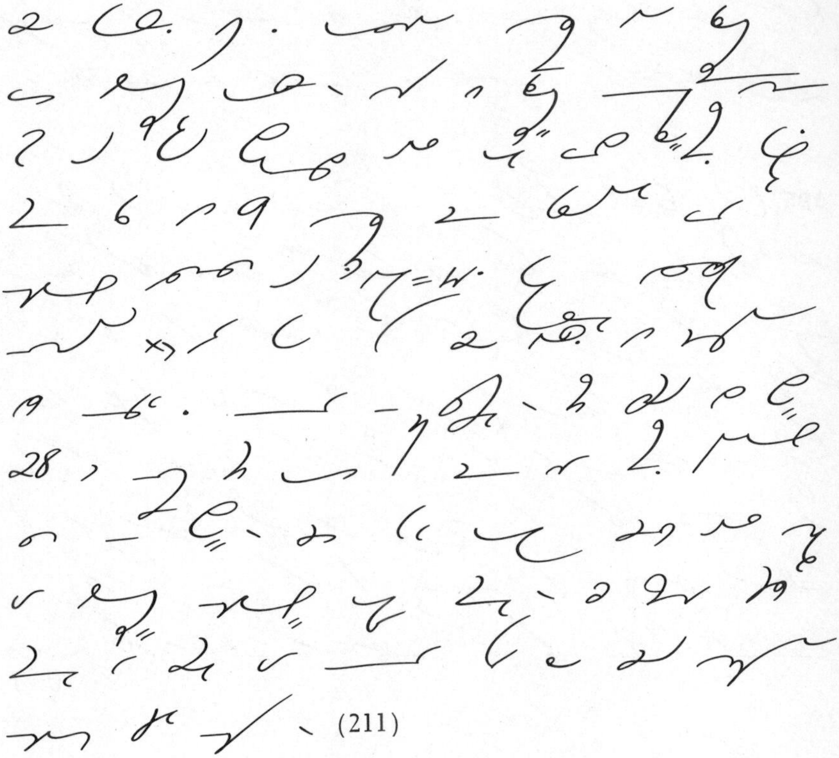

(211)

Building Speed Through Reading

197. HINTS FOR SUCCESS

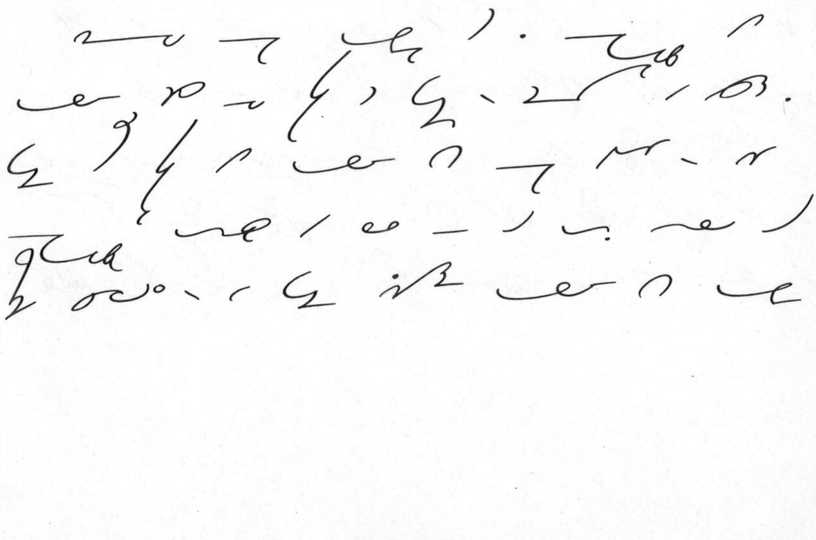

(261)

Lesson 28

BUILDING PHRASING SKILL

Adjective and Adverb Phrases

Drill 1

Drill 2

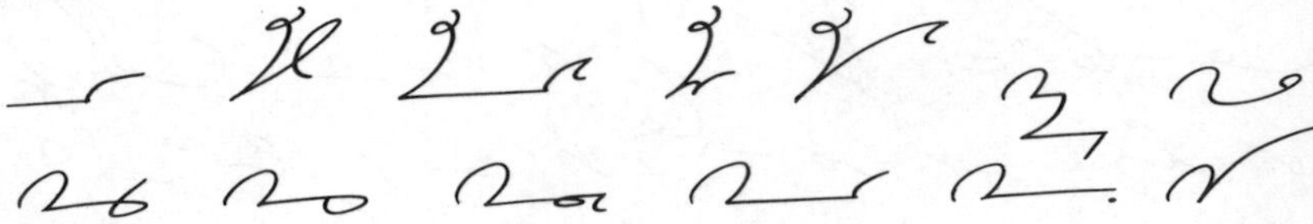

Drill 3

KEY

Any information, any more, any one, any other, any time, each day, each month, each morning, each one, each other, each time, few days, few minutes, few months.

More than, several days, several months, several other, several times, this information, this letter, this matter, this may, this means, this month, this morning, this time.

Easily understood, so far, so little, so long, so much, so that, so well, very glad, very good, very important, very many, very much, very well.

Brief-Form and Phrase Letters

198. 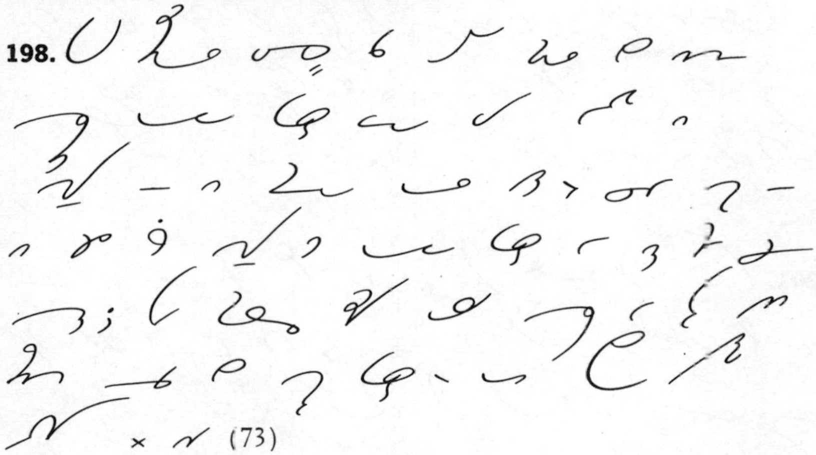

(73)

199. 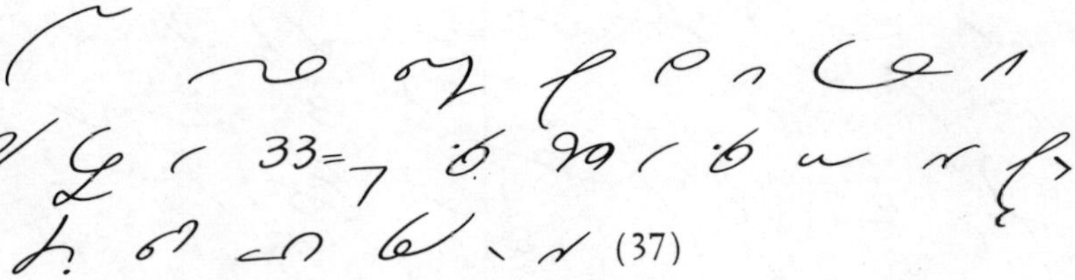

(37)

200. 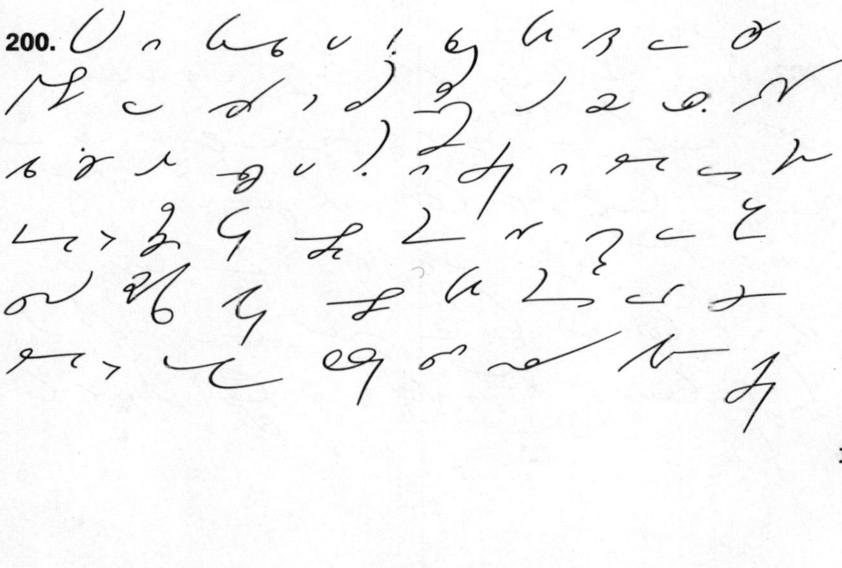

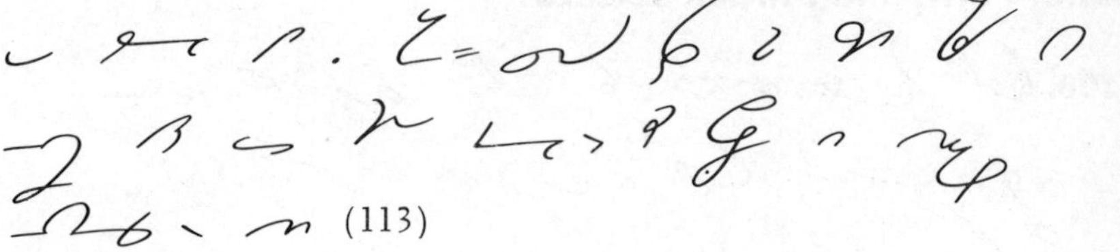

(113)

201.

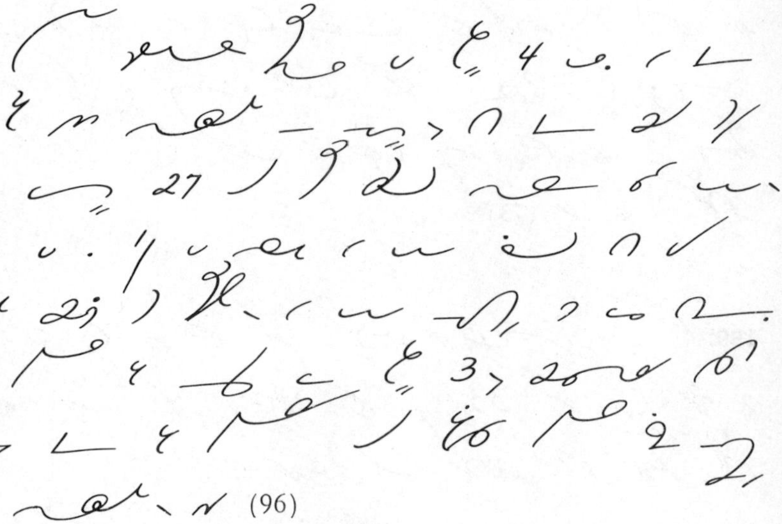

(96)

202.

 (89)

203. 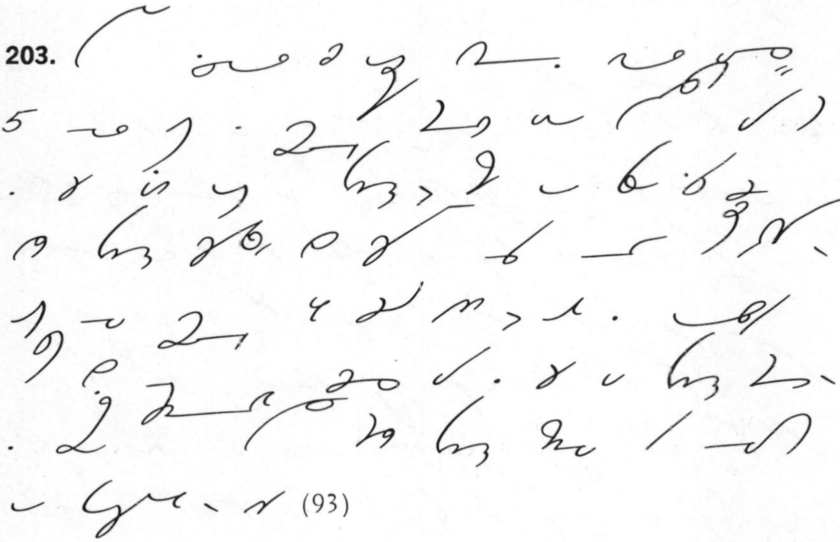 (93)

204. 

(98)

205.

(137)

206.

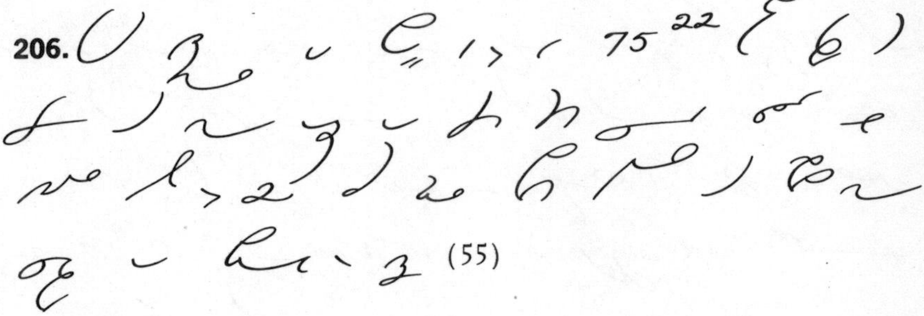

(55)

Lesson 29

PROGRESSIVE SPEED BUILDING

Half-Minute Progressive Speed Builder (80-120)

VOCABULARY PREVIEW

KEY

Appreciate, retail, catalogue, assistance, to us, merchandise, notify. We shall be glad to see, appointment, to make, promised, quotation, immediate, cabinets.

(½ MINUTE AT 80)

207. Dear Mr. Miller: Please refer to our order No. 901 and let us know when the balance of this order/will be shipped. We need the goods soon so that we may complete an order for a customer. Yours very truly,//

(½ MINUTE AT 90)

208. Gentlemen: We should appreciate it very much if you would send us a copy of your new retail catalogue. It/would be of great assistance to us in our Purchasing Department.

May we have it by next week if possible. Yours truly,//

(½ MINUTE AT 100)

209. Dear Mr. Hill: This is in reply to your recent letter in which you said that you wish to show us samples of your new line of merchandise./

If you will notify us when you can be in Chicago, we shall be glad to see you. Please telephone me for an appointment. Cordially yours,//

(½ MINUTE AT 110)

210. Gentlemen: Will you please inform us when you expect to make shipment on our order No. 7428. You promised that you would deliver by/October 15.

If we don't hear from you by the first of next week, we shall have to cancel the order, as we cannot wait much longer. Yours very truly,//

(½ MINUTE AT 120)

211. Gentlemen: We have received the quotation that you sent us on September 29, but we have no immediate need for these cabinets and shelves.

We are filing/the information that you sent us so that we may get in touch with you when we do need new shelves.

We appreciate your sending us the information. Sincerely yours,//

Minute Progressive Speed Builder (70-90)

VOCABULARY PREVIEW

KEY

Mimeographing, binding, let us know, it has been, stencils, difficult, exactly.

(1 MINUTE AT 70)

212. Dear Mr. Lawson: We plan to purchase a quantity of paper for use in mimeographing/a 100-page manual for our office personnel.

In addition to the paper on// which the material will be printed, we shall need stencils and heavy paper for binding the///300 copies. Please let us know whether we can expect a discount on this order. Yours truly, (1)

(1 MINUTE AT 80)

213. Dear Mr. Brown: It has been a pleasure to serve your paper needs for the past several years, and we appreciate/ your inquiry about quantity buying of the paper and stencils you will need for the mimeographing//job you describe.

We shall be glad to give you a 10 per cent discount on this purchase. If you will refer to///page 18 of our catalogue, you will see that we have three qualities of stencils and of paper. Yours truly, (2)

(1 MINUTE AT 90)

214. Dear Mr. Lawson: The discount you suggest in your letter of May 10 is satisfactory; we shall be glad to give you/the order. I should like to inquire whether it might be possible to break up the order into two parts. It is difficult//to estimate exactly how many stencils we shall need, and we wish to avoid getting too many.

Could we place an order///for 100 stencils and order the paper later when we know exactly how many more stencils we shall need? Yours truly, (3)

Reading and Writing Practice

215.

216.

(117)

217.

(277)

218.

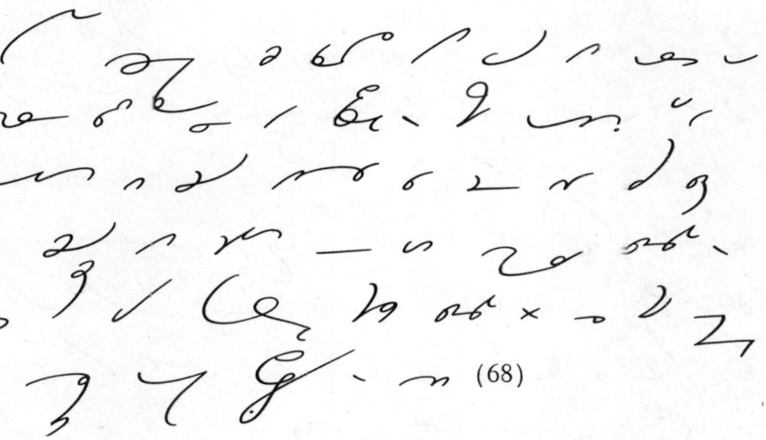

(68)

219.

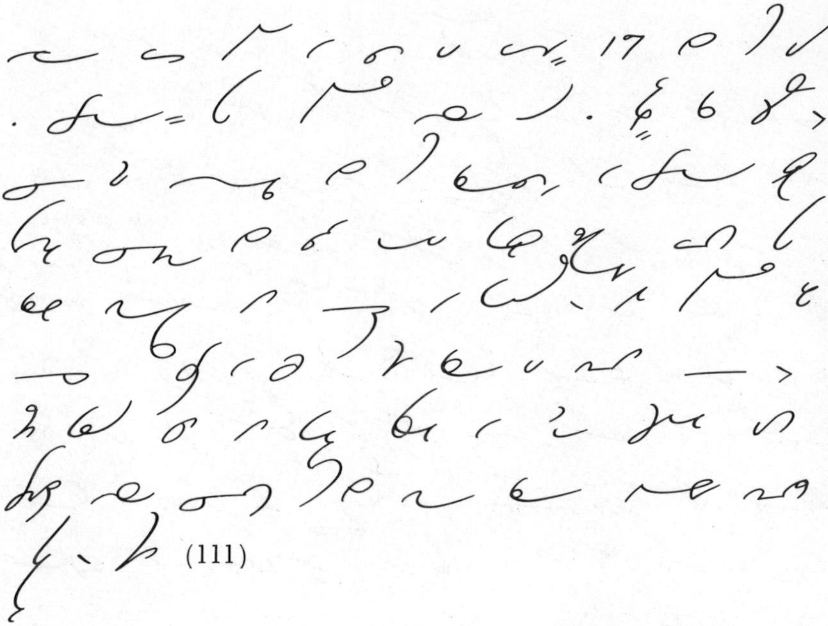

(111)

220.

(91)

Lesson 30

BUILDING SUSTAINED SPEED

Five-Minute Speed Builder

The following correspondence is between Morris R. Ward, 23 Canada Drive, Hartford 9, Connecticut, and Mr. Porter.

VOCABULARY PREVIEW

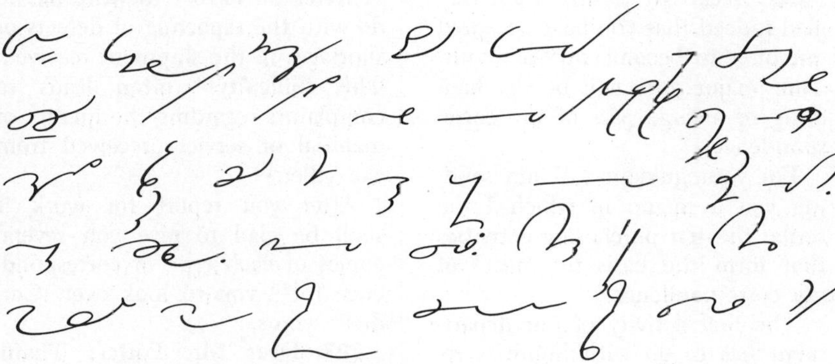

KEY

Porter, personnel, succeed, assistant, promoted, enjoyable, pamphlets.
Acquaint, to do, duty, correspondence, memo, describe, activities, inquiries.
Constantly, specifications, we want, fourth, consists, rejecting, in the market, fifth, notifying.
Corrections, canceling, one of the most, annoying, defects, shortages, difficulty.
Complaints, quality, I shall be glad, similar, I shall be able, eagerly, forward.

221. Dear Mr. Porter: I have written your personnel manager telling him that I wish to accept your company's[1] offer to succeed your assistant, who has been promoted. I am sure that I shall be very happy with[2] you and that my work will be most enjoyable.

I expect to arrive in Chicago by the middle of this[3] month and will report to work on the 15th. I should appreciate your sending me in advance any company[4] pamphlets that will serve to acquaint me with the work I am to do there, so that I may be better prepared for[5] the job. Sincerely yours,

222. Dear Mr. Ward: I am very glad indeed that you have accepted our offer to become my[6] assistant. Your major duty will be the handling of a large part of my correspondence.

For your guidance, I[7] am sending you a memo in which I describe the ten purchasing activities that form the basis for most[8] of my correspondence.

The first activity of our department has to do with inquiries regarding[9] materials or services that we have been requested to purchase for the company.

The second concerns calls[10] that we receive constantly from those who have something they wish to sell us.

The third deals with our requirements, the[11] specifications for the merchandise we want, and the time limits set for the delivery of our orders.

The[12] fourth activity consists of writing letters rejecting offers of items for which we are not in the market[13] or that are out of our field.

The fifth activity involves a very pleasant type of letter to write[14] — acceptances of offers.

The other five types have to do mainly with the following up of orders for prompt[15] delivery and the notifying of sellers of changes or corrections in our orders. Sometimes, but not[16] very often, we have to write letters canceling orders.

One of the most annoying types of letter we have[17] to write has to do with the reporting of defects or shortages in the shipment received. This difficulty[18] often leads to complaints regarding the quality of material or services received from the seller.[19]

After you report for work, I shall be glad to give you several copies of each type of correspondence for[20] you to look over. Cordially yours,

223. Dear Mr. Porter: Thank you very much for sending me a description of[21] the types of correspondence that your department handles. I am studying similar letters in a business[22] correspondence book so that I shall be able to write letters that will be a credit to the company and[23] to you.

I am eagerly looking forward to beginning my duties with you on the 15th. Sincerely yours,[24] (480)

Reading and Writing Practice

224.

(127)

225.

(184)

226.

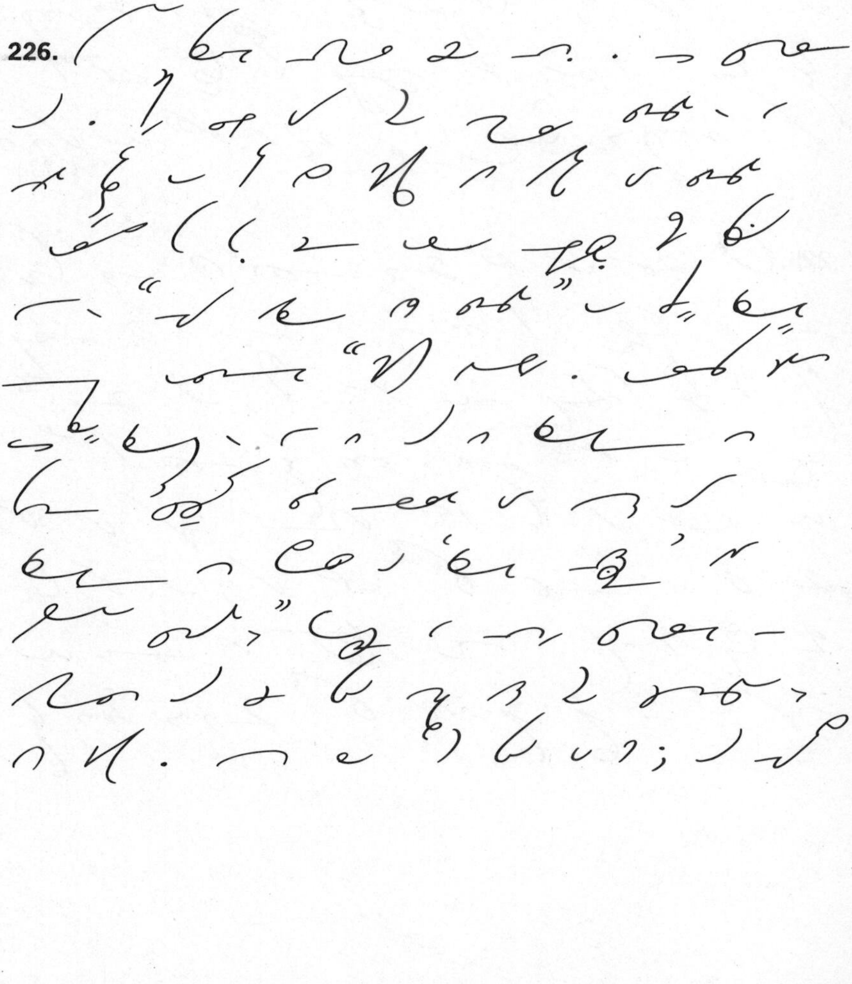

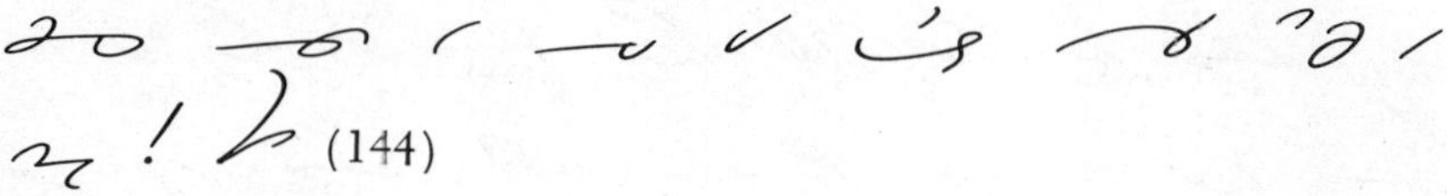
(144)

227. 
(175)

228. 

(198)

* * *

7

The Personnel Department

Spelling and Penmanship Improvement Drills for Chapter 7

SPELLING

When a word ends in y preceded by a vowel, the y is usually retained before all terminations.

annoy, annoyance
betray, betrayal
buoy, buoyancy
convey, conveyance
convoy, convoyed
delay, delayed
destroy, destroyer
display, displayed
obey, obeying
pray, prayer
stray, straying
sway, swaying

Exceptions

day, daily
lay, laid
say, said
slay, slain

PENMANSHIP

1.
2.
3.
4.
5.

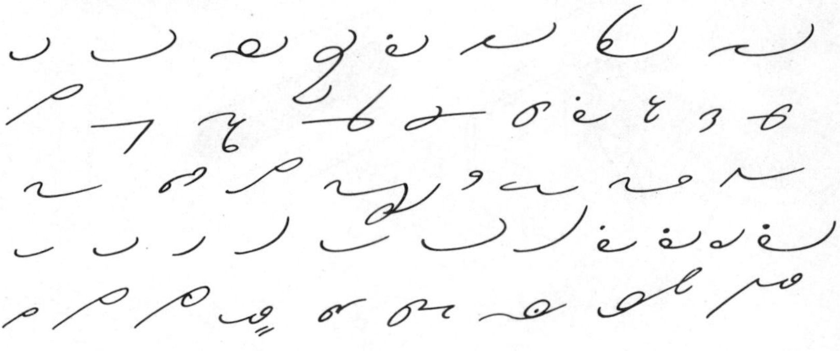

KEY

1. Rd, ld, card, favored, heard, told, build, called.
2. Day, much, copy, made, same, out, her, also, yours, now.
3. You will, with us, and that, you will find, he is, on our, your letter, it will.
4. Are, rd, there, and, will, ld, emt-emd, her, heard, either, held.
5. Tea, day, die, Roy, youth, ounce, create, radio, drawee.

Lesson 31

BUILDING TRANSCRIPTION SKILL

Transcription English Pointers

THE USES OF THE COMMA (CONTINUED)

A portion of a sentence that can be omitted without changing the basic meaning of the sentence must be set off by commas. Such portions are known as *interrupting*, or *parenthetic*, *elements*. This rule applies to words, phrases, and clauses.

The following sentences illustrate the punctuation of clauses that are set off by commas according to this rule.

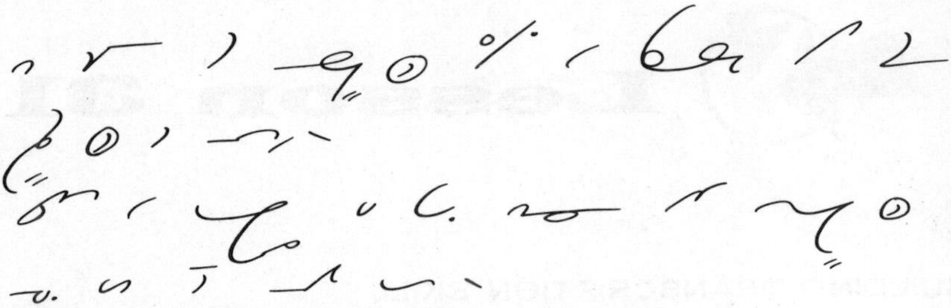

Our prospects for next year, however, are brighter.
Nevertheless, ours is the most elaborate window display in town.
To begin with, we didn't make a cent of profit on that item.
You have, I feel sure, every reason to feel encouraged.
We can only make one suggestion, knowing how he feels.
The graduate student, having completed the required courses, chose the subject of his thesis.
The index cards, being in alphabetic order, are now ready for filing.
Your statement for March, including the balance due from February, is enclosed.
I took the liberty of presenting your name to the Club, knowing of your interest in its work.

(Concluded on page 215)

Transcription Speed Builder

229. 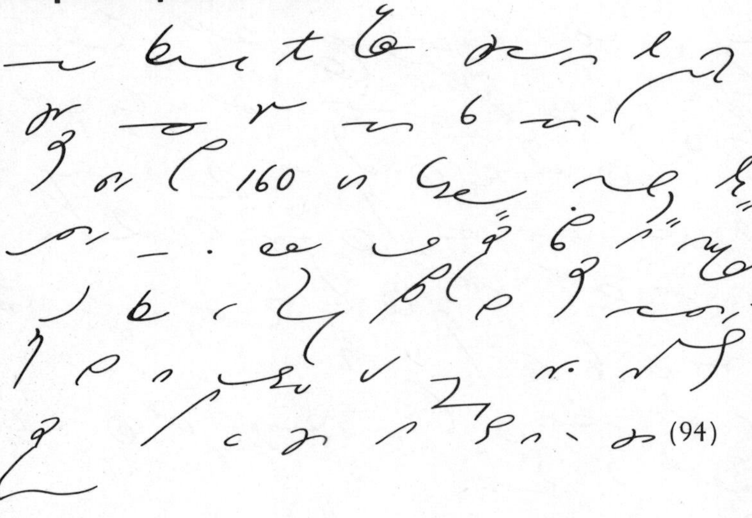 (94)

230.

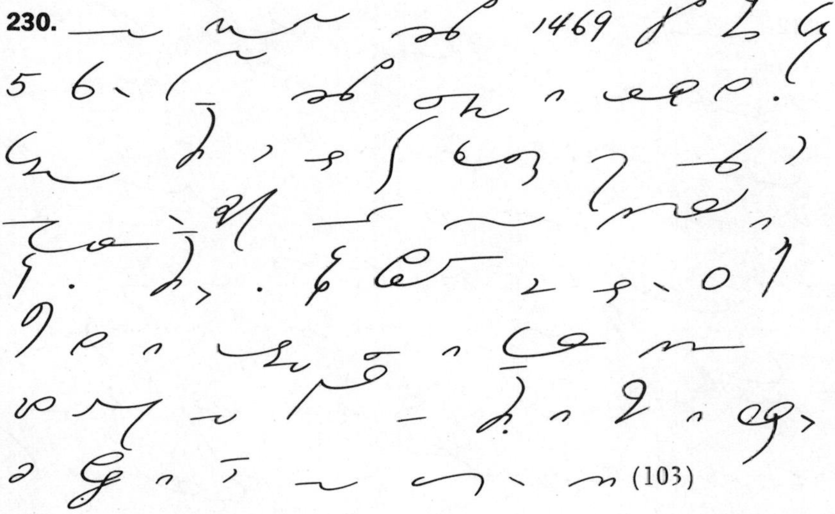

(103)

231.

(134)

232.

(121)

233.

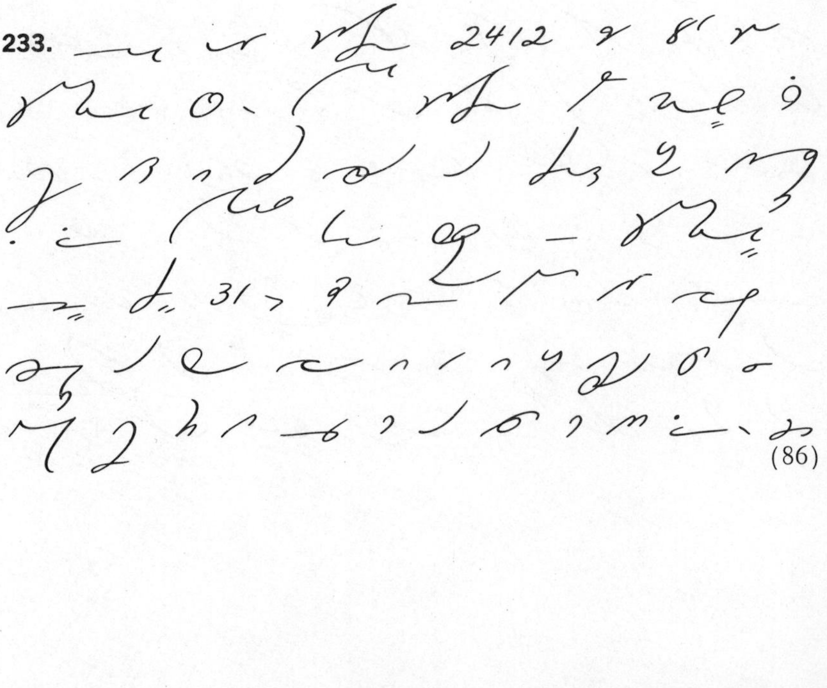

(86)

234.

(89)

235.

(134)

236.

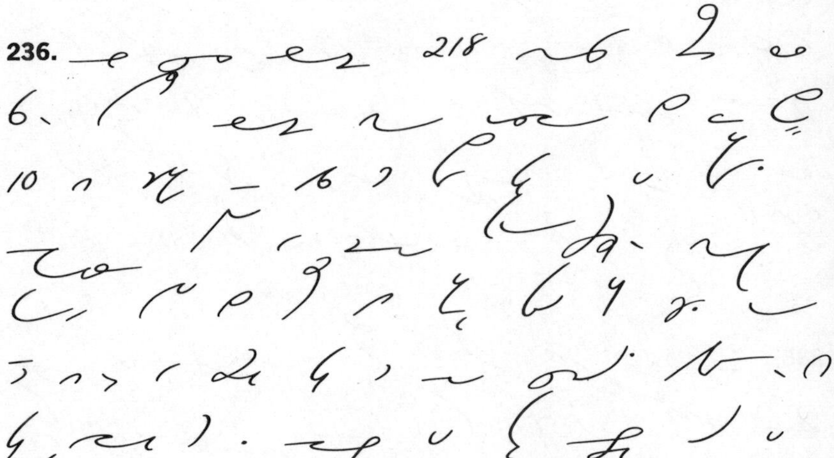

(179)

Lesson 32

MASTERING SHORTHAND THEORY

Word Endings

-ification

-ing

-ingly

-ings

-less

KEY

Clarification, classification, identification, justification, notification, qualifications, specifications.

Accounting, addressing, asking, being, interesting, maturing, owing, willing.

Accordingly, approvingly, exceedingly, increasingly, seemingly, unknowingly, willingly.

Buildings, dealings, furnishings, hearings, proceedings, savings, surroundings, things.

Needless, carelessly, unless, useless, thoughtless.

Reading and Writing Practice

237.

(238)

238. 28

(126)

239.

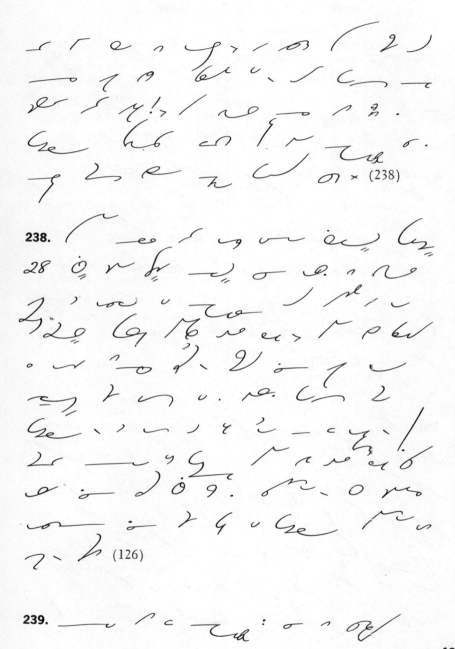

(140)

240.

(131)

241.

(140)

Building Speed Through Reading

242. HINTS FOR SUCCESS

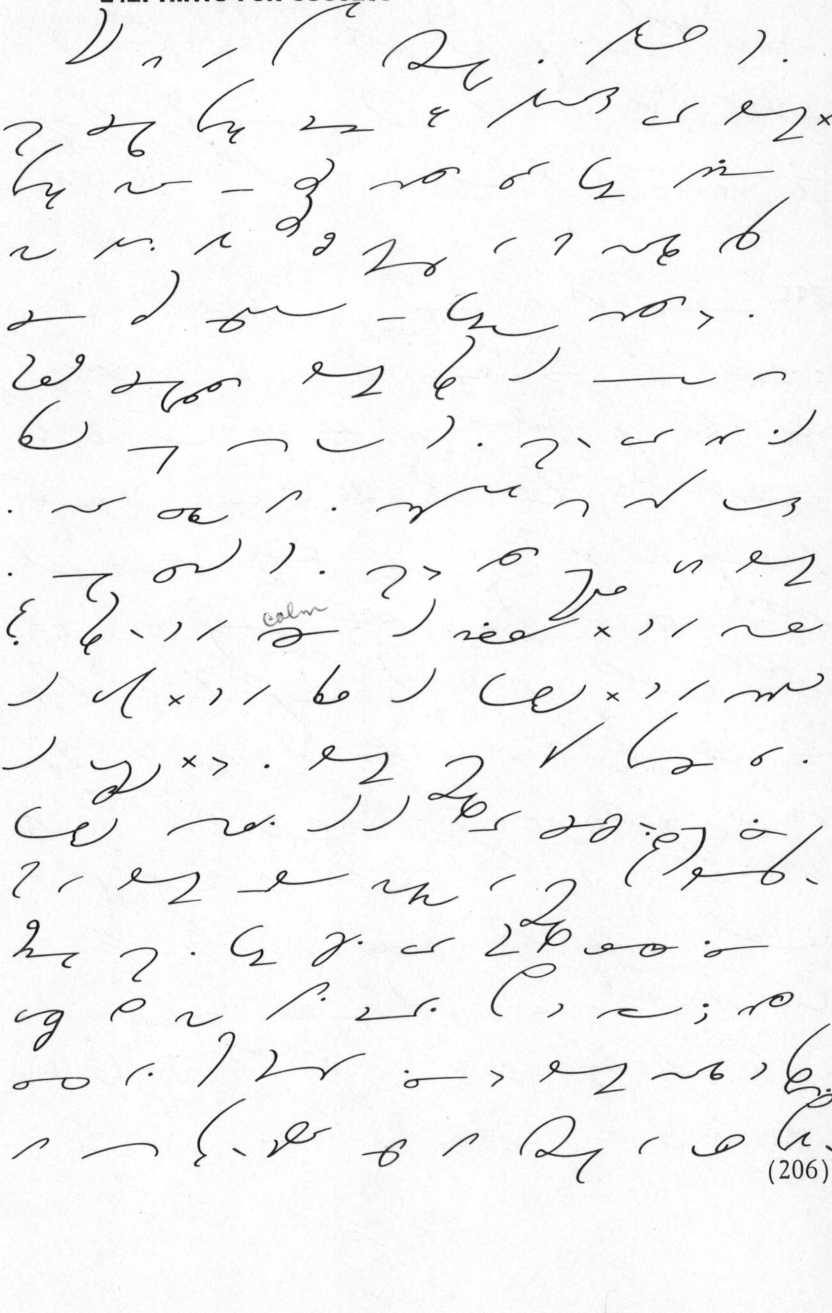

(206)

Lesson 33

BUILDING PHRASING SKILL

Conjunctive and Relative-Pronoun Phrases

Drill 1

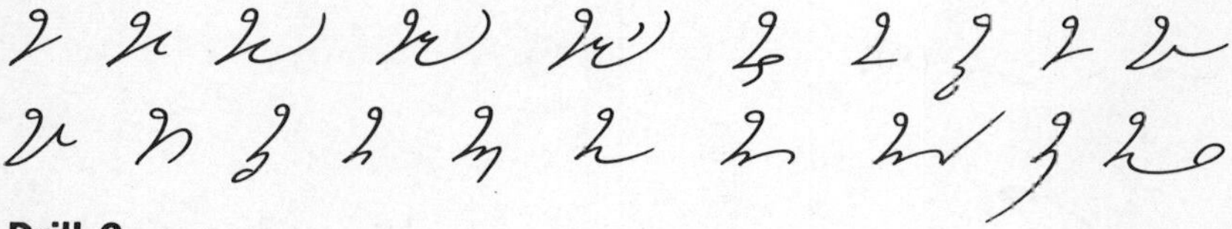

Drill 2

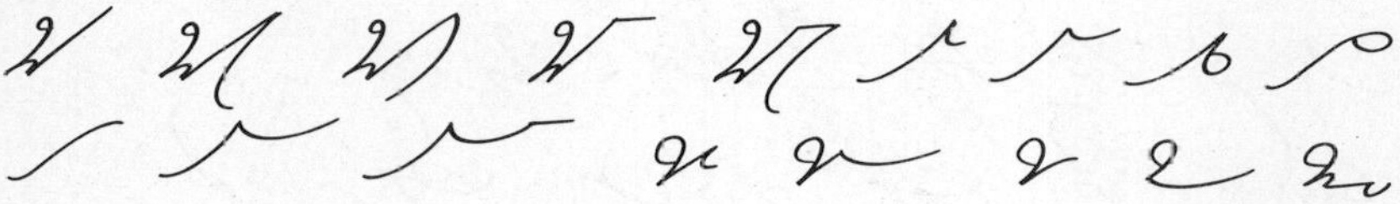

Drill 3

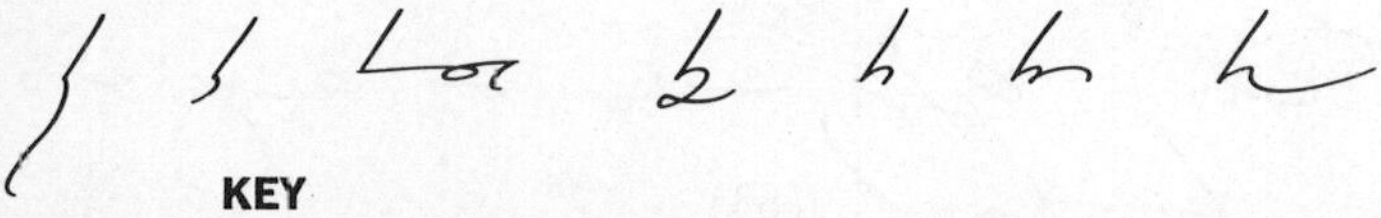

KEY

If it, if it is, if it is not, if it was not, if it wasn't, if necessary, if not, if so, if the, if there are, if there is, if this, if we, if you, if you wish, if you are, if you can, if you could, if you have, if you like.

If you would, if you would be, if you would have, if you would not, if you would not be, and is, and are, and say, and that, and the, and will, and will not, as it is, as it will, as the, as well, as you know.

Which have been, which is, which means, which we are, which you, which you can, which you will.

Brief-Form and Phrase Letters

243.

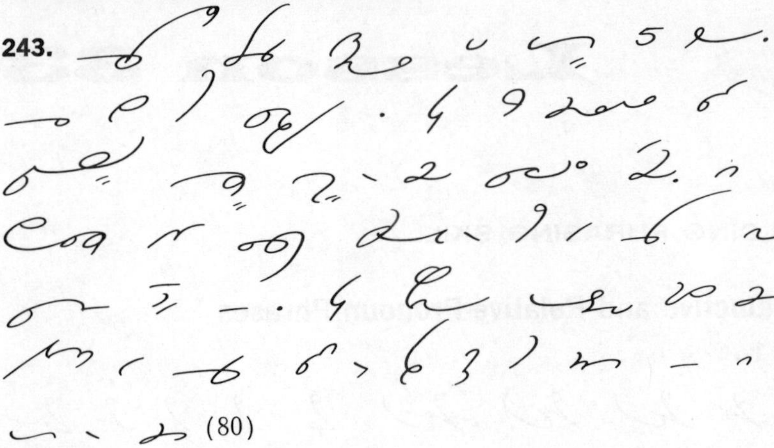

(80)

244.

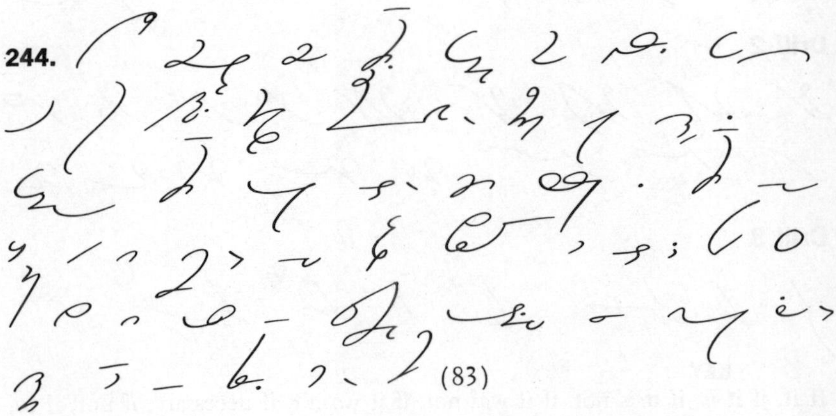

(83)

245.

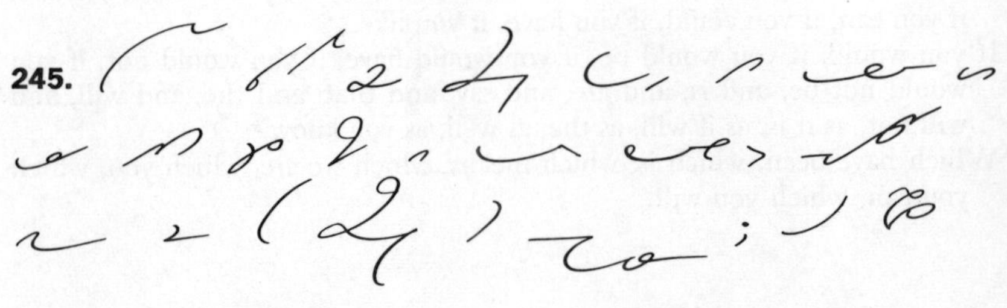

(68)

246.

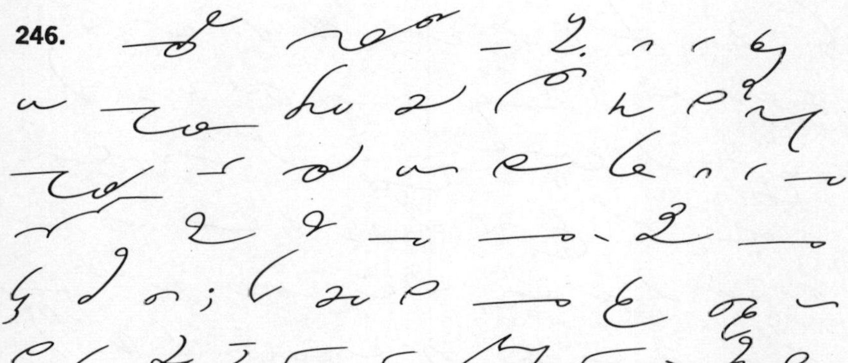

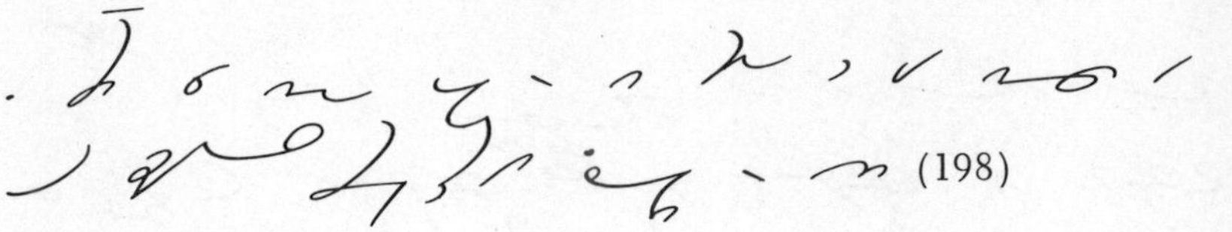

(198)

247.

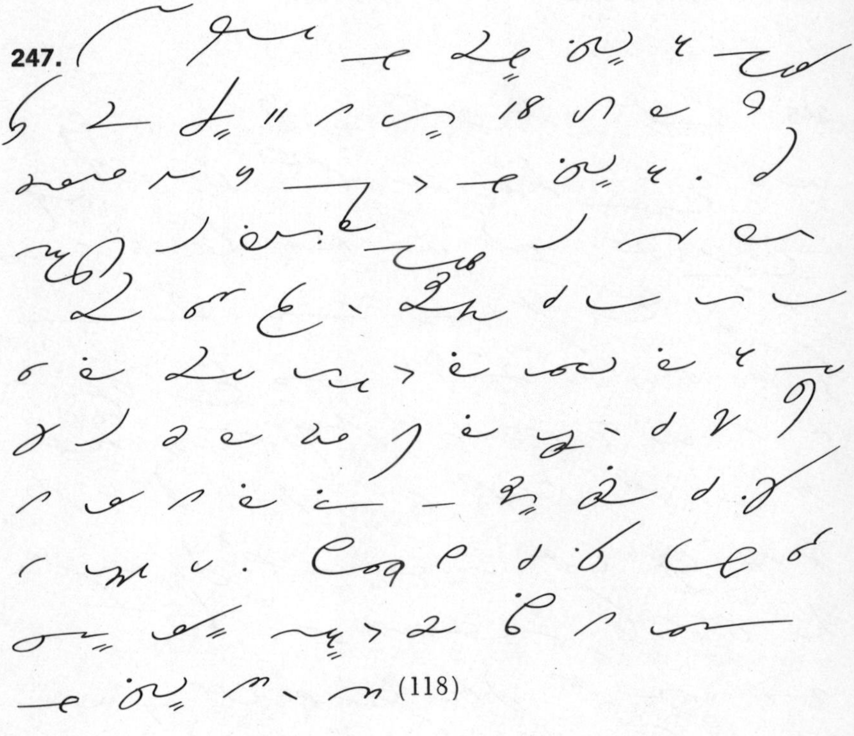

(118)

248.

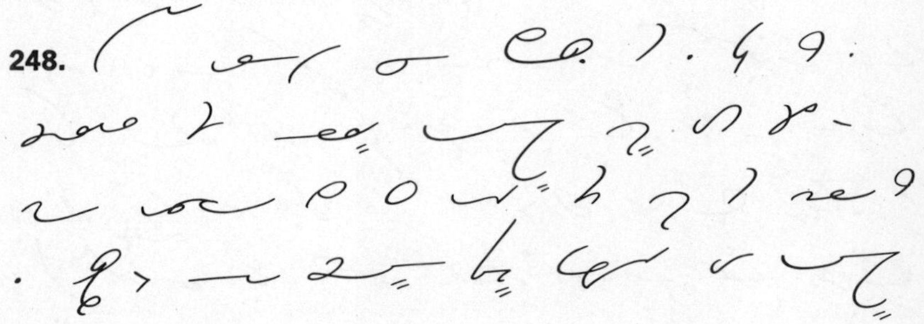

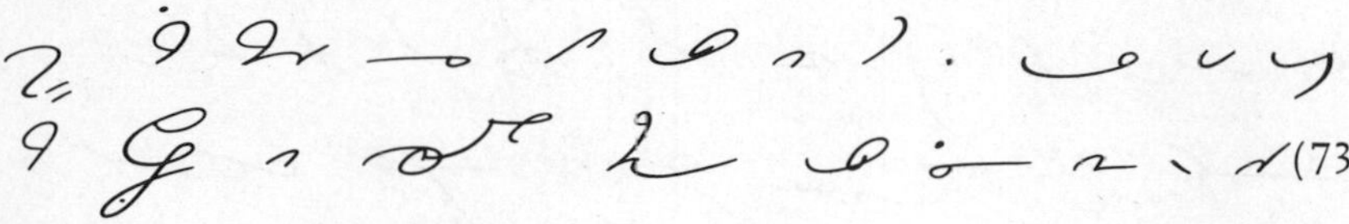

(73)

249.

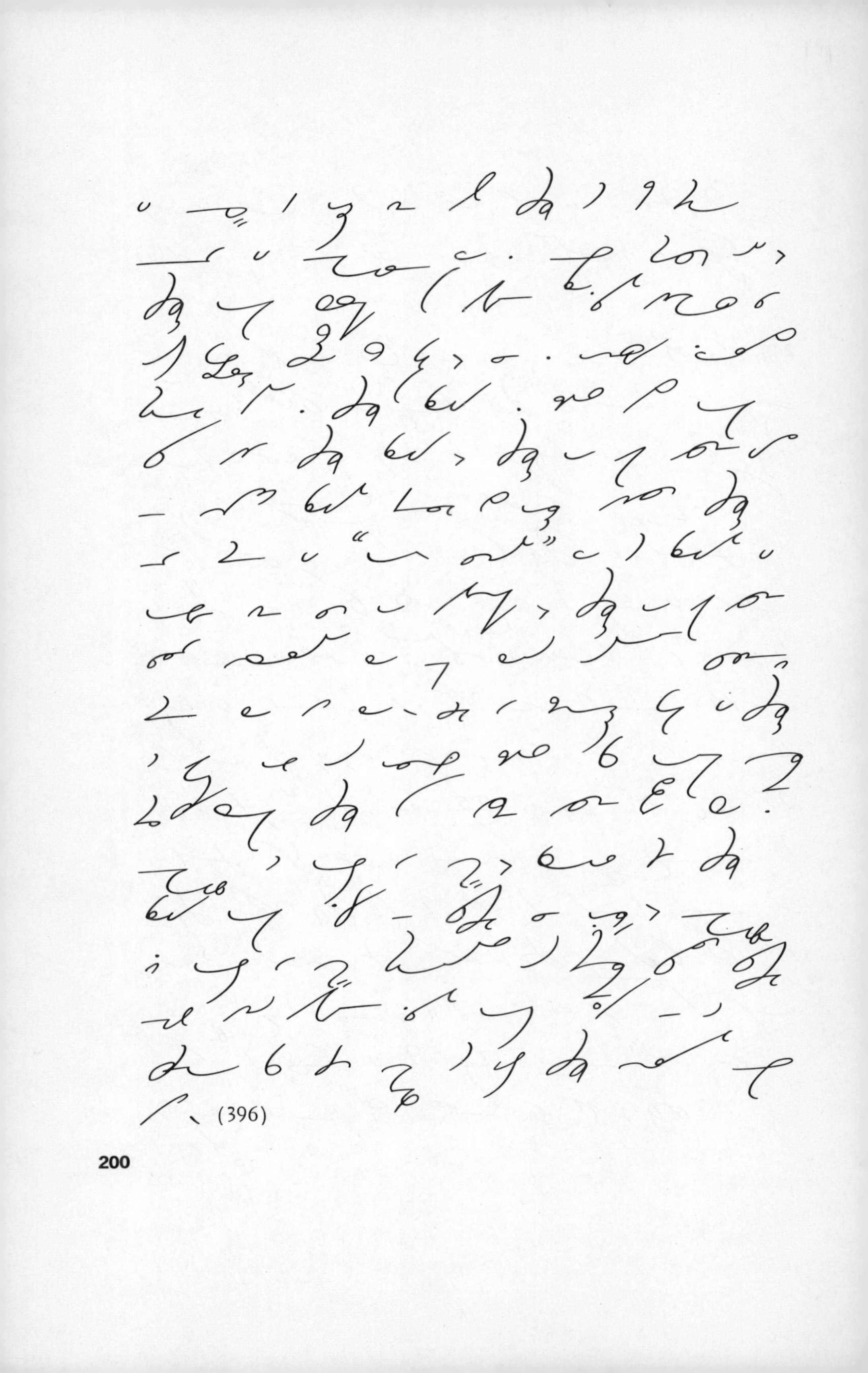

(396)

Lesson 34

PROGRESSIVE SPEED BUILDING

Half-Minute Progressive Speed Builder (90-125)

VOCABULARY PREVIEW

KEY

Employee, survey, secure, advancement, as soon as, calendar, remind. Birthday, heartiest, occurred, celebrate, application, tardiness.

(½ MINUTE AT 90)

250. Memo to Mr. Steel: We have just completed an employee survey and find that a steady, secure job is considered/nearly four times more important to workers than their base rate salary. We thought, as you will recall, that salary would be first choice.//

(½ MINUTE AT 100)

It was rated third place. Opportunity for advancement placed second. I will send you the complete results as soon as they can be typed in/proper form, which will probably be next week.

251. Dear Mr. Graham: A note on my calendar reminds me that you will have another birthday soon.//

(½ MINUTE AT 110)

I should like to take this opportunity to extend my heartiest personal wishes for many happy returns of the day.

It occurred to me/this morning that there might be some birthday plans being made to celebrate this occasion. If I can be of assistance to you, please call on me. Yours truly,//

(½ MINUTE AT 120)

252. Dear Mr. Price: Thank you for your letter of March 10. We are sending you an application blank. Please fill in this form and return it to our office.

We have several/positions open in which we think you will be interested. If you can bring in the application in person, we will arrange an immediate interview. Yours truly,//

(½ MINUTE AT 125)

253. Memo to All Employees: I have delayed this memo in the hope conditions would improve. But I must report that it has come to my attention that there is a great deal/of unexplained tardiness among our employees. Remember, if you are unable to report for work on time, you should immediately get in touch with your department head.//

Minute Progressive Speed Builder (80-100)

VOCABULARY PREVIEW

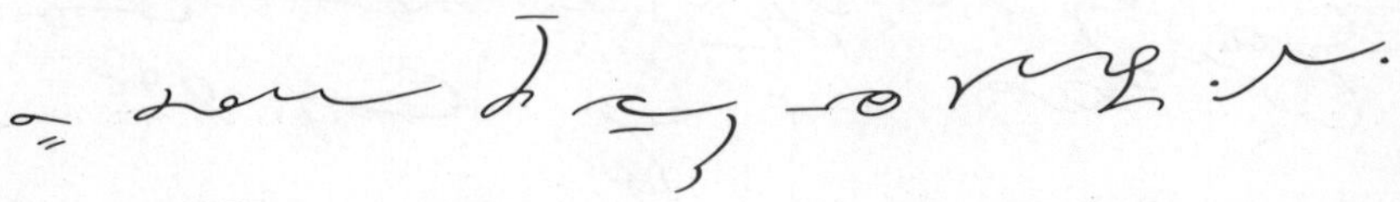

KEY

England, secretarial, interview, qualifications, inquiry, stenographic, handling.

(1 MINUTE AT 80)

254. Gentlemen: In June of this year I shall be graduated from New England College with a major in business./I have trained for secretarial work and should like to know whether there is an opening in your company//for someone of my background.

I am enclosing a data sheet with this letter; it will give you details of my///background. I shall appreciate an interview with you to discuss my qualifications. Very truly yours, (1)

(1 MINUTE AT 90)

255. Dear Miss Mason: Thank you for your inquiry about the possibilities for employment as a secretary in our/firm. We do not employ girls for immediate secretarial positions. All stenographic employees begin in our//stenographic pool and advance to secretarial positions as they show themselves capable of handling such jobs.

I///am enclosing our application blank. You may fill in the form and mail it back to us if you are still interested in a position. Very truly yours, (2)

(1 MINUTE AT 100)

256. Dear Mrs. Mansfield: Enclosed is the application form you asked me to fill in to make application for a job in your stenographic/pool. Your system of advancing persons from the pool into more responsible jobs sounds like a very good one, as it gives you a chance to//observe a girl's work habits and training before you have placed her in a job that she may not be able to handle.

I am very confident/// of my ability to handle a job in your company and do not object to competing with others. Very truly yours, (3)

Reading and Writing Practice

257.  (86)

258. 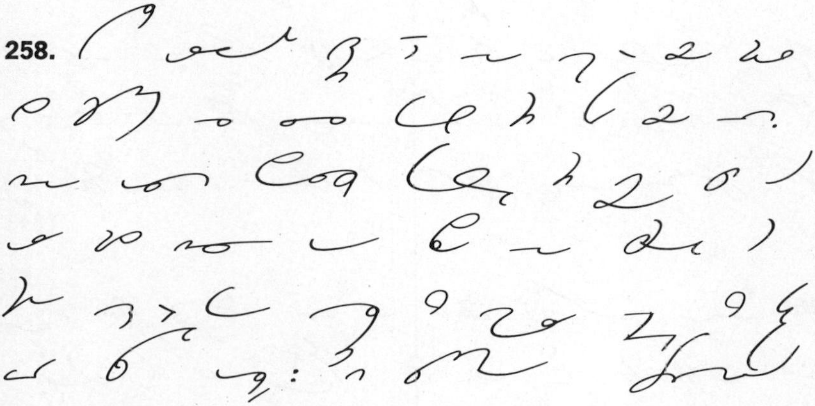

(99)

259.

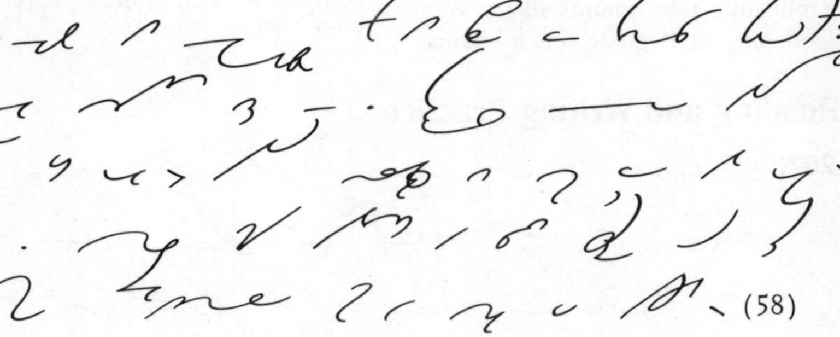

(58)

260.

(84)

261.

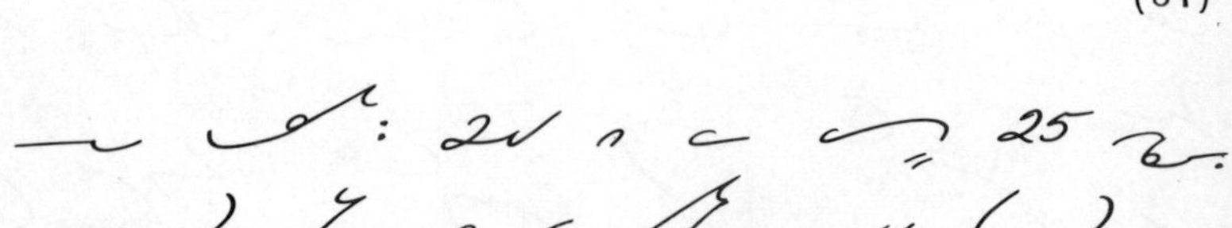

(60)

262.

(75)

263.

(204)

264.

(89)

Lesson 35

BUILDING SUSTAINED SPEED

Five-Minute Speed Builder

The first two letters are between Miss Ruth Jones, 195 Remington Avenue, Chicago 32, Illinois, and Mr. Brown. The last two are between Mr. Brown and Miss Mary Scott, 115 West Commerce Street, Aurora, Illinois.

VOCABULARY PREVIEW

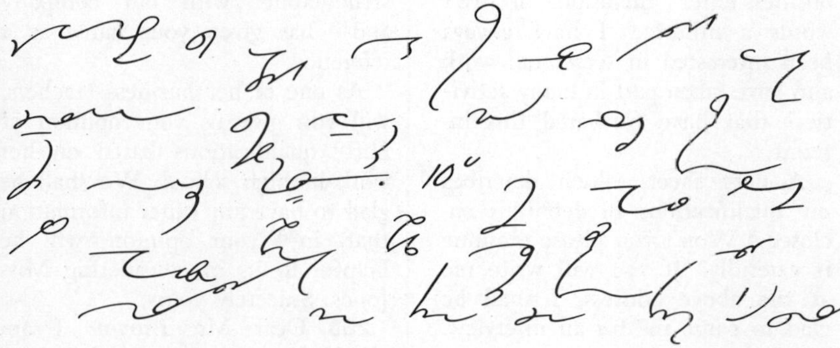

KEY

Stenographer, I wish, reputation, themselves, I have been, myself, dictation, always been.

Secretarial, activities, qualifications, won't, carefully, I shall be glad.

Interview, glad to receive, Friday morning, ten o'clock, convenient, employ, telephone.

Daily, employees, we hope you will be, we hope to see, give us, we shall be glad, any other.

Graduated, one of our, junior, senior, bookkeeping, shorthand, accurate.

265. Dear Mr. Brown: I have heard that you have an opening in your company for a stenographer, and I wish[1] to apply for that position.

I should like very much to work for the National Company, Mr. Brown, because[2] its reputation, the nature of its business, and the officers themselves have made it *the* company for[3] which I have been preparing myself.

I know that you need someone who is both interested and properly trained.[4] I have just completed the business course at Central High School, where I made very good grades. My rate of typing is[5] 70 words a minute, and I can take business-letter dictation at 125 words a minute.[6] I have always been interested in secretarial work and have taken part in many activities[7] that have furthered this interest.

A data sheet, which describes my qualifications in detail, is enclosed.[8] Won't you please examine it carefully? If you will write me at the above address, I shall be glad to come in[9] for an interview. Sincerely yours,

266. Dear Miss Jones: We were glad to receive your letter of October 15 and the data sheet you enclosed. We[10] shall be pleased to have you come in for a personal interview Friday morning[11] at ten o'clock if this time is convenient for you.

The duties of the person whom we shall employ consist of[12] (1) taking dictation, (2) typing, (3) filing, (4) answering the telephone, and (5) meeting customers.

Our[13] office hours are from nine to five daily, Monday through Friday, making a total of 35 hours a week. The[14] beginning salary is $195 a month, with a $10 increase at the end of[15] two months if the employee's work is satisfactory.

We hope you will be interested in this position,[16] because your qualifications fit our needs quite well. We hope to see you in our office on Friday morning.[17] Cordially yours,

267. Dear Miss Scott: Miss Ruth Jones has applied for a position as stenographer with our company and[18] has given your name as a reference.

As one of her business teachers, will you give us your opinion of her[19] qualifications based on her work in high school. We shall be glad to have any other information that, in[20] your opinion, will be helpful to us in considering Miss Jones. Sincerely yours,

268. Dear Mr. Brown: I am glad[21] to give you the following information about Miss Ruth Jones.

She was graduated last spring as a business[22] major from our high school, and we considered her one of our best and most popular students. During her junior[23] and senior years, she was assigned on many occasions to work in the local school office. She did her work well,[24] obeying instructions carefully and intelligently. She has had two years of bookkeeping, shorthand, and typing;[25] and, as I have said, she was a thorough and accurate student. I know that she would take an interest in[26] your work and that she would never be guilty of betrayal of office secrets.

Miss Jones's father died recently,[27] and she and her mother have moved to Chicago. If you decide to employ her, I know you will be pleased with[28] her. Yours very truly, (564)

Reading and Writing Practice

269.

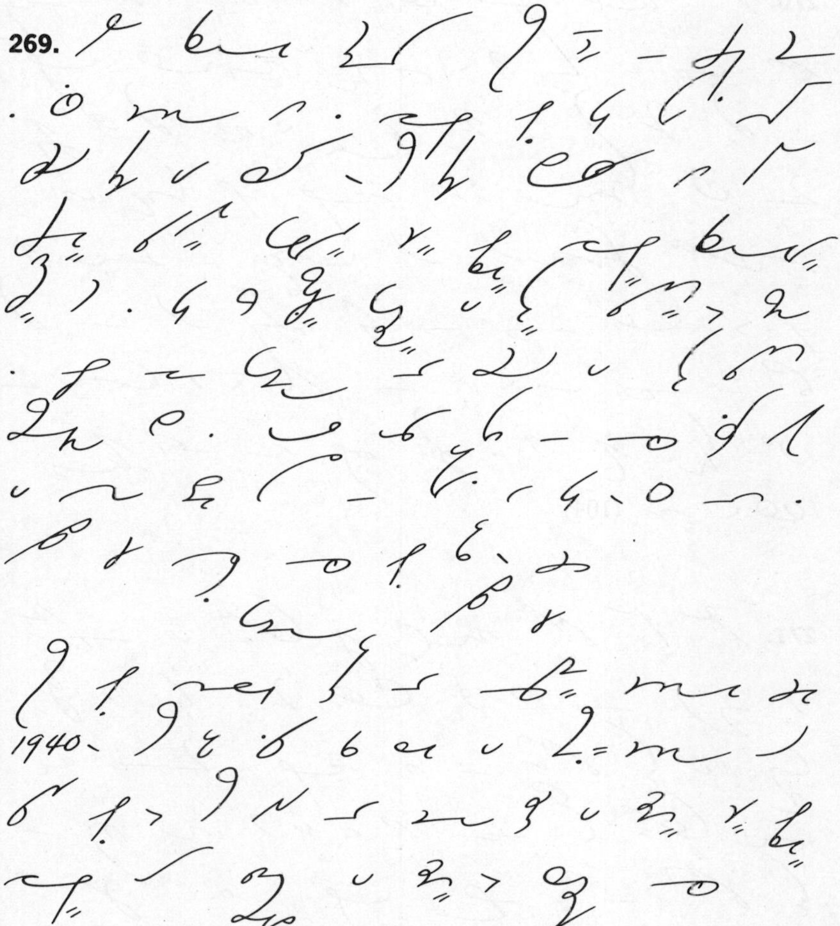

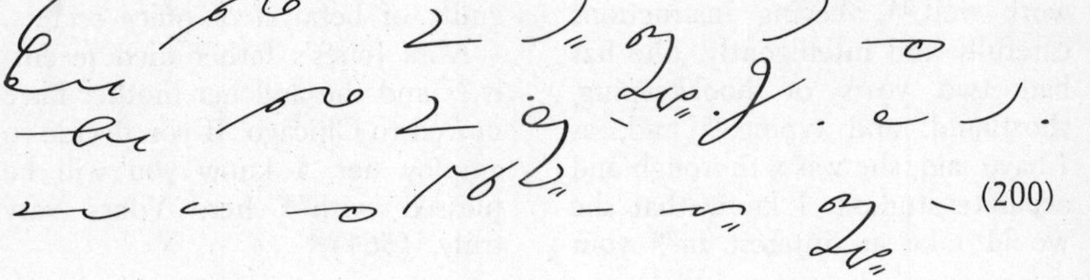

(200)

270.

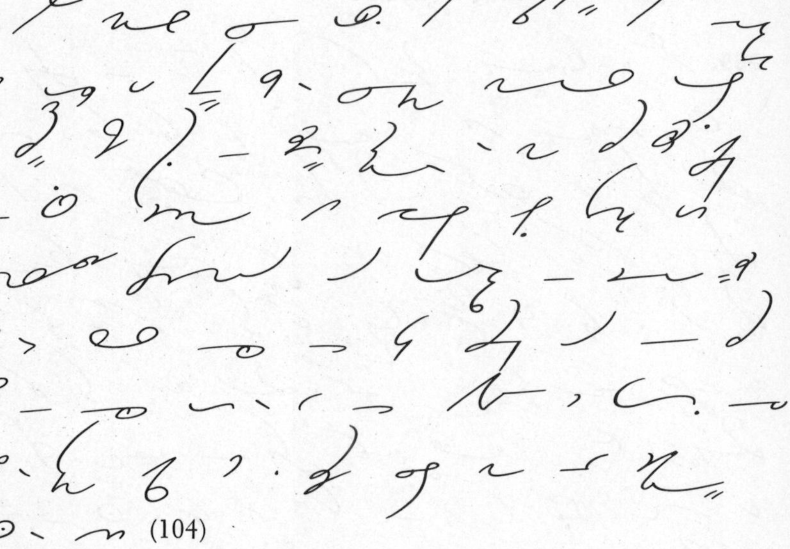

(104)

271.

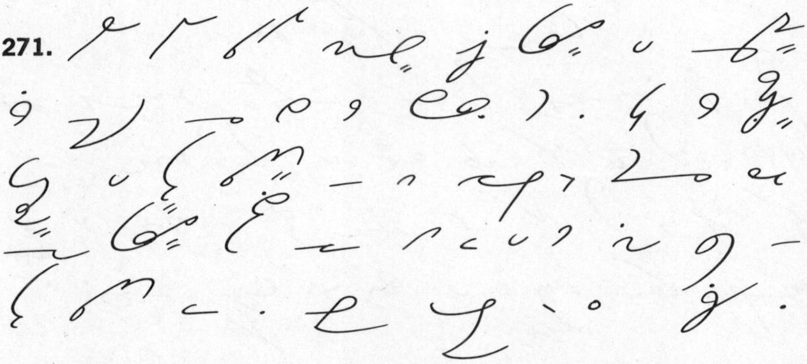

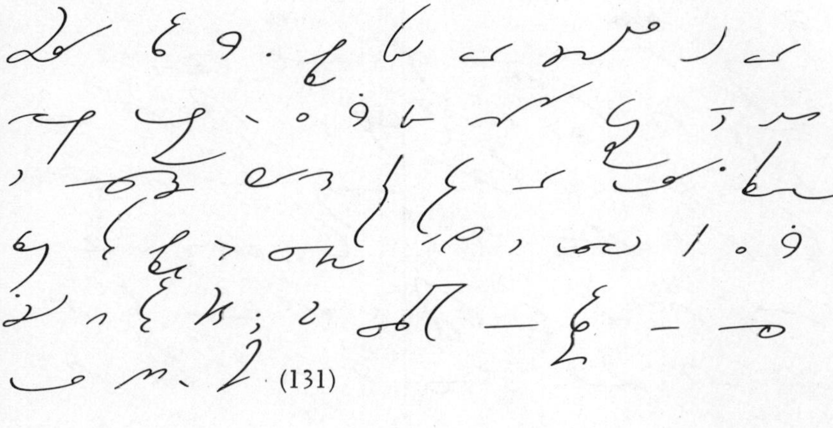

(131)

272.

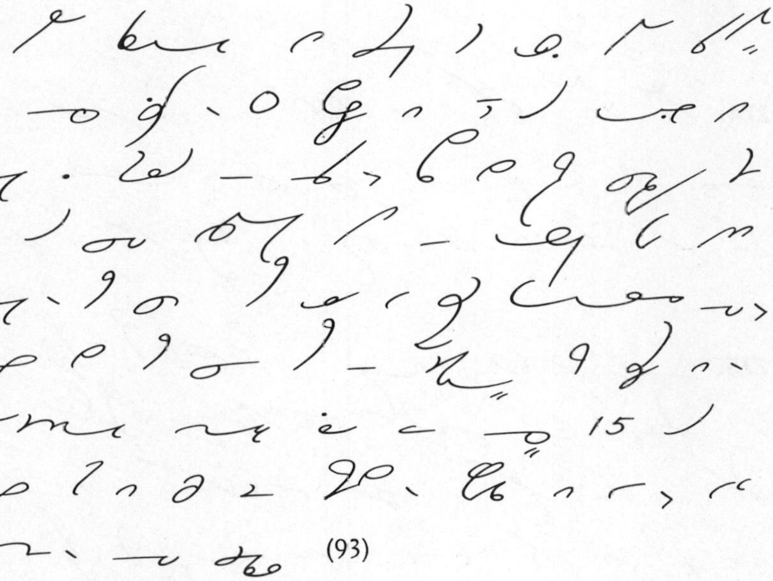

(93)

273.

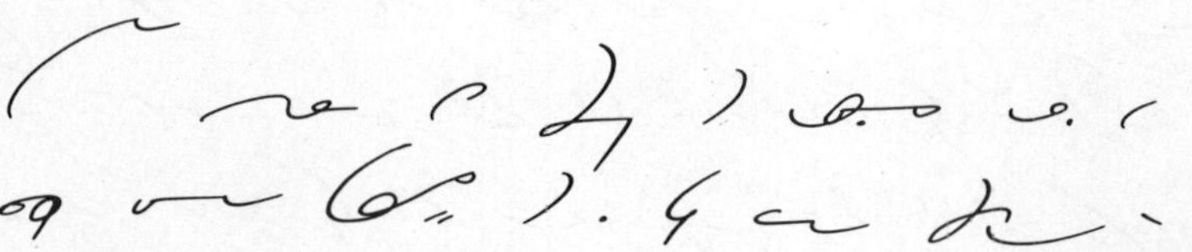

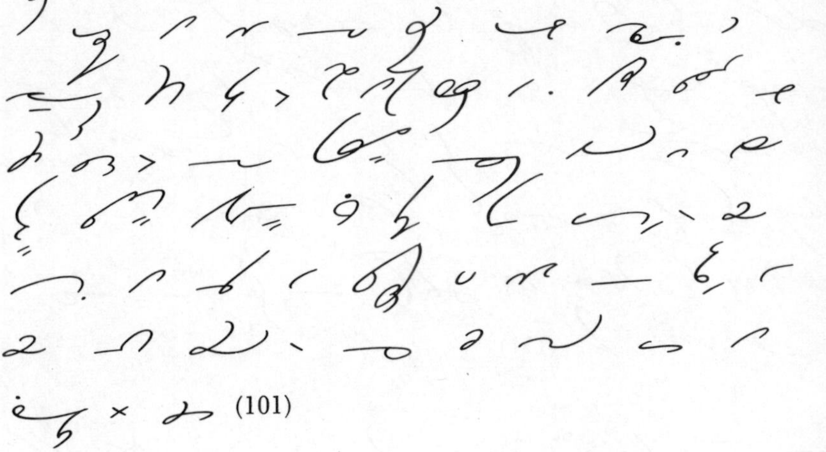

(101)

274.

(30)

275.

(86)

8

The Manufacturing Department

Spelling and Penmanship Improvement Drills for Chapter 8

SPELLING

In words with an *ei* or *ie* combination, the *i* precedes the *e* except when it follows the letter *c*, or when the combination has the sound of long *a*.

chief	niece	relieve
field	pier	variety

After c

conceit	deceive	receive

Sounds like a

eight	reign	freight

Exceptions

ancient	leisure	weird
forfeit	neither	seize
height		

PENMANSHIP

1.
2.
3.
4.
5.

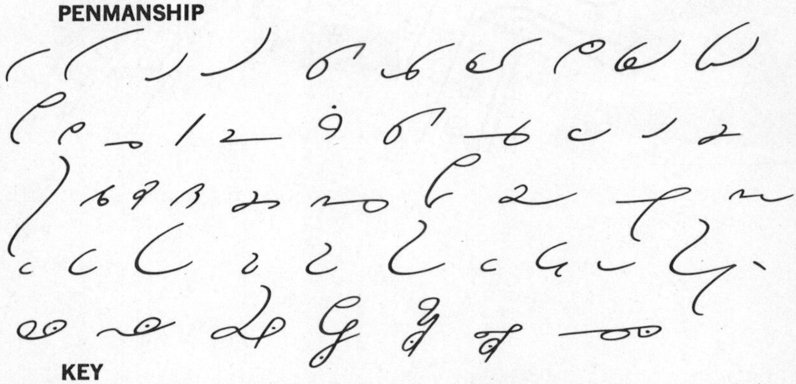

KEY

1. Ten-den, tem-dem, ent-end, emt-emd, attention, written, certain, deny, point, bond.
2. About, they, any, which, some, has, attention, matter, or, there, send.
3. Have been, to see, we shall, to us, Sincerely yours, you may, about the, we will, may be, one of our.
4. All, per, bill, so, fr, value, all presents are valuable.
5. Area, create, variation, appreciate, association, initiation, mania.

Lesson 36

BUILDING TRANSCRIPTION SKILL

Transcription English Pointers

THE USES OF THE COMMA (CONCLUDED)

1. A comma should precede the conjunctions *and, or, nor, but* used to connect the co-ordinate clauses of a compound sentence.

We have examined the credits to your account, and we find that our records agree with yours.
He is a good medical risk, but for several reasons we must reject his application.

If, however, a comma occurs within either or both of the clauses, a semicolon is used before the conjunction.

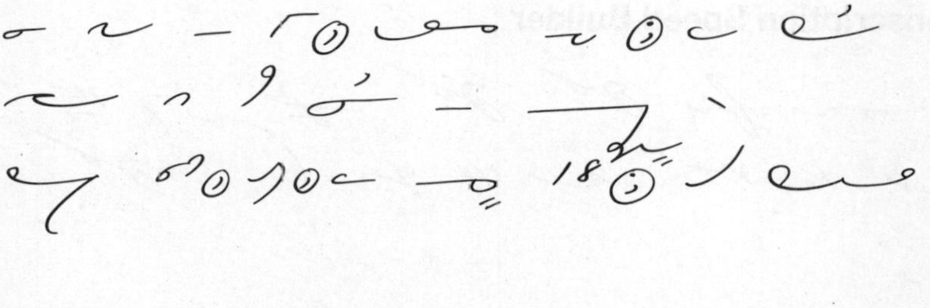

When you are in town, let me know; or I'll call you if I'm in Manchester.
He will be with us, therefore, on May 18; and I will let you know later the exact time and place.

Do not mistake a simple sentence containing a compound predicate for a true compound sentence. Compound predicates are not usually separated by commas.

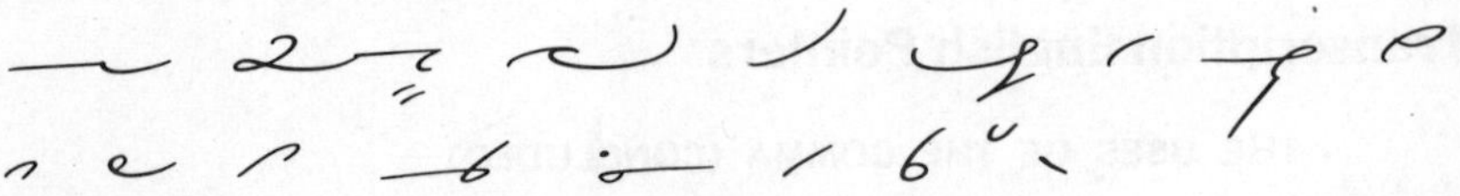

Mr. Williams called and left the message that you were to meet him at six o'clock.

2. If the clauses of a compound sentence are very short, the comma may be omitted.

You may come by subway or you may take a taxi.

3. A comma precedes a brief quotation.

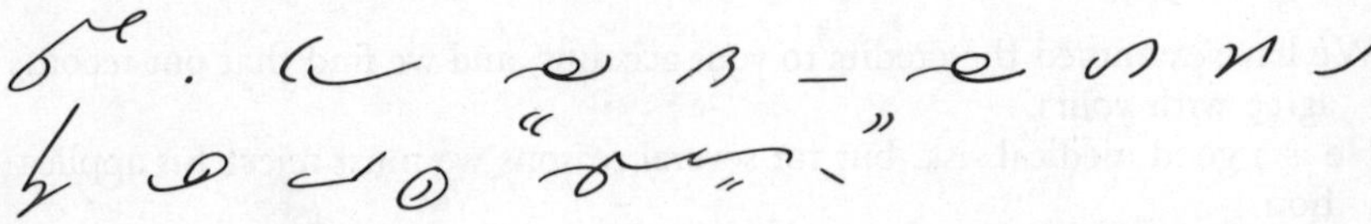

Address a postal card to us in care of this station and just write on it, "Catalogue."

Transcription Speed Builder

276. 

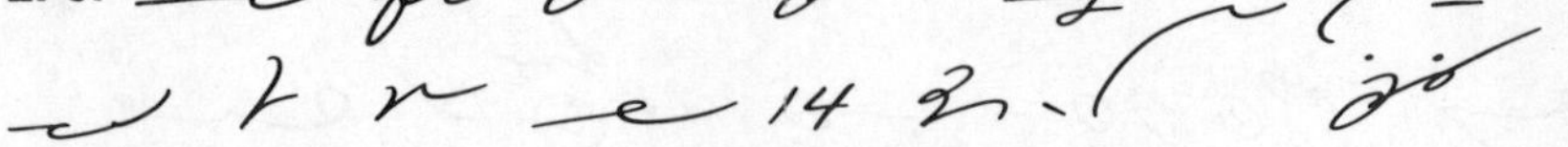

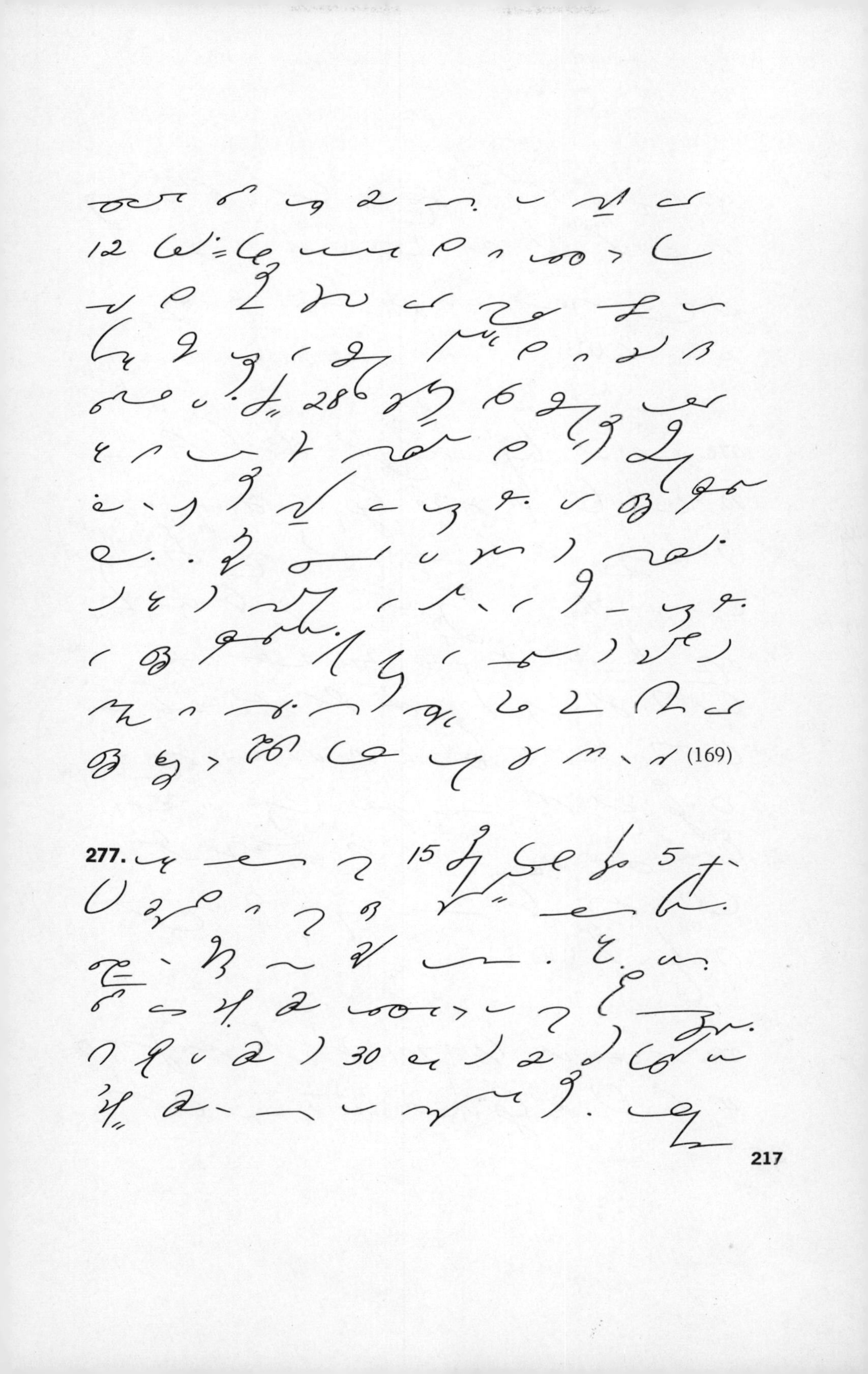

12 ... 28 ... (169)

277. ... 15 ... 5 ... 30 ...

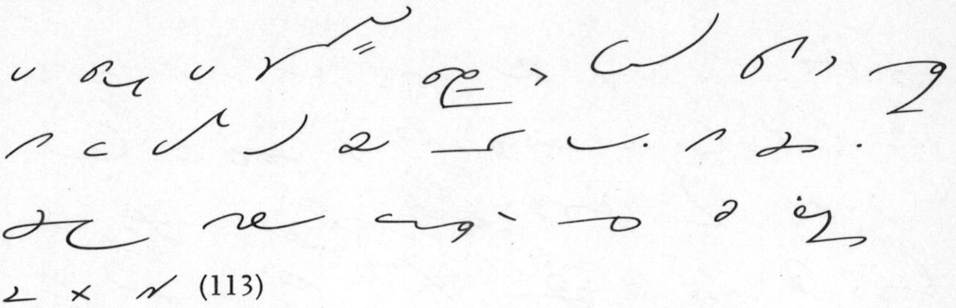

278.

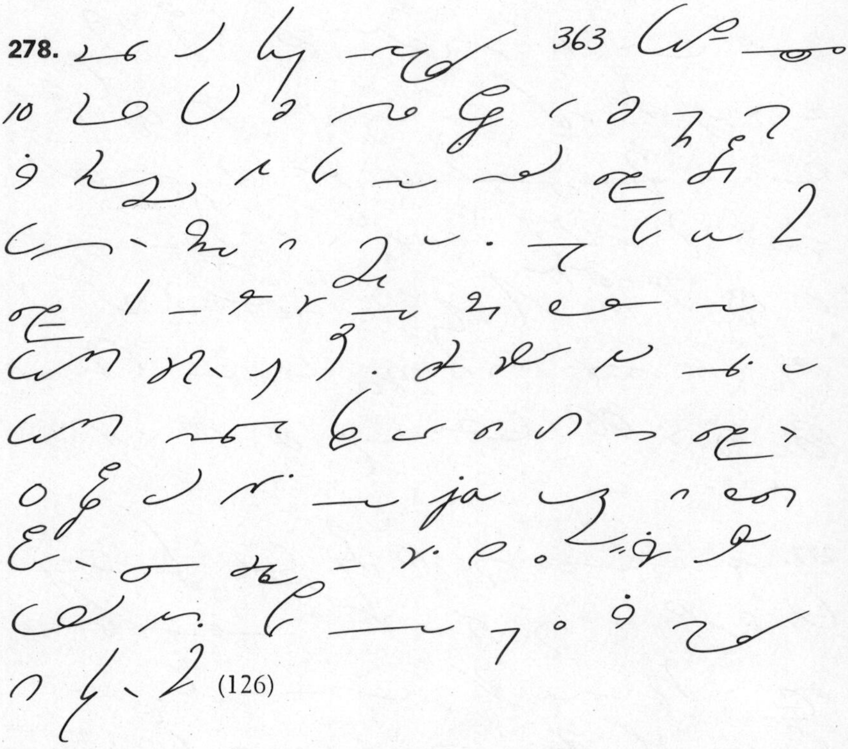

279.

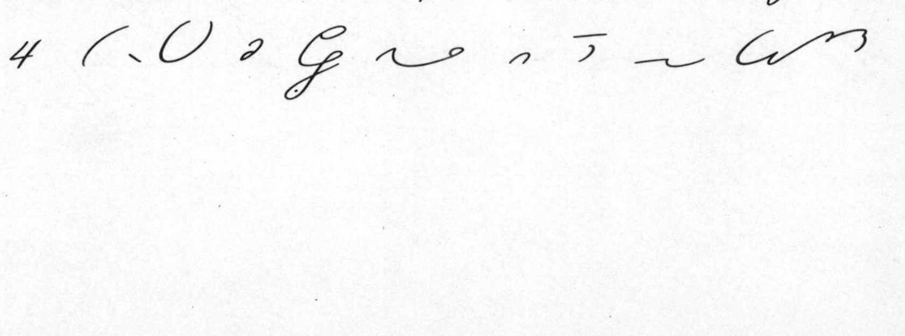

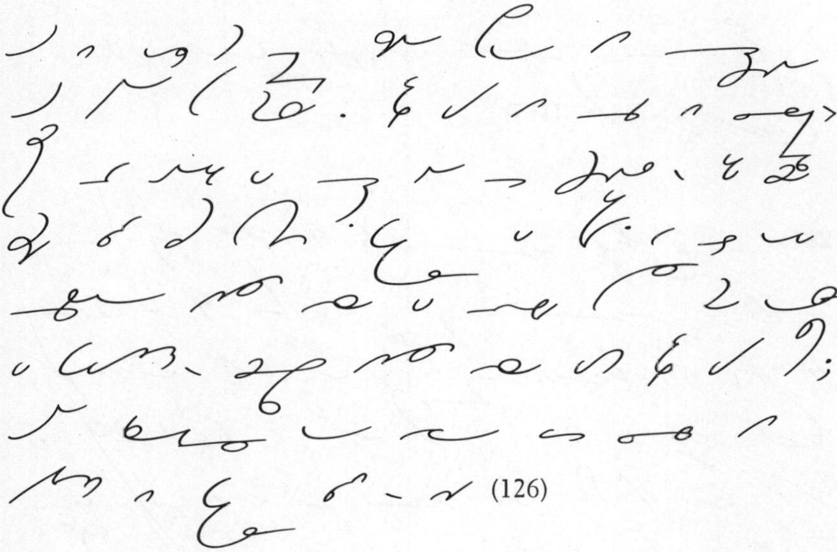

(126)

280.

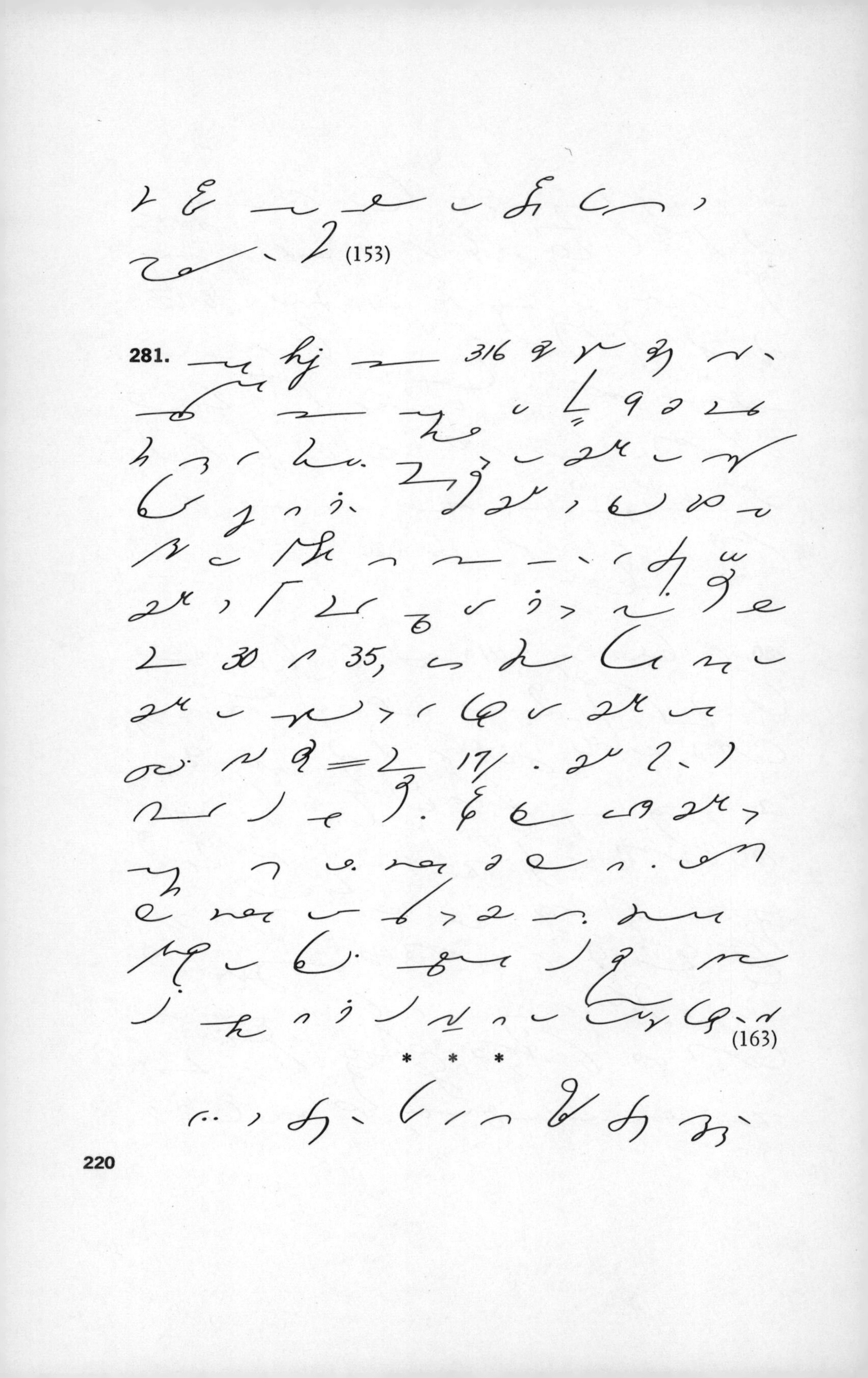

(153)

281. 316 … 30 … 35 … 17 …

(163)

* * *

Lesson 37

MASTERING SHORTHAND THEORY

Word Beginnings

In-

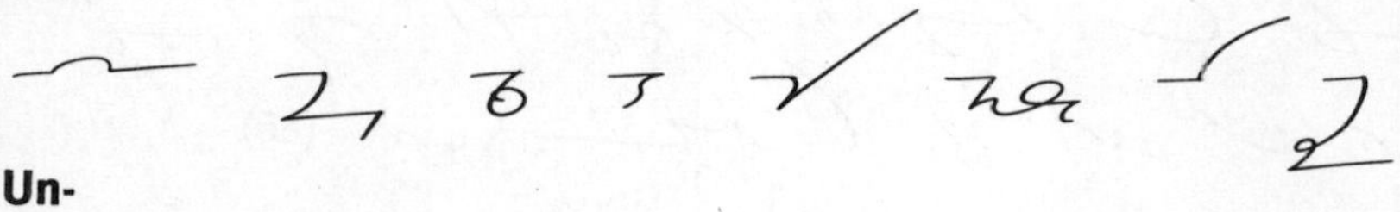

Un-

Per-

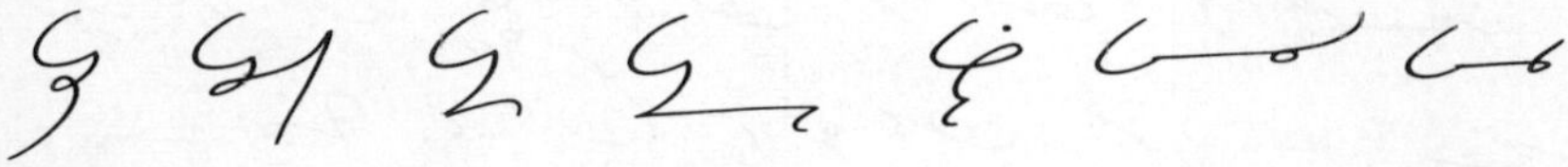

Pro-

Pur-

KEY

Income, information, inside, insist, instead, insurance, intend, investment.
Uncommon, uncomfortable, unless, unpaid, unreasonable, unsatisfactory.
Perceive, percentage, perfect, performance, perhaps, permanent, permit.
Approaching, problems, proceeds, process, promise, promote, proper.
Purchasing, purchaser, purple, purport, purposely, purse, pursue, pursuant, pursuit.

Reading and Writing Practice

282. 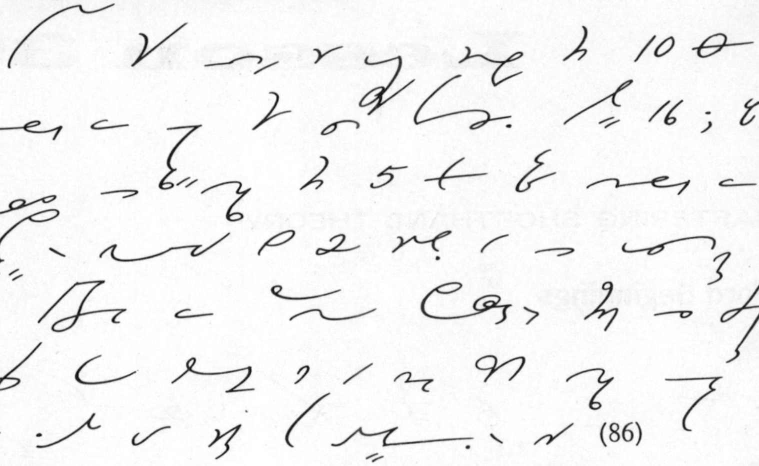 (86)

283.  (130)

284.

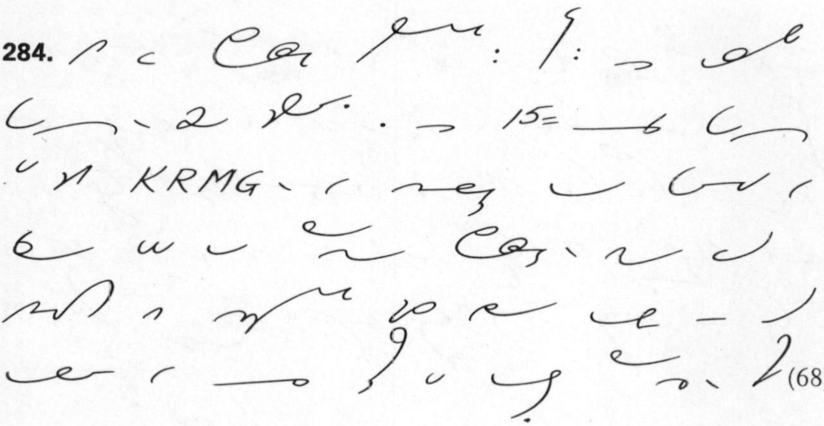

(68)

285.

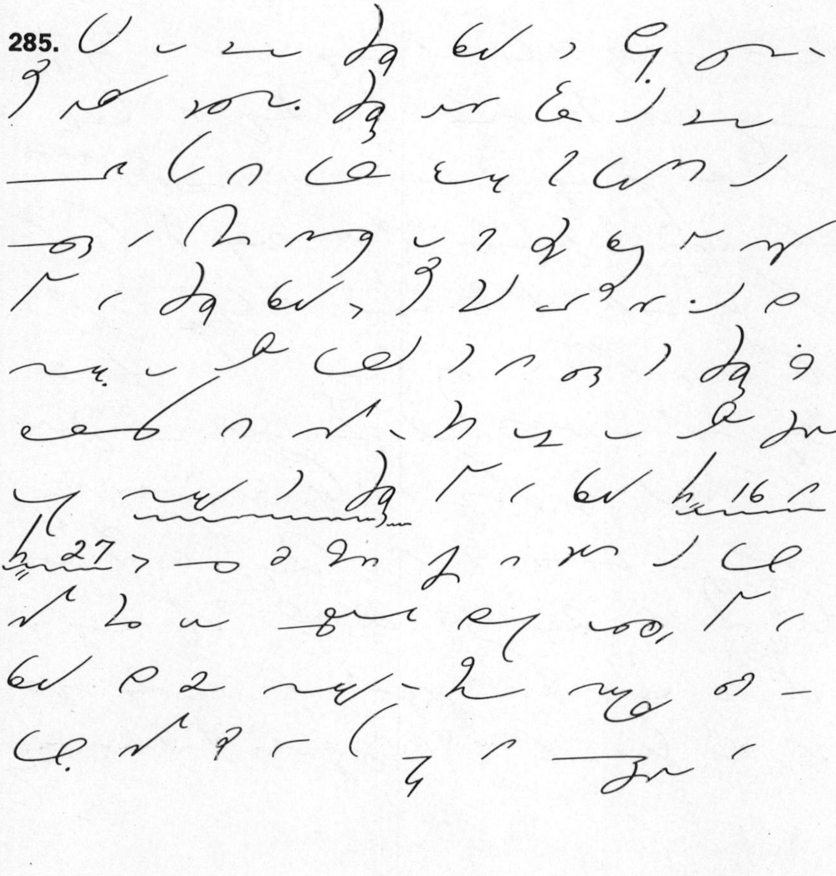

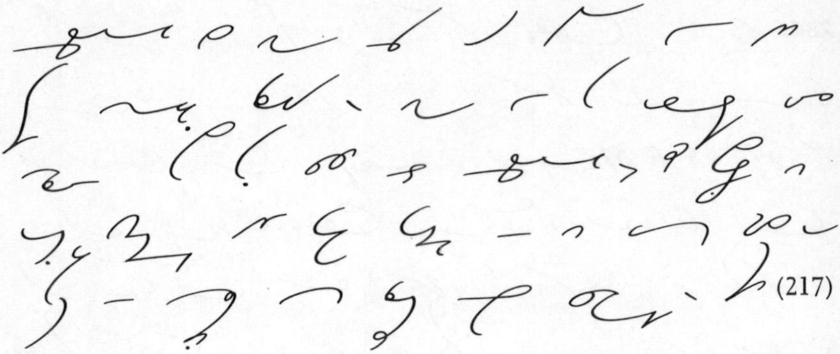

(217)

286.

(238)

287.

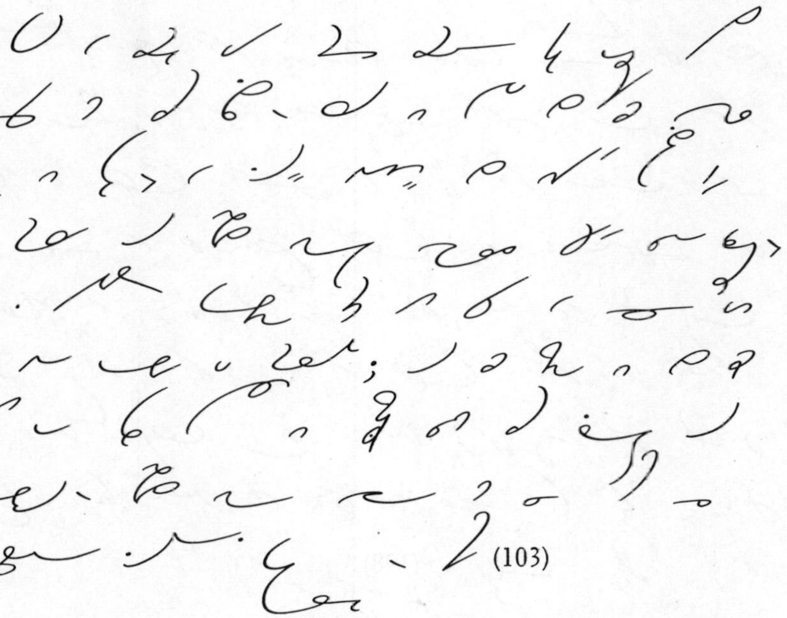

(103)

Building Speed Through Reading

288. HINTS FOR SUCCESS

(198)

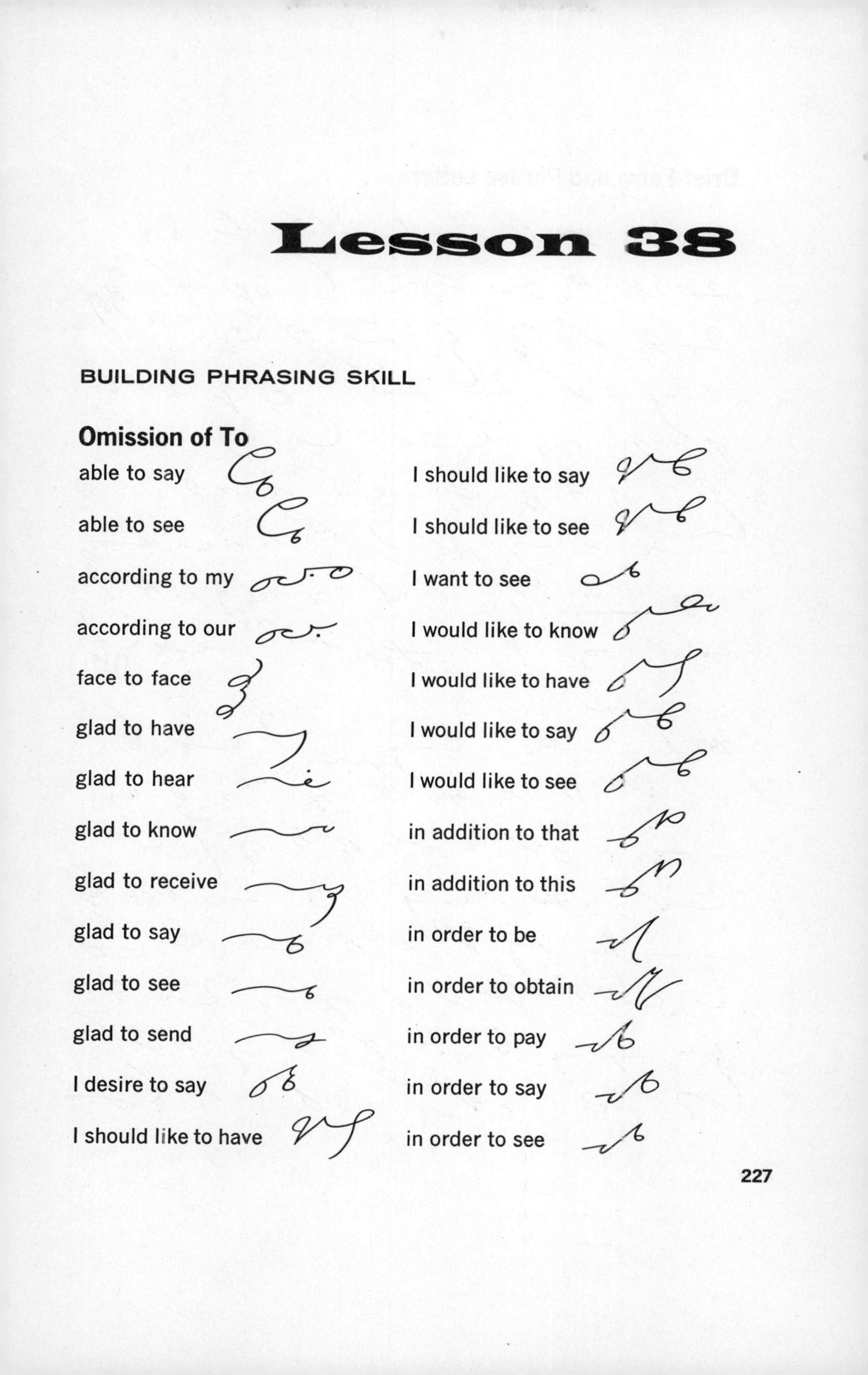

Lesson 38

BUILDING PHRASING SKILL

Omission of To

able to say
able to see
according to my
according to our
face to face
glad to have
glad to hear
glad to know
glad to receive
glad to say
glad to see
glad to send
I desire to say
I should like to have

I should like to say
I should like to see
I want to see
I would like to know
I would like to have
I would like to say
I would like to see
in addition to that
in addition to this
in order to be
in order to obtain
in order to pay
in order to say
in order to see

Brief-Form and Phrase Letters

289.

(115)

290.

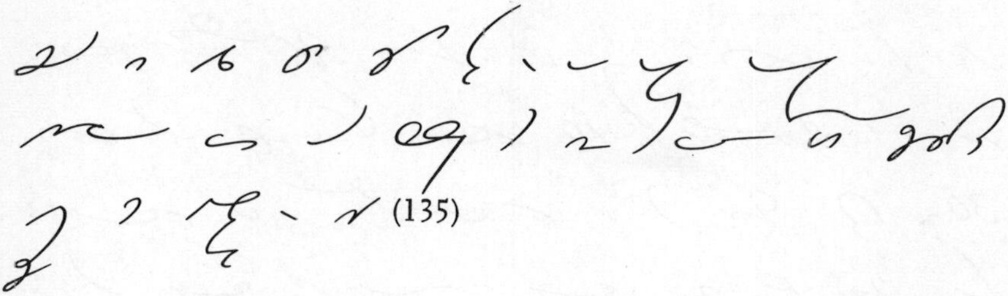

291. 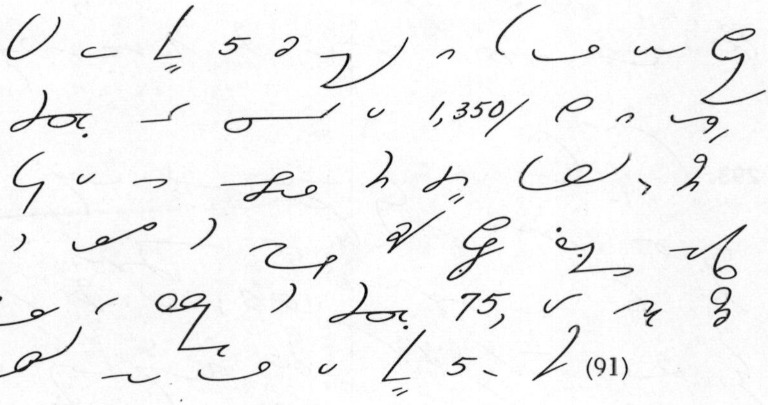

292. 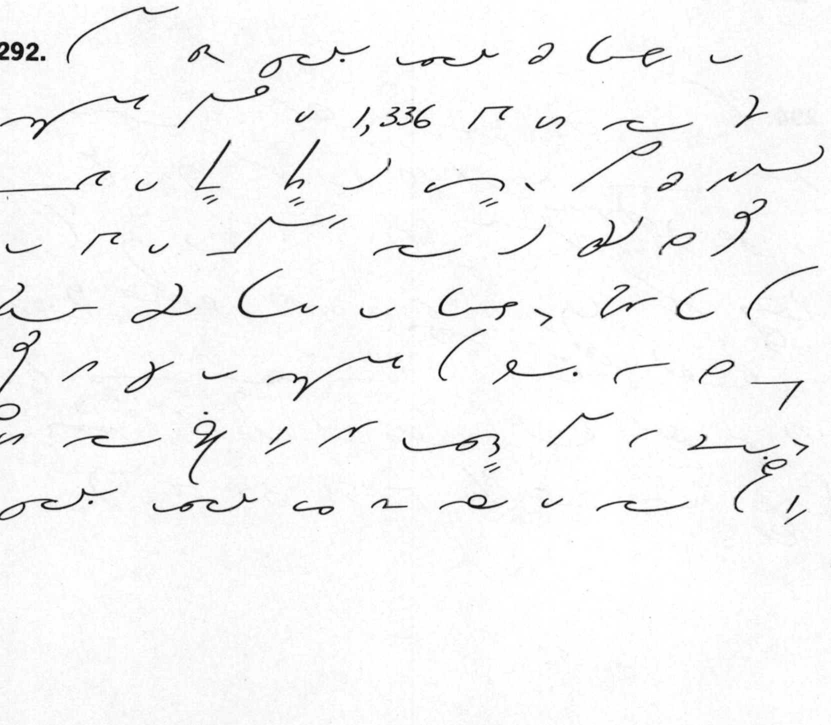

(152)

293.

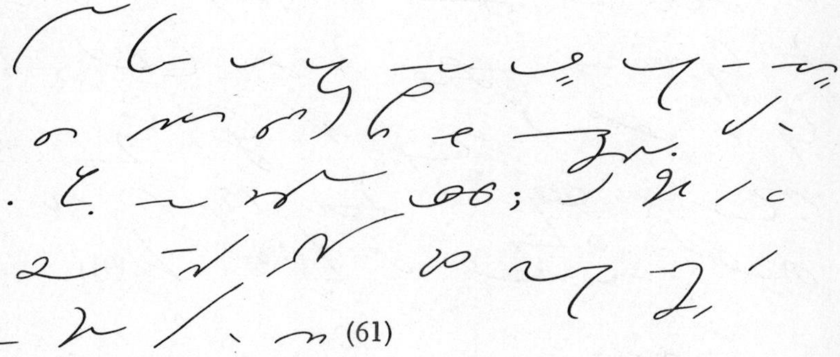

(61)

294.

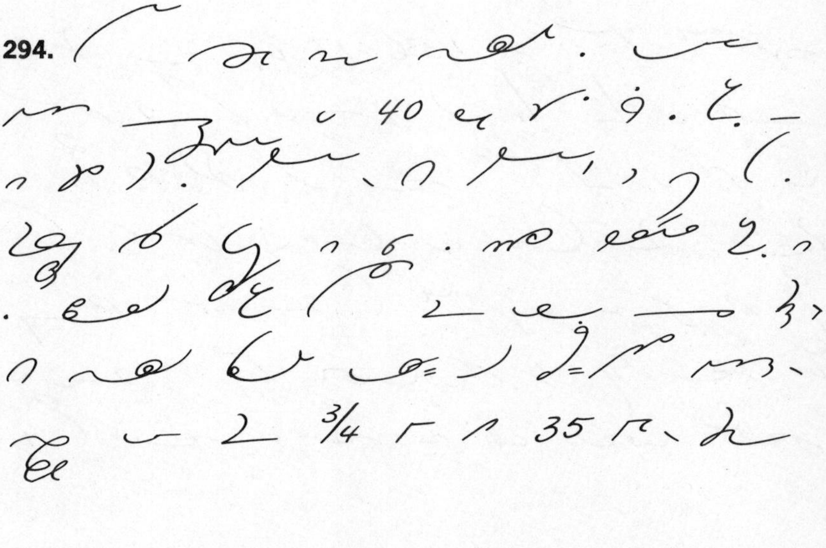

(304)

295. 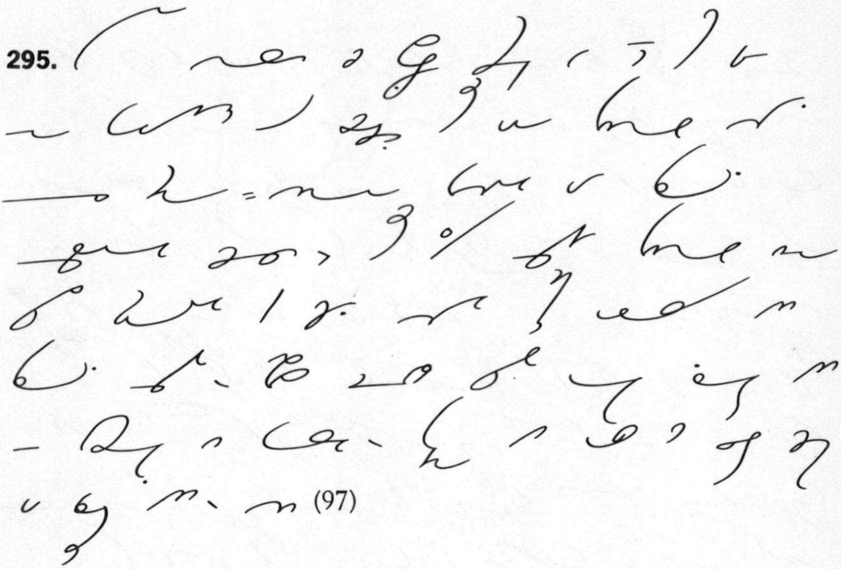 (97)

296.  (142)

Lesson 39

PROGRESSIVE SPEED BUILDING

Half-Minute Progressive Speed Builder (90-125)

VOCABULARY PREVIEW

KEY

Director, we are sending you, booklets, manufacture, distribution, publication, throughout the.
Wholesale, Pacific, territories, Portland, proposal, equipped, appreciate.

(½ MINUTE AT 90)

297. Dear Miss Lane: At the suggestion of your State Director, we are sending you a group of booklets about the manufacture/of the goods we produce at our several manufacturing plants. This is the same material that we send to the trade.//

(½ MINUTE AT 100)

Because you are concerned with the distribution of merchandise, we believe you will be interested in our trade publication. This/publication is mailed the first of each month to about 20,000 merchants throughout the country—those who are in the retail and wholesale trade.//

(½ MINUTE AT 110)

Enclosed is a copy of the March issue. If you wish to receive this publication monthly, let us know.

We appreciate this opportunity/ to be of service. Sincerely yours,

298. Gentlemen: Since our last letter to you, we have decided to separate the Pacific Coast into four territories.//

(½ MINUTE AT 120)

A dealer at Portland will be appointed to handle our manufacturing business there.

Before we present our proposal to you, we should like to have you answer/the following question:

Have you a place where you can store repair parts and machinery equipped and ready for immediate shipment to prospects in your territory?//

(½ MINUTE AT 125)

If you have a storage place for this material, we should like very much to have you handle the Pacific Coast territory for us. We are sure that you will find/it profitable to handle our line of repair parts and machinery.

We should appreciate having your answer as soon as possible. Very truly yours,//

Minute Progressive Speed Builder (80-100)

VOCABULARY PREVIEW

KEY

Thank you for the, manufacture, discontinued, Oklahoma City, warehouse, mechanical.

(1 MINUTE AT 80)

299. Dear Mr. Archer: Thank you for the order you sent us for 80 machines. I hope it will be all right if we/delay shipment on these items for thirty days. We are making a style change in the machine, and manufacture//is being discontinued while the equipment is made ready for the new model.

If it is necessary///for you to have immediate shipment, we can get them from our Oklahoma City warehouse. Yours very truly, (1)

(1 MINUTE AT 90)

300. Dear Mr. Perry: I appreciate your writing to me to explain why you cannot make immediate shipment of my/order for 80 of your machines.

I don't know whether to ask that you send me machines from your Oklahoma City warehouse//or to wait for the new ones. What changes are being made in the design? Do the changes relate only to design or are///there internal changes also?

If you will answer these questions, I shall be glad to give you my choice of action. Yours truly, (2)

(1 MINUTE AT 100)

301. Dear Mr. Archer: I am sorry

I was so vague in my letter to you about the changes that are being made in the new model of/our machine.

The mechanical workings of the machine will be unchanged. We have found it necessary to change the design of the machine//to keep it in line with modern trends. Actually, there are very few changes; but there are enough to make it necessary to shut down///manufacturing for a few weeks.

We shall be glad to do whatever you suggest with regard to shipment of the machines. Sincerely yours, (3)

Reading and Writing Practice

302. 

(98)

303. 

(266)

304.

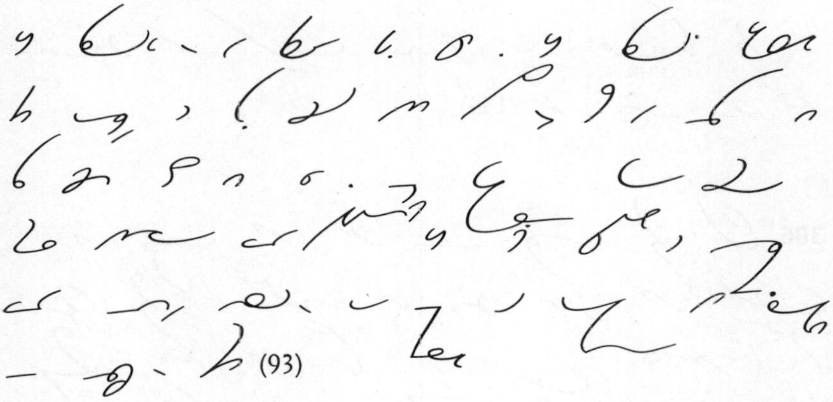

(93)

305.

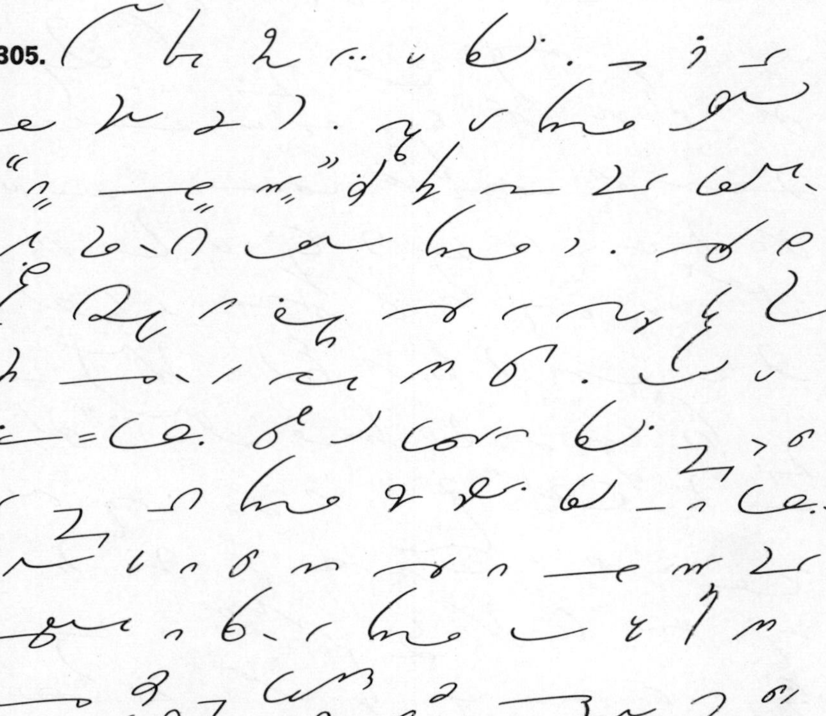

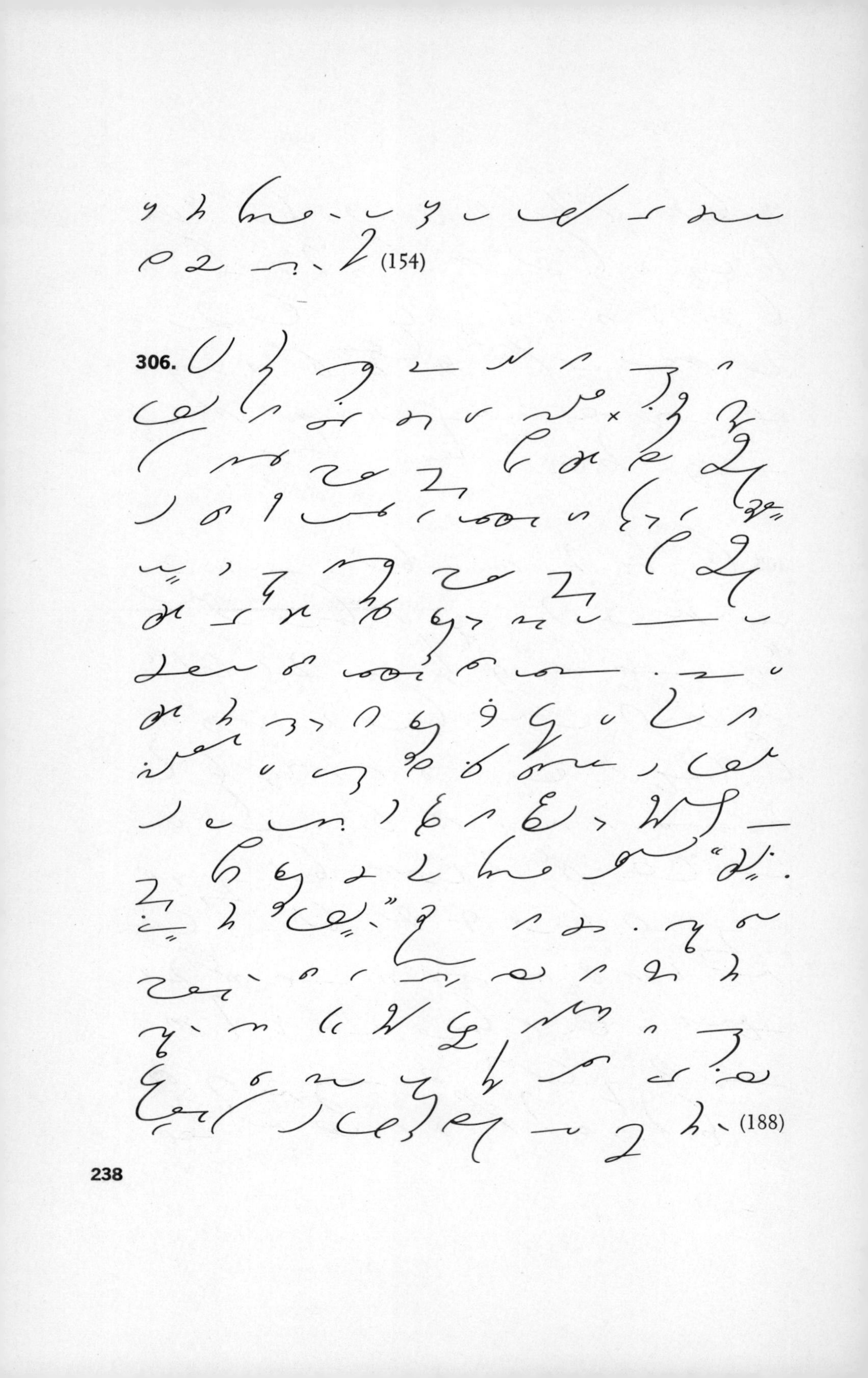

(154)

306.

(188)

Lesson 40

BUILDING SUSTAINED SPEED

Five-Minute Speed Builder

The following correspondence is between Edward P. Erickson, School of Commerce, Ohio State University, Toledo 5, Ohio, and Barry L. Parsons, Educational Director, General Manufacturing Company, 1739 Brookdale Road, Wichita 6, Kansas.

VOCABULARY PREVIEW

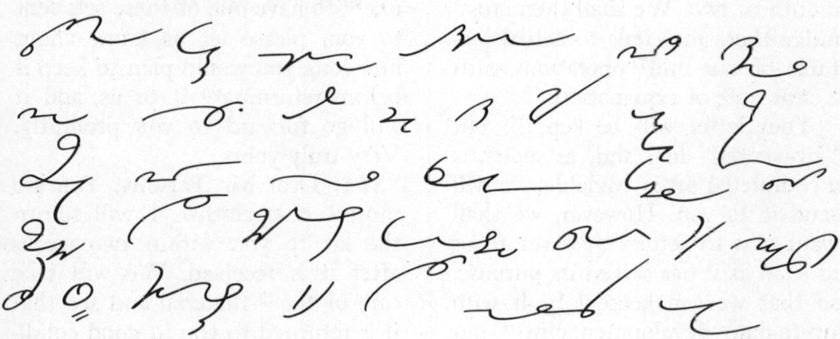

KEY

Educational, processes, instructor, industrial, one of these, thank you for your letter.

One of our, gathering, index, as soon as, to us, up-to-date, response, I shall be glad.

Available, one of them, gladly, salesmen, personnel, week or two.

As a result, demand, if you would like to have, please let us know, how long, forward, co-operative.

Via, Eye, photographs, $100, to make, unlimited, will you please.

307. Dear Mr. Parsons: The other day I ran across an ad in Manufacturing News in which you offer to[1] send business schools free of charge an educational kit showing basic processes of manufacturing. I[2] am an instructor of industrial management and should appreciate very much receiving one of these[3] kits for use in my class. Sincerely yours,

308. Dear Mr. Erickson: Thank you for your letter of January 9,[4] asking for one of our Manufacturing Educational Kits.

Although this kit has been mentioned in the trade[5] papers, we are still in the process of gathering materials for it. It is our aim to complete this kit[6] within the coming month or two. We shall then cross-index these materials to actual pictures of our mill[7] operations with a clear note of explanation.

Your letter will be kept in our "kit-wanted" file; and, as soon[8] as a completed set is available, we will send it to you. However, we shall want you to return this[9] set to us as soon as it has served its purpose, so that we can keep it fresh with up-to-date developments in[10] our industry.

Thank you again for your interest in writing to us. Sincerely,

309. Dear Mr. Parsons: Thank you[11] very much for your prompt response to my request. I shall be glad to wait until the kit is ready for distribution.[12] Yours truly,

310. Dear Mr. Erickson: On January 10 we wrote you in reply to your request for[13] one of our Educational Kits, telling you that it was still in the process of being completed. These sets[14] are now available. If you still feel that you could use one of them, we shall gladly send it to you. Our salesmen[15] are using these kits in educating department-store personnel regarding basic manufacturing[16] processes, and several of our dealers have already asked for kits to keep for a week or two. As a result,[17] we are having requests for more sets than we have made up.

Because of the demand for these sets, we are asking each[18] of the persons to whom we send them to return them to us as soon as they have served their purpose. If you would like[19] to have one of these sets sent to you, please let us know about how long you would plan to keep it before returning[20] it to us, and it will go forward to you promptly. Very truly yours,

311. Dear Mr. Parsons: You are most[21] co-operative. I will return the kit to you within two weeks after it is received. We will take care of the[22] material and see that it is returned to you in good condition. Sincerely yours,

312. Dear Mr. Erickson: As[23] you requested in your letter of April 12, one of our Educational Kits and a book, "Education[24] via the Eye," containing photographs showing the story of manufacturing, are being sent to you[25] via insured parcel post, being insured for $100.

When you see this material, you

will realize[26] why we are unable to make up these sets in unlimited quantities. As we are having many requests[27] from our salesmen and our dealers for this material, we necessarily must limit the time that any[28] one person may keep one of these sets.

We appreciate your co-operation in helping us maintain our[29] schedule. During the summer, if there is not so much call for these sets as there is at the present time, we will gladly[30] send you another one if you are teaching the course at that time.

When you are through with this set, will you please return[31] it via insured parcel post. Sincerely yours, (630)

Reading and Writing Practice

313.

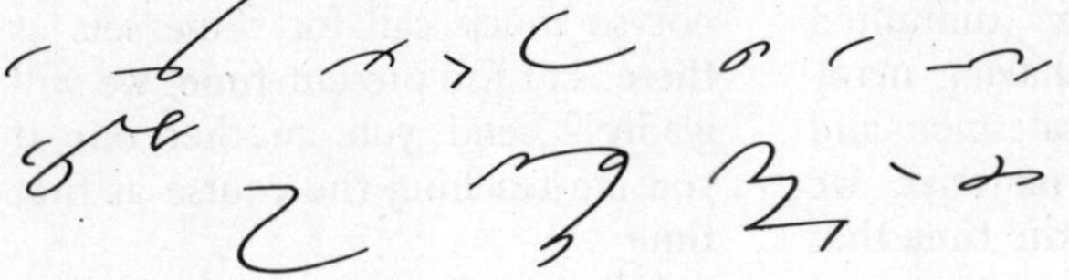

(183)

314. 

(162)

315.

(142)

316. MEETING THE NEEDS OF MILLIONS OF PEOPLE

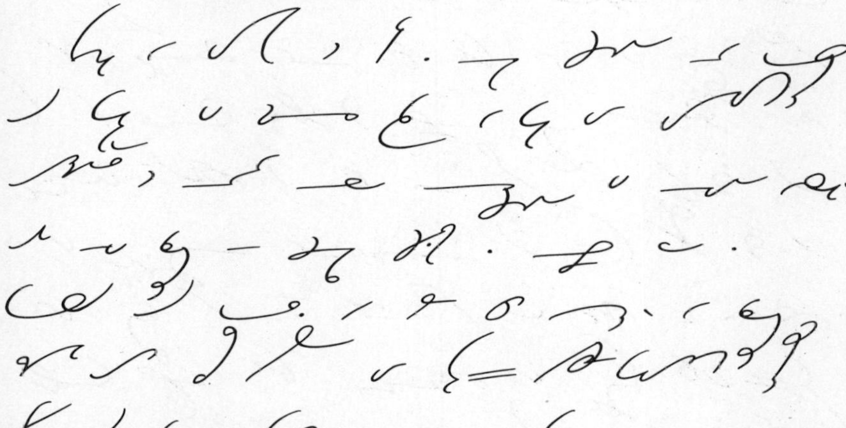

(296)

PART III Vocational Dictation and Transcription

In Part III you will become acquainted with the types of material you would take from dictation and transcribe in eight different vocations. You will also learn the terms and expressions that are peculiar to each of these vocations. The vocations with which you will work are:

Chapter	*Business or Profession*
9	Advertising, Publishing, and Printing
10	Aviation
11	Banking
12	Law
13	Petroleum
14	Medicine
15	Utilities
16	Government

9

Advertising, Publishing, and Printing

Word Study for Chapter 9

ADVERTISING, PUBLISHING, AND PRINTING

Backbone. The spine of a book; the part of the cover displayed as the book stands on the shelf.

Ben Day. A process (named for the inventor) for shading the background of a line of engraving.

Blurb. A laudatory announcement of a book, often printed on the jacket or outer paper cover. (Slang or colloquial.)

Boldface. Type of a heavier weight than lightface, which is the standard weight. Boldface is indicated in manuscript by a wavy underscore below the word or words.

Caption. The headline of an item in a newspaper; the heading of a chapter, section, page, or article.

Chase. A rectangular steel or iron frame into which pages of type are fastened, or "locked up," for printing or for making plates.

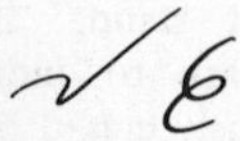

Coated Paper. Paper that has been coated, or covered, with a preparation of mineral matter and an adhesive and made smooth or glossy. Coated paper is especially suitable for halftone engravings.

Collate. To examine sets of printed sheets, to verify the order and the number of pages, plates, maps, and so on. Also, to gather such sheets into sets.

Colophon. A distinctive emblem used by a publisher on the title page of a book, at the end of a book, or on the cover; formerly, an inscription at the end of the book giving information about the making of the book.

Cut. An engraving. Drawings without shading are reproduced as line cuts. Drawings with shadings or photographs are reproduced as halftones.

Delete. The proofreading term meaning to "take out." It is usually expressed by the Greek letter *delta.* (δ)

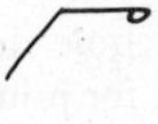

Dummy. A page-by-page layout for a book, folder, or other printed piece. Also, blank sheets bound to represent a projected book.

Electrotype (Electro). A metal facsimile plate of type or engravings from which printing is done.

Engraving. The process of producing designs on wood, metal, or stone; the book so prepared; a picture printed from such a block.

Folio. The page number. A sheet folded once, thus making four pages to the sheet; hence, a book of the largest dimensions – more than 11 inches in height.

Form. A page or pages of type or other matter, locked in a metal frame or chase; by extension, the printed sheet made from the metal form.

Galley. A shallow oblong metal tray to hold type that has been set for printing. The proof of this type is called *galley proof.*

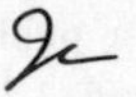
Halftone. A metal plate for reproducing varying degrees of lights and shadows, as in photographs. The gradation is effected by fine dots and produced by putting a screen between the object and the camera.

Italic. A style of type characterized by sloping or slanted letters. Italic is indicated in manuscript by a straight line below the word or words.

Layout. The make-up of a book, periodical, newspaper, or advertisement.

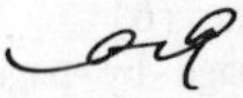
Linotype. A machine for casting type in lines, for printing.

Manuscript. Handwritten or typewritten material as distinguished from printed material.

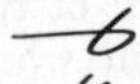
Mat. Short for *matrix*, a die or mold for a type face.

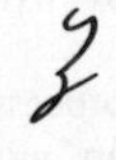
Offset. A smudge or transfer of undried ink from a freshly printed sheet upon another sheet; also a kind of lithography.

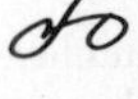
Pica. Standard measure for type composition; 12-point type. Six picas equal 1 inch.

Proof. An impression taken for the purpose of correction or examination; also called a *proof sheet.*

Roman. The style of type most commonly used in books and in all classes of ordinary reading matter; it is light-faced and upright, with serifs and shaded strokes.

Rout. To cut off. Usually the expression is "Rout off" or "Rout out." The term is applied, as a rule, to cuts or engravings from which some mark is to be removed.

Royalty. Payment to the writer of a book or the author of a work of art for each copy sold or used. Royalty may be either a percentage of the selling price or a fixed sum.

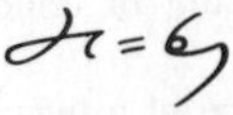
Sans-serif. "Without serifs"; a term that describes any type face in which the individual characters do not have the fine cross strokes at the top and bottom.

Script. Type, printing, or engraving that has the appearance of handwriting.

Signature. A folded printed sheet ready to be bound into a book or a pamphlet. A signature is usually 16 pages, but it may be 8, 32, or 64 pages.

Stet. "Let it stand." A proofreader's mark to indicate that previously erased or crossed out material is to be retained. The word *stet* may be written, or the process indicated by a series of dots below the words that are to remain.

Type. Small pieces of metal, each having a letter or other character in relief on the metal. A type face is a "family" of type with similar characteristics.

Lesson 41

BUILDING TRANSCRIPTION SKILL

Transcription English Pointers

THE USES OF THE APOSTROPHE

How to Form Possessives

The possessive form of a noun or a pronoun is used in the place of a phrase beginning with *of*. "The stenographer's notes" means "the notes of the stenographer." "Nobody's business" means "the business of nobody." An *s*-ending noun followed immediately by another noun is usually a possessive.

A. 1. The possessive singular of a noun or of an indefinite pronoun is formed by adding *'s* to the nominative, except where the noun or pronoun ends in *s* or a sibilant sound.

boy, boy's
man, man's
the employee's records
one, one's
other, other's
anybody, anybody's

When a singular noun or an indefinite pronoun ends in *s* or a sibilant sound, only an apostrophe is added. If, however, a new syllable is formed in the pronunciation of the possessive, the *'s* is added.

the hostess' gown
Frances' book
my boss's mail
the witness's testimony

2. The possessive plural of a noun or of an indefinite pronoun is formed by adding an apostrophe to the regular plural of the noun or pronoun.

buyer, buyers'
boys, boys'
ladies, ladies'
others, others'

When the plural ends in a letter other than *s*, the possessive plural is formed by adding *'s*.

businessmen, businessmen's women, women's
children, children's

B. The possessive forms of personal pronouns do not require the apostrophe. Each pronoun has its own possessive form.

he, his	it, its	you, yours	who, whose
she, hers	we, ours	they, theirs	

Caution: Guard against confusing personal possessive pronouns with similarly spelled contractions; for example:

its with *it's*, which means "it is"
theirs with *there's*, which means "there is"
whose with *who's*, which may mean either "who is" or "who has"

(Concluded on page 283)

Transcription Speed Builder

317.

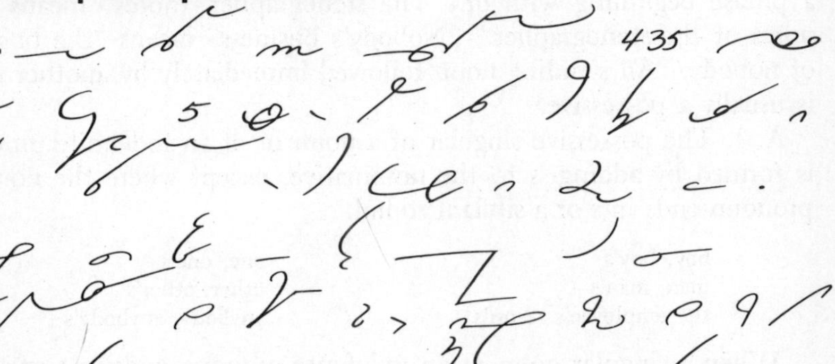

(67)

318.

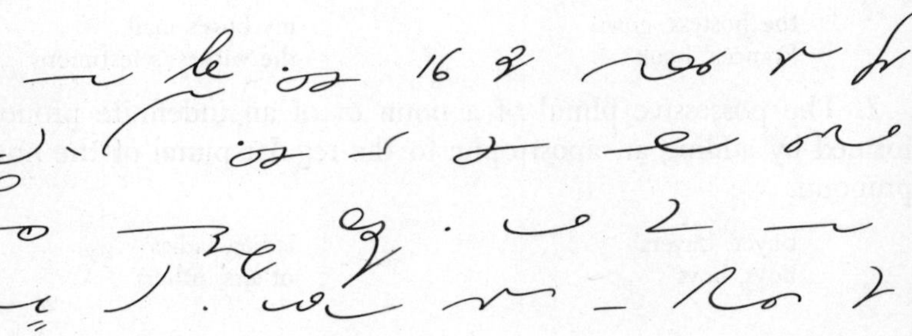

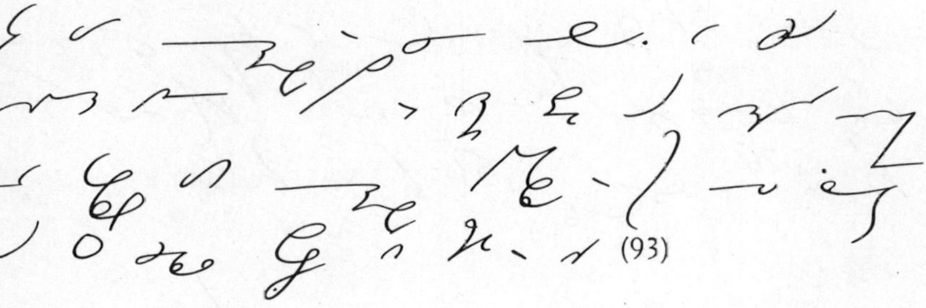

(93)

319.

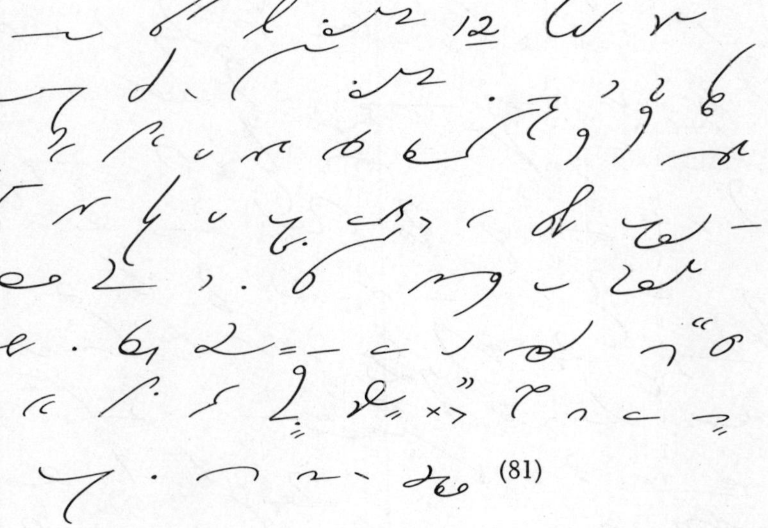

(81)

320.

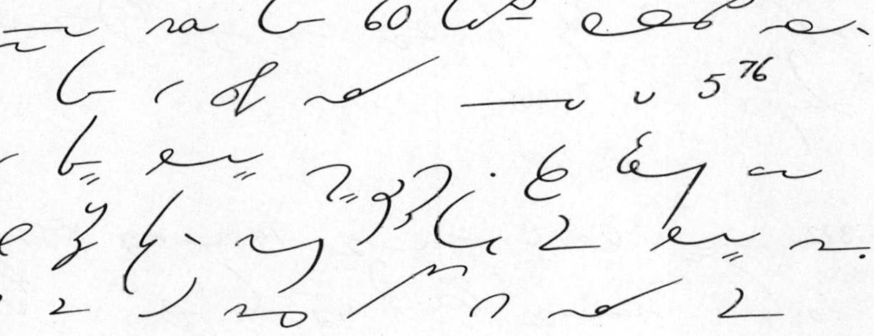

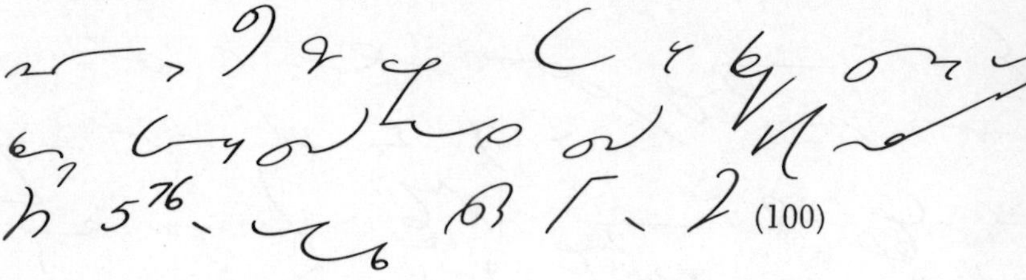

321.

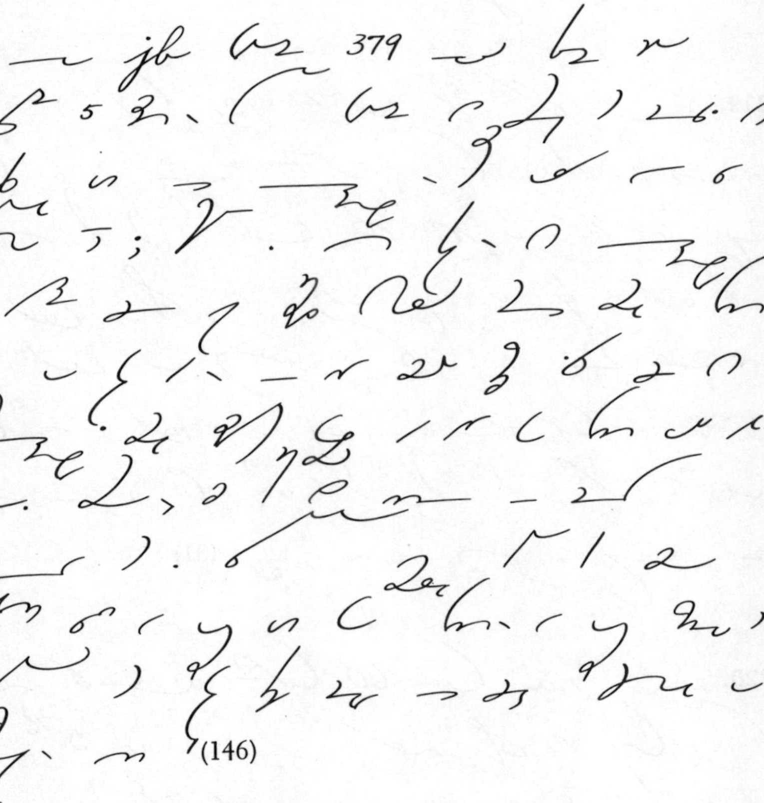

322.

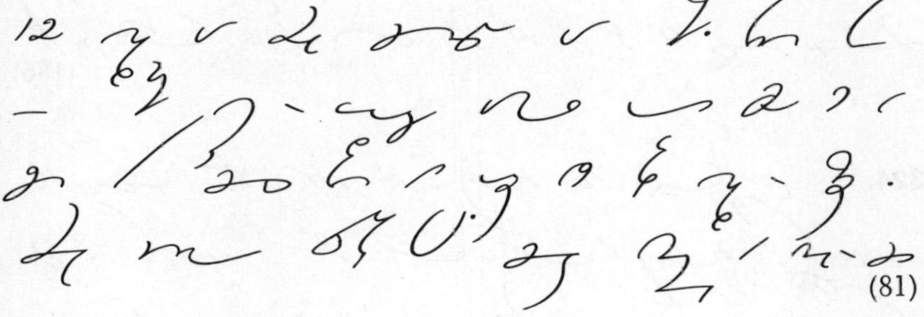

(81)

323.

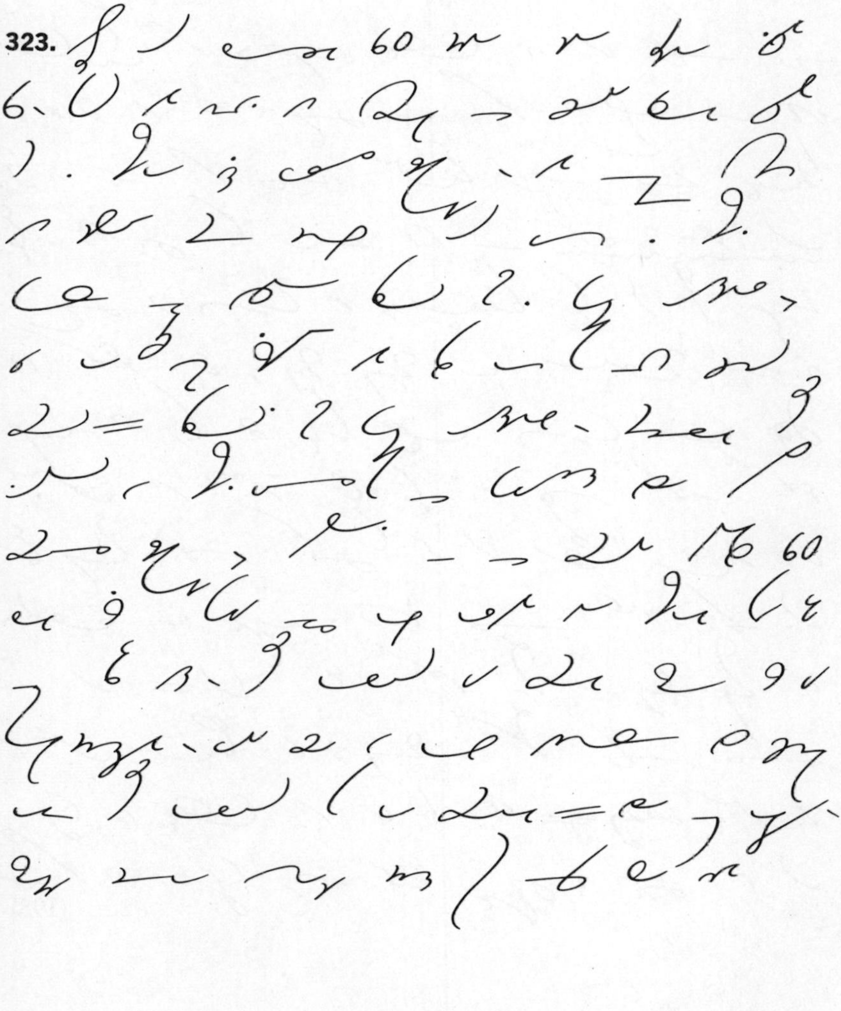

(186)

324. 

(198)

Lesson 42

MASTERING SHORTHAND THEORY

Word Endings

-cial, -tial

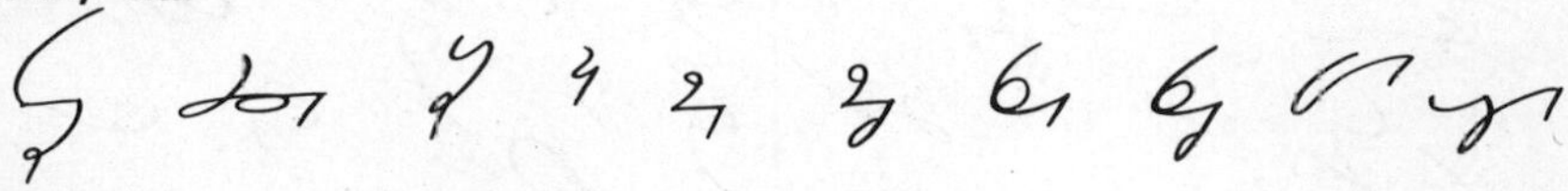

-sion

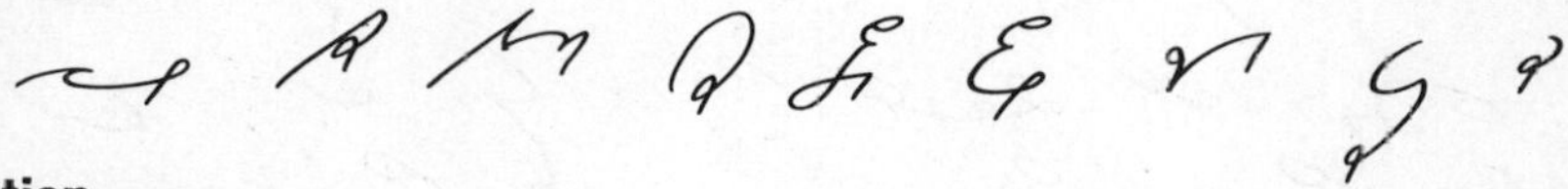

-tion

-cient, -ciency

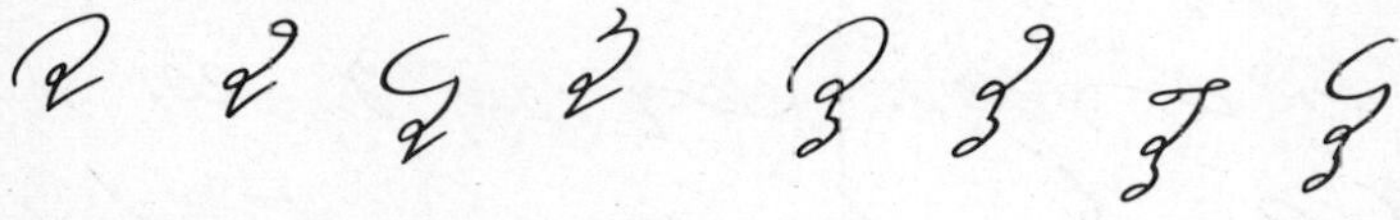

KEY

Beneficial, financial, official, social, essential, essentially, partial, partially, potential, residential.

Collision, decision, discussion, division, expansion, expression, extension, provision, session.

Action, cancellation, distribution, expiration, intentions, operation, selection.

Deficient, efficient, proficient, sufficient, deficiency, efficiency, inefficiency, proficiency.

Reading and Writing Practice

325.

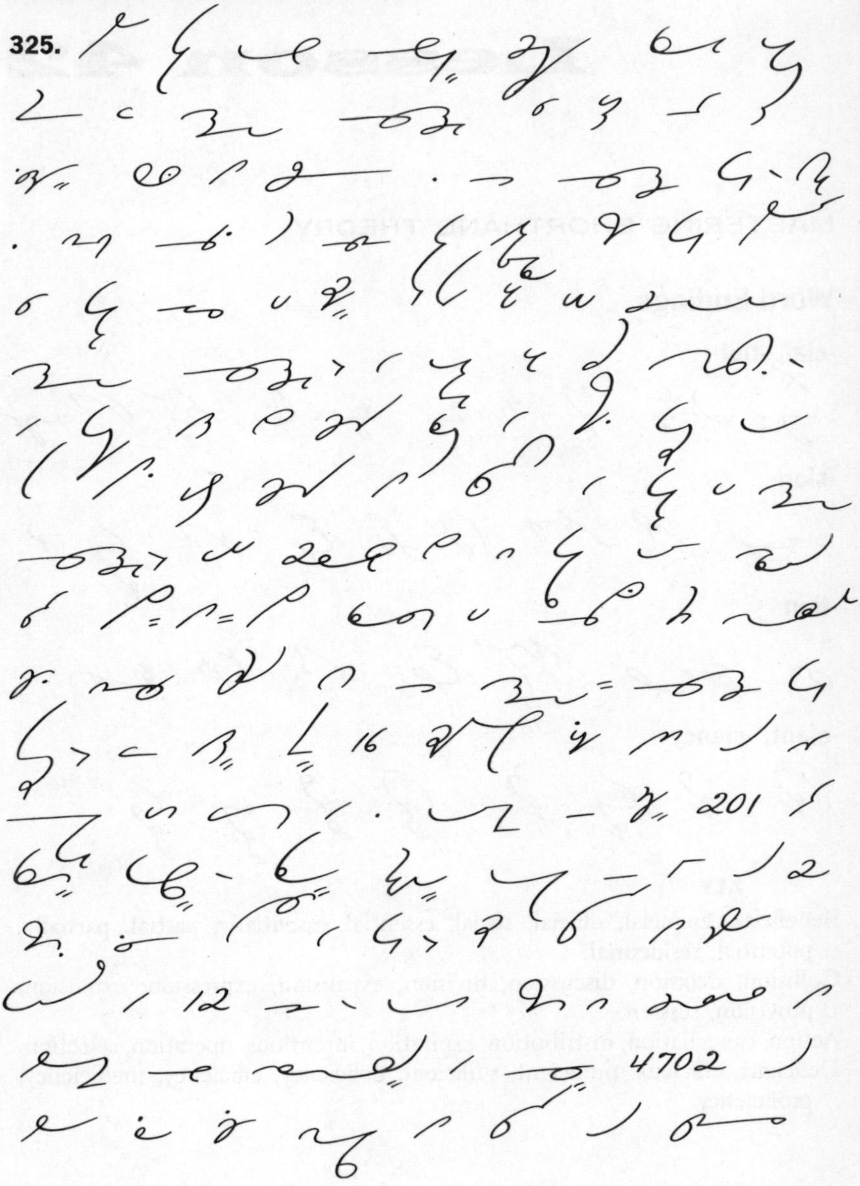

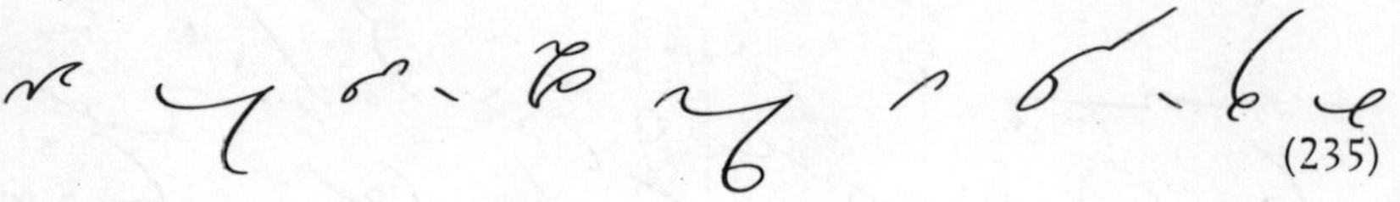

(235)

326.

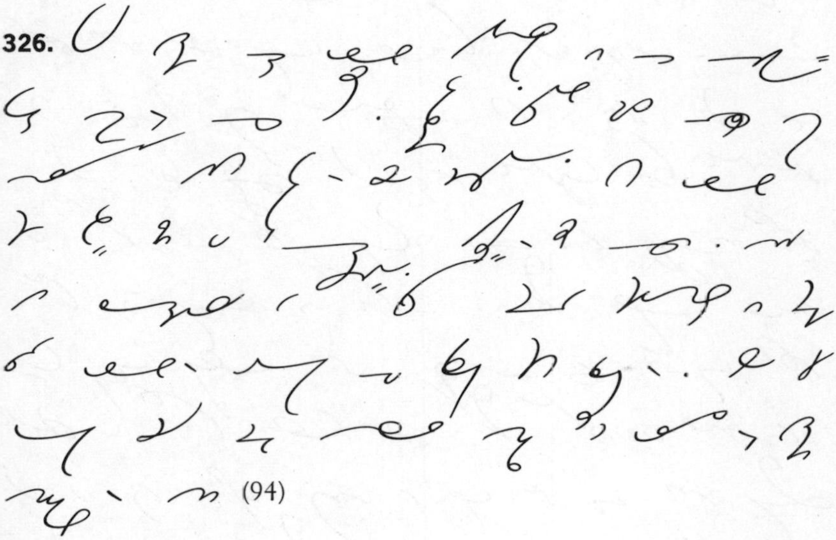

(94)

327.

(258)

328.

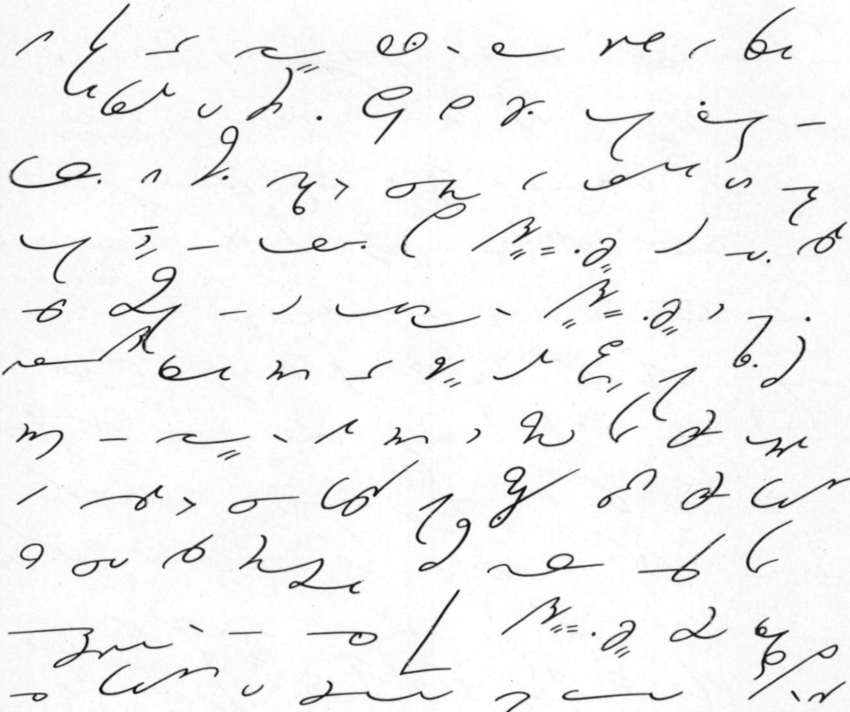

(227)

329.

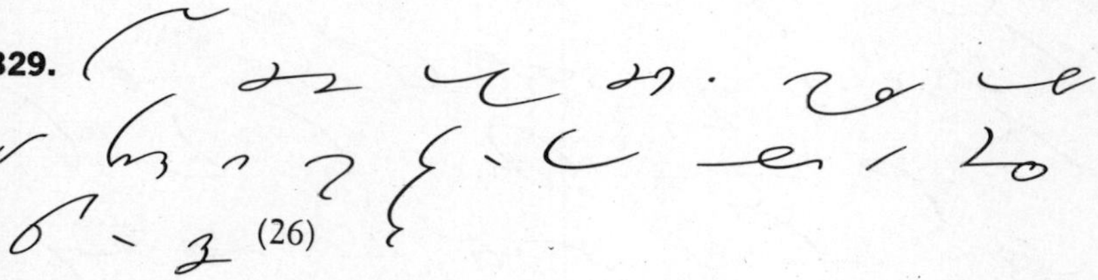

(26)

Building Speed Through Reading

330. HINTS FOR SUCCESS

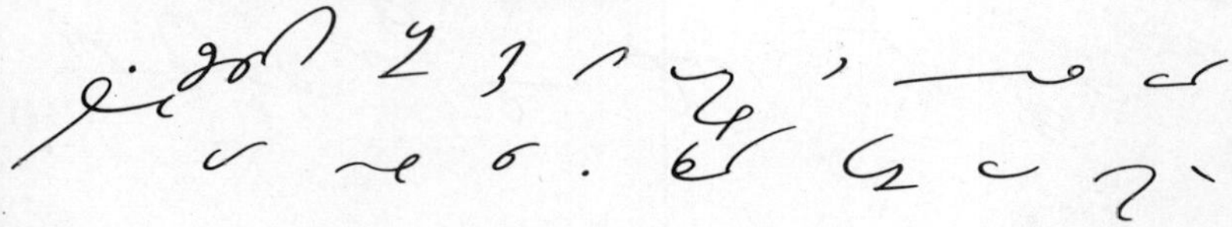

(244)

Lesson 43

BUILDING PHRASING SKILL

Verbal Phrases

Drill 1

Drill 2

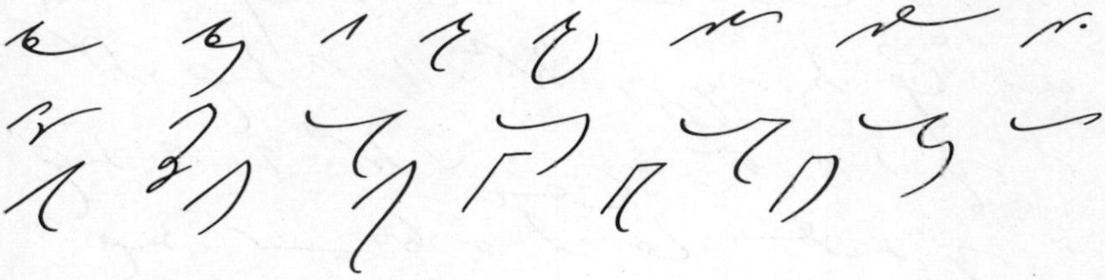

KEY

To fill, to find, to finish, to fit, to follow, to get, to give, to go, to keep, to know, to make, to pay, to place, to please, to prepare, to present, to print, to protect, to provide, to put, to say, to see.

To sell, to serve, to ship, to speak, to spend, to talk, to tell, to think, to understand, to visit, will be, will have, will not be, will prove, will you, would be, would have, would have been, would not, would not be, would not have.

Brief-Form and Phrase Letters

331.

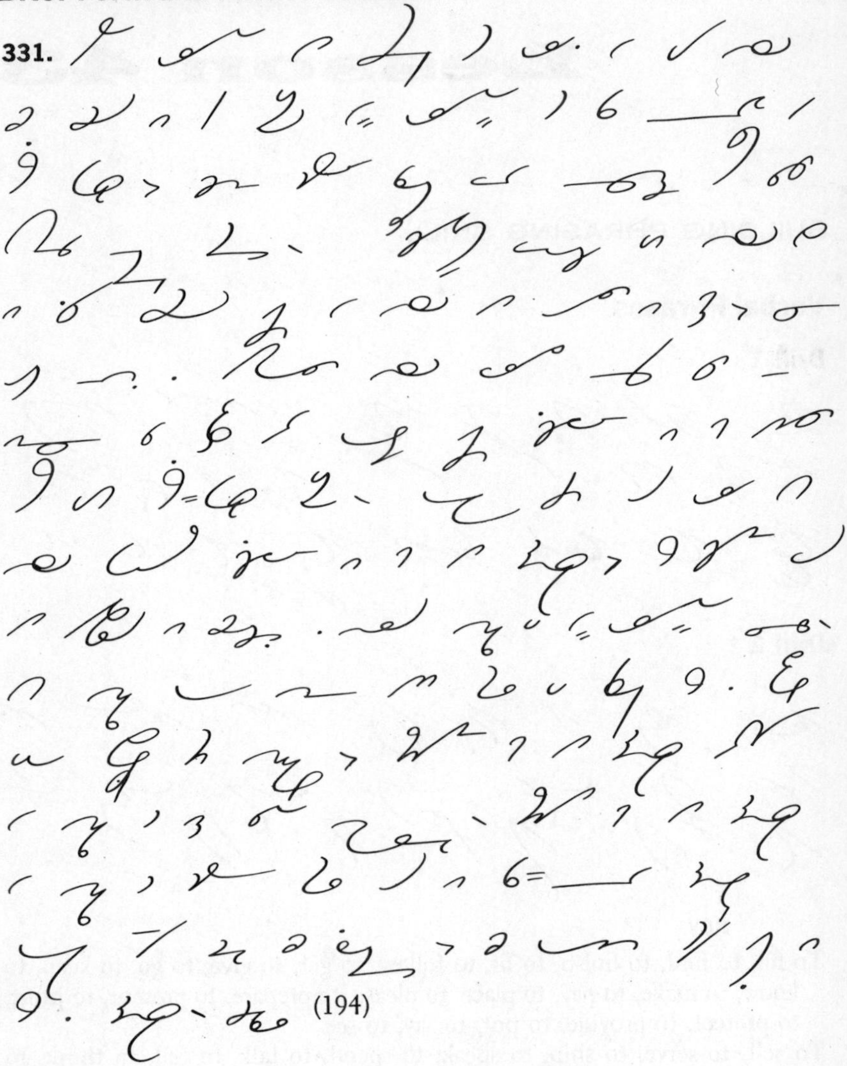

(194)

332.

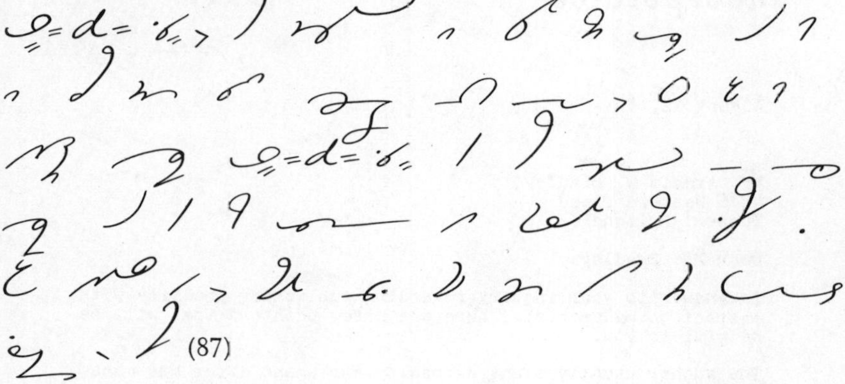

(87)

333.

Craig & Smither, Incorporated

TELEPHONES: LO 4-3001 LO 4-3002 LO 4-3003

158 West 45 Street, New York 72, New York

August 12, 19--

Mr. Arnold W. Bradley
4418 Western Place
Tucson, Arizona

Dear Mr. Bradley:

In answer to your inquiry regarding publishing practice with respect to manuscripts, here are a few pointers that will be helpful to you.

The author usually signs a royalty agreement after his manuscript has been accepted. Once in a while the agreement is signed before the manuscript is written. (This possibility might arise in the case of a well-known author.)

After the manuscript has been accepted, an arrangement is made with the editorial committee for a conference whenever the committee in its judgment decides one is necessary. I shall be glad to make an appointment for you if you will let me know the most convenient time for you to come to New York. At that time we can dispose of several matters you have mentioned in your letter, such as format, size and face of type, and color of the cover stock.

We shall need your help also in preparing copy for our initial announcement and future advertisements. Please do not consider this last job an imposition on your time, as we have found that the author benefits as much as the publisher when he participates in writing the sales promotion material.

We are very much pleased with the progress you have made thus far and look forward to a large sale next year on your book.

Sincerely yours,

William N. Morris
Editor-in-Chief

HK

Long Letter
Full-Blocked Style
Standard Punctuation

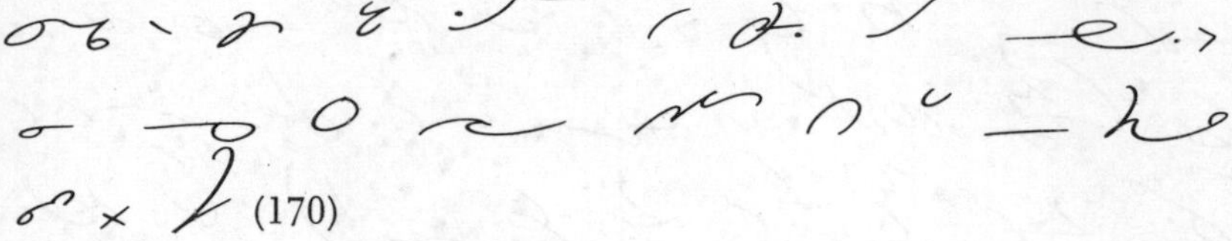

(170)

334.

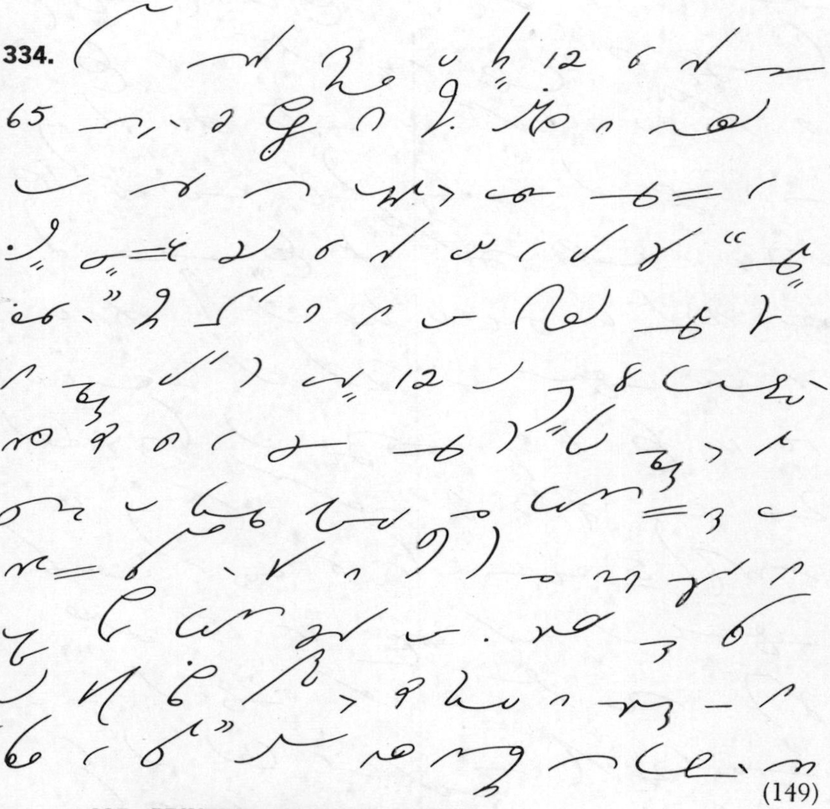

(149)

335. PRINTING AND PUBLISHING

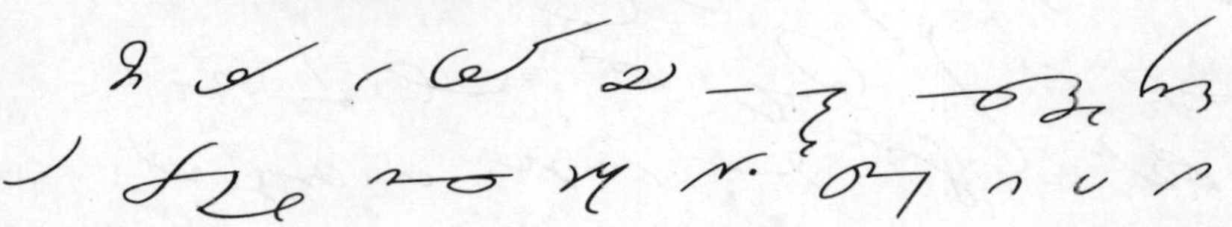

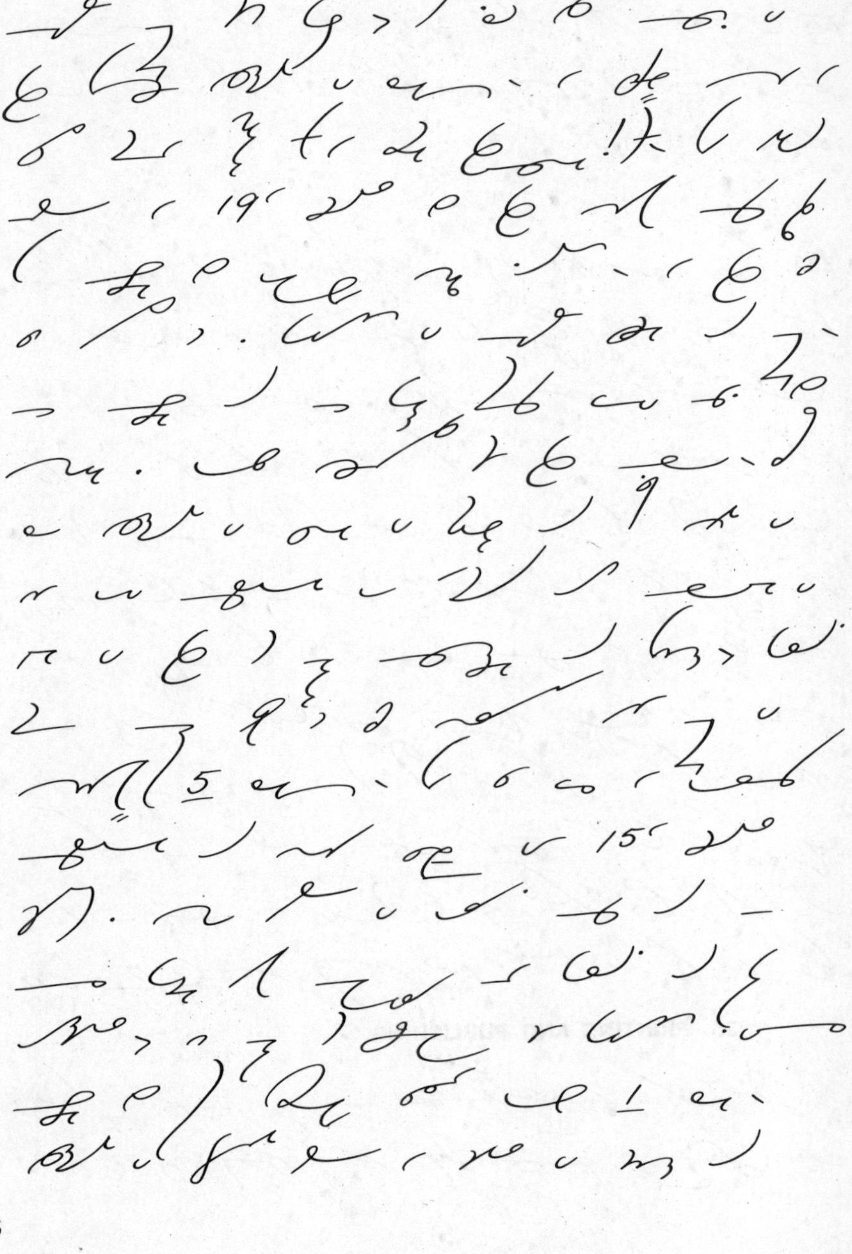

(458)

Lesson 44

PROGRESSIVE SPEED BUILDING

Half-Minute Progressive Speed Builder (100-135)

VOCABULARY PREVIEW

KEY

Articles, education, to correspond, conscious, ten years, background, to present.

Realistic, I hope you can, to me, controversial, associate, grudge, convictions.

(½ MINUTE AT 100)

336. Gentlemen: I am sending you a series of nine articles that I have written on education. I have written these articles with the idea of/starting them in September and ending in May to correspond with the school year. This is the time when people are most conscious of education.//

(½ MINUTE AT 110)

I think that my ten years of teaching experience and my three degrees in education have given me the background necessary to present a/realistic picture of education in this country. I hope you can use the articles. If not, please return them to me soon. Yours very truly,//

(½ MINUTE AT 120)

337. Dear Mr. Jameson: I am in accord with your objective in writing articles on education that will bring the public to demand some reforms. I must explain,/however, why we cannot take sides on a controversial issue.

A magazine can publish a statement that the views expressed do not reflect those of the publisher.//

(½ MINUTE AT 130)

Nevertheless, the reading public will always associate a thought with the publication in which it was read. Those readers who do not agree with you would hold a grudge against/our magazine.

If you wish to revise your articles according to the enclosed suggestions, we shall consider publishing them. May we hear from you soon? Yours very truly,//

(½ MINUTE AT 135)

338. Gentlemen: Thank you for returning my articles. I appreciate the time that you took to read them and the suggestions you made.

I feel, however, that it would be contrary to my/convictions to make the changes you suggest.

If you feel that you cannot accept the articles as they are written, I have no choice but to offer them to some other publisher. Yours very truly,//

Minute Progressive Speed Builder (90-110)

VOCABULARY PREVIEW

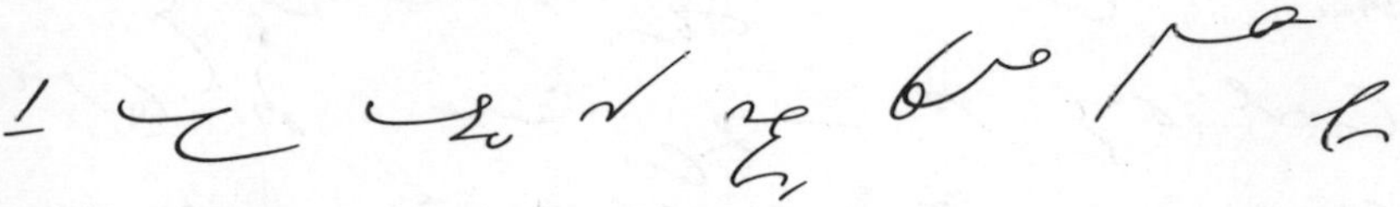

KEY

100, will you please, let us know, your order, unexpected, bindery, deadline, typical.

(1 MINUTE AT 90)

339. Gentlemen: On July 15 we ordered 100 copies of *Principles of Good Selling*, by Adams. Delivery/ was promised September 1. It is now September 5, and we have not received the books. Classes begin on Monday, and we must//have the books by that time. Will you please check this shipment and send the books immediately. If there is a reason why we cannot///have immediate shipment, I hope you will let us know so that we can make plans to get books from another source. Yours truly, (1)

(1 MINUTE AT 100)

340. Dear Mr. O'Neal: We appreciated very much your order for 100 copies of *Principles of Good Selling*, by Adams. I/am sorry the books did not reach you by the time we promised, but unexpected difficulties arose. We were without electrical power//in the bindery for over a week because of some faulty wiring.

Repairs were made as promptly as possible and binding was resumed ///immediately. The incident, however, threw us behind schedule in our work. Your order should go out within the next three days. Yours truly, (2)

(1 MINUTE AT 110)

341. Dear Mr. O'Neal: Thank you for writing us that the books have been received. We deeply appreciated your patience during our trouble at the bindery./We try always to have all school orders delivered by September 1 and are very much disturbed when we are not able to meet this deadline.

We are//confident that you understand that the recent delay is not typical of our service, as your previous dealings with us have shown. Mr. Brown, our///representative in your territory, will have the pleasure of calling on you soon to talk over your present book needs. Thank you. Yours very truly, (3)

Reading and Writing Practice

342.

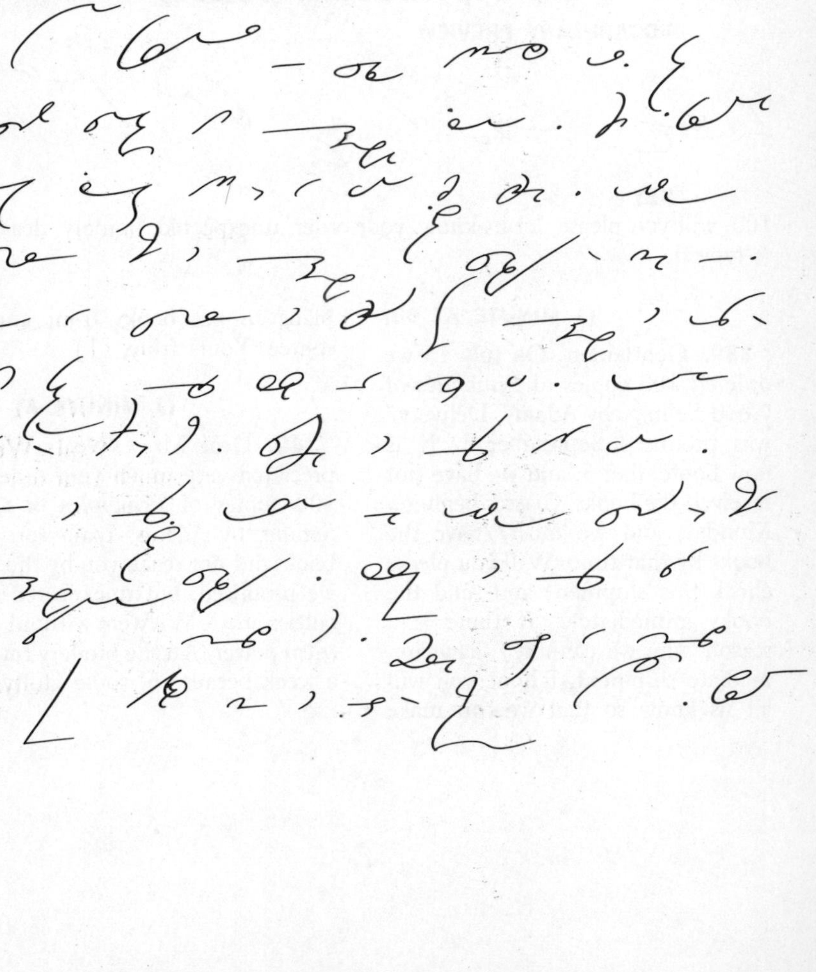

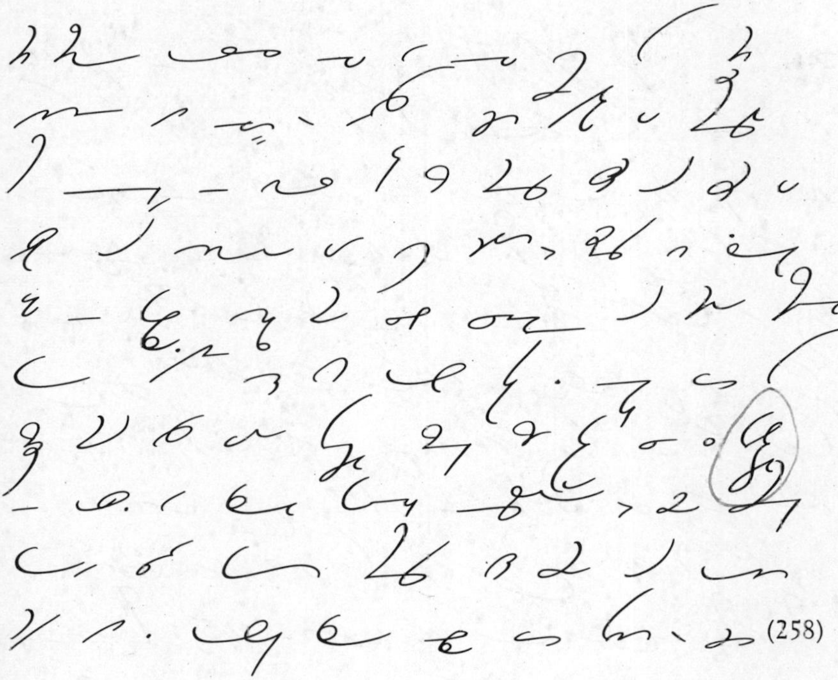

(258)

343.

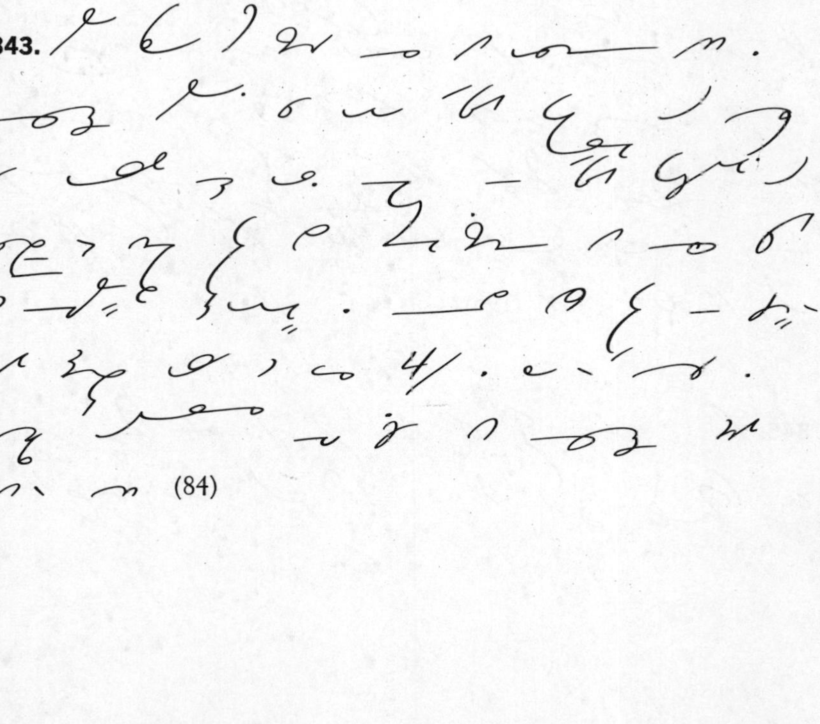

(84)

344.

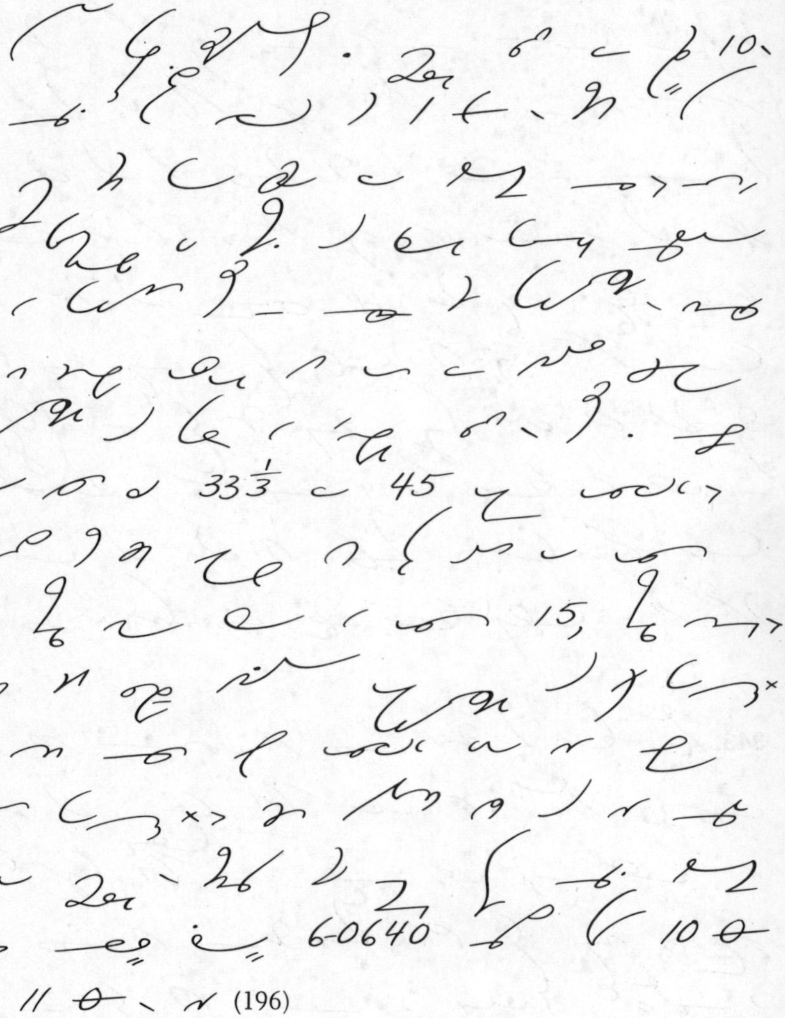

(196)

345.

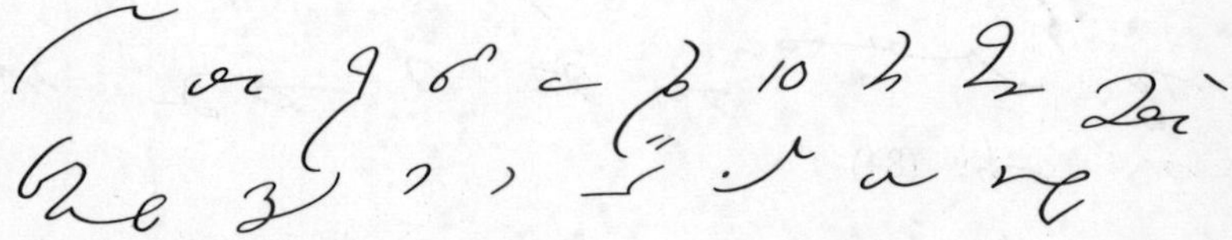

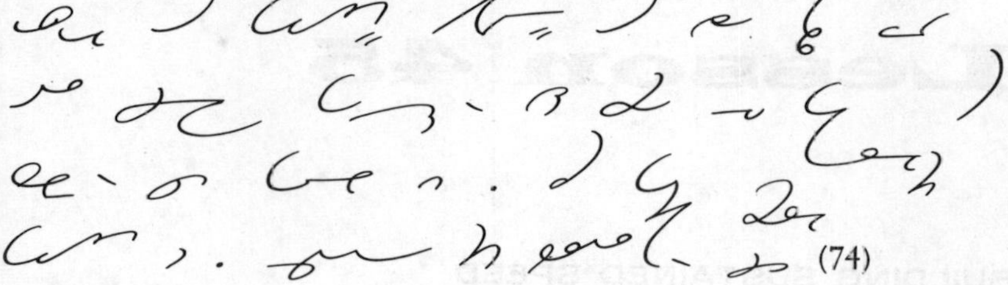

(74)

346. 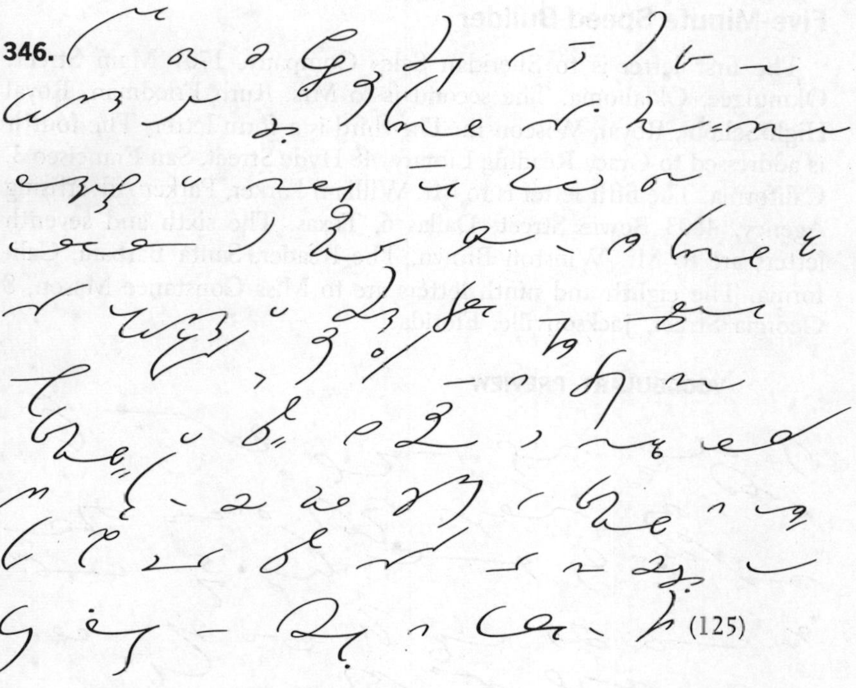

(125)

347. 

(24)

Lesson 45

BUILDING SUSTAINED SPEED

Five-Minute Speed Builder

The first letter is to Sheridan Sales Company, 1701 Main Street, Okmulgee, Oklahoma. The second is to Mrs. Ruth Friedman, Royal High School, Royal, Wisconsin. The third is a form letter. The fourth is addressed to Grace Reading Library, 48 Hyde Street, San Francisco 3, California. The fifth letter is to Mr. William Parker, Parker Advertising Agency, 4803 Bowie Street, Dallas 6, Texas. The sixth and seventh letters are to Mr. Winston Brown, The Reader, Santa Barbara, California. The eighth and ninth letters are to Miss Constance Mason, 8 Georgia Street, Jacksonville, Florida.

VOCABULARY PREVIEW

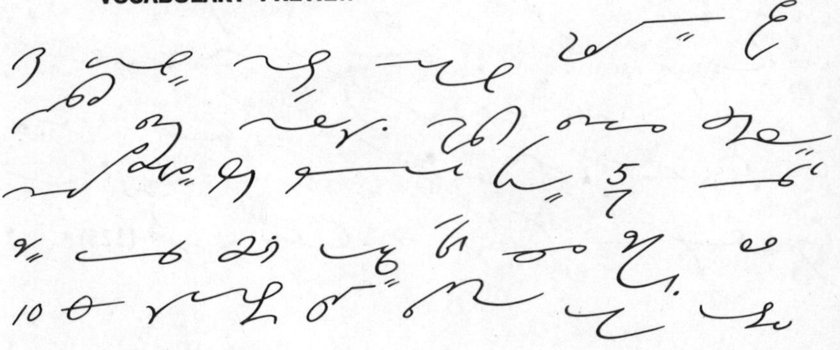

KEY

Thank you for, Oklahoma's, classified, marketplace, Friedman, exhibit.
Tentatively, University, clear understanding, competitive, economy; San Francisco, California.
Commodity, tariff, terminals, Baltimore, 500 pounds, many thanks.

Yesterday, on the matter, warehouse, Los Angeles, transportation, namely, establishing, early.
10 a.m., stenographic, out of town, educational, will you please, let us know.

348. Gentlemen: Thank you for placing your advertisement in the Tulsa Times — Oklahoma's greatest classified[1] marketplace.

As an experienced ad writer on your type of advertising, I should like to introduce myself[2] to you. I hope you will call me to help on this ad or on any future advertising. Sincerely,

349. Dear[3] Mrs. Friedman: Thank you very much for your recent invitation to exhibit our textbooks at the Business[4] Education Conference scheduled for March 11.

I cannot promise definitely that I shall be there[5] at that time, as I am already tentatively scheduled for a five-day exhibit beginning March 8 at[6] Bucknell University. If I find I cannot possibly get to the Business Education Conference[7] meeting, I will notify you immediately.

Please extend my very best wishes to your colleagues. Cordially,[8]

350. Dear Student: We hope that you enjoyed Today's Business as much as we enjoyed sending it to you during the[9] school year.

But, even more important, we hope our approach to financial reporting has helped give you a clear[10] understanding of the vital part finance plays in our competitive business economy.

Now that your classes[11] are over, we wish you much success and hope we may serve you again at some future stage of your business career.[12] Sincerely,

351. Gentlemen: Thank you for your letter of November 21 requesting rates on books shipped from the[13] East and from Chicago to San Francisco, California.

Your commodity takes group listing No. 18[14] in our West Coast commodity tariff.

On the attached rate sheet, we have underscored the rates from Chicago and[15] from our Eastern terminals—New York, Philadelphia, and Baltimore—to San Francisco, California. You[16] will notice that these rates are based on volume and include rates on shipments weighing under 500 pounds and[17] 500 pounds and upward. Rates include pickup and delivery to you at San Francisco.

Cars are shipped every[18] Thursday from our Eastern terminals—New York, Philadelphia, and Baltimore—and every Monday from[19] Chicago. They are shipped direct to San Francisco; there are no stops and the normal running time is six to seven[20] days from Chicago.

Thank you for your inquiry and your interest in our service. Very truly yours,

352. Dear[21] Mr. Parker: Many thanks for your most welcome letter of September 7 in which you tell us that your client,[22] Graphic Sales Company, will be with us in the forthcoming March service issue of Yesterday Magazine.[23] Very truly yours,

353. Dear Mr. Brown: I have a report from our business manager on the matter of who shall[24] pay the freight on the book shipments made from our New York warehouse. We will accept your suggestion that this charge be made[25] on a basis of Los Angeles shipments.

As yet we have not set up a system that will catch all these omissions;[26] and, if you will be kind enough to call any of them to our attention, we shall be very glad to make[27] any adjustments. Very truly yours,

354. Dear Mr. Brown: This will answer your letter of May 5 regarding[28] transportation charges on books to your store.

To take the action that you recommend—namely, to bill you for transportation[29] from Los Angeles on those occasional orders that we must refer to our New York office—involves[30] establishing a company policy. If we do this for your bookstore, we should by all means do it for all[31] the other bookstores in that territory. The final word on this must come from our New York office. I am, therefore,[32] sending a copy of your letter to our New York office and asking for instructions on what action should[33] be taken. Very truly yours,

355. Dear Miss Mason: Your cooperation in filling out the application blank[34] is appreciated, and we are scheduling an interview for the early part of next week. Will May[35] 30 at 10 a.m. be satisfactory with you? I am sorry that we cannot make an appointment for[36] you to come in this week; but Mrs. Johnson, who is head of the stenographic pool, is out of town. It is she[37] who always interviews prospective stenographers after I have talked with them.

I am writing to the persons[38] you listed as references on your application blank. Perhaps we will have their answers by the time you come[39] in to meet us personally. Sincerely yours,

356. Dear Miss Mason: Thank you for the interest you have shown in working[40] for our company. Mrs. Johnson and I were both very happy to meet you and to consider you for[41] placement in our stenographic pool. We were both impressed with your educational and experience background.[42] You also made very good grades on your skill tests.

On behalf of the company, I am offering you a job[43] with us beginning June 15. I believe that the rate of pay and salary increases was discussed with you[44] at the time you were here. With your background, you should be able to advance quickly to a secretarial[45] position. Will you please let us know whether to expect you June 15. Sincerely yours, (915)

Reading and Writing Practice

357.

(120)

358.

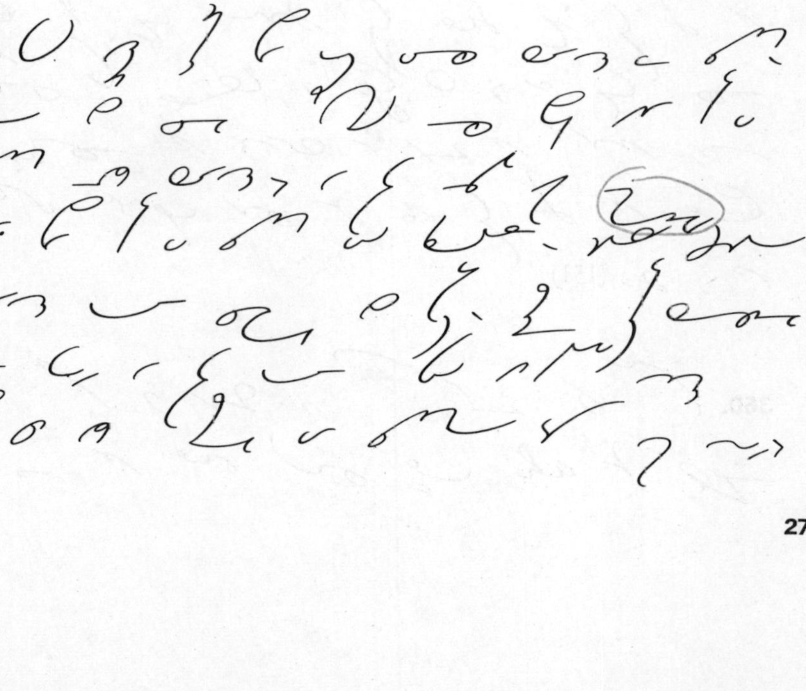

(133)

359.

(151)

360.

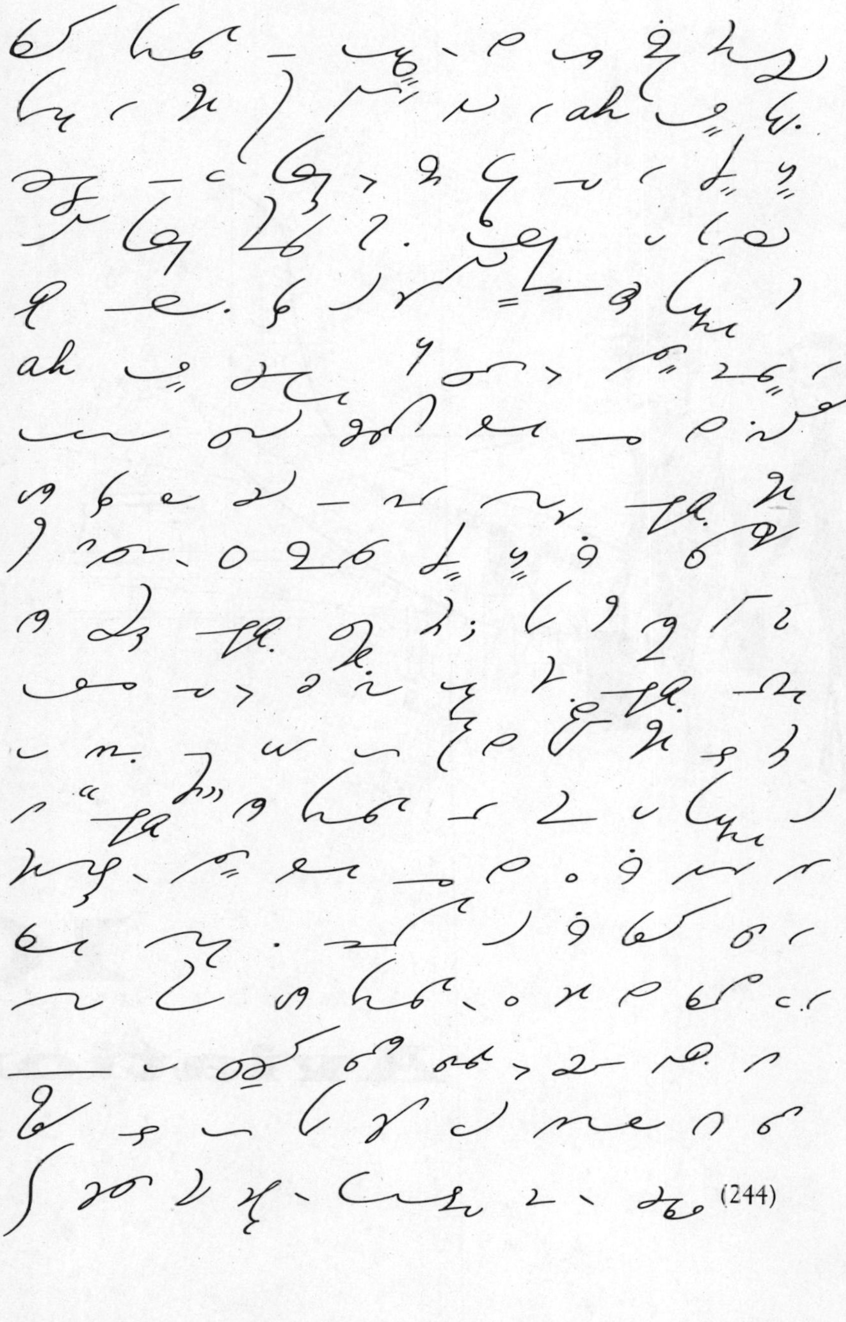

(244)

10

Aviation

Word Study for Chapter 10

AVIATION

Aerodynamics. The branch of dynamics that treats of the motion of air and other gaseous fluids and of the forces acting on solids in motion relative to such fluids.

Aeronautics. The science and art of flight.

Aileron. A hinged or moveable portion of an airplane wing, the primary function of which is to control lateral or rolling motion of an airplane. It is usually part of the trailing edge of a wing.

Air-borne. Wholly free from contact with the ground, and supporting itself in the air.

Airfoil. Any surface, such as an airplane wing, aileron, or rudder, designed to obtain reaction from the air through which it moves.

Airframe. A term used to denote either the fuselage or a complete airplane minus the power plant and its controls.

ATC. Airways Traffic Control, the division of CAA that maintains airways navigational aids and polices airplane traffic flying on established airways.

Altigraph. An instrument that records vertical distances above the sea level.

Altimeter. An instrument that measures the vertical distance of an aircraft from either sea level or the ground.

Amphibian. An airplane designed to rise from and alight on either land or water.

Apron. The paved area of a landing field adjacent to a hangar. Used to load, service, or repair aircraft.

Bank. To incline an airplane laterally; that is, to rotate it about its longitudinal axis.

Barograph. An instrument for recording the barometric or static pressure of the atmosphere.

Bulkhead. A closed or solid frame; a partition in a plane.

C.A.V.U. Abbreviation for "ceiling and visibility unlimited."

Ceiling. The height above the ground of the lowest level of a bank of clouds. *Absolute Ceiling*. The maximum altitude above the sea level attainable by an aircraft. *Service Ceiling*. The altitude at which an airplane ceases to climb at a rate greater than 100 feet a minute.

CAA. Civil Aeronautics Administration, the Government agency that enforces rules and regulations established by CAB.

Cockpit. The "driver's seat." The compartment up forward, sometimes called "the office," from which the flight crew operates the ship.

Configuration. Arrangement of parts within a structure; the figure or contour.

Cowling. A removable covering extending over or around the engine and sometimes over a portion of the fuselage as well.

Drag. Air resistance.

Empennage. The tail surfaces. The vertical fin and rudder and the horizontal stabilizers.

Fin. A fixed or adjustable airfoil. Its purpose is to afford directional stability.

Fuselage. That part of the airplane to which the wings and the empennage are attached, and which is designed to hold the crew, the passengers, and the cargo.

Glider. An aircraft heavier than air, similar to an airplane but without an engine.

Ground Loop. An uncontrollable violent turn of an airplane while taxiing, or during the landing or take-off run.

Gyroscope. A steering apparatus or a balancing device dependent on centrifugal force.

Helicopter. A type of rotor plane whose support in the air is normally derived from airfoils mechanically rotated about an approximately vertical axis.

Instrument Landing. The art of landing an aircraft largely or entirely by the use of instruments.

Mach Number (also, Mach.). A number representing the ratio of velocity of air flow (air speed) to the velocity of sound.

Nacelle. An enclosed shelter on an aircraft for passengers or for a power plant.

Pressurization. The keeping of the air pressure inside a plane at or near normal sea-level pressure, even though the plane climbs up where the outside pressure is much lower.

Propeller Pitch. The distance a propeller would advance in one revolution if there were no "slippage."

Radio Beam. A radio code signal sent out continually by a directional radio transmitter on the ground and aimed along the airway. It is heard by the pilot through earphones.

Stabilizer. A normally fixed surface of a plane, the function of which is to lessen the pitching motion; also called "tail plane."

Stacking. A term describing the "holding" procedure when aircraft are waiting their turns to land at an airport during instrument-flying conditions.

Tachometer. An instrument that measures in revolutions a minute the rate at which the crankshaft of an engine turns.

Wind Sock. A device at an airport to show the direction of the wind.

Lesson 46

BUILDING TRANSCRIPTION SKILL

Transcription English Pointers

THE USES OF THE APOSTROPHE (CONCLUDED)

Rules regarding the formation and use of the possessive are as follows:

1. The sign of the possessive is added to the last word of a compound expression.

the secretary-treasurer's report
the editor-in-chief's duties
my father-in-law's home
anybody else's

Note: This rule does not apply to compounds in which the first element is a possessive noun.

a worm's-eye view
robin's-egg blue

2. Joint possession of two or more nouns is indicated by making only the last noun possessive.

Fulton & Lee's annual sale
Bob and Ann's new car

3. Separate ownership is indicated by adding the sign of the possessive to each noun.

Both Mr. Hall's and Mr. Booth's offices are in the Wrigley Building.

4. Often the noun following the possessive is omitted (that is, it is understood), in which case the possessive form is still used.

The proof has just come from the printer's (plant).

5. When a noun that ordinarily would be in the possessive case is followed by an explanatory word or phrase, the sign of the possessive is added to the explanatory word only.

That is Mr. Prescott, the bookkeeper's, job.

6. The possessive form, properly used, is confined to nouns and pronouns that refer to persons or animals.

the teacher's explanation	the dog's collar

When reference is made to inanimate things, an *of* phrase should be used.

the facade of the store	*not* the store's facade

Exceptions: In certain commonly used expressions, however, especially in phrases pertaining to time or measurements and in phrases implying personification, the use of the possessive has come to be considered correct.

an hour's delay	at arm's length	the law's delay
a dollar's worth	a stone's throw	for heaven's sake

Note that when a preposition intervenes in such expressions the possessive is not used.

two months of waiting	a year of experience

7. In company and organization names containing possessives, more often than not the apostrophe is omitted. Likewise, many geographic names and many titles of publications do not include the apostrophe.

Miners National Bank	Pikes Peak	Harpers
Eastern Teachers Association	Governors Island	

However, the form that the organization, the publication, or the National Geographic Board uses should be followed.

Dairymen's League	Saint John's, Newfoundland	Reader's Digest

8. A noun or a pronoun that precedes a verbal noun (a gerund) should be in the possessive form. Verbal nouns are recognized by their *ing* endings.

I am sure that Louise's typing of the table is accurate.
His disappointment over our not accepting his bid was great.

The omission of the possessive in this construction is a common transcription error.

9. The possessive forms of abbreviations are written thus:

Finley & Co.'s proposal	the CIO's president
The Y.M.H.A.'s new building	Barclay Bros.' option

Transcription Speed Builder

361.

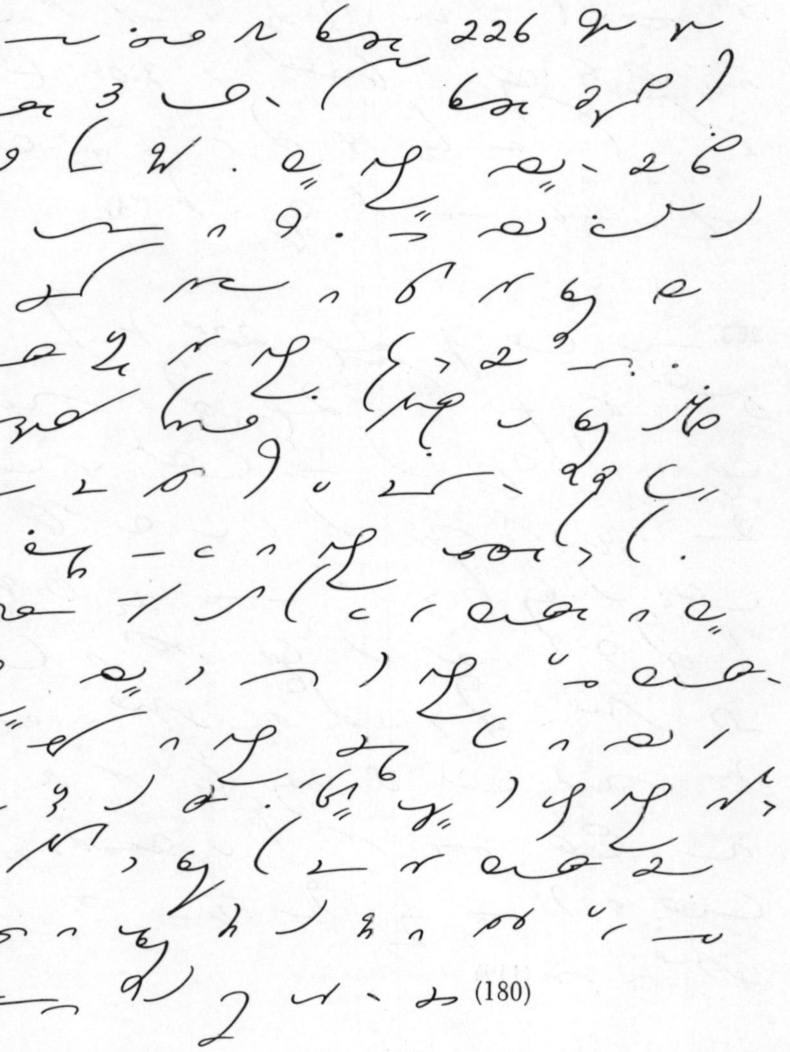

(180)

362.

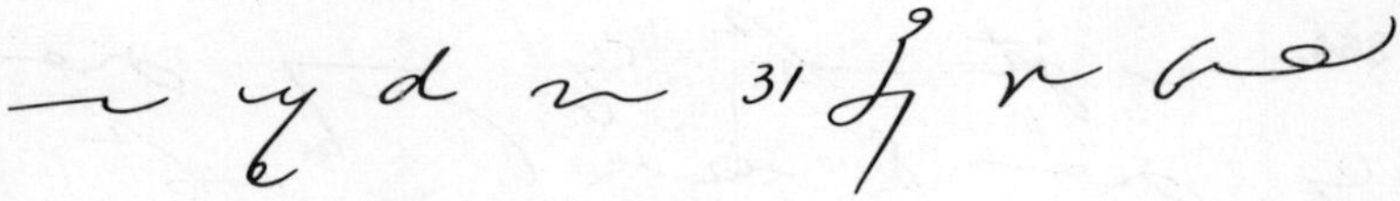

3 … 3:05 … 14 … (54)

363. … 225 … (119)

364. …

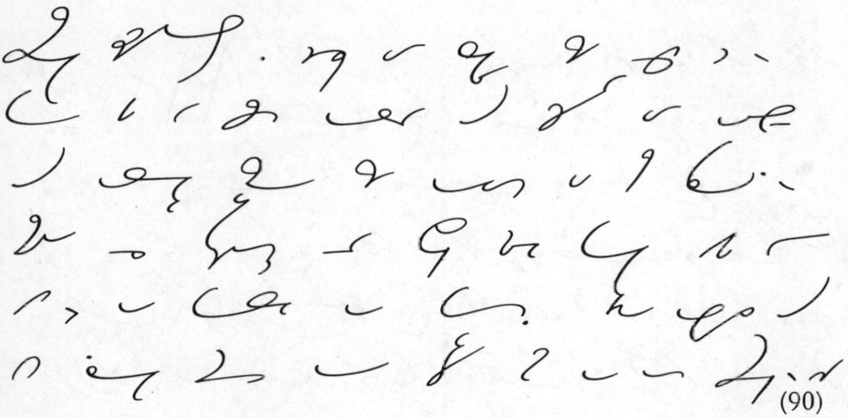

(90)

365.

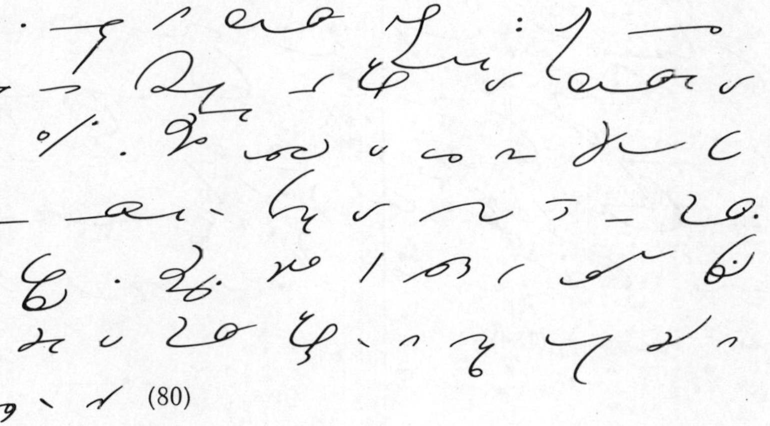

(80)

366.

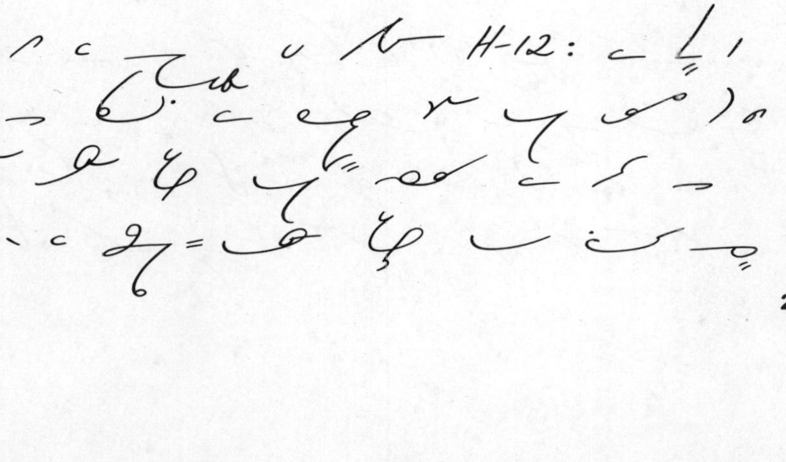

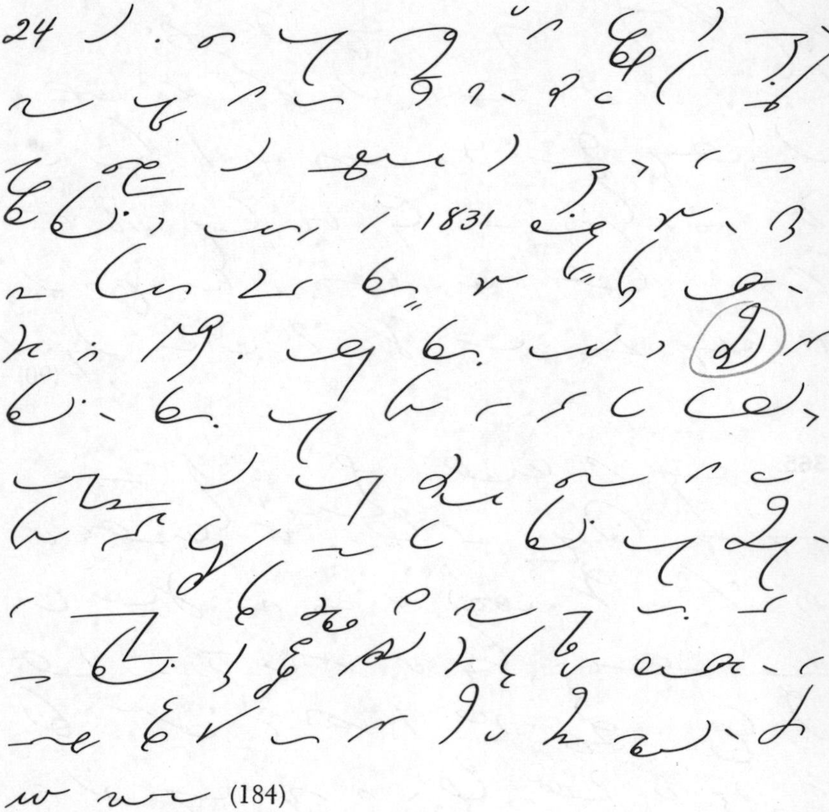

367.

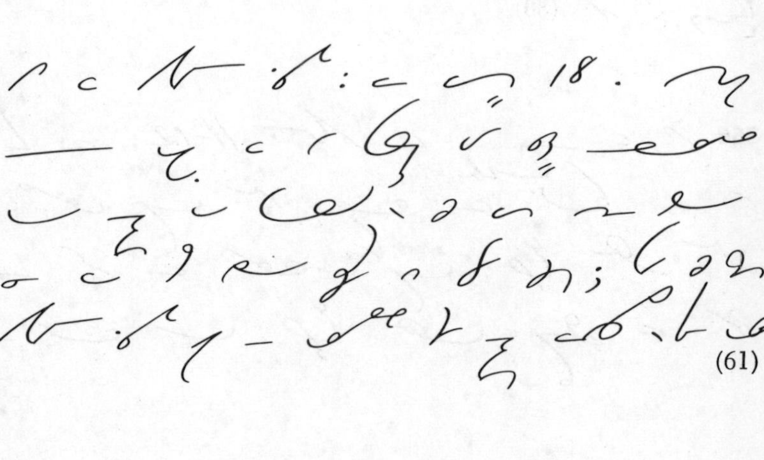

Lesson 47

MASTERING SHORTHAND THEORY

Word Endings

-ual, -tual

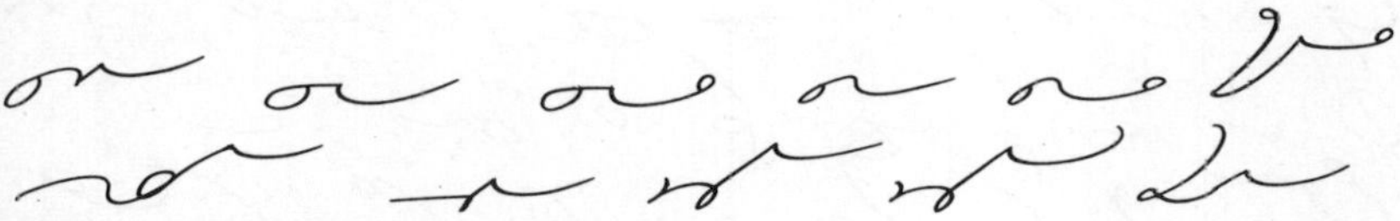

-ulate

-ure, -ture

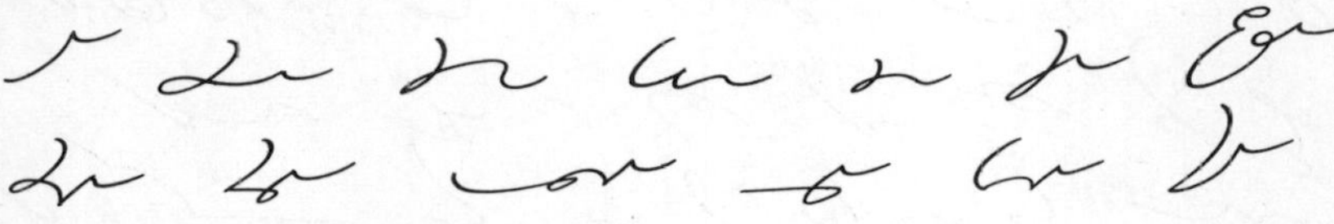

KEY

Actual, annual, annually, equal, equally, eventually.
Gradual, mutual, schedule, scheduled, virtual.
Accumulate, accumulation, accumulated, congratulate, calculate.
Insulation, insulator, population, speculation, stimulate, stimulates, tabulation.
Endure, failure, figure, procure, secure, feature, expenditure.
Fixture, furniture, lecture, mature, picture, venture.

Reading and Writing Practice

368.

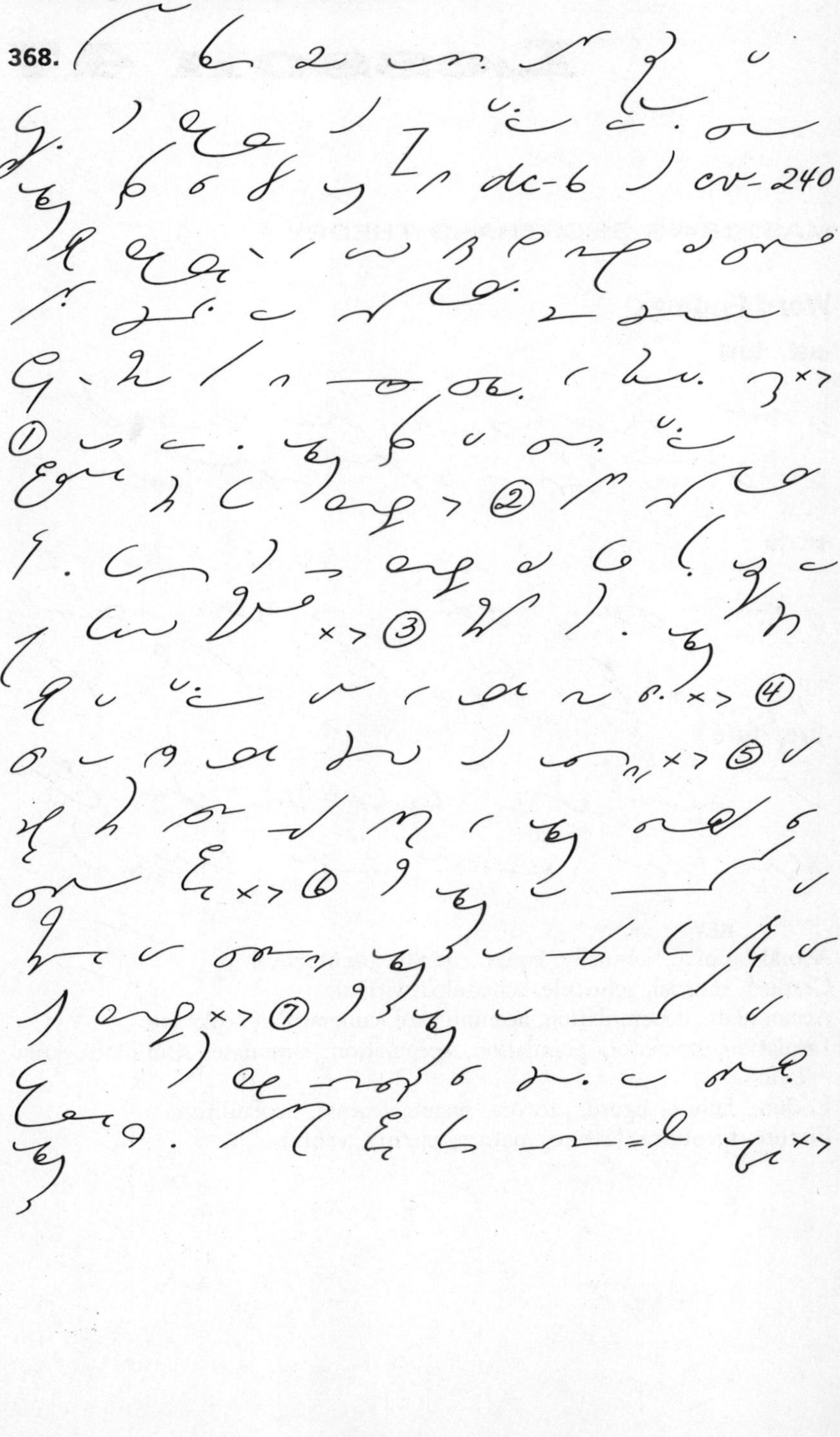

(340)

369.

XL-422

120

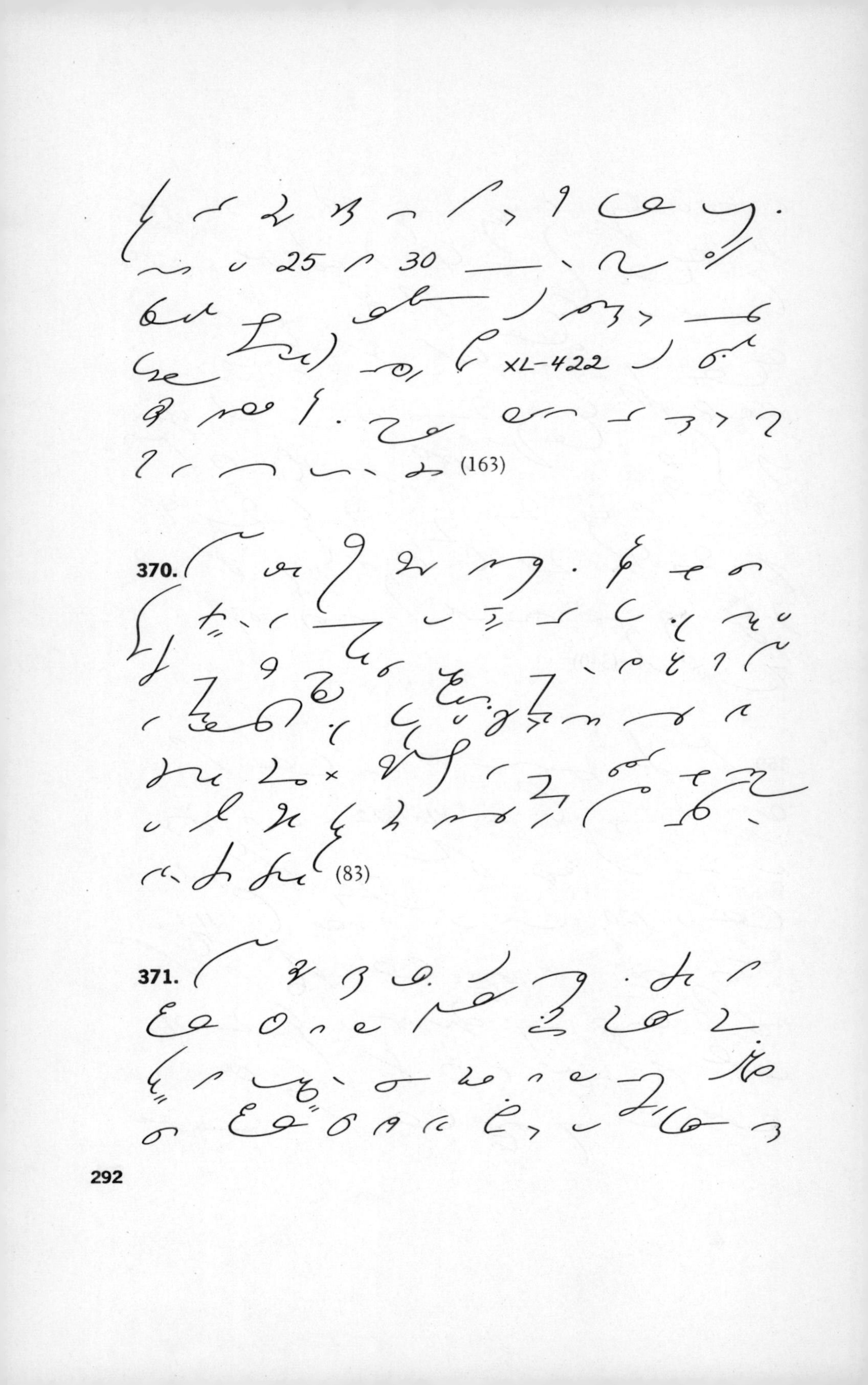

25 30 XL-422 (163)

370. (83)

371.

(194)

Building Speed Through Reading

372. HINTS FOR SUCCESS

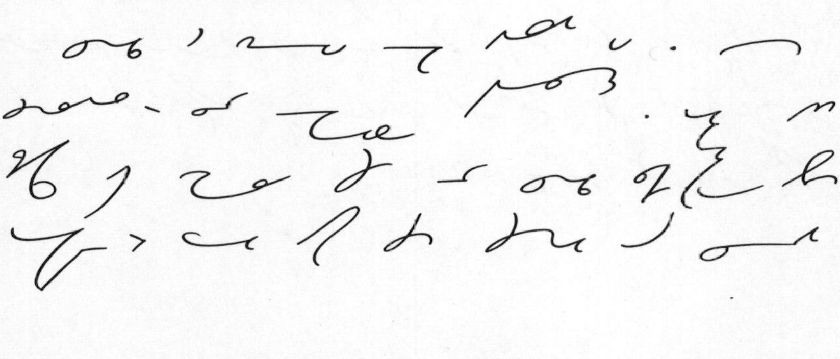

(256)

Lesson 48

BUILDING PHRASING SKILL

Many, Us

about how many	many thanks
as many	many things
good many of the	many times
good many of them	so many
good many of these	so many things
great many	so many times
how many	very many
how many of them	before us
how many of these	between us
how many times	for us
many of the	give us
many of these	help us
many of those	reach us
many others	send us

Brief-Form and Phrase Letters

373.

(112)

374.

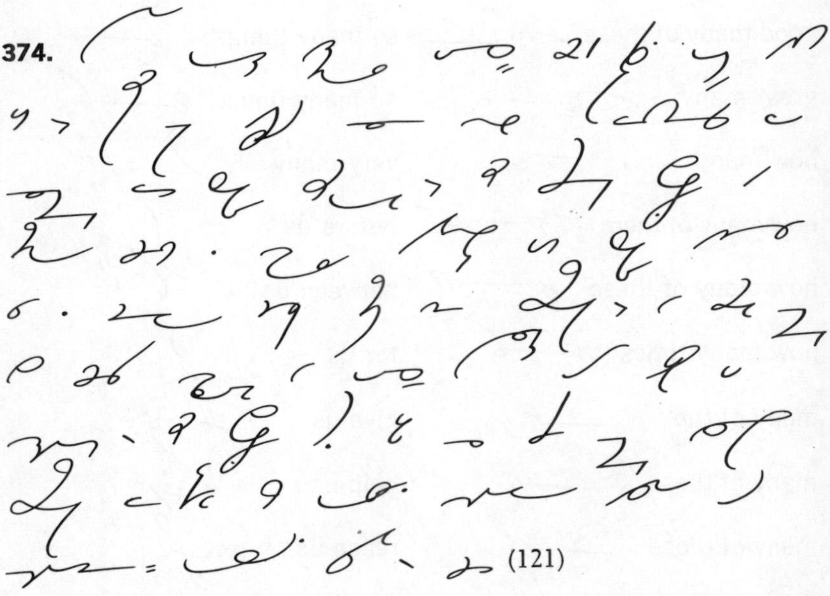

(121)

375.

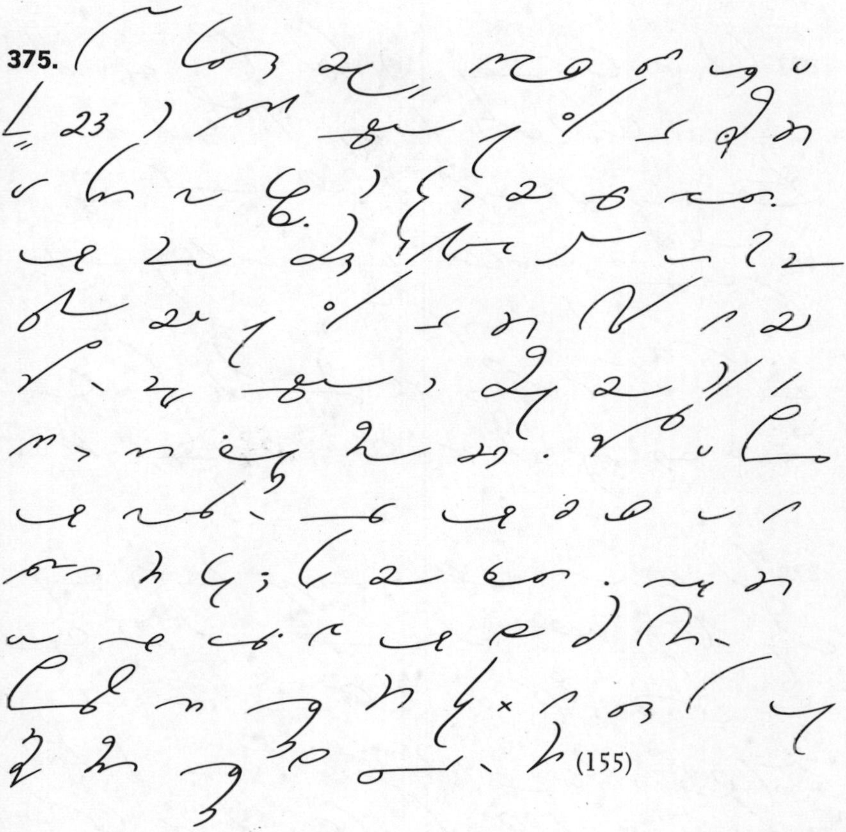

(155)

376.

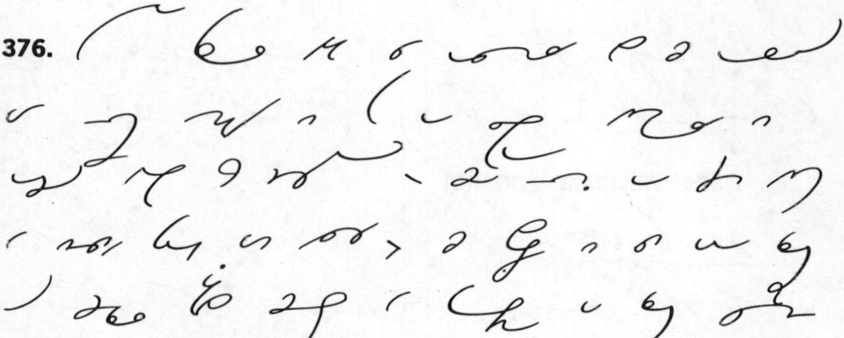

(70)

377 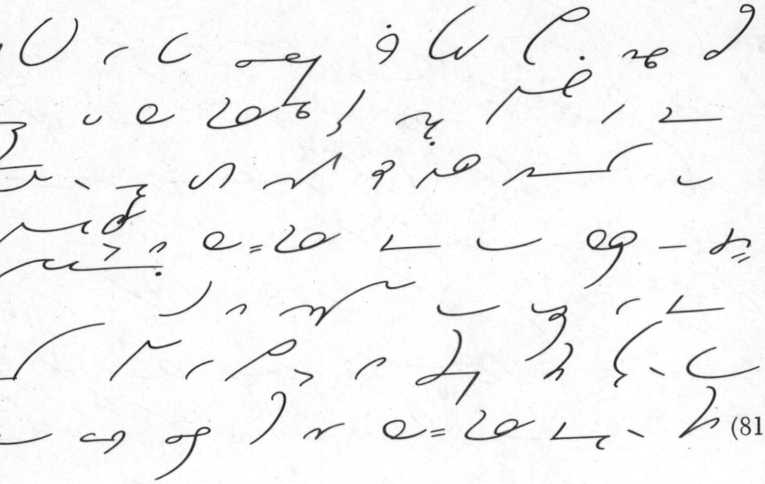 (81)

378. 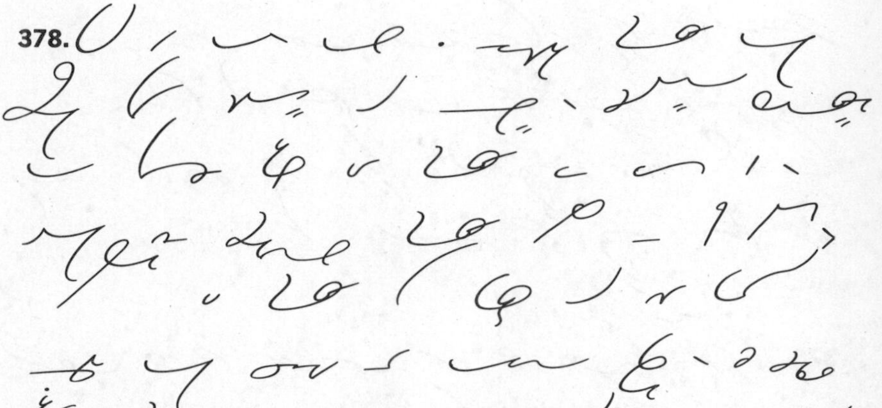 (77)

379. WELCOME ABOARD!

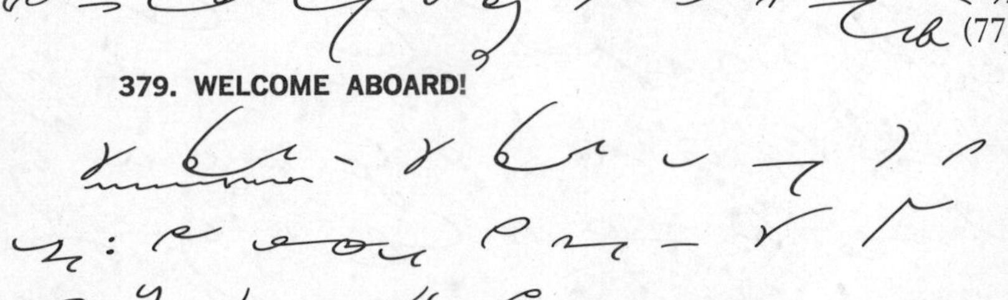

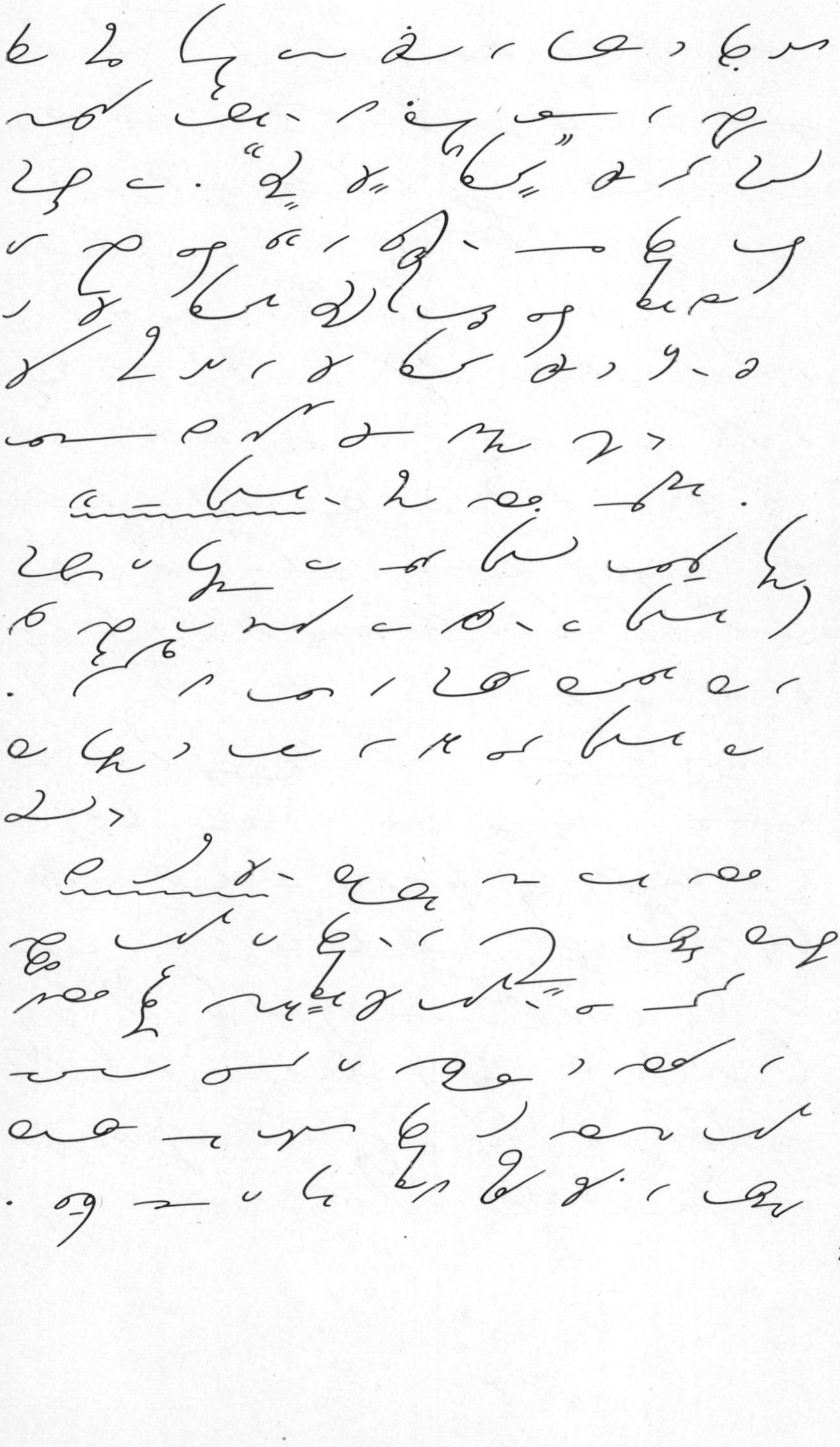

(397)

Lesson 49

PROGRESSIVE SPEED BUILDING

Half-Minute Progressive Speed Builder (100-135)

VOCABULARY PREVIEW

KEY

Stewardess, disappointing, mechanical, inconvenienced, attitude, easier, to do, will you please.

Application, to us, earliest, background, vacancy, retained, to serve you.

(½ MINUTE AT 100)

380. Dear Mrs. Patton: Miss Taylor, your stewardess, told me about the disappointing experience you had recently when your flight to Dallas/was delayed because of mechanical difficulties.

I sincerely hope that you were not too inconvenienced by this delay.//

(½ MINUTE AT 110)

We appreciate your understanding attitude and co-operation, which made the work of our staff much easier.

We are usually able/to do a much better job of operating on time. We shall look forward to serving you again to prove that we can give you better service. Cordially yours,//

(½ MINUTE AT 120)

381. Dear Miss Adams: We wish to acknowledge receipt of your recent inquiry regarding employment with our company.

In order that we may be informed completely/as to your training and previous experience, will you please fill in the enclosed application blank and return it to us at your earliest convenience.//

(½ MINUTE AT 130)

If the application does not provide enough space to give all your training and experience, please add enough pages to give us a complete background.

We appreciate your/interest in employment with our airlines. If a suitable vacancy is not available now, your application will be retained for later consideration. Yours truly,//

(½ MINUTE AT 135)

382. Dear Mr. Green: As you requested, we have booked you for flight No. 161 on Thursday, April 16, which leaves New York at 4:15 p.m. and arrives in Chicago at/7:30 p.m. We have left the return trip open.

Do you wish to call for your ticket in person or shall we deliver it to you?

It has been a pleasure to serve you. Yours very truly,//

Minute Progressive Speed Builder (90-110)

VOCABULARY PREVIEW

KEY

Senior, United States, stewardess, graduate, glamorous, one of our.
I should like to know, constantly, will you please, permanently, as soon as, seniority.

(1 MINUTE AT 90)

383. Dear College Senior: Now is the time to make application to the United States Airlines to become a stewardess. As/a college graduate, you have an excellent opportunity to enter the most exciting and glamorous career for women.//

If selected, you will attend a three months' training course in Chicago. On completion of this course, you will begin///to fly on one of our many flights.

If you wish to receive more information, mail the enclosed card today. Sincerely yours, (1)

(1 MINUTE AT 100)

384. Gentlemen: I have read your booklet about a career as airline stewardess with United States Airlines.

I should like to know whether a/stewardess is based at the same city all the time or whether she must constantly change bases. Can you tell me also how long a stewardess//is assigned to the same flight and whether she can progress to one of her choice?

Will you please enclose an application blank with your answers ///to these questions. If I receive favorable answers to the questions I have asked, I shall wish to apply for the program. Sincerely yours, (2)

(1 MINUTE AT 110)

385. Dear Miss Reynolds: We appreciate the interest that you have shown in becoming an airline stewardess. I feel sure that you will never regret a/decision to enter this field of work.

If a stewardess desires, she may be permanently based in the city of her choice as soon as there is an opening//for her there. In answer to your second question, choice of flights is based on seniority where there is a great demand for a particular flight.///

I hope that you will consider these answers favorable and that we may soon receive your application to become an airlines stewardess. Yours very truly, (3)

Reading and Writing Practice

386.

(85)

387.

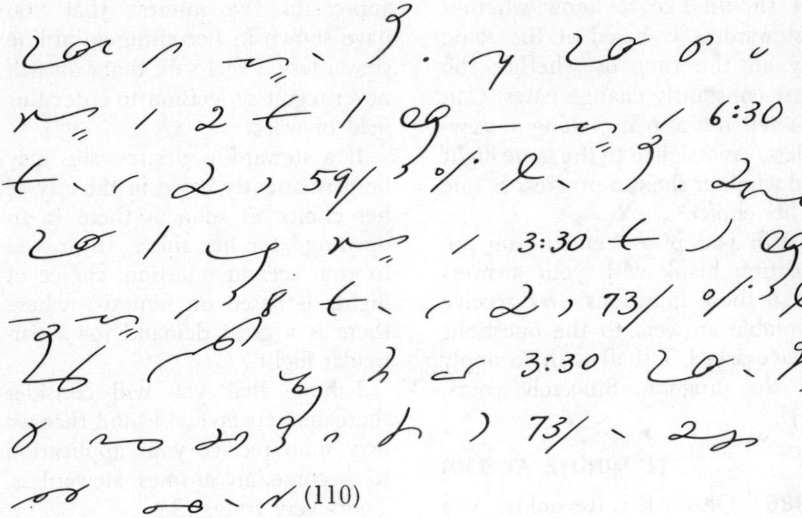

(110)

388.

(114)

389. 17 (134)

390.

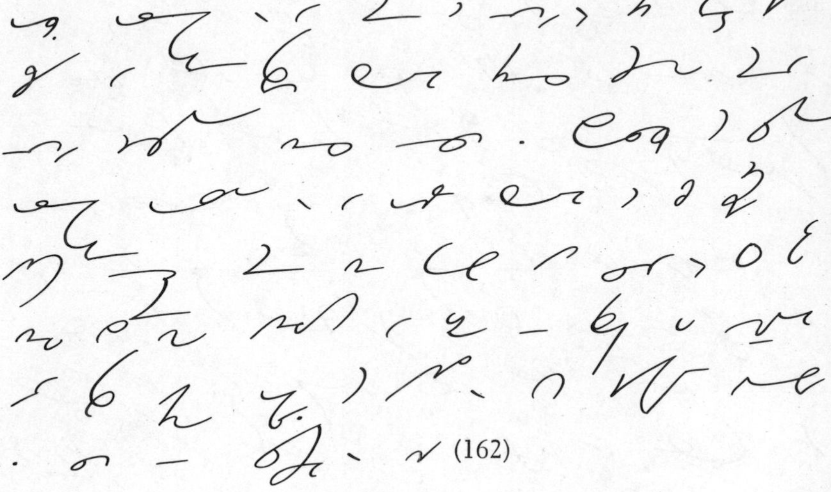

(162)

391.

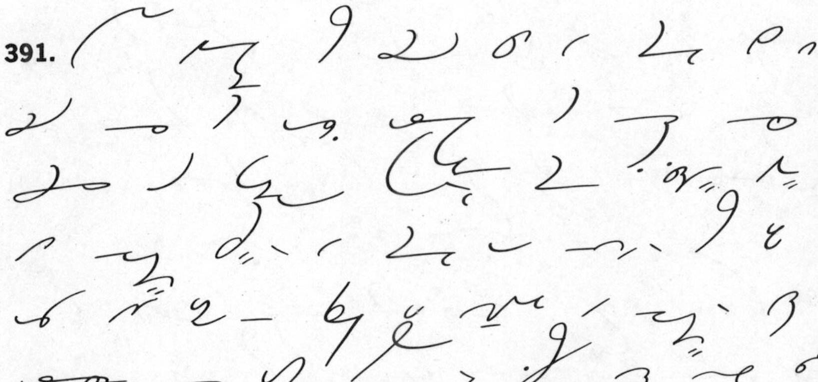

(116)

Lesson 50

BUILDING SUSTAINED SPEED

Five-Minute Speed Builder

The following correspondence is between Henry E. Dunn, 100 North Street, Pittsfield, Massachusetts, and Daniel B. Pierce, Engineering Department, Airways, Inc., Columbus 8, Ohio.

VOCABULARY PREVIEW

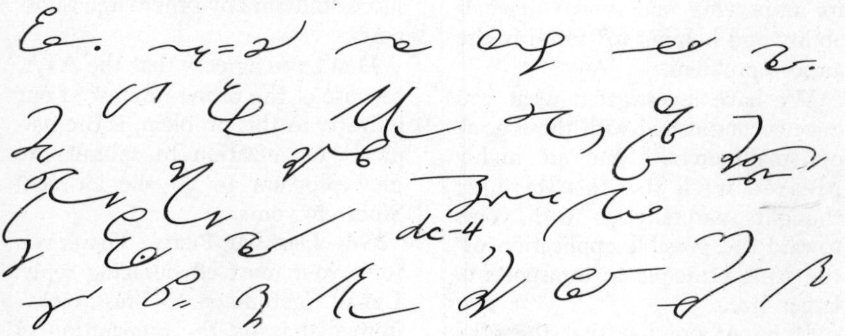

KEY

Experimenting, cross-wind, gear, aircraft, merit, concerning.
Convinced, potential, operational, dependability, simplify, airport, investigated.
Accomplished, established, we should like to see, manufacturers, burden, anyone.
Benefit, appropriate, concerted, DC-4, temporary, conclusive.
Incident, ATA, thank you for your, desirability, supervised, appointment, next time, to do so.

392. Dear Mr. Pierce: I have been experimenting for some time with a device that I think will greatly improve our[1] present landing gears. I am calling the device a "cross-wind landing gear." This new gear has been put through many severe[2] tests on small aircraft, and I should like to interest you in the application of this principle to transport[3] planes of larger sizes.

I should like to prepare a testing program for you if you think my suggestion has[4] merit. Enclosed are the details of the gear. Sincerely yours,

393. Dear Mr. Dunn: I have discussed with Mr. Green your[5] letter of May 11 concerning the use of your cross-wind landing gears. We are convinced that there is potential[6] value in such a device; both for improving operational dependability and helping to[7] simplify the airport problem.

We have investigated what you have accomplished with these gears on small aircraft[8] and are highly pleased with the results. Our thoughts naturally go with yours toward the possible application of[9] the same principle to transports of larger sizes.

It is our opinion that the principle is well established,[10] and we should like to see an active program leading to the use of proved designs for large transport airplanes. We[11] feel that the airlines, the manufacturers, and the military services should all have an interest in[12] such a development for commercial and military purposes. If a proper program is developed[13] for the sharing of costs among these interested parties, we believe that it could be easily accomplished[14] without serious burden to anyone and with great benefit to all.

We feel that it would be highly[15] appropriate for you to prepare and propose such a program for concerted action. The procurement of a[16] DC-4 airplane for development test purposes for a temporary period should not be too difficult[17] or too expensive. It is our feeling that the development and proving of the detailed problems and[18] principles on a DC-4 would be conclusive in demonstrating the value of, and in solving the problems[19] incident to, applying cross-wind landing gears successfully to any other large transports.

Don't you agree[20] that the ATA, because of the prime interest of our industry in this problem, is the natural[21] organization to submit the final program to all the airlines? Sincerely yours,

394. Dear Mr. Pierce: Thank you for[22] your most encouraging reply. I shall "get down to brass tacks" immediately on the preparation of the[23] type of program you suggested.

Yes, I agree with you that the ATA is the logical organization[24] to handle this important matter after we iron out all the major problems and decide on the[25] desirability of the program.

We shall want to conduct a series of carefully supervised tests with several[26] transports of larger sizes.

May I have an appointment to discuss this further with you the next time I am[27] in Columbus, which I think will be the 30th of this month? I shall try to have the outline of the program[28] ready to bring with me so that we may go over it together.

If you have any additional suggestions[29] that you wish to give me before then, please feel free to do so. Sincerely yours, (594)

Reading and Writing Practice

395.

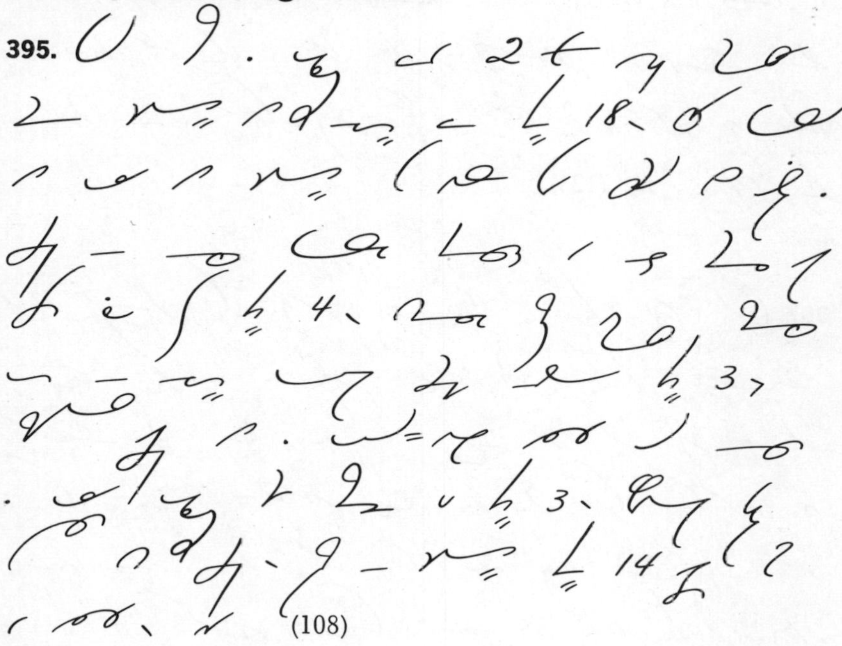

(108)

396.

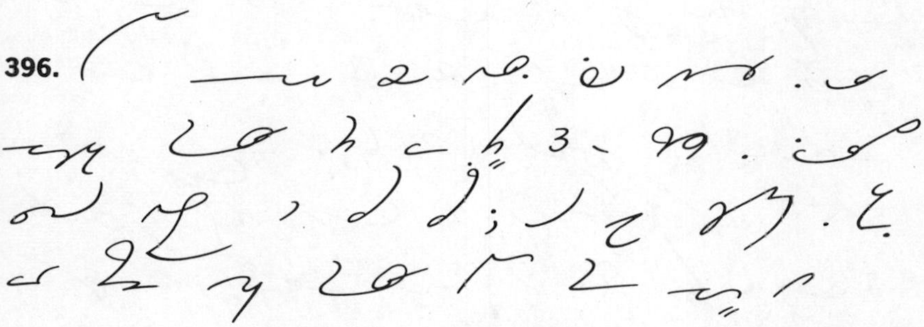

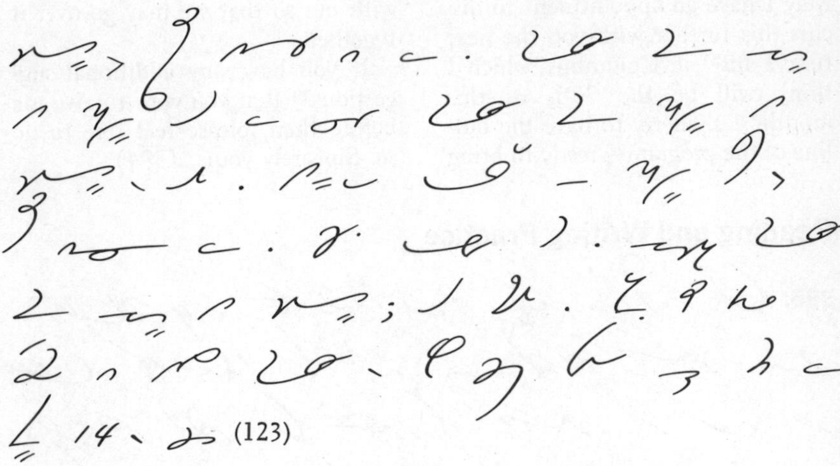
(123)

397.
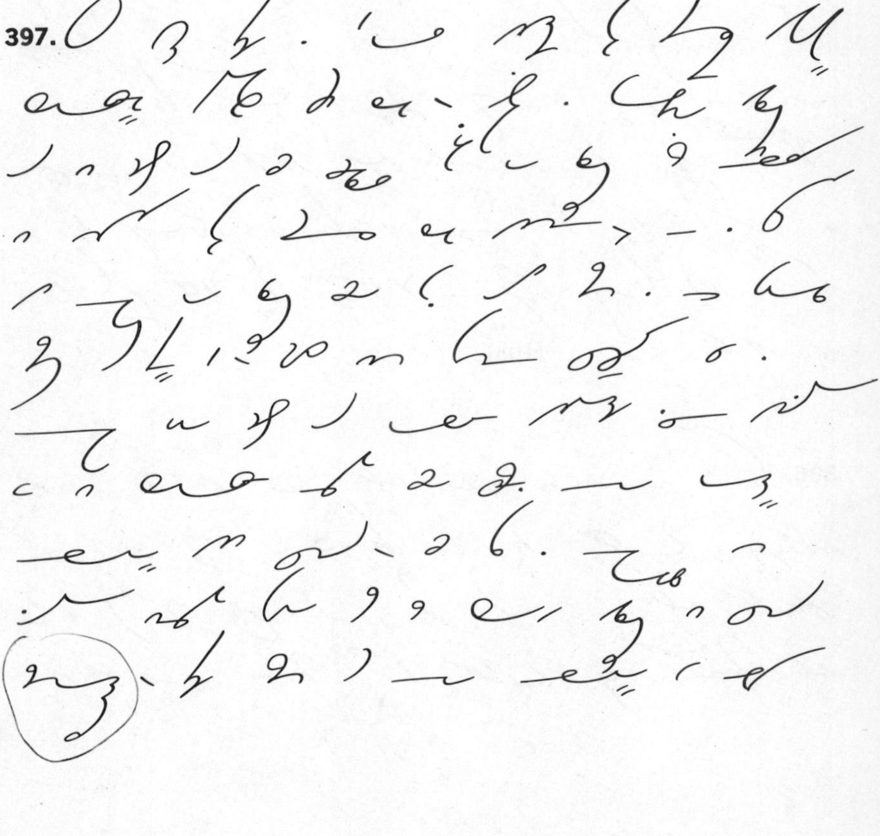

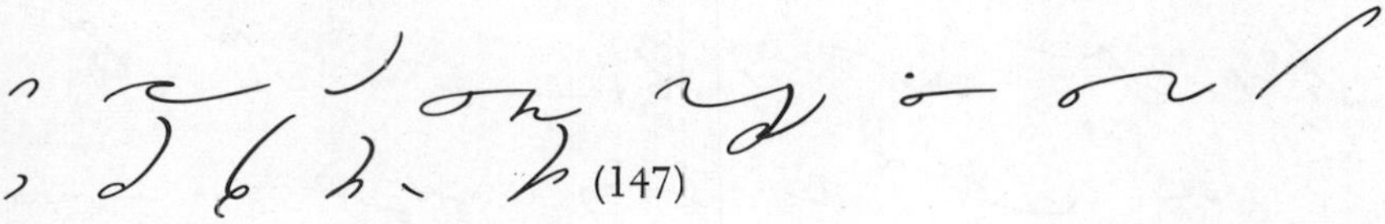

(147)

398.

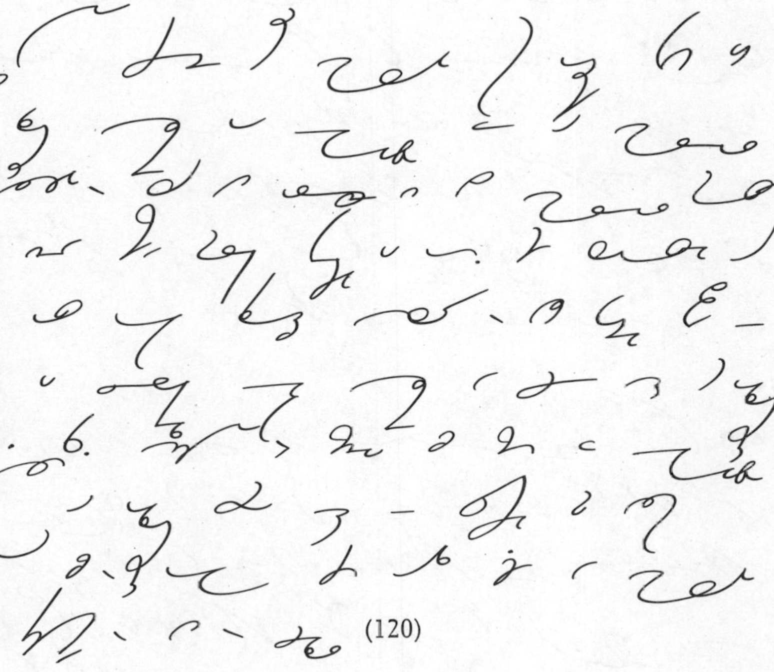

(120)

399.

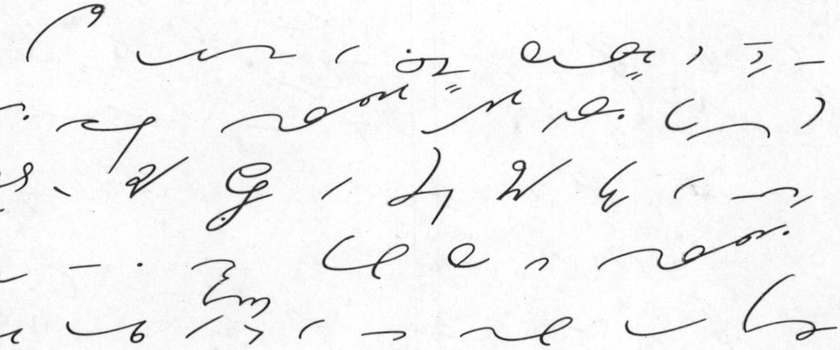

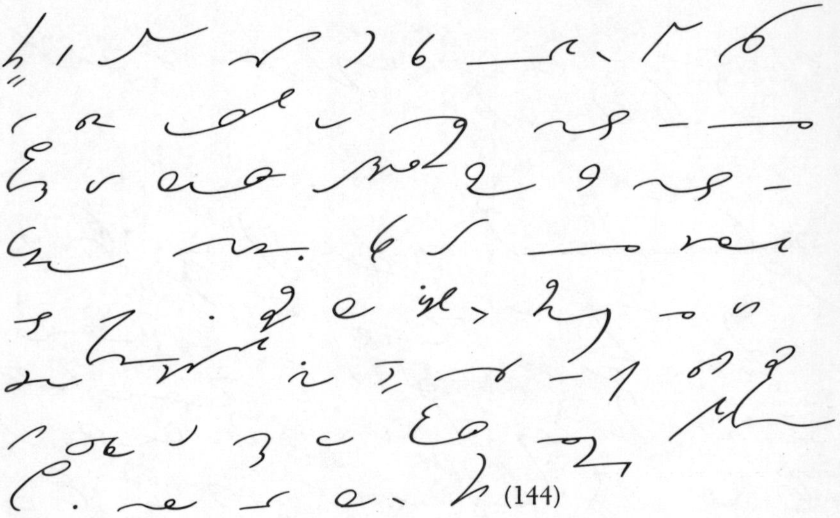

(144)

400.

(115)

11 Banking

Word Study for Chapter 11

BANKING

Acceptance. A time draft on which the drawee has formally written "Accepted" and his signature.

Accrued. Earned or accumulated but not yet due, as interest.

Amortization. The gradual reduction of a debt by means of equal periodic payments sufficient to meet current interest and extinguish the debt at maturity.

Assignee. Any person to whom a property or a right is assigned.

Bearer. The person in possession of a bill or note that is payable to "bearer."

Big Board. The New York Stock Exchange.

Bond. An interest-bearing certificate of indebtedness issued by a government or by a corporation; also, a writing under seal by which a person binds himself to pay a sum of money or to do a certain thing.

Call Loan. A loan made on a day-to-day basis, callable on twenty-four hours' notice.

Capital Stock. The investment in a corporation for which shares of stock have been issued.

Cashier's Check. A check drawn on a bank by itself and signed by its cashier.

Clearinghouse. A place where the banks in a city may daily exchange checks, drafts, notes, and the like, and settle the resulting balances.

Collateral. Property pledged as security for the payment of a debt.

Commercial Paper. Short-term negotiable instruments (drafts, notes, acceptances) arising out of commercial transactions calling for the payment of money.

Cover. To buy stocks or commodities that one has previously sold short in order to protect oneself when the market rises.

Curb. A market trading in securities not listed on the New York Stock Exchange. Formerly, actually on the *curb*; hence, the name.

Dishonor. To refuse to accept a draft, check, or note that is duly presented for acceptance; also, to refuse to pay a draft, check, or note that is duly presented for payment.

Dividends. The proportion of the net earnings of a corporation paid to the stockholders as their share of the profits.

Equity. The value of collateral over the amount of the obligation it covers.

Escrow. A written agreement between two or more parties by which a bond, a deed, or other paper and certain funds, securities, or other property are deposited with a third party, known as an *escrow agent*, for safekeeping, the instrument and the property to be delivered only on the fulfillment of the conditions set forth in the agreement.

Federal Reserve Bank. One of twelve banks created under the Federal Reserve Act to serve as bankers for member banks of the Federal Reserve System.

Fiduciary. A corporation or a person to whom property is entrusted.

Hypothecate. To pledge without delivery of title or possession. The term is applied today to the deposit of stocks, bonds, and the like, as security for a loan.

Letter of Credit. A written notice by a bank that the person named therein is entitled to draw on the bank up to a certain amount.

Liquidation. The payment of debts. The settling of accounts and the distribution of assets in the process of winding up an estate or business.

Margin. The money deposited with a broker by a customer to protect the broker against loss resulting from transactions made by the broker on the customer's behalf.

Negotiable Instruments. Checks, notes, drafts, bills of exchange, or other commercial paper that may be transferred by the owner to another by the owner's indorsement.

Odd Lot. A smaller unit of trade than the standard unit on an exchange, such as less than 100 shares of stock.

Over the Counter. A term referring to dealings in securities that are not listed on any stock exchange.

Point. The unit of fluctuation on a marker; usually $1.

Revocation. The act by which a power or an authority or a license is withdrawn by the one having the right so to withdraw.

Right. The privilege offered to stockholders to purchase shares of a new stock issue in proportion to their holdings at a set time.

Scrip. A provisional document certifying that the holder is entitled to receive something else; as, stocks, bonds.

Short. One who sells securities that he does not possess or has not contracted for at the time of the sale, expecting to profit by a fall in prices; a bear.

Stop-Loss Order. An order to a broker authorizing him to sell at the market when a stock is at or below a specified quotation, or to buy when it is at or above a specified price.

Surety. A person who engages to be answerable for the debt or default of another.

Usury. Interest at a higher rate than is allowed by law.

Lesson 51

BUILDING TRANSCRIPTION SKILL

Transcription English Pointers

THE USES OF THE HYPHEN

How to Write Compound Words

Whether to write a compound word as a solid word (as *halftone*), as two words (as *half dollar*), or with a hyphen (as *half-truth*) presents a perplexing problem to the transcriber.

It must be realized from the outset that authorities do not agree on the rules for forming compounds and that practice gradually changes. Over a period of years the elements of a compound word may either grow apart or grow together. The following rules, however, represent sound standard practice. Observance of them will result in consistent transcripts. Directions are also included for writing those compound expressions that are "manufactured" – that do not occur in the dictionary.

1. When two or more words convey a *single thought*, they should be hyphenated.

a never-to-be-forgotten war	to dry-clean
a hard-and-fast rule	to blue-pencil
a well-known lawyer	to double-check

Do not confuse compound adjectives with constructions in which two or more independent adjectives precede a noun.

an unsavory police record	a charming little fellow

Exceptions:

a. When one of the elements of a compound adjective is an adverb ending in *ly*, the adjective is not hyphenated. The *ly* indicates the relationship between the two words – that the first modifies the second and, therefore, the hyphen is not needed.

a poorly arranged outline | a highly valued painting

Some adjectives, however, end in *ly*. Such adjectives, when they form part of a compound adjective, should be hyphenated.

a friendly neighbor | a queenly woman
a friendly-acting neighbor | a queenly-looking woman

b. No hyphen is inserted in two-word proper nouns used as adjectives.

a North American Indian | a Wall Street broker
the Jersey City police | a New York Central train

But, two two-word names used before a noun are usually joined by a hyphen.

the New York-San Francisco flight

2. When two or more words used as a single modifier follow the word they modify, then no hyphen is used.

a lawyer well known in our city | the regulation above mentioned
an editorial a full column wide | files are up to date
ability in letter writing | a war never to be forgotten

3. When a series of hyphenated words has a common basic element, the hyphen follows each word. A space is left after each word except the last in the series to indicate the omission of the basic element.

hard- and soft-coal dealers | long- and short-term notes
round-, square-, or oval-shaped trays

(Concluded on page 350)

Transcription Speed Builder

401.

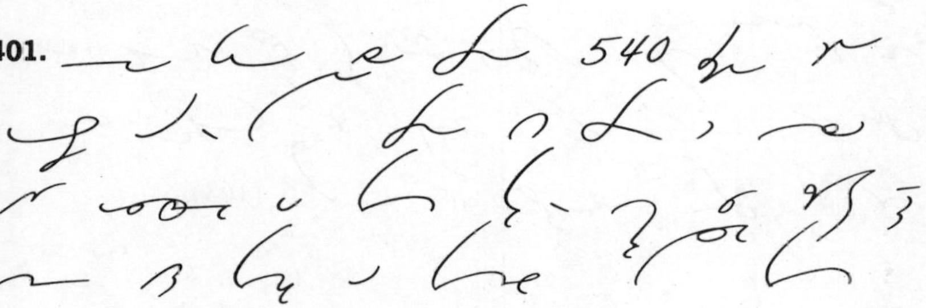

(77)

402.

(168)

403. 26 14 25 25 21 5 26 26 28 (212)

404. 75

(54)

405.

(98)

406.

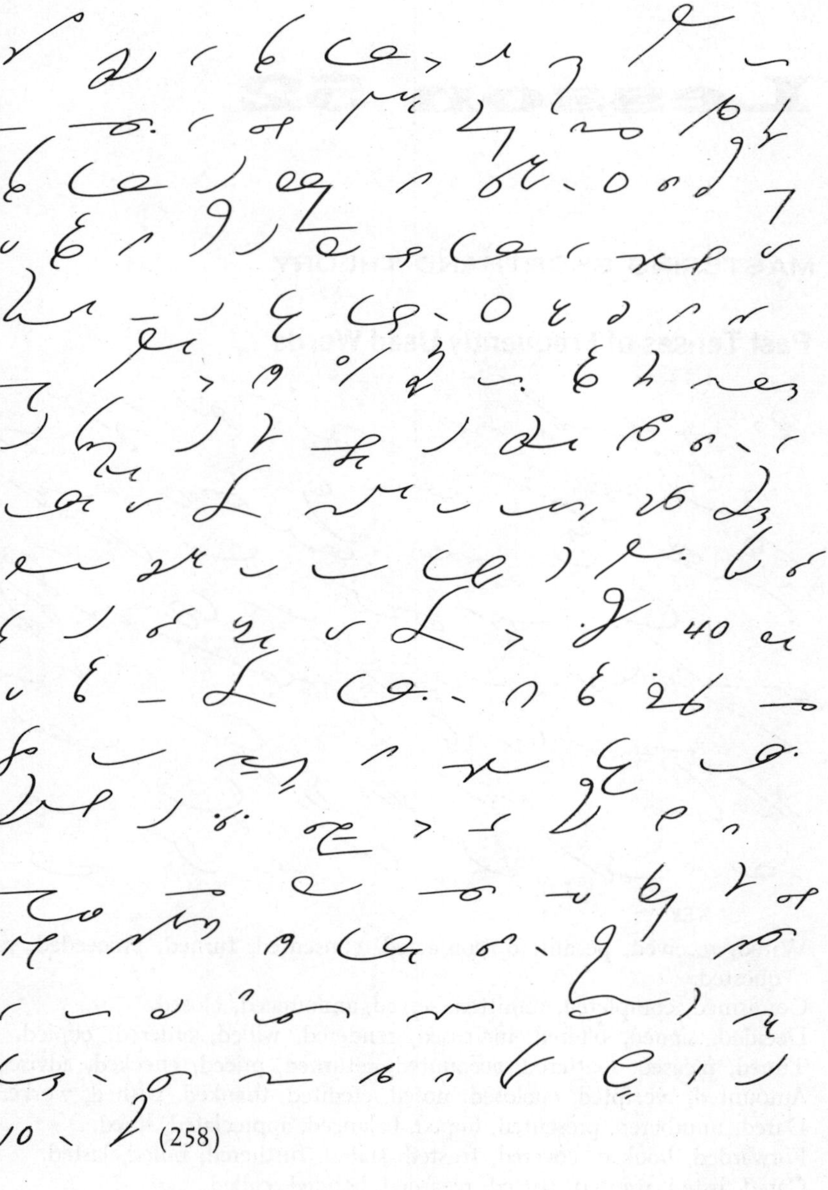

(258)

Lesson 52

MASTERING SHORTHAND THEORY

Past Tenses of Frequently Used Words

KEY

Wired, received, permitted, contacted, consented, turned, proceeded, requested.
Confirmed, completed, remitted, served, announced, closed.
Decided, signed, offered, increased, rendered, willed, ordered, copied.
Timed, pleased, mattered, accounted, returned, priced, checked, advised.
Amounted, receipted, enclosed, noted, credited, thanked, wished, worked.
Dated, numbered, presented, hoped, balanced, appreciated, lined.
Forwarded, booked, covered, trusted, stated, furthered, billed, lasted.
Cared, listed, wanted, parted, regarded, handed, called.

Reading and Writing Practice

407.

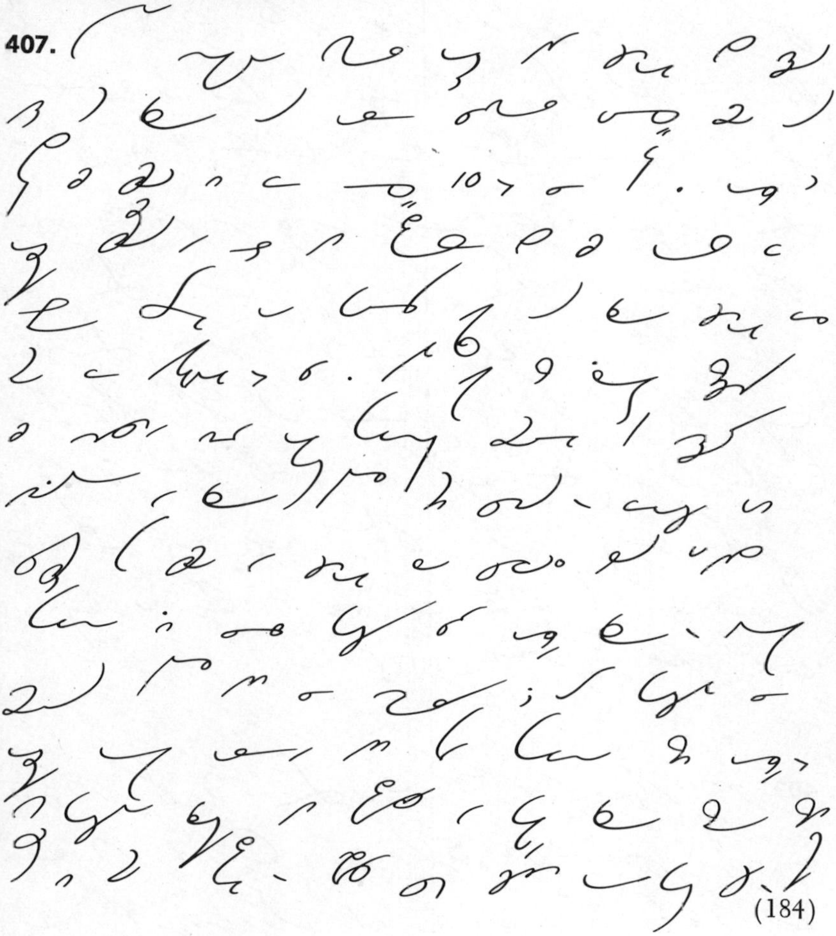

(184)

408.

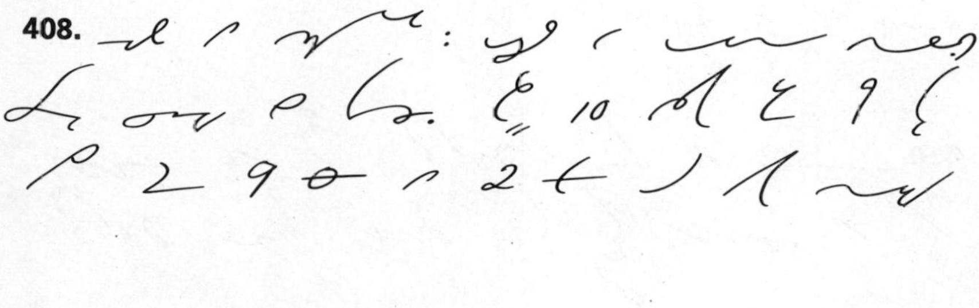

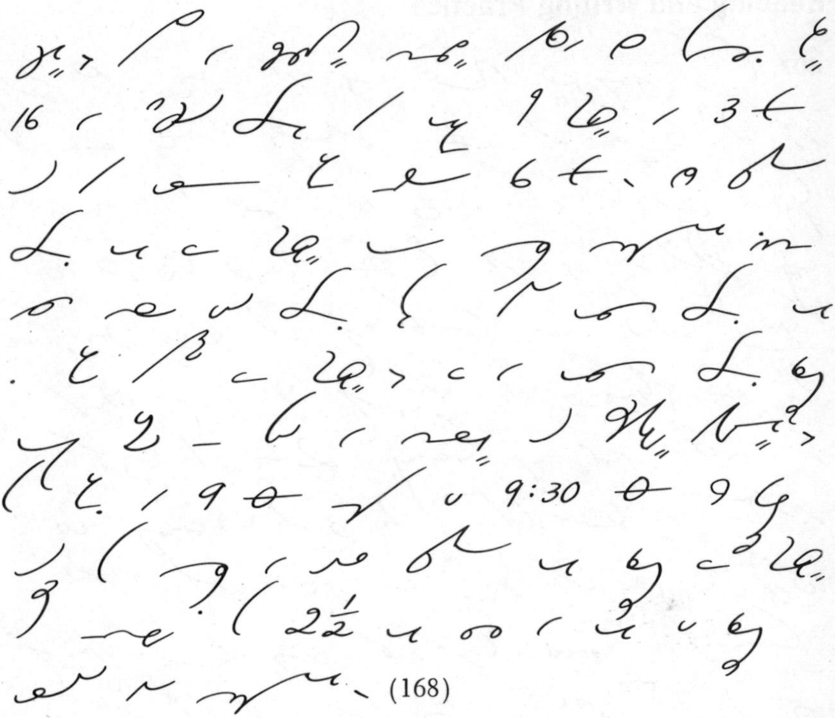

(168)

409. 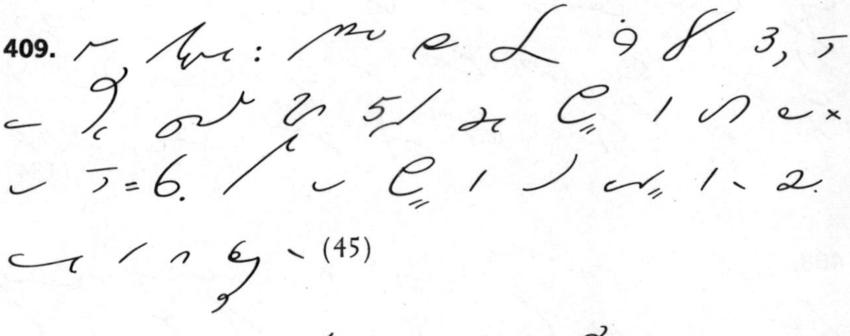

(45)

410. 

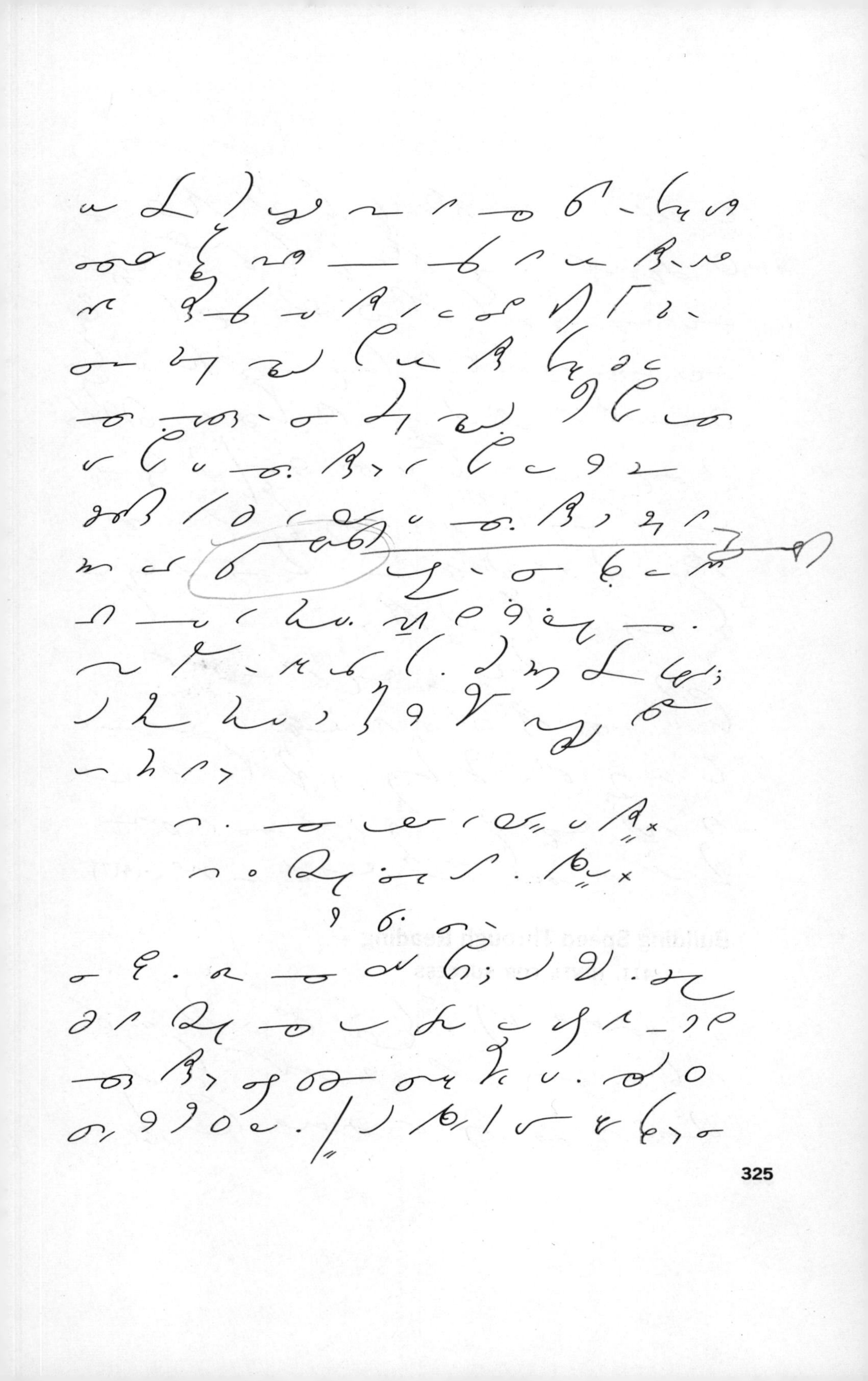

(417)

Building Speed Through Reading

411. HINTS FOR SUCCESS

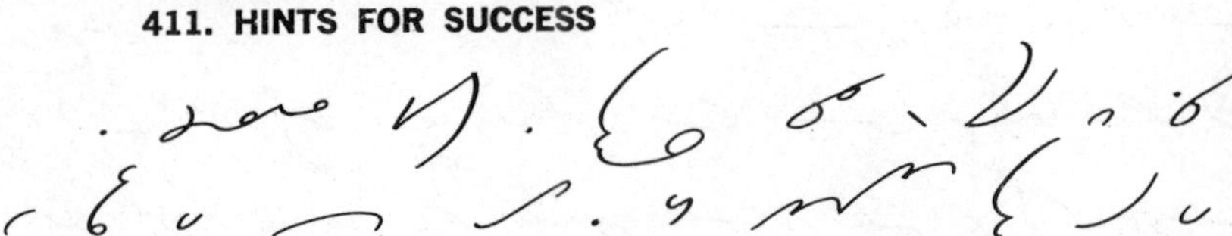

(230)

Lesson 53

BUILDING PHRASING SKILL

Let, Year

and let	during the last year
and let us	during the past year
do not let	during the year
let me	for a number of years
let us	for next year
let us have	for some years
let us know	for the last year
let us make	for the past year
let us say	in the last year
let us see	last year
please let	next year
please let me	one year
please let us	some years ago
please let us have	years ago

Brief-Form and Phrase Letters

412.

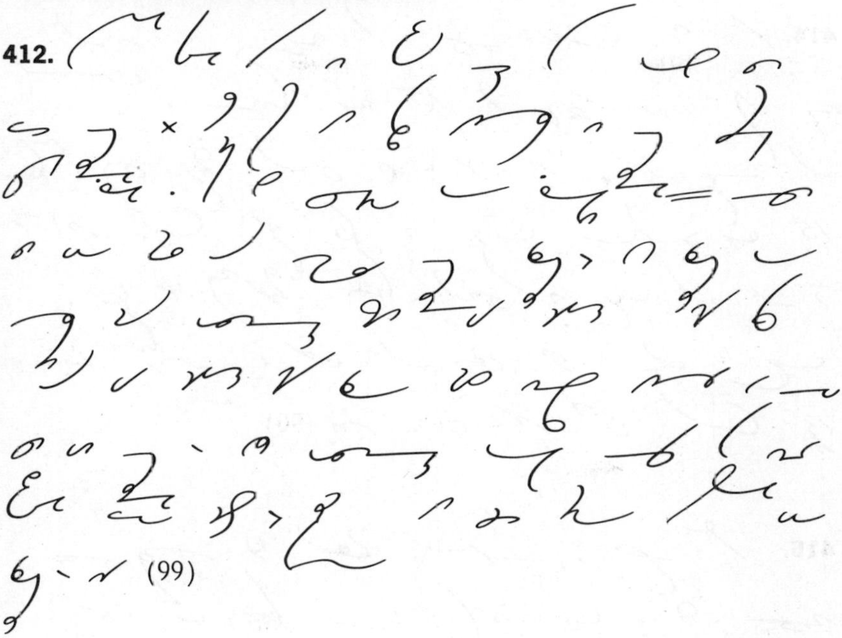

(99)

413.

(94)

414.

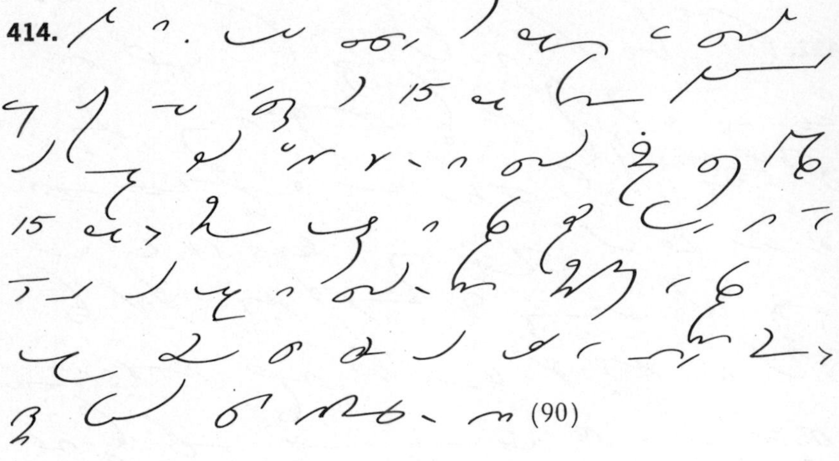

415.

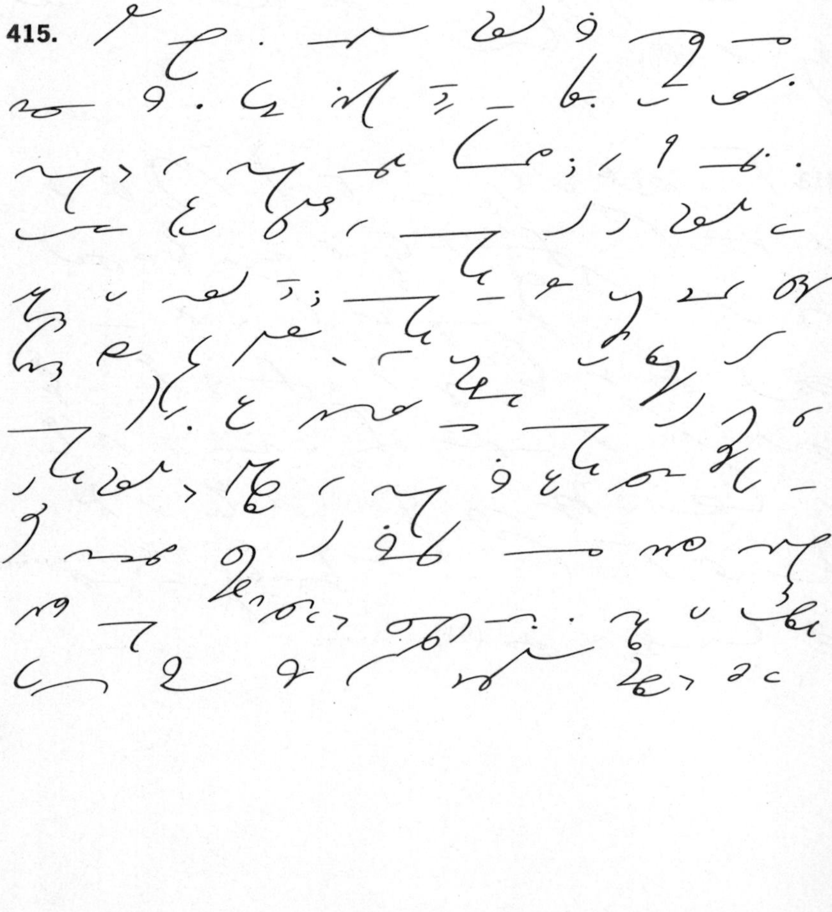

Monarch AIRLINES INC. GENERAL OFFICES
UNIVERSITY AIRPORT
WASHINGTON 1, D. C.

May 22, 19--

Mr. Roger Burke
Mid-West Airlines
377 North First Street
Madison, Wisconsin

Dear Mr. Burke:

Subject: Airplane and Engine Overhauling

We are looking into the feasibility of providing for airplane and engine overhaul on an annual reserve basis with particular reference to DC-6 and CV-240 type airplanes. It occurred to us that you may be either actually doing the same thing or contemplating some similar approach. If you are, would you mind answering the following questions?

1. Are you on a reserve basis of accruing overhaul expenditures for your present aircraft?

2. Do you contemplate such a program for new aircraft either presently being received or to be procured eventually?

3. If you do have a reserve for this type of overhaul, what are the rates you are using?

4. How are these rates and figures regulated?

5. What steps have you taken in order to keep the reserve equalized with actual expense?

6. If reserves are maintained, what adjustments of the accumulated reserves are made upon disposition of the individual aircraft?

7. If reserves are [...] have arisen in [...] utilizing reserv[...] upon your income[...]

The question of providing [...] is not acute after the ai[...]

Mr. Roger Burke 2 May 22, 19--

only three months, but a real problem does exist in respect to airplanes on which overhaul periods exceed 8,000 hours.

We realize that this problem has many angles and facets. Therefore, before we venture to take any steps in this direction, we should like to receive as much information as possible as well as to benefit as much as we can from the experience that other companies have had.

We shall appreciate receiving any comments you have in connection with such a proposal.

Very truly yours,

A. G. Lane, Vice-President

CHK

P. S. I have just learned that I must be in Chicago during the next few weeks. As I need the above information as soon as possible, I would appreciate it if you would address your letter to me in care of the Hotel Madison in that city. Thank you for your co-operation.

Two-Page Letter
Blocked Style, with Subject Line and Postscript
Standard Punctuation

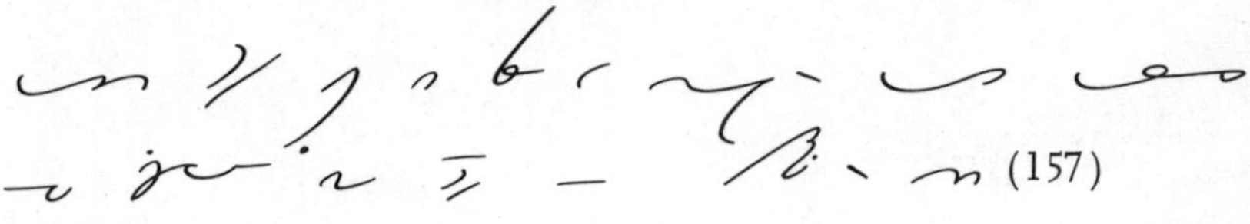

(157)

416.

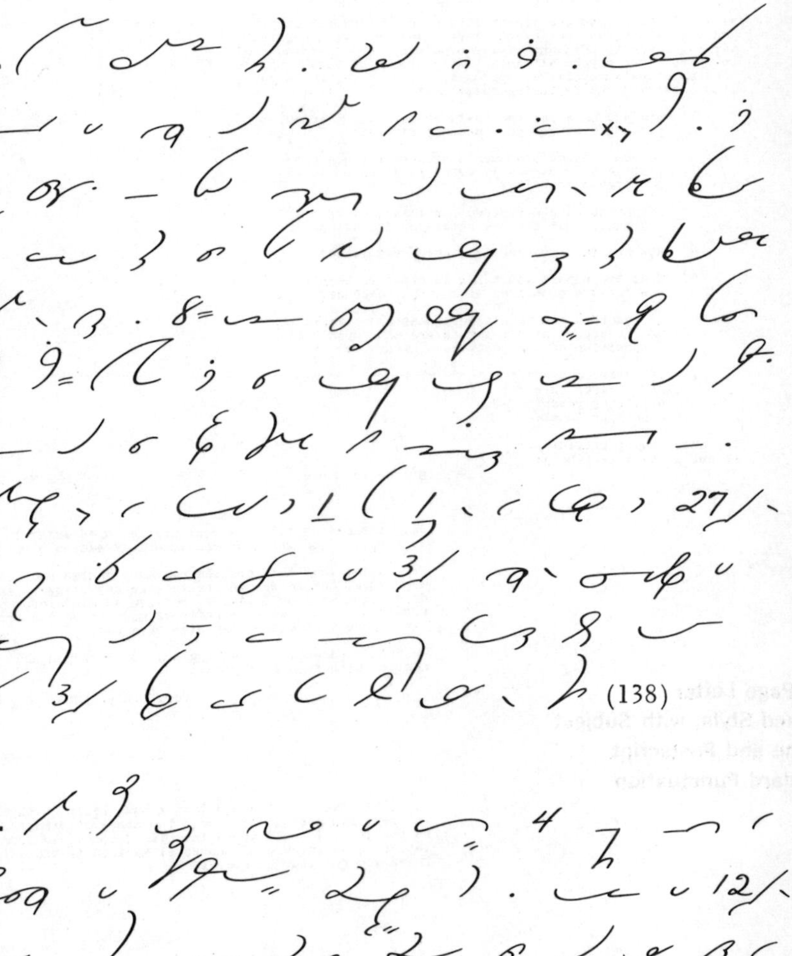

(138)

417.

(53)

418. BANKING IS A UNIQUE SERVICE

(331)

419. THE SECRET OF SUCCESSFUL SAVING

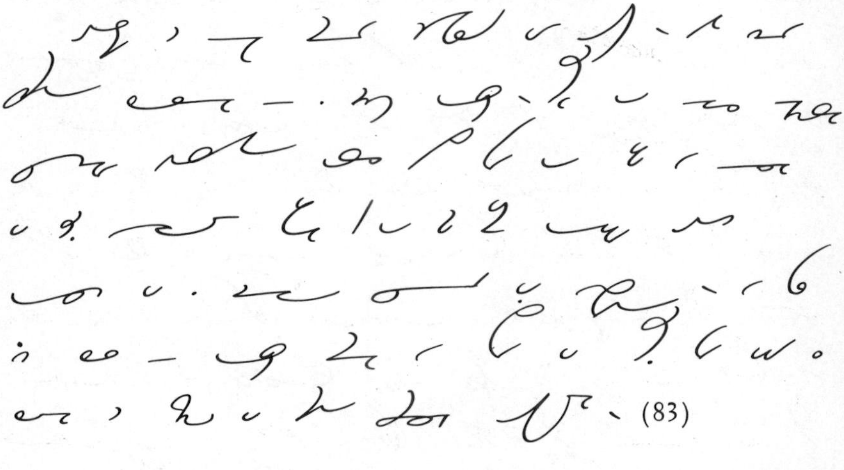

(83)

Lesson 54

PROGRESSIVE SPEED BUILDING

Half-Minute Progressive Speed Builder (110-140)

VOCABULARY PREVIEW

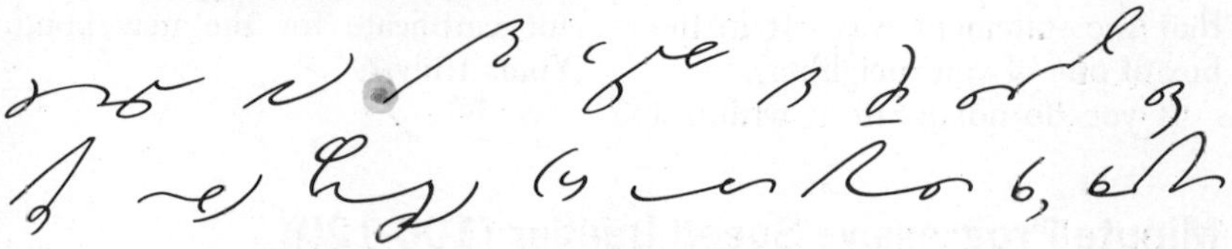

KEY

Signature, it is not, to do so, self-addressed, to us, few hundred, week or ten days, useful.

Digest, correspondent, I hope you will find, post office, locate, duplicate, 6 per cent, certificate.

(½ MINUTE AT 110)

420. Dear John: Enclosed are the signature cards for your use in sending us the official signatures of your president and treasurer, in connection with/the new account that you will be establishing with us. It is not necessary that you consider the statement on the back unless you wish to do so.//

(½ MINUTE AT 120)

I am also enclosing a self-addressed stamped envelope for your convenience in returning the cards to us when they are completed.

At your request, I have ordered/ a few hundred checks imprinted for your use and numbered, beginning with No. 1. They will be shipped to you direct from our printer within a week or ten days.//

(½ MINUTE AT 130)

I am also sending a rubber addressing stamp, which your remittance clerk will find useful in addressing these collections to us.

I am putting your name on our mailing list to/receive Trends, a weekly digest of current events. This is a service we maintain for our correspondent banks. I hope you will find it to be useful and interesting. Yours truly,//

(½ MINUTE AT 135)

421. Dear Mr. Smith: We are sorry that you did not receive your last bank statement. According to our records, your statement was mailed on July 31.

May we suggest that you check with your post/office. It may be that the statement was left in the box of one of your neighbors.

If you do not locate it within a week, we shall be glad to issue a duplicate. Very truly yours,//

(½ MINUTE AT 140)

422. Gentlemen: Your check for $79.61, representing the balance due on your 6 per cent bond, has been received and credited to your account.

We think that the permanent/certificate will be ready for delivery in about four months, and at that time we shall be glad to comply with your request to exchange your present certificate for the new bond. Yours truly,//

Minute Progressive Speed Builder (100-120)

VOCABULARY PREVIEW

KEY

There is not, to do this, constantly, loyal, I did not, I have been, ten years, worthy.

Community, Chamber of Commerce, embarrassing, insufficient, individualize, economically, imperative.

(1 MINUTE AT 100)

423. Dear Bank Customer: This letter will answer your inquiry of November 22 about the holding of checks when there is not/sufficient money in your account to cover them. I know this seems to you like a very small favor; but, as much as I should like to help you,//the Federal Government does not allow us to do this.

I hope you will call on us often to be of service to you in ways that are///possible. The bank is constantly making an effort to find more ways to be of service to its many loyal customers. Yours very truly, (1)

(1 MINUTE AT 110)

424. Gentlemen: I received today the form letter that you write to persons asking you to hold checks. I did not realize that my problem was such a common/one. I still do not feel, though, that mine is a "form" account.

I have been banking with you for over ten years. This should be long enough to be classed as a good// customer and worthy of some favors. I am a leader in the community, having just been elected president of the Junior Chamber of/// Commerce. This is why it is so embarrassing when my checks are returned marked "Insufficient funds." Isn't it possible to make an exception in my case? Sincerely yours, (2)

(1 MINUTE AT 120)

425. Dear Mr. Bailey: You are right – yours is not a "form" account. We consider each of our customers as an individual and try to individualize our/service as much as possible. The large number of letters we receive makes it economically imperative that we use form letters. I am sorry you felt// you were not given personal consideration.

Because banks handle the money of other people, they are regulated by state and Federal laws. These laws are very///strict, and failure to abide by them can mean death to a bank.

I wish it were possible to make an exception in your case, but we just cannot do so. Sincerely yours, (3)

Reading and Writing Practice

426.

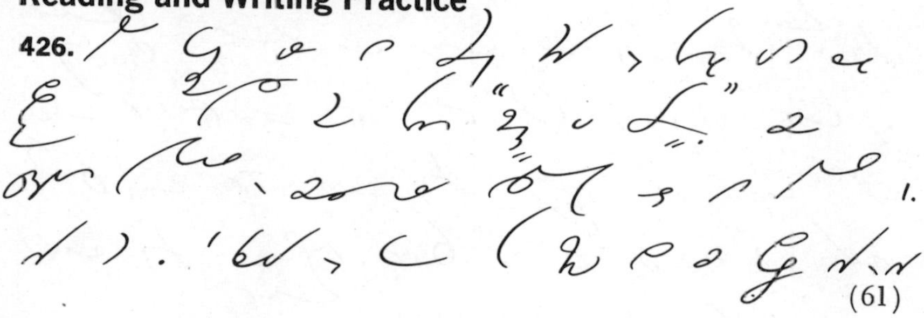

(61)

427.

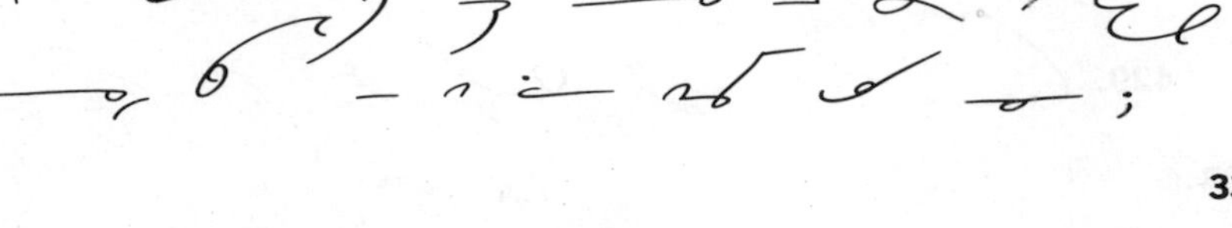

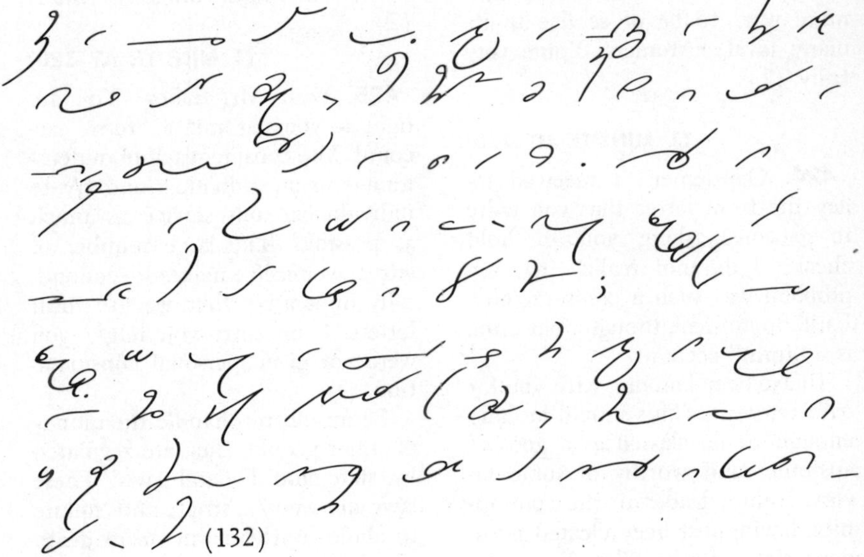

(132)

428.

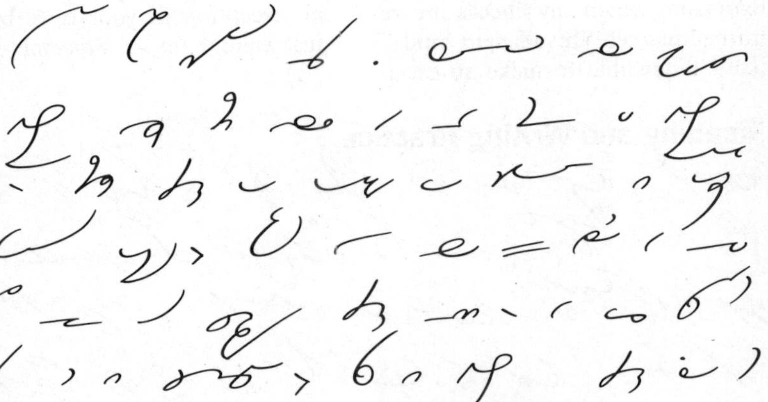

(74)

429.

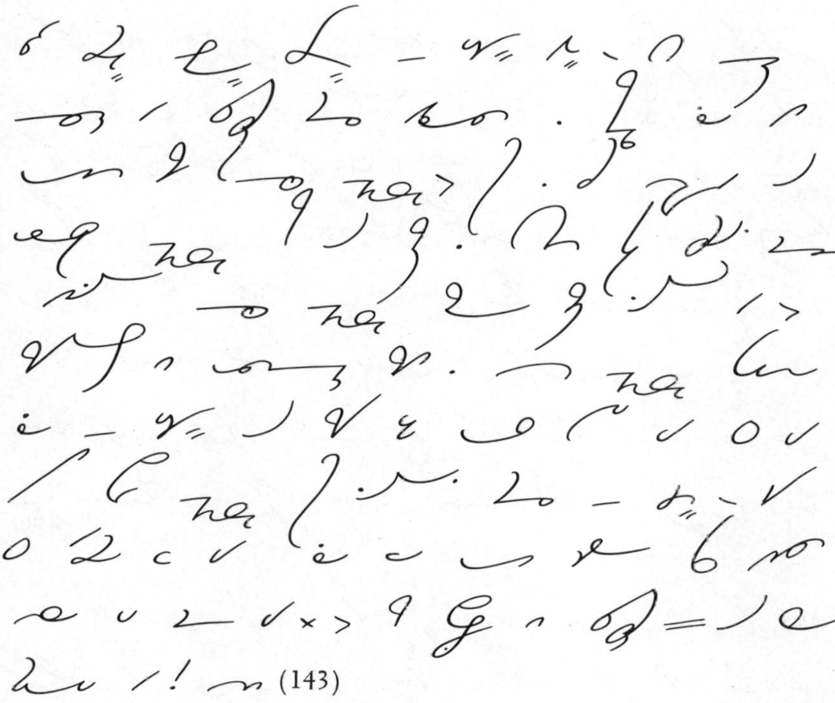

(143)

430. 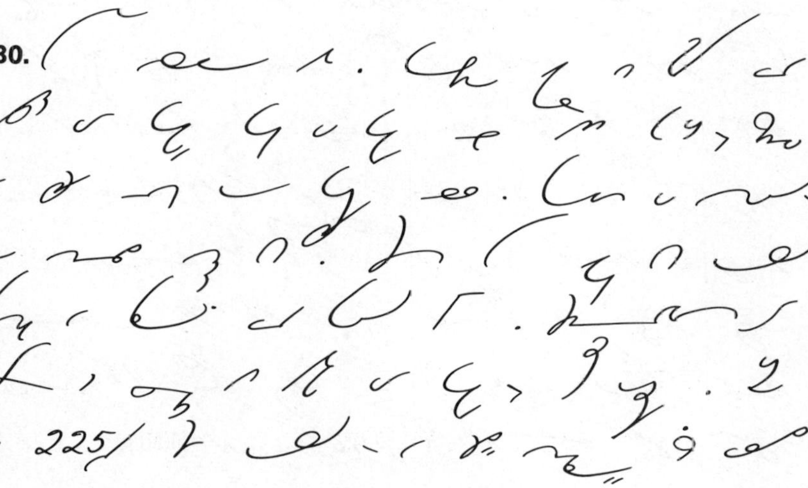

(189)

431.

(110)

Lesson 55

BUILDING SUSTAINED SPEED

Five-Minute Speed Builder

The following correspondence is between E. R. Bradshaw, President, the National Bank of Commerce, Hopkins Building, Wilkes-Barre, Pennsylvania, and Mr. E. V. Curtis, 15 Columbia Street, Wilkes-Barre, Pennsylvania.

VOCABULARY PREVIEW

KEY

Curtis, resident, community, attractive, permanent, cordial.

Commerce, industrial, real estate, characterized, friendly, disposal.

Financial, transactions, Bradshaw, thank you, few months, particulars, borrower, rigid.

Formula, extending, substantial, shorter, discussion, one of our, assist, orderly.

With the understanding, appreciated, assistance, clients, William, machinery, hesitancy.

432. Dear Mr. Curtis: We are glad to learn that you have become a resident of our city, and we are confident[1] that you will find this community a good one in which to live – attractive and pleasant in every way[2] as a permanent home.

A cordial welcome awaits you at the National Bank of Commerce. If there is any[3] information in regard to our industrial or real estate conditions that you may desire, or if there[4] is any way in which you think our service can be of value to you, we shall welcome your visit at the first[5] opportunity.

Our bank is characterized by friendly co-operation and places at your disposal[6] the most complete equipment for the handling of financial transactions of any kind, including personal[7] loans.

I am looking forward to meeting you personally. Very truly yours,

433. Dear Mr. Bradshaw: Thank you very[8] much for your welcoming letter of April 26. I am going to take advantage of your offer[9] to help me by asking about your personal-loan service. I wish to begin my own law practice and may[10] need a small loan within the next few months.

Will you please give me full particulars on your personal-loan service?[11] Cordially yours,

434. Dear Mr. Curtis: We were very much pleased to receive your letter of April 30 in[12] which you ask about our personal-loan service.

Our personal loans are made on the basis of the steady income[13] of the borrower and the recommendation of relatives or friends. No rigid formula is used for[14] extending credit. Each loan is "made to measure" to fit your particular need.

In many cases, where the[15] borrower and his wife are homeowners and have a substantial income and credit standing, no recommendation[16] is required.

Loans are usually made for a period of twelve months. They may be made, however, for shorter[17] periods or for a longer time. In the latter case the monthly installments will be smaller.

You are cordially[18] invited to write us or come in for a friendly discussion with one of our loan officers. Their primary[19] interest is to assist you to plan your financial affairs on an orderly basis. Yours very truly,[20]

435. Dear Mr. Curtis: Our Finance Committee today considered your application for a personal loan[21] and has approved it with the understanding that the loan is to be paid in full within one year.

Mr. Barnes, the[22] head of our Personal Loan Department, has the papers for you to sign in his office. Come in at your convenience[23] and sign them – the money will then be yours.

This opportunity for serving you is very much appreciated[24] and we hope that you will call on us again whenever our bank may be of assistance to you. Sincerely[25] yours,

436. Dear Mr. Bradshaw: One of my clients, William Snyder, who is also a personal friend of mine, is[26] here in the interest of his company, which is buying some machinery.

The purpose of this letter is[27] to tell you that, should Mr. Snyder desire to cash any checks at your bank, you need have no hesitancy in[28] doing so. I have known Mr. Snyder for twenty years; he has always met his obligations and has never[29] written a check that has not been paid.

Any consideration or courtesy extended Mr. Snyder[30] will be greatly appreciated. Very truly yours, (610)

Reading and Writing Practice

437.

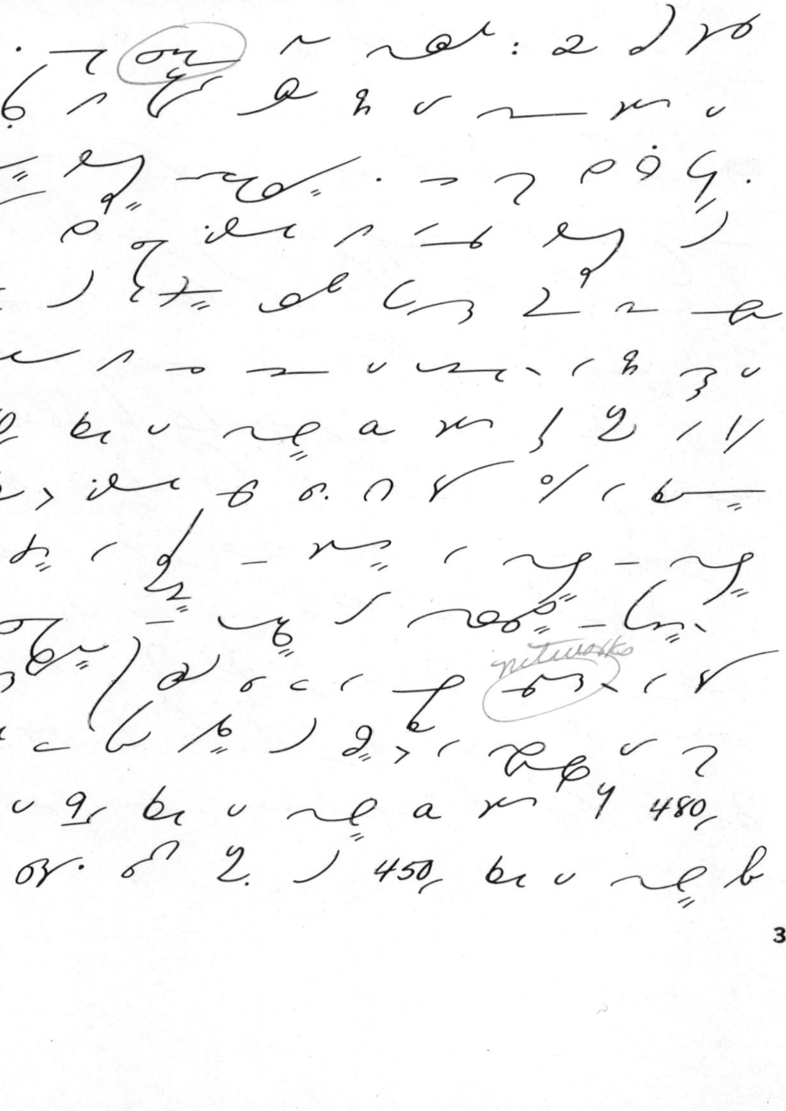

240 (259)

438.

18 (134)

439.

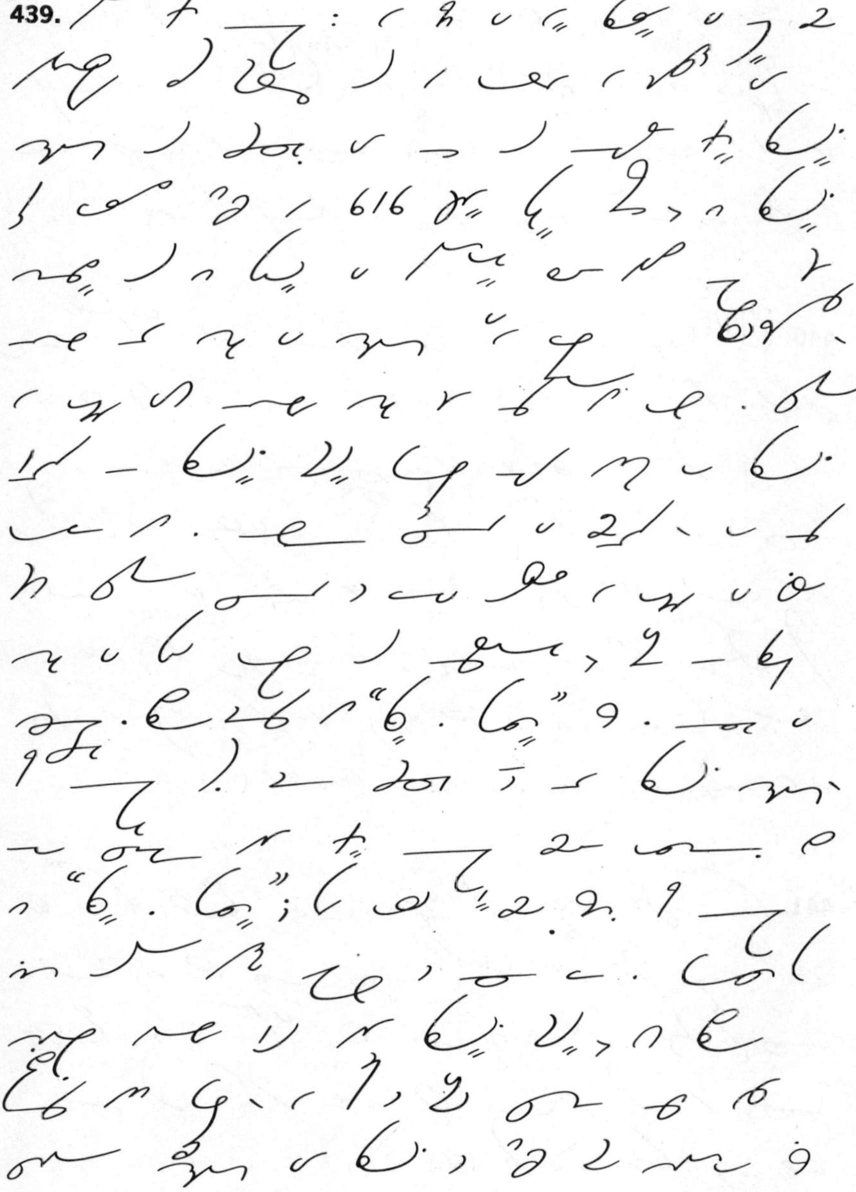

(298)

440.

(87)

441.

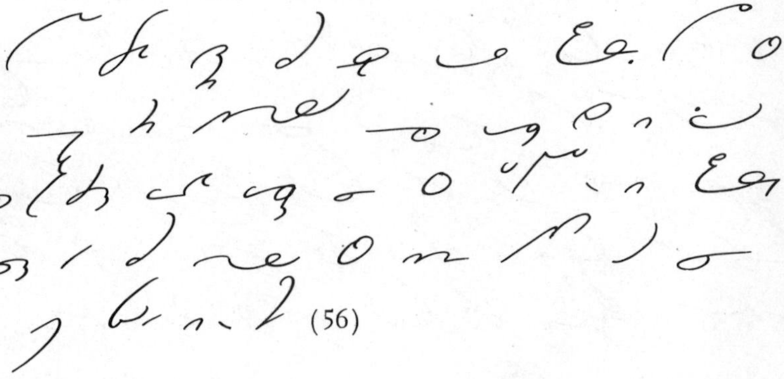

(56)

12
Law

Word Study for Chapter 12

LAW

Affiant. One who makes a statement under oath.

Allegation. That which is alleged or asserted.

Bailee. A person who receives the custody of goods in trust for a specific purpose other than as owner.

Beneficiary. The person designated to receive the income of a trust estate or the proceeds of an insurance policy.

Chattel. Any item of movable or immovable property except real estate, or the freehold, or things that are parcel to it. *Chattels personal* may be goods, furniture, and so on. *Chattels real* may be rights in land, such as leases, mortgages, and the like.

Codicil. A supplement to a will.

Demurrer. A pleading by a party to an action that, assuming the truth of the matter alleged by the opposite party, sets up that it is insufficient in law to sustain his claim.

Deponent. One who makes an affidavit or testifies in writing under oath.

Dower. The interest that the law gives a widow in the realty of her deceased husband.

Emblements. The growing crop or vegetable growth, or profits of a crop.

Equity. A body of laws based on natural principles of justice. The value of property in excess of liens against it.

Escheat. Reversion of property to the state in default of a person who can inherit it.

Estoppel. A bar to the proof of some fact because it is contrary to one's prior acts or admissions.

Garnishee (v.). To attach salary, wages, or other income to pay a debt.

Hereditaments. Any property that can be inherited.

Indigent. Destitute of property, poverty-stricken.

Infant. In common law, a person under twenty-one years of age. By statute in many states, however, a woman ceases to be an infant at eighteen years of age.

Inquest. A judicial inquiry. An inquiry made by a coroner and a jury as to the death of the person who has been killed or has died under suspicious circumstances or in prison.

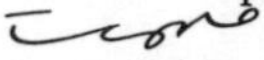

Interlocutory. Incident to a suit still pending.

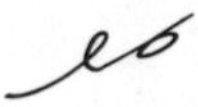

Intestate. Not having made a will; also one who dies without having made a lawful will.

Legacy. A gift of property by will; a bequest.

Lien. A charge on real or

personal property for the satisfaction of some debt or duty.

Praecipe. A writ commanding a person to do something or to appear and then show cause why he should not.

Probate. To prove legally and officially, as a will; also, having jurisdiction over wills.

Replevin. An action to recover the possession of chattels unlawfully taken.

Subpoena. A writ commanding attendance in court at a certain time and place.

Tort. A civil wrong independent of a contract for which a civil suit can be brought.

Waiver. A voluntary relinquishment of some right.

Writ. An instrument in writing, under seal, issued by the proper authority, commanding a person to do or not to do something.

LEGAL PHRASES OF LATIN ORIGIN

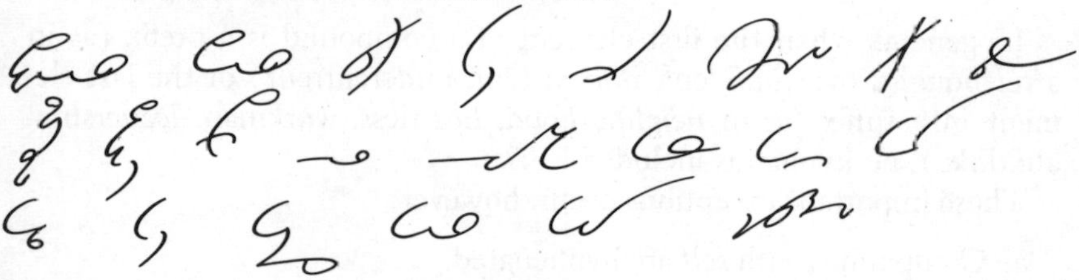

A posteriori	ā' pŏs-tē'rĭ-ō'rī	From effect to cause.
A priori	ā' prī-ō'rī	From cause to effect.
Ad valorem	ăd vȧ-lō'rĕm	According to the value.
Bona fide	bō'nȧ fī'dē	In or with good faith.
Caveat emptor	kā'vē-ăt ĕmp'tôr	Let the buyer beware.
De facto	dē făk'tō	Actually.
De jure	dē jōō'rē	By lawful title.
Et al.	ĕt ăl	And others.
Ex officio	ĕks ŏ-fĭsh'ĭ-ō	By virtue of an office.
Ex post facto	ĕks pōst făk'tō	Having a retroactive application.
Habeas corpus	hā'bē-ăs kôr'pŭs	A writ to produce a person in court.
In re	ĭn rē'	Concerning.
Modus operandi	mō'dŭs ŏp'ĕ-răn'dī	Manner of operation.
Per annum	pĕr ăn'ŭm	Annually.
Per capita	pĕr kăp'ĭ-tȧ	For each person.
Per diem	pĕr dī'ĕm	By the day.
Per se	pûr sē	By itself.
Prima facie	prī'mȧ fā'shĭ-ē	At first view.
Pro forma	prō fôr'mȧ	As a matter of form.
Pro rata	prō rā'tȧ	Proportionately.
Pro tem	prō tĕm'	Temporarily.
Status quo	stā'tŭs kwō	The state in which.

Lesson 56

BUILDING TRANSCRIPTION SKILL

Transcription English Pointers

THE USES OF THE HYPHEN (CONCLUDED)

In general, when the first element of a compound is a prefix (as in *afterthought, overconfident, nonexistent, undercurrent*) or the last element in a suffix (as in *neighborhood, heartless, workman, leadership, childlike*), no hyphen is included.

These important exceptions occur, however:

a. Compounds with *self* are hyphenated.

self-reliance
self-addressed

b. When the second element of a word that contains a prefix begins with a capital, a hyphen follows the prefix.

un-American Trans-Jordan anti-Semitic pre-Victorian pro-Israel

c. When the last letter of a prefix is the same as the first letter of the word to which it is joined, a hyphen is inserted.

co-operate
re-enter
semi-invalid
anti-imperialistic
pre-establish

d. When, in adding a suffix, the same letter occurs three times, the hyphen is inserted.

bell-like
shell-less

e. The hyphen is required in several verbs beginning with *re,* in which *re* means "again," to distinguish the verbs from other identically spelled words of different meanings.

to re-collect the cards	to recollect the terms
to re-cover the book	to recover a loss
to re-form the pattern	to reform a drunkard
to re-mark the merchandise	to make a remark

The compounding of numerals follows these rules:

a. Spelled-out compound numerals below 100 should be hyphenated: *twenty-five, eighty-one.*

b. When it is necessary to spell out numerals over 100, no hyphen should appear in the hundreds and thousands.

One hundred twenty-five tons were shipped last June.
Nineteen hundred and fifty-eight (the style used in invitations).
One thousand nine hundred and fifty-eight (the style used in legal documents).

c. When a fraction is spelled in words, the numerator and denominator should be separated by a hyphen – as, *seven-eighths* – unless the numerator or the denominator already contains a hyphen.

thirty-two fifty-sixths	two thirty-seconds

It is better and clearer to use figures for such awkward fractions.

$^{32}/_{56}$ ths	$^{2}/_{32}$ ds

Civil, military, and naval titles are not hyphenated.

Attorney General	Brigadier General
Chief Justice	Lieutenant Commander
Under Secretary	Rear Admiral

But, if a title represents two offices, it is hyphenated: Secretary-Treasurer.

Transcription Speed Builder

442.

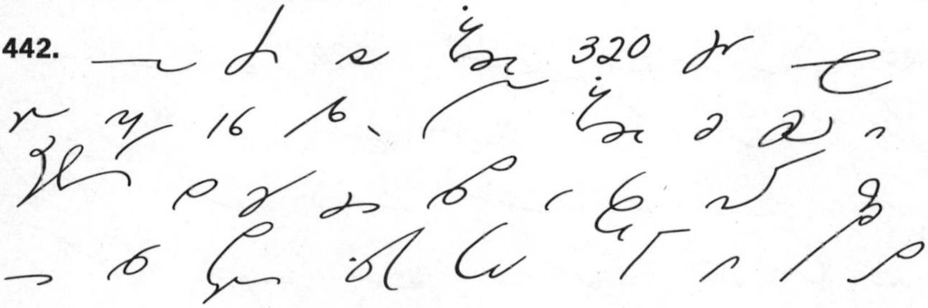

(203)

443.

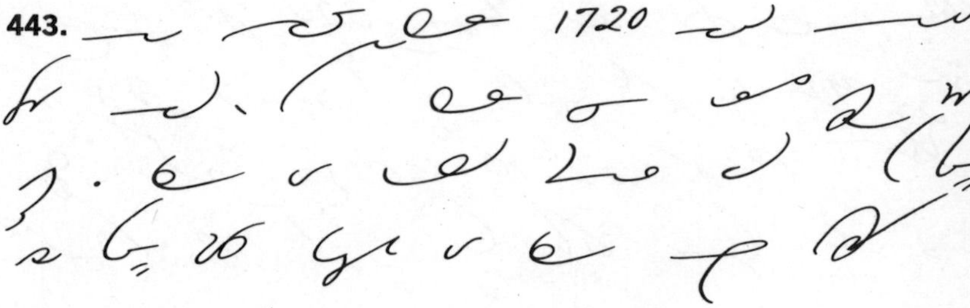

(167)

444.

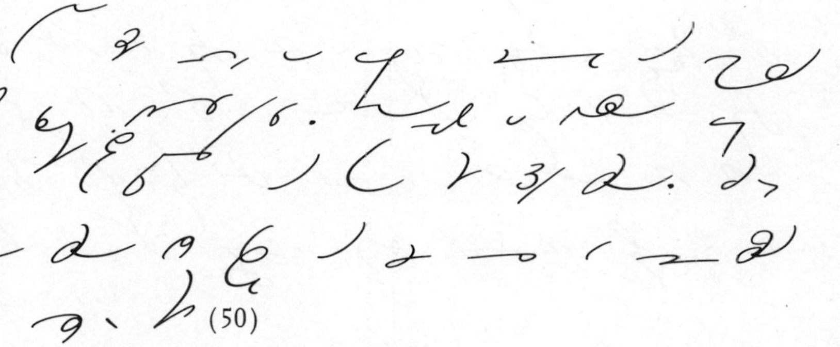

(50)

445.

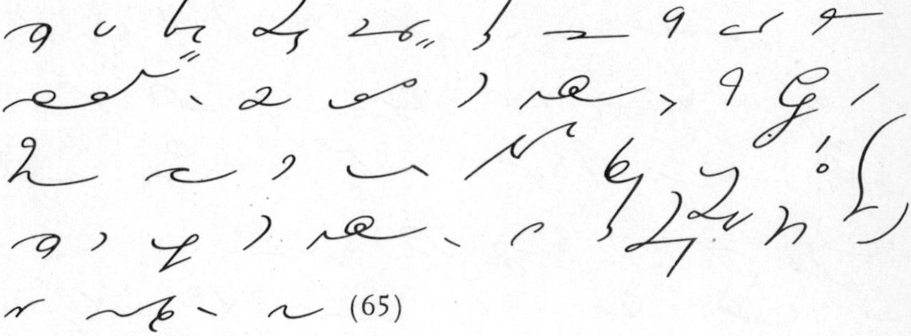

(65)

446.

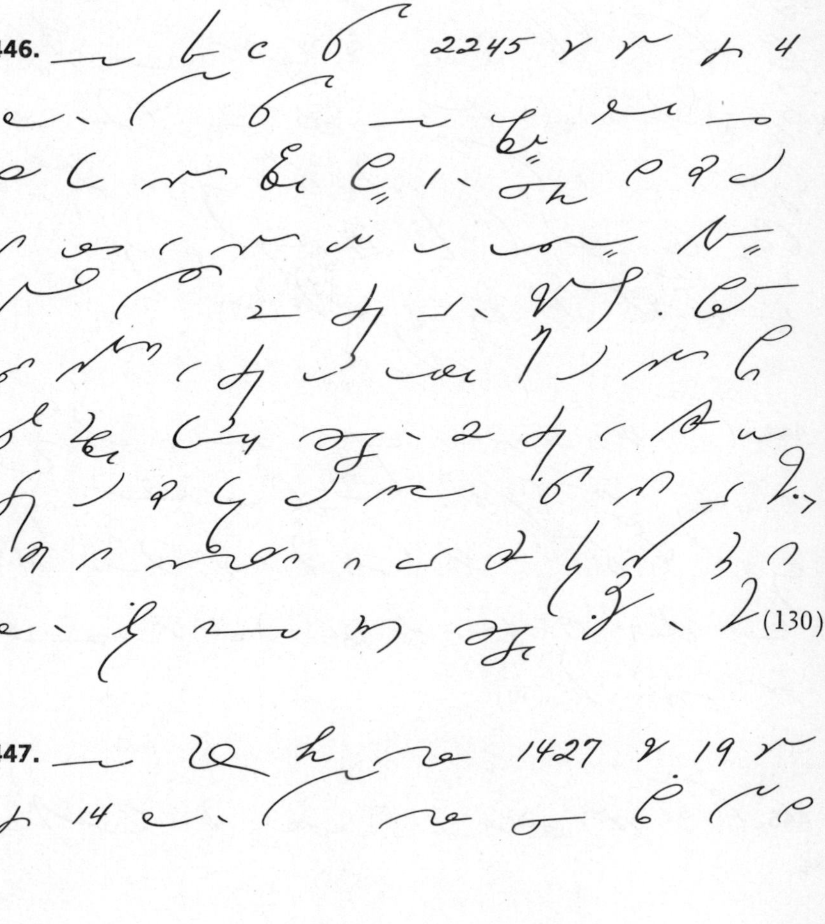

(130)

447.

(146)

448.

(105)

Lesson 57

MASTERING SHORTHAND THEORY

Rd and Ld

Rd

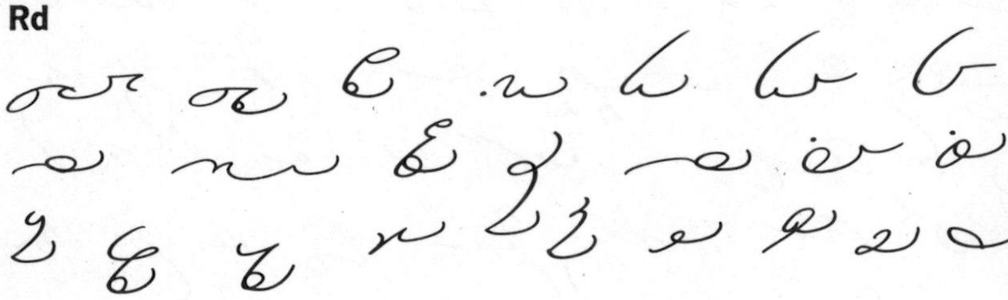

Ld

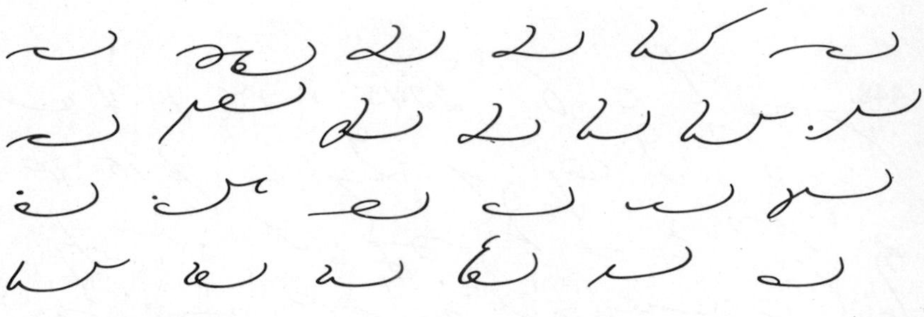

KEY

Accordance, answered, appeared, award, board, border, burden.
Card, colored, expired, favored, guard, harder, hired.
Offered, prepared, repaired, stored, suffered, third, tired, word, yard.
Called, canceled, failed, field, folded, gold.
Cold, drilled, filed, filled, fold, folder, handled.
Held, holders, mailed, old, rolled, settled.
Shoulder, soiled, sold, spoiled, told, yield.

Reading and Writing Practice

449. 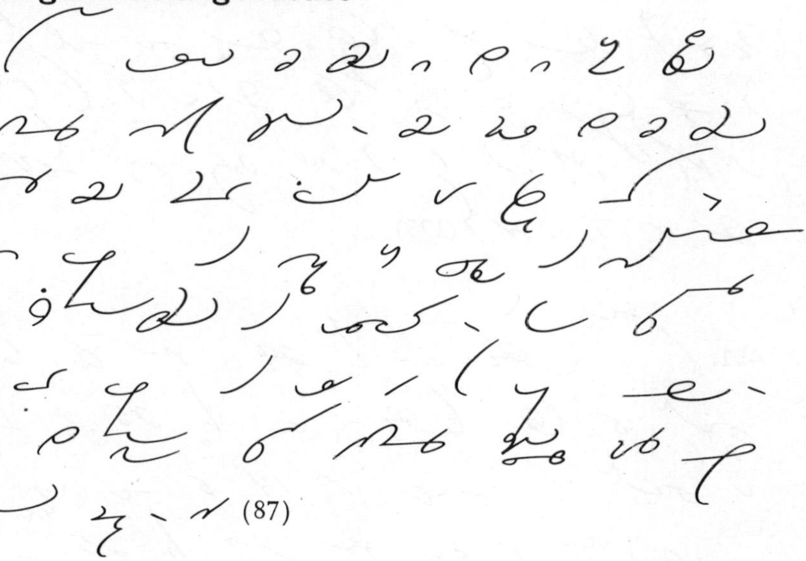

(87)

450. 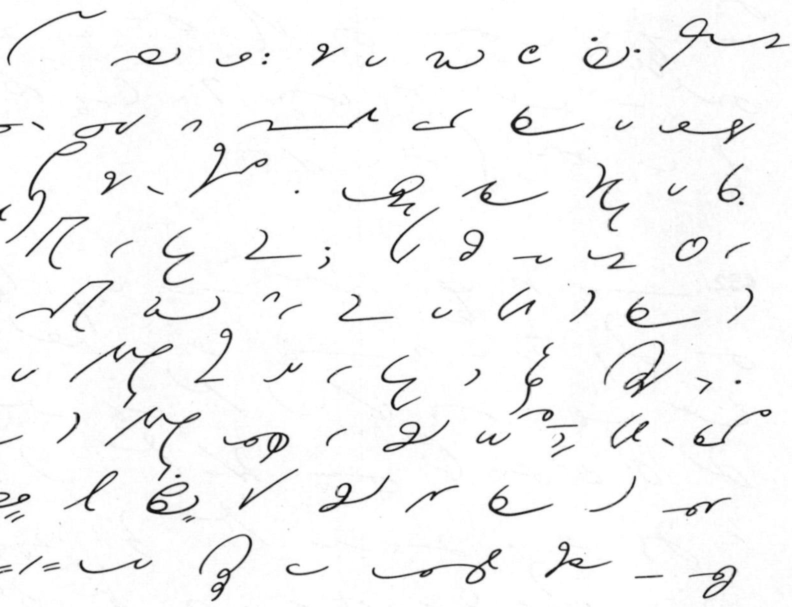

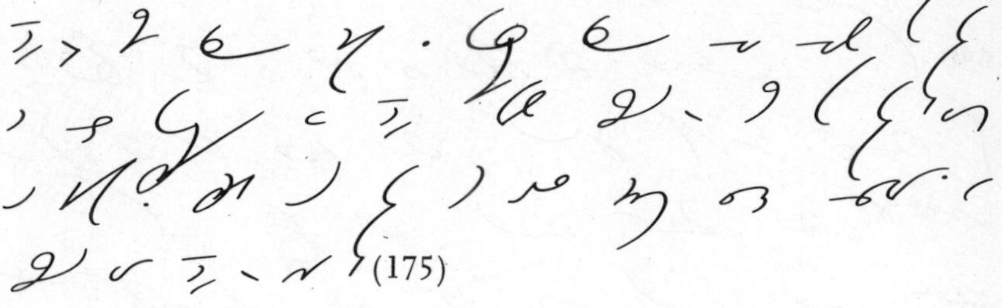

(175)

451.

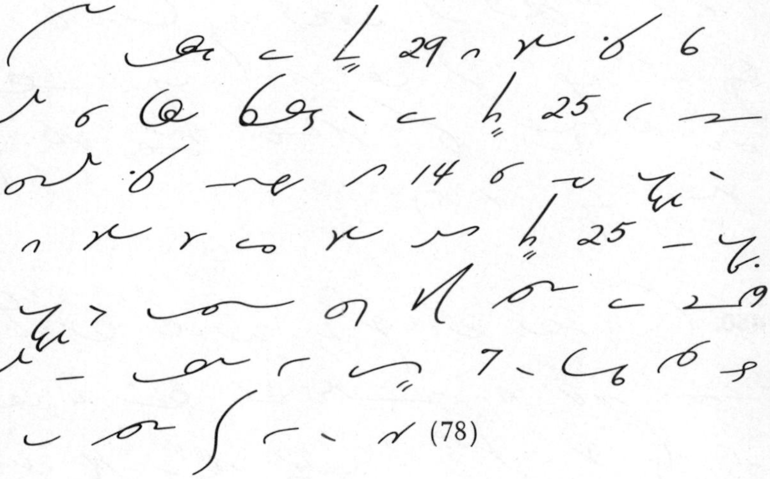

(78)

452.

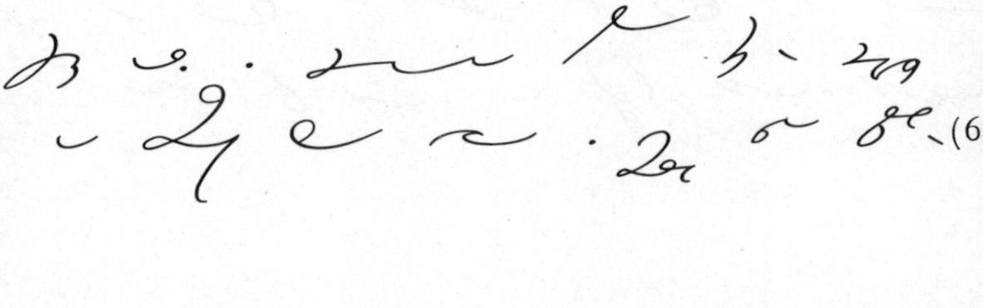

(68)

453. 

454. 

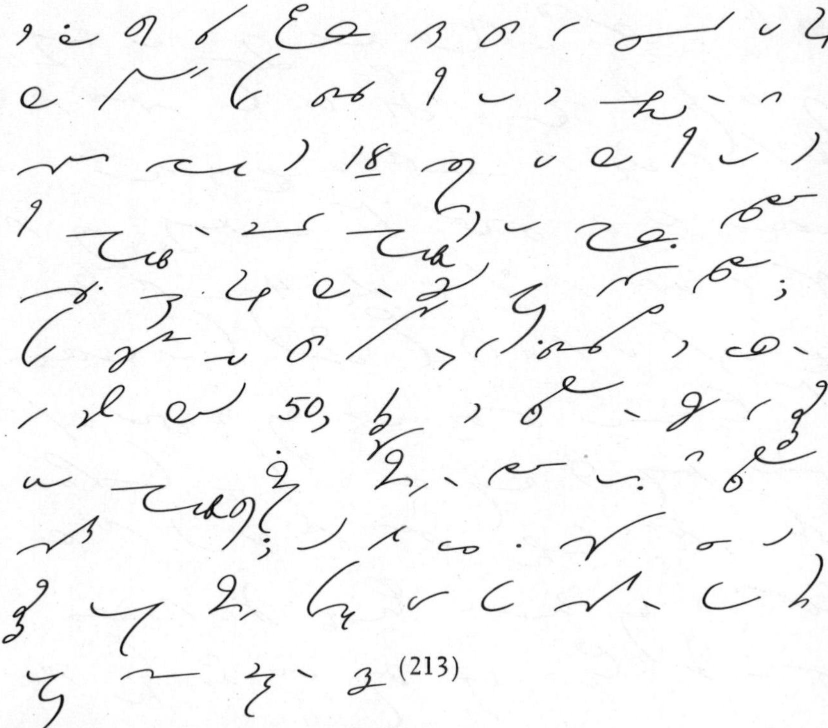

(213)

Building Speed Through Reading

455. HINTS FOR SUCCESS

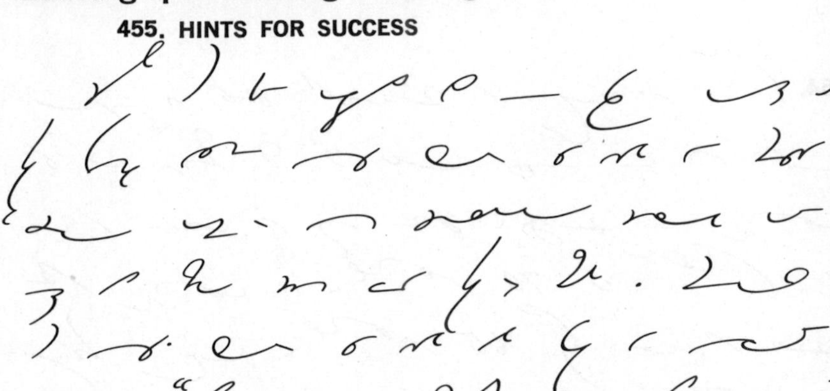

(255)

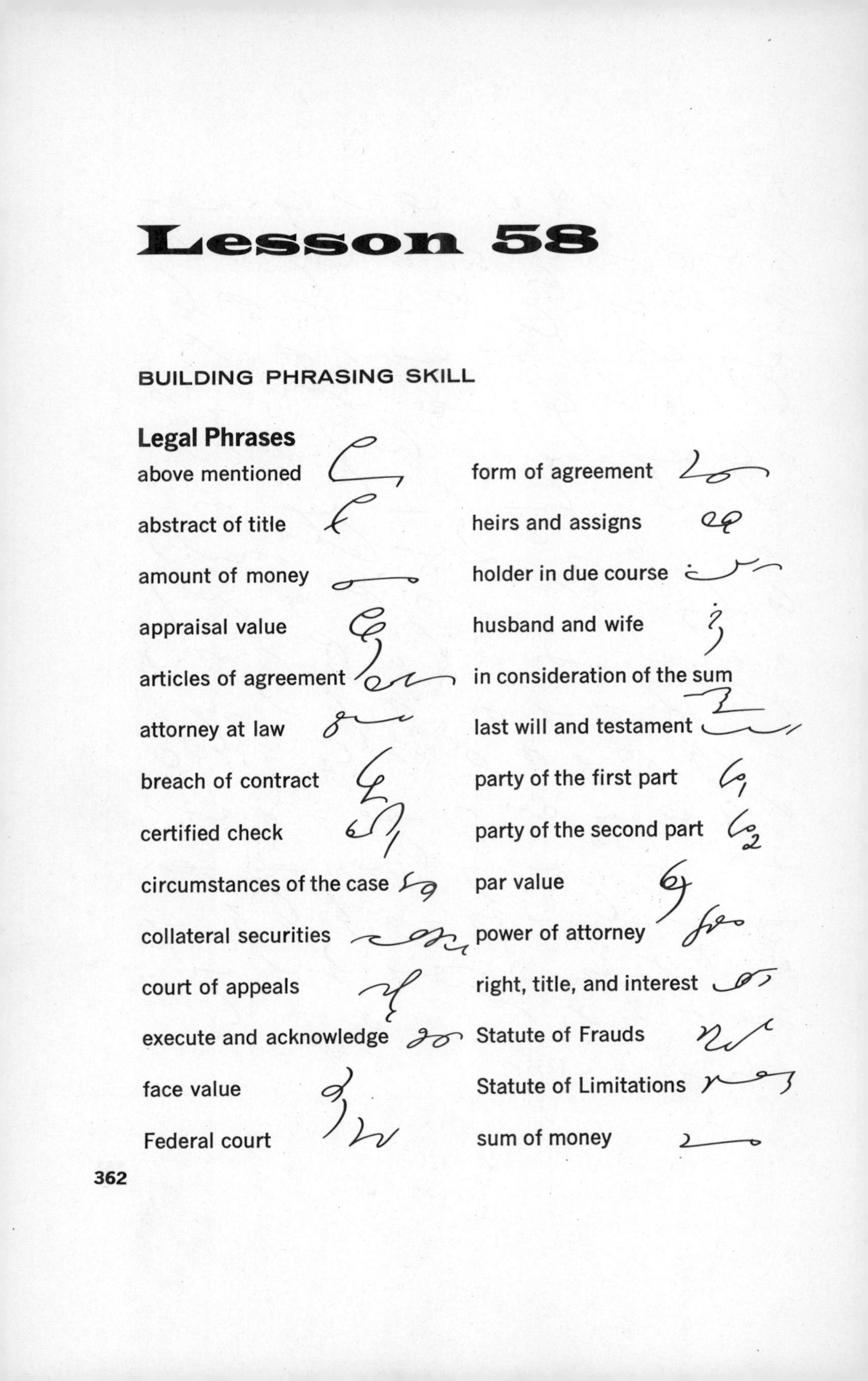

Lesson 58

BUILDING PHRASING SKILL

Legal Phrases

above mentioned
abstract of title
amount of money
appraisal value
articles of agreement
attorney at law
breach of contract
certified check
circumstances of the case
collateral securities
court of appeals
execute and acknowledge
face value
Federal court
form of agreement
heirs and assigns
holder in due course
husband and wife
in consideration of the sum
last will and testament
party of the first part
party of the second part
par value
power of attorney
right, title, and interest
Statute of Frauds
Statute of Limitations
sum of money

Brief-Form and Phrase Letters

456.

457.

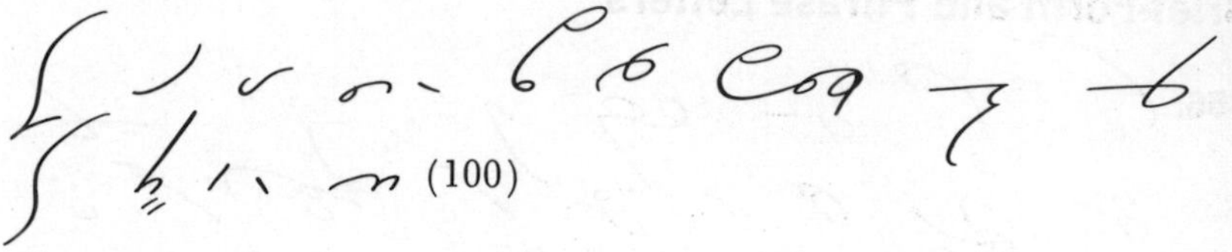

458. 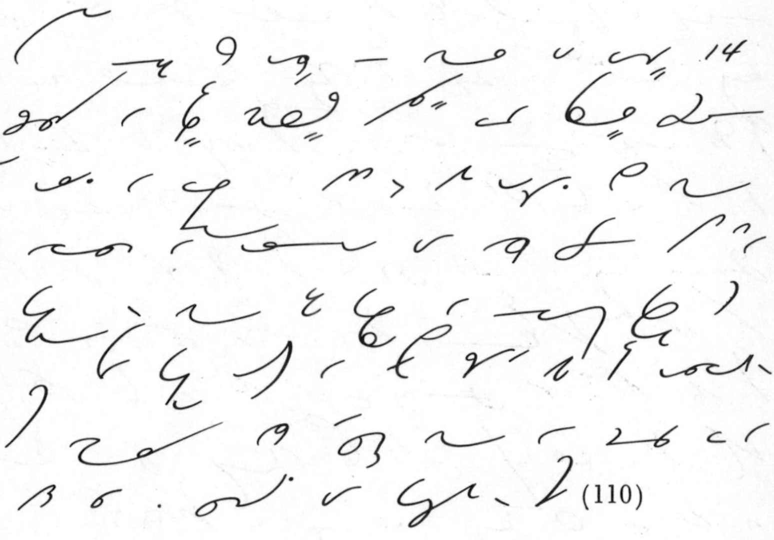

459. 

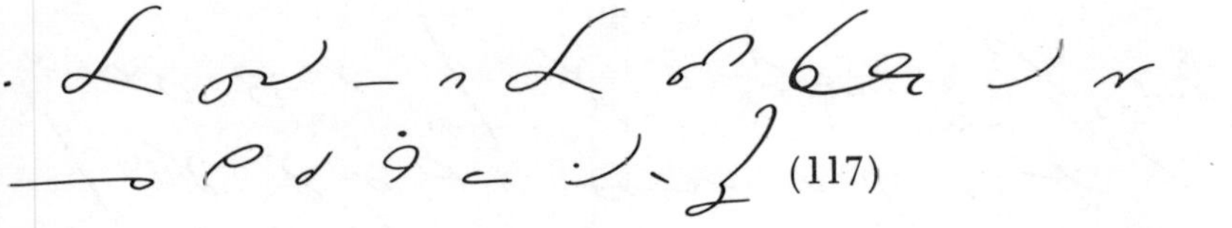

(117)

460.

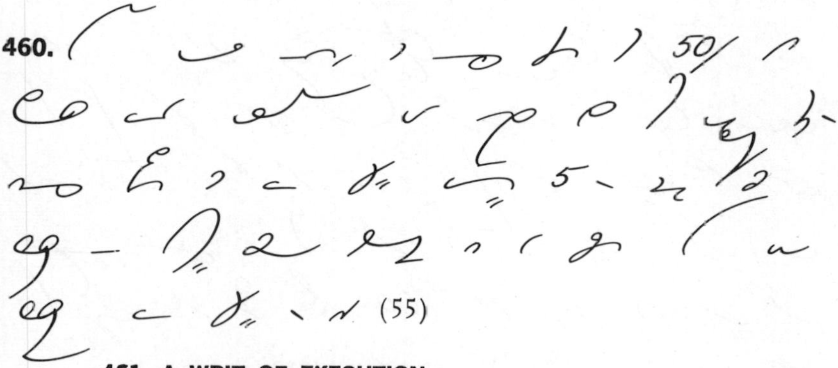

(55)

461. A WRIT OF EXECUTION

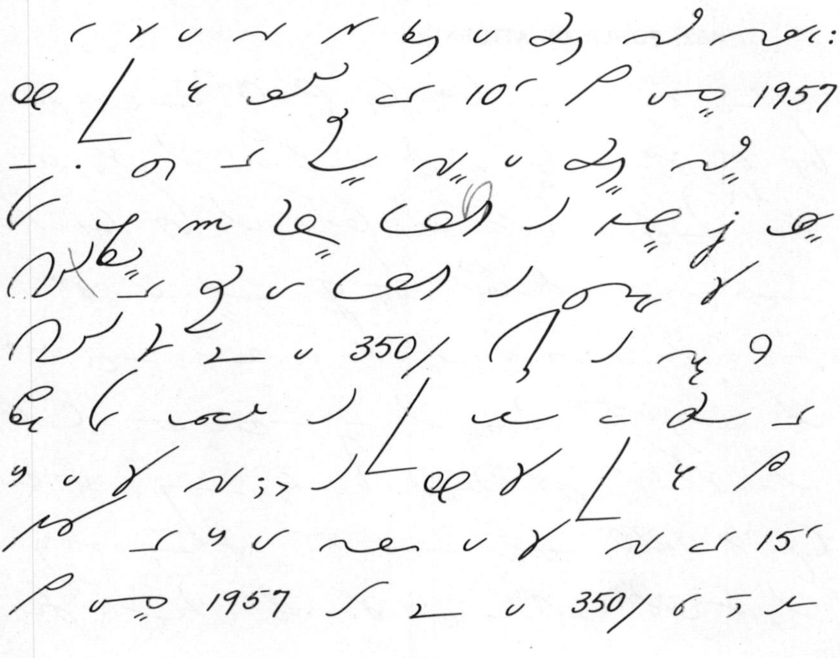

(232)

462. POWER OF ATTORNEY

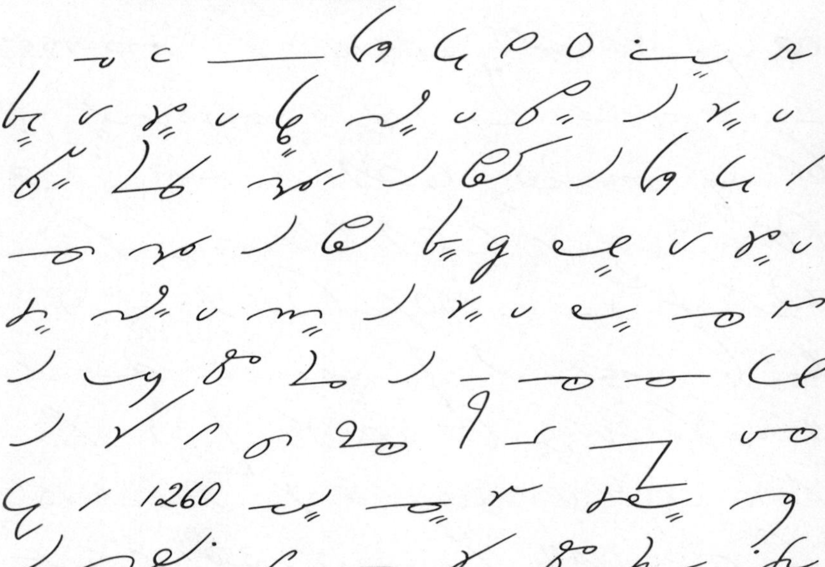

(205)

463. PROXY

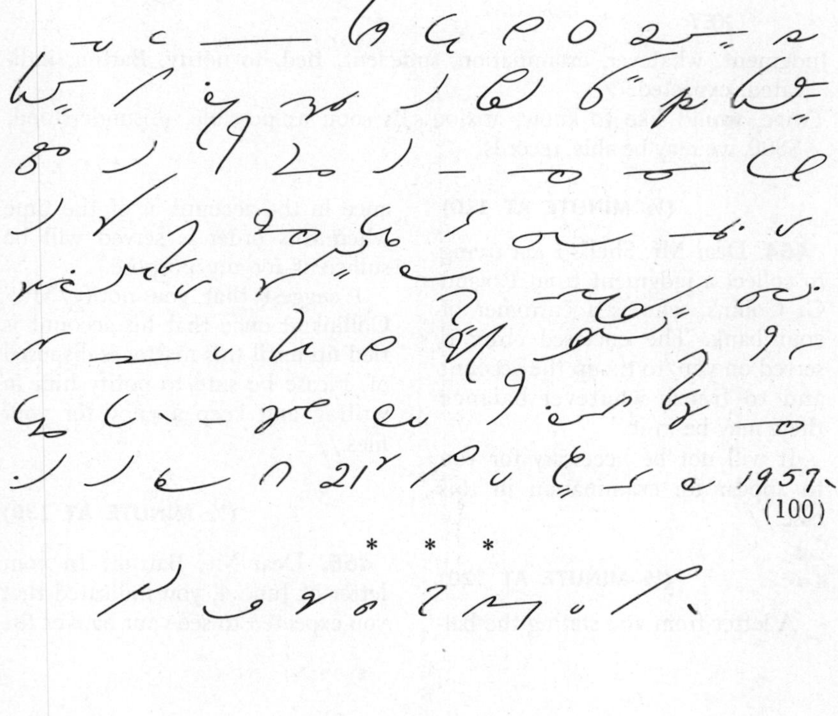

(100)

* * *

Lesson 59

PROGRESSIVE SPEED BUILDING

Half-Minute Progressive Speed Builder (110-140)

VOCABULARY PREVIEW

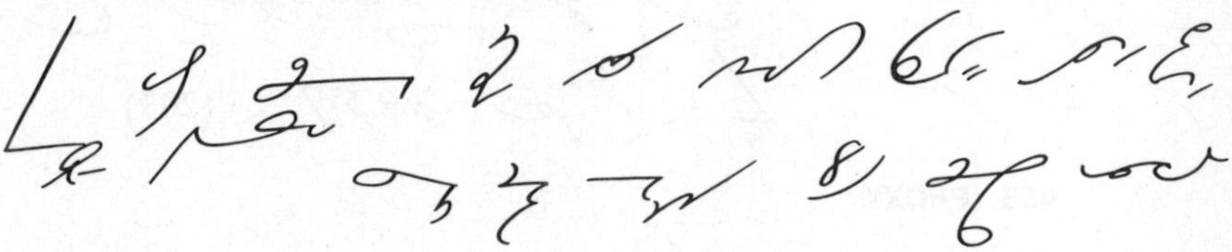

KEY

Judgment, whatever, examination, sufficient, tied, to notify, Barton, indicated, expected.

Twice, would like to know, anxious, as soon as possible, misunderstood, $800, we may be able, records.

(½ MINUTE AT 110)

464. Dear Mr. Shell: I am trying to collect a judgment from Roland C. Collins, who is a customer of your bank. The enclosed order is served on you/to tie up the account and to freeze whatever balance there may be in it.

It will not be necessary for you to appear for examination in this case.//

(½ MINUTE AT 120)

A letter from you stating the balance in the account as of the time when this order is served will be sufficient for my purpose.

I suggest that you notify Mr./ Collins at once that his account is tied up until this matter is disposed of. Please be sure to notify him in writing and keep a copy for your files.//

(½ MINUTE AT 130)

465. Dear Mr. Barton: In your letter of June 4, you indicated that you expected to see your banker the following day and then write to me.

Mr. Miller has called at my/ office twice since then and would like to know whether any progress is being made toward a settlement. He is anxious to get the matter closed as soon as possible. Very truly yours,//

(½ MINUTE AT 135)

466. Dear Mr. Sherman: Since receiving your letter of January 14, we have had a further talk with Robert Powers.

From what he tells us, it would appear that you must have misunderstood/his letter to you. He states that, on your paying to the First National Bank the $800 covering his payment to you last summer, he is ready to pay the balance. Yours truly,//

(½ MINUTE AT 140)

467. Mr. Bates: There is a good chance that we may be able to settle your claim against the express company without going to court. If we can do this, it will save a great deal of time and expense./

I suggest, therefore, that you come into the office on Monday or Tuesday, bringing with you all the records, correspondence, and other material relating to the case. Very truly yours,//

Minute Progressive Speed Builder (100-120)

VOCABULARY PREVIEW

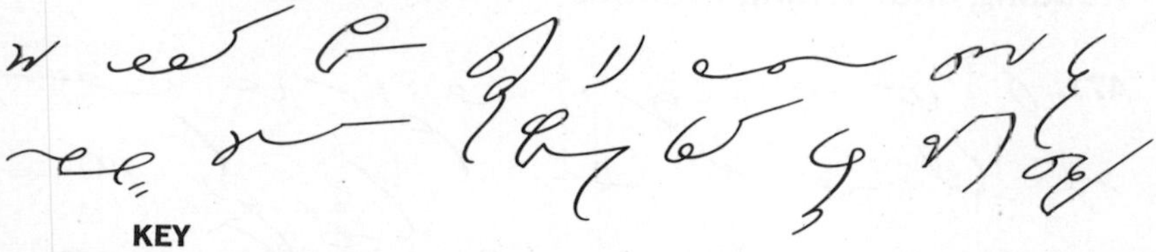

KEY

Suit, rerented, apartment, advisable, $100, illegal, out-of-court, possible. Christmas, settlement, I hope it will be, pointed, previous, he should not have, accepted.

(1 MINUTE AT 100)

468. Dear Mr. Fagan: Regarding your claim against Richard T. Brown, which you presented in your letter of December 10, it would seem that you/do have cause for suit if Mr. Brown forced you to pay rent until January 1 and then rerented the apartment before that time.

As//the amount of your claim is only $125, it might be advisable for you to sue for $100 in///the small-claims court. If I handle the case for you, my fee would be $30. Let me know whether you still wish me to bring suit. Yours very truly, (1)

(1 MINUTE AT 110)

469. Dear Mr. Fagan: I shall begin work immediately on your suit against Richard T. Brown for $125 for illegal collection of/rent.

I shall try to get an out-of-court settlement, but it is possible that Mr. Brown will insist on going to court. If he does, we will prepare the//case and schedule it for hearing in a couple of weeks if possible.

No, it will not be necessary for you to appear in court. Go ahead and///take your Christmas vacation. If I need further information, I shall get in touch with Mr. Johnson, as you suggested. Have a happy Christmas. Yours very truly, (2)

(1 MINUTE AT 120)

470. Dear Mr. Fagan: I have made a settlement of your rent claim against Mr. Richard T. Brown, and I hope it will be to your satisfaction. I called on Mr. Brown to/see whether an out-of-court settlement could be made.

He pointed out that, when you moved into the apartment, he allowed you a week's free rent because you were still paying//rent at your previous place. In view of this consideration, he felt that he should not have to pay the $125. He agreed to pay///$100, and I accepted.

I am charging you only $10 for my services, as there was no court action. My check for $90 is enclosed. Yours truly, (3)

Reading and Writing Practice

471.

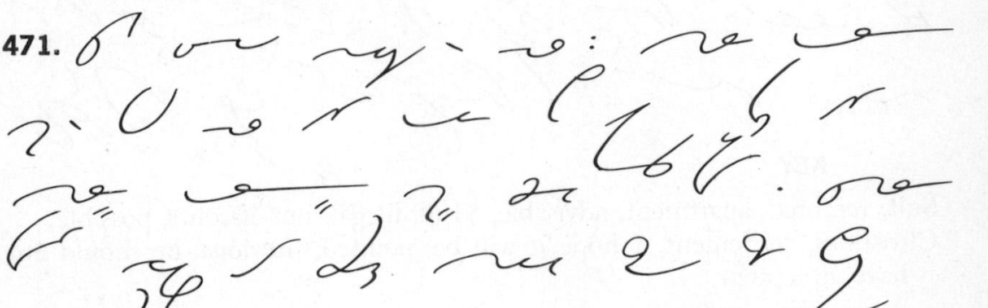

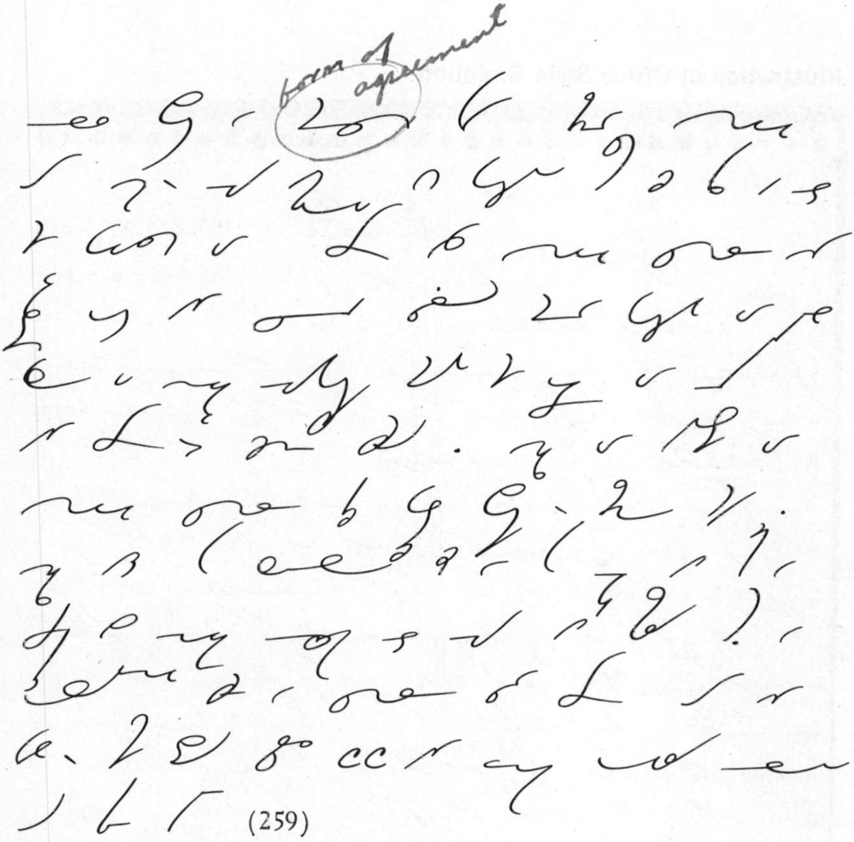

(259)

472. 

(73)

Illustration of Office Style Dictation

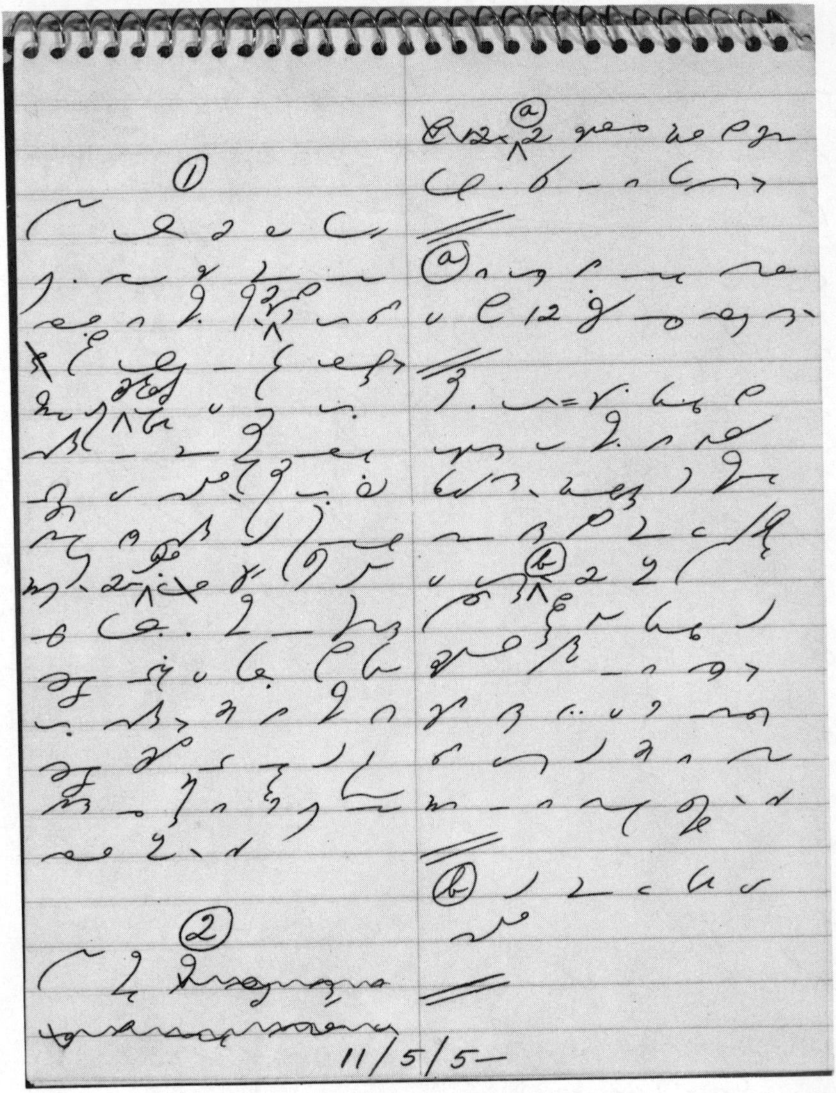

This page of notes shows one way of indicating changes in dictation. If time permits, some stenographers prefer to indicate changes with a red pencil.

473.

(97)

474.

(107)

475.

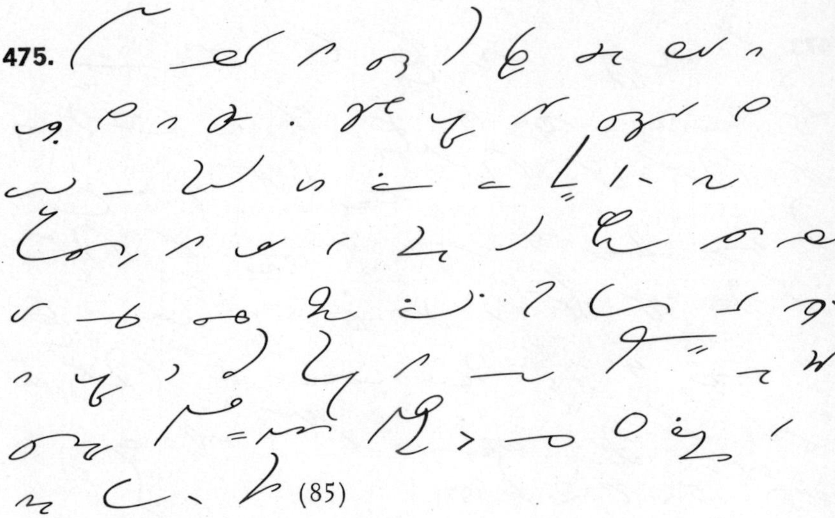

(85)

476.

(122)

Lesson 60

BUILDING SUSTAINED SPEED

Five-Minute Speed Builder

The first three letters are between Mrs. Ernest P. Chapman, 1712 Sheridan Drive, Charlotte 6, North Carolina, and Charles Carter, Assistant Trust Officer, Citizens National Bank, Charlotte 1, North Carolina. The last two are written by George T. Holden, 239 West College Avenue, to Frank E. Hardy, Esq., Register of Probate, Danbury Probate Court, and to George Coleman, Esq., 1512 State Street, all of Danbury, Connecticut.

VOCABULARY PREVIEW

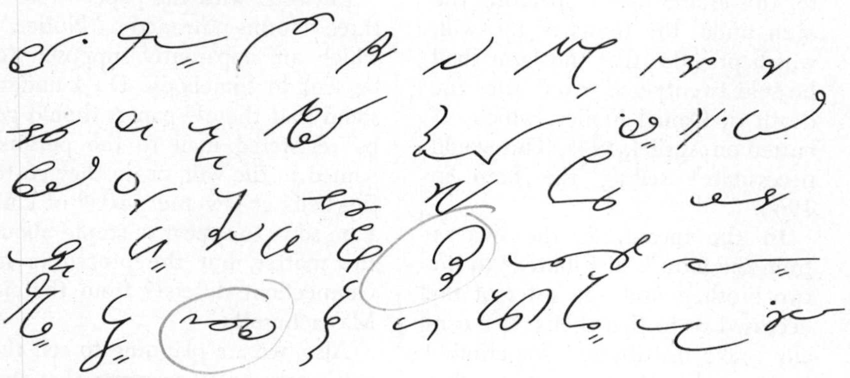

KEY

Ascertaining, Daniel, to make, deceased, it is not, distributed, trustee, estate.
Necessitate, heirs, response, disappointed, for so long a time, Hardy, forwarding, promptly.
Apparently, I understand, registered, next of kin, stupid, about the matter, real estate.

License, Petition, parties, expiration, devisees, legatees, Coleman. Danbury, Probate, unanswered, specifies, auction, operative, Albany, will you please, whether or not.

477. Dear Mr. Carter: I am interested in ascertaining the status of the Daniel Frailey farm. If the[1] farm is available for sale, I should like to make arrangements to purchase it. Your records will show that I am[2] a cousin of the deceased.

It is not clear in my mind just how the farm is being operated at present,[3] but I assume that the income is being distributed among my cousin's brothers and his sisters. Is[4] this correct? Yours truly,

478. Dear Mrs. Chapman: We have your letter of October 27, asking for[5] information regarding the Daniel Frailey farm. The First National Bank of Charlotte is trustee for this estate[6] and is operating the farm under the terms of the will, which provides that the farm shall be sold twenty-one years[7] after the death of Daniel Frailey, which occurred on April 4, 1945. This would necessitate[8] selling the farm in 1966.

In the meantime, the income from the farm is distributed[9] to the two brothers and one sister of the deceased or to their heirs. We usually make distribution sometime[10] in December. You may know that Frailey Fruits are grown on this farm.

We do not have the latest addresses of[11] the two brothers and shall appreciate it if you will supply these to us, so that our records will be complete.[12] Very truly yours,

479. Dear Mr. Carter: Thank you very much for your immediate response to my inquiry[13] and for the information contained in your letter. I am naturally very much disappointed to find[14] that the farm cannot be sold for so long a time, but I realize that there is nothing I can do to change the terms[15] of the will.

I am enclosing the addresses of the two brothers. Sincerely yours,

480. Dear Mr. Hardy: Re: Estate[16] Alice C. Boardman. Thank you for forwarding the papers in this case so promptly.

Enclosed with the papers were[17] three forms headed "Notice," which are apparently supposed to be sent to somebody. Do I understand that these[18] papers should go by registered mail to the persons named in the will, or do they go to the heirs at law and next[19] of kin? I am sorry to appear so stupid about the matter, but the procedure in Connecticut differs[20] from that in Massachusetts.

Also, we are planning to sell the real estate, and I presume that this will be[21] by license. Will you send me a Petition for License to Sell as well as the necessary forms to notify[22] the parties in interest. These parties, I presume, in case of sale before the expiration of a year,[23] would be all heirs or next of kin, rather than the devisees or legatees under the will. Sincerely yours,

481. Dear[24] Mr. Coleman: In talking with Mr. Hardy at Danbury Probate Court, I learned that you have been away on[25] vacation. This probably accounts for my unanswered letter of July 22.

Since I wrote the letter,[26] I have obtained the license to sell real estate and am enclosing it. I notice the license specifies sale[27] at public auction, but I assume that the license is also operative for private sale.

Title is to[28] be taken in the name of Ruth Lord, whose residence is Albany, New York. I should like to arrange to complete[29] the sale sometime before August 15.

Will you please let me know whether or not you will be able to handle[30] this for me. I can arrange to meet you sometime before the fifteenth. Yours very truly, (616)

Reading and Writing Practice

482.

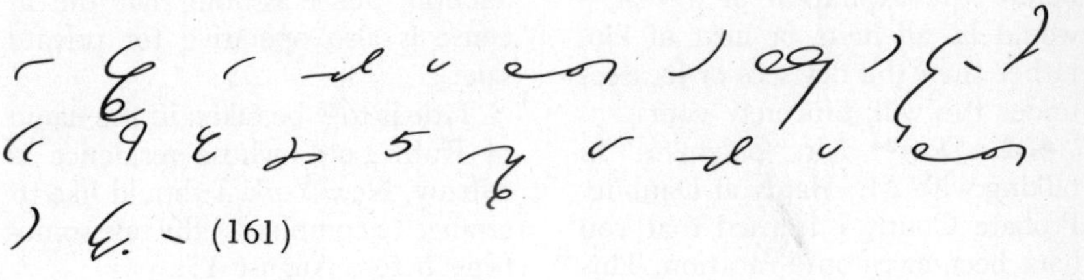

(161)

483.

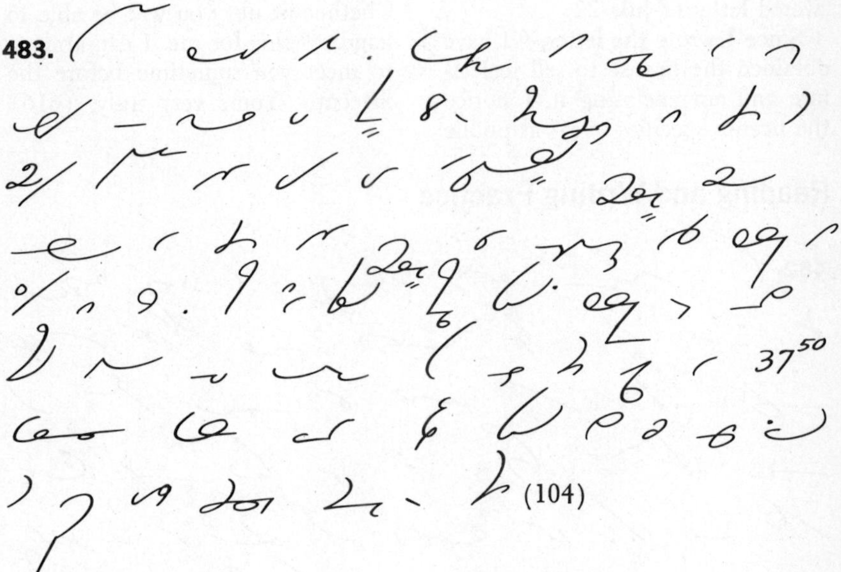

37^{50}

(104)

484.

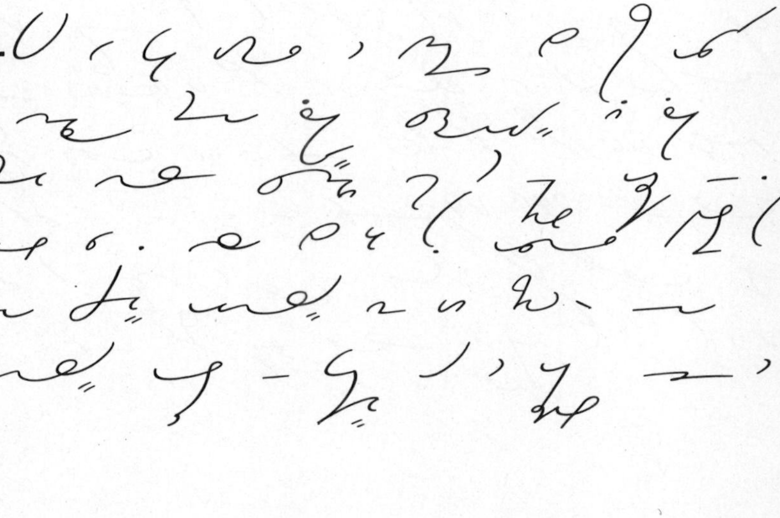

47280 ... 17 ... 5 ... (119)

485. ... 22 ... (136)

486. ...

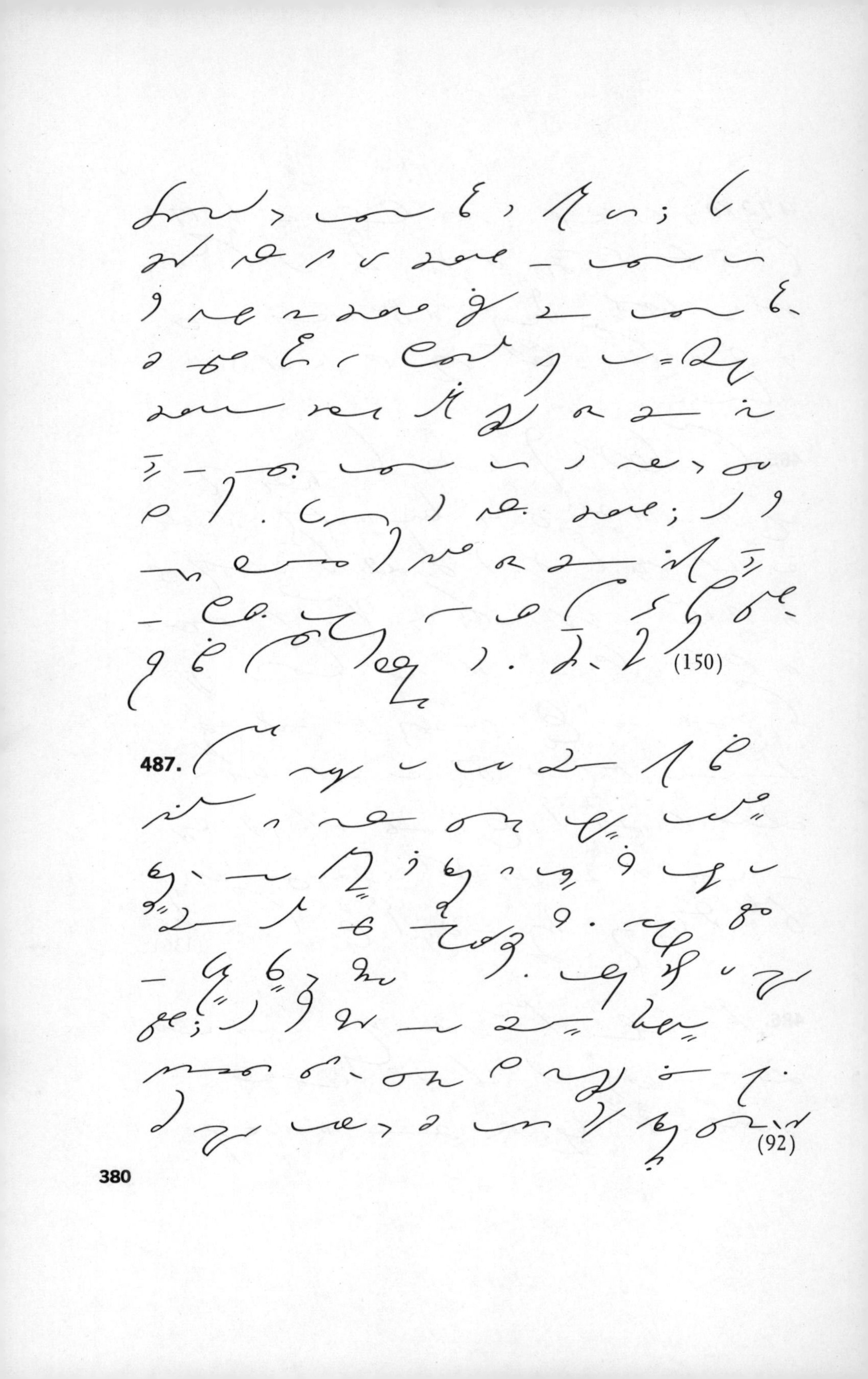

(150)

487.

(92)

13

Petroleum

Word Study for Chapter 13

PETROLEUM

Acetone. An inflammable liquid used in making chloroform and as a solvent for fats, camphor, and resins.

Acetylene. The most brilliant of the illuminating gases.

Acidizing. A process used in treating oil-producing zones. Acid is injected opposite the formation to be acidized. Pressure is applied, which forces the acid into the formation, where it eats out passages through which the oil will travel into the well.

Adsorption. The adhesion, in a thin layer, of gases or dissolved substances to a solid surface.

Anticline. A dome caused by upfolding of rock strata. Oil and gas are trapped in porous structures on the tops of these domes.

Barrel-miles. A measure of pipeline traffic for carrying a definite quantity of oil a certain distance; number of barrels of oil times number of miles shipped.

Benzene. A colorless, volatile, inflammable liquid used as a solvent.

Carbon Monoxide. A colorless, odorless, very poisonous gas resulting from the incomplete combustion of carbon when burned with an insufficient supply of air or oxygen.

Cleavage. A tendency of some rocks, because of their composition, to split in one direction.

Combustion. The process of burning; the chemical process of combining oxygen with a fuel to obtain heat and sometimes light.

Cracking. The process by which the complex hydrocarbons of petroleum and similar oils are broken up into lighter hydrocarbons suitable for producing commercial gasoline.

Crude Oil. Oil in its natural state.

Dew Point. The temperature at which moist air begins to condense or form deposits of liquid.

Distillation. The process of separating a volatile fluid or fluids from a heavier fluid by evaporation and condensation.

Ethylene. A colorless gaseous compound contained in illuminating gas.

Flash Point. The temperature to which an oil must be raised to produce enough vapor from a momentary flash when the vapor is ignited under certain standard conditions.

Flow Tank. The tank to which oil is piped from a well and where it is freed from gas and water before it is put into the stock tank.

Geophysics. The science treating of the agencies that modify the earth; especially, the causes of the movements and warpings of the solid part of the earth.

Gusher. An oil well with a large natural flow of oil.

Helium. An inert, colorless gas found in the air and in certain natural gases.

Iso. A prefix denoting similarity; as *isomers.*

Kelly. A square, hollow steel shaft screwed to the drill pipe in a rotary-drilling apparatus. The kelly fits through a square hole in the rotary table, the driving mechanism that rotates the drill string.

Migration. The underground movement of oil or gas not artificially effected.

Mud. A mixture of clay, water, and special materials used to support the walls and control pressure in a rotary-drilled well.

Naphtha. Any of several volatile inflammable liquids obtained by distilling petroleum; used in dry cleaning, varnish making, and as a fuel.

Nitroglycerin. A colorless, heavy, oily liquid used as an explosive.

Offset Well. A well drilled opposite another well on an adjoining property.

Oil Sand. A term loosely applied to porous sandstone and other formations from which petroleum is obtained.

Permeable. Easily penetrated by water, oil, and other fluids.

Petroleum. In general, an oily, dark-colored, inflammable liquid mixture of highly complex hydrocarbons, occurring naturally and obtained by drilling into earth or rock.

Refinery. A building and apparatus for separating many products from crude petroleum.

Residuum. A by-product obtained on the distillation of crude petroleum after the constituents boiling below 620°F. have been removed.

Rig. The derrick and auxiliary structure necessary before the drilling of a well can be started. The complete equipment of a drilling or a pumping well.

Seismograph. The foremost scientific instrument used for the location of hidden earth structures that may contain oil or natural gas. Originally used to record earthquakes and still so used.

Sluice. A channel or passage for water or other liquids.

Specific Gravity. The ratio of the weight of a substance to that of an equal volume of some standard substance.

Thermal. Relating to heat or heating.

Viscosity. The property of an oil that determines its rate of flow.

Wildcat. An exploratory oil well drilled in an area or structure not known to contain oil.

Lesson 61

BUILDING TRANSCRIPTION SKILL

Transcription English Pointers

HOW TO USE QUOTATION MARKS

1. The *exact* words of a writer or a speaker are enclosed in double quotation marks.

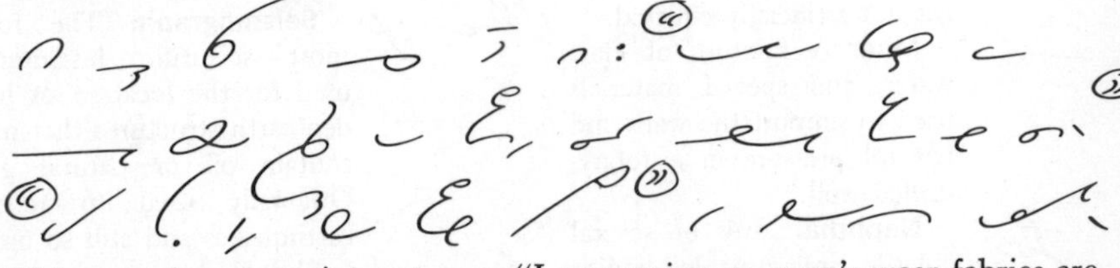

This news item may interest you: "Lower prices on men's wear fabrics are expected when the mills open next week."
"Order being shipped air express today," the telegram reads.

2. When the words of a writer or a speaker are indirectly quoted, they are *not* enclosed in quotation marks. Indirect quotations may usually be recognized by the introductory word *that;* also, by the fact that the person of the noun or pronoun and often the tense of the verb have been changed from their original forms.

Direct: The letter contained one encouraging sentence: "We are considering your proposal."
Indirect: The letter contained the encouraging information *that they were* considering *my* proposal.

Other marks of punctuation in relation to quotation marks are placed as follows:

a. The period and the comma are placed *inside* the closing quotation mark, regardless of the construction of the sentence.

Somewhere in the letter include this comment: "The New York office of the company confirmed the report but would make no statement."
Unfortunately he has gained the reputation of being "high hat."
The teacher dictated the article on "The Genius of American Business," which begins on page 50 of our text.

b. The semicolon and the colon are *always* placed outside the closing quotation mark. The question mark and the exclamation point are placed *inside* the closing punctuation mark if they are an integral part of the quotation; otherwise, they are placed *outside* the closing punctuation mark.

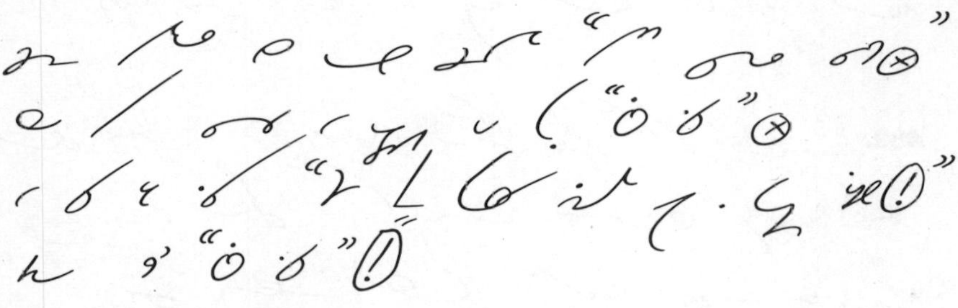

We cannot disregard that last sentence, "Do you agree with us?"
Where did he get the reputation of being "high hat"?
The ad was headed "For the June bride who wants to be a perfect hostess!"
Sure, he's "high hat"!

(*Concluded on page 417*)

Transcription Speed Builder

488.

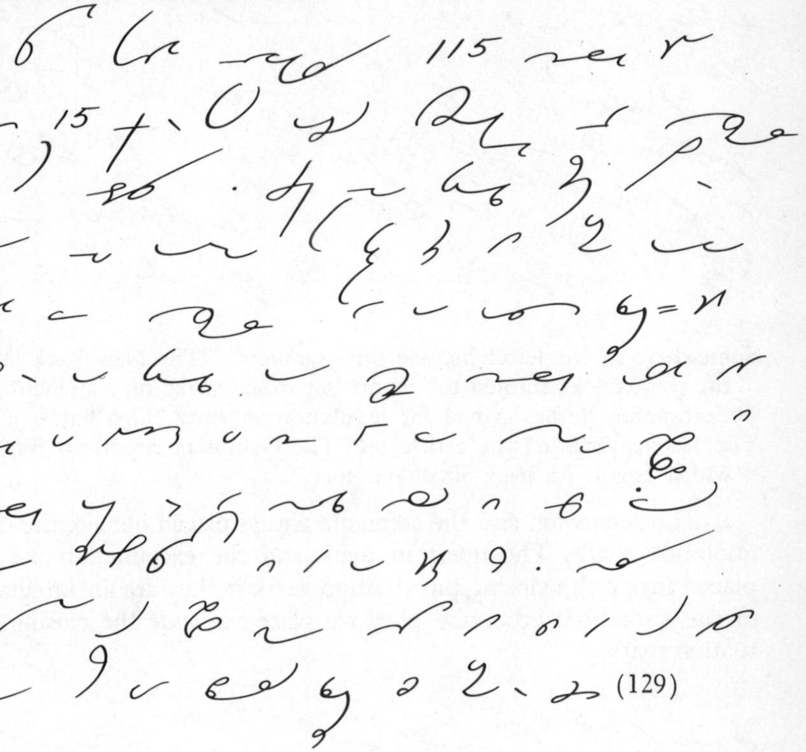

(129)

489.

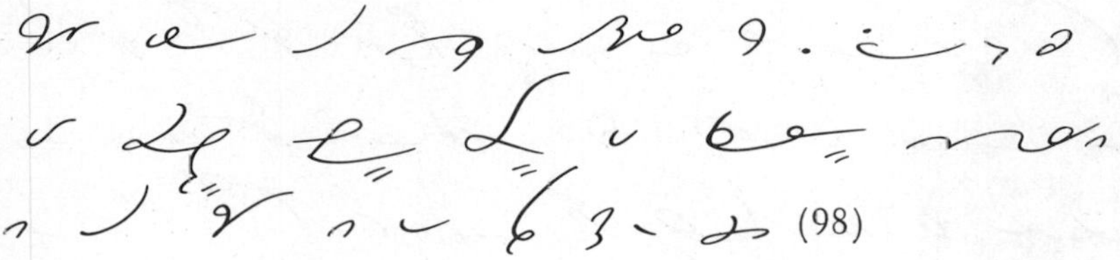
(98)

490.

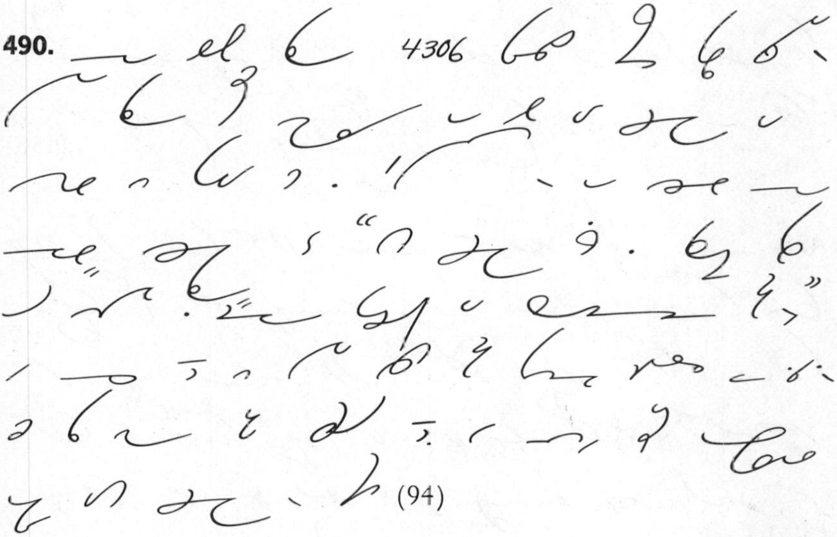
(94)

491.

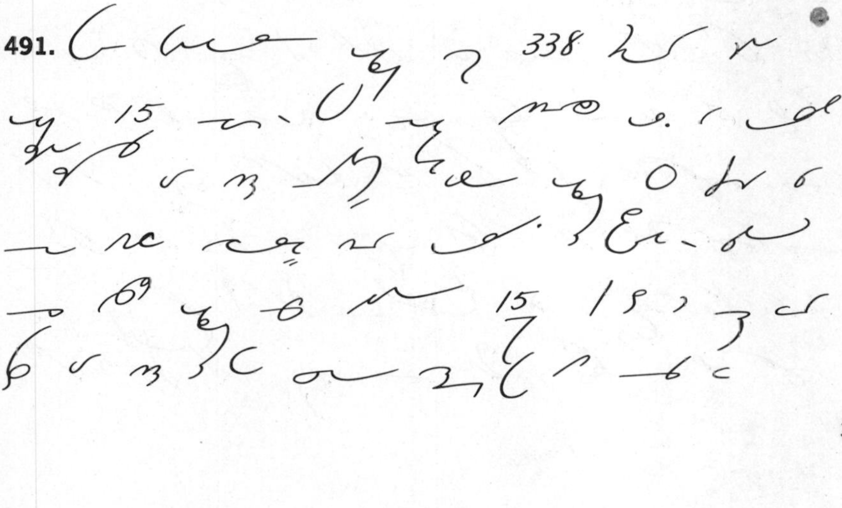

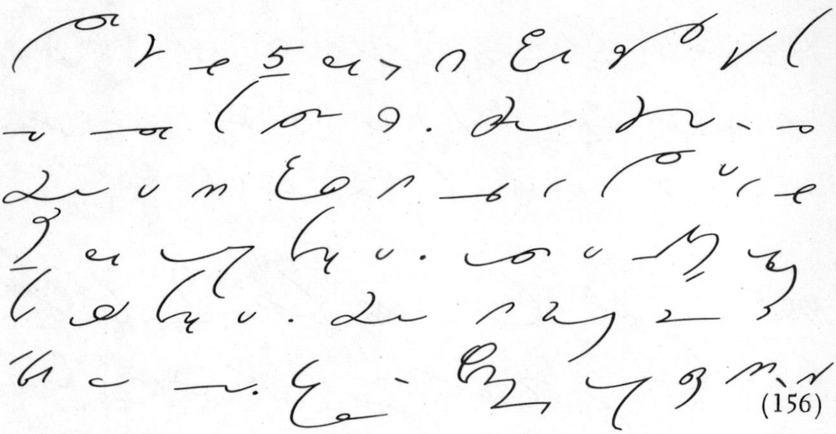

(156)

492.

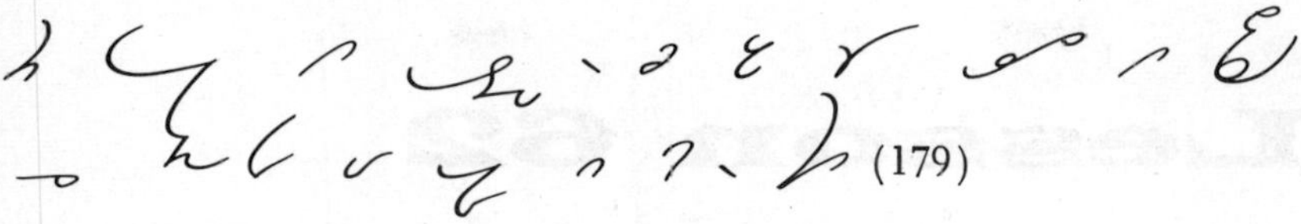

(179)

493.

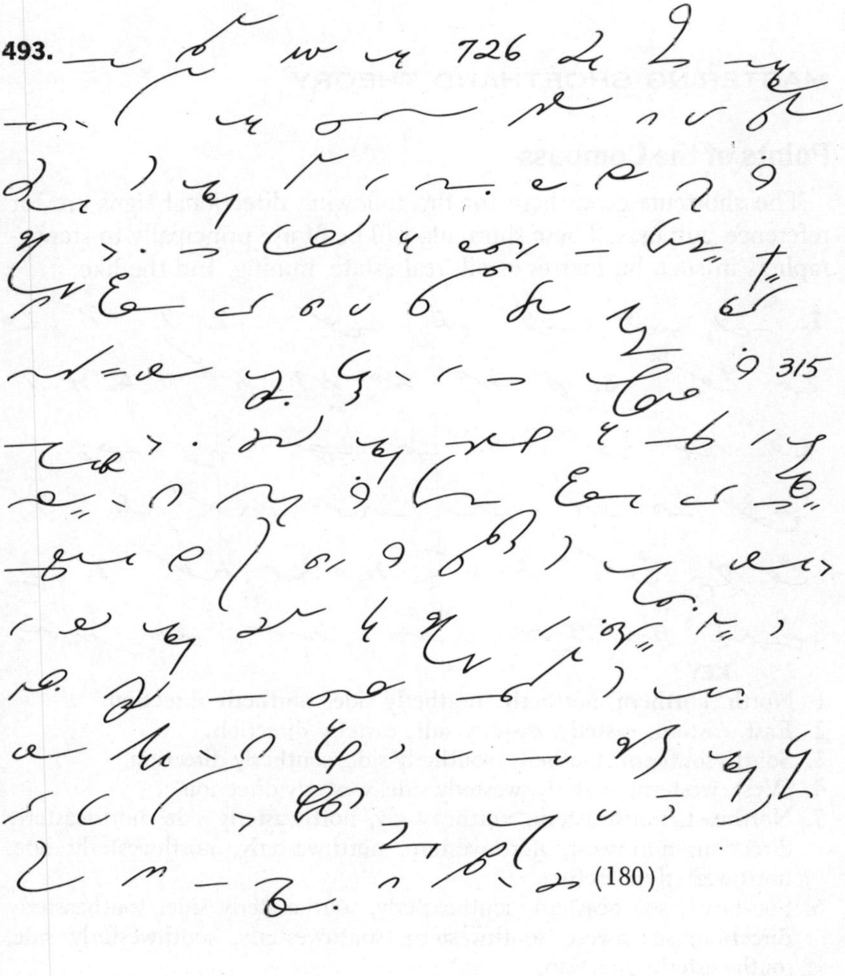

(180)

Lesson 62

MASTERING SHORTHAND THEORY

Points of the Compass

The shortcuts given here for the following directional signs are for reference purposes. These shortcuts will be of use principally to stenographers in such businesses as oil, real estate, mining, and the like.

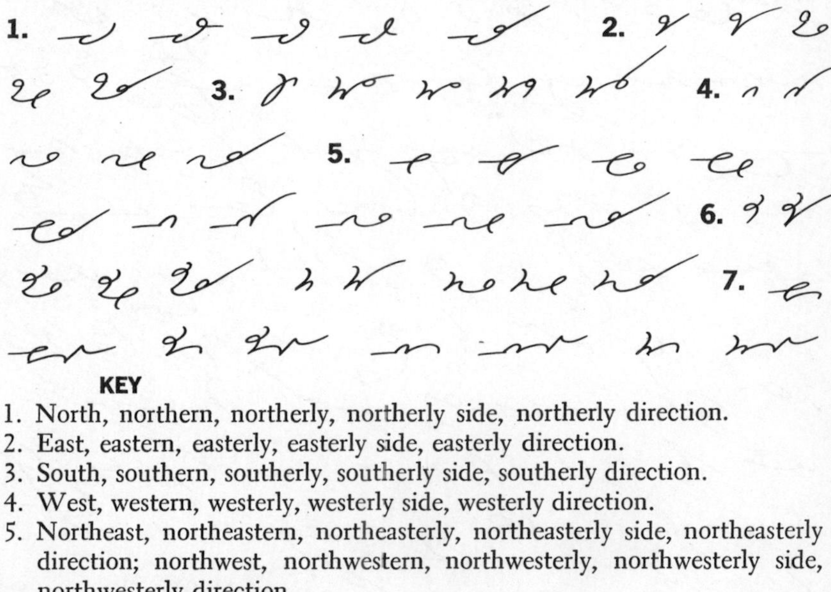

KEY

1. North, northern, northerly, northerly side, northerly direction.
2. East, eastern, easterly, easterly side, easterly direction.
3. South, southern, southerly, southerly side, southerly direction.
4. West, western, westerly, westerly side, westerly direction.
5. Northeast, northeastern, northeasterly, northeasterly side, northeasterly direction; northwest, northwestern, northwesterly, northwesterly side, northwesterly direction.
6. Southeast, southeastern, southeasterly, southeasterly side, southeasterly direction; southwest, southwestern, southwesterly, southwesterly side, southwesterly direction.
7. Northeast corner, northeast quarter, southeast corner, southeast quarter, northwest corner, northwest quarter, southwest corner, southwest quarter.

Reading and Writing Practice

494.

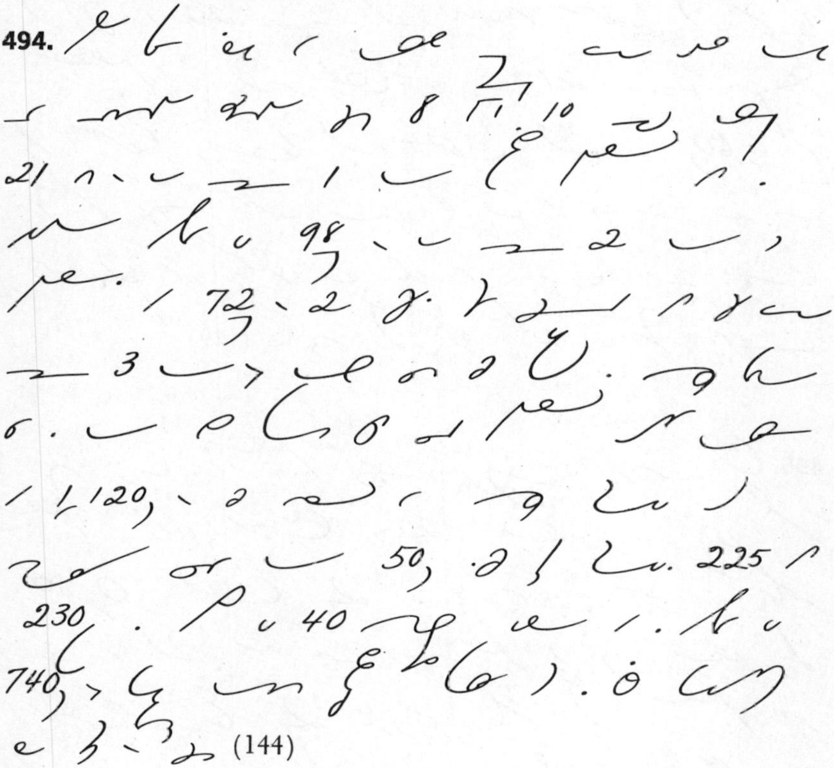

(144)

495.

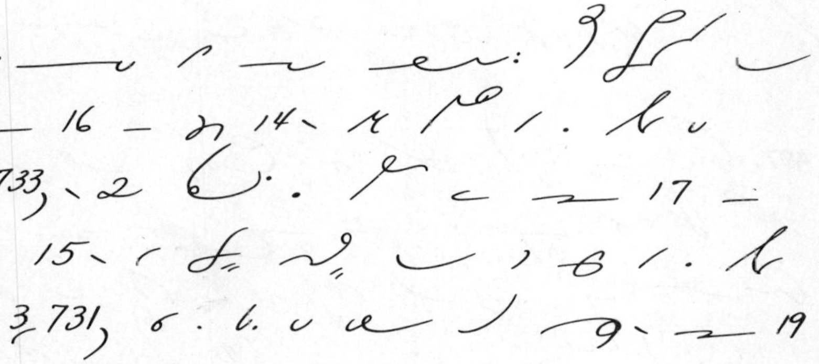

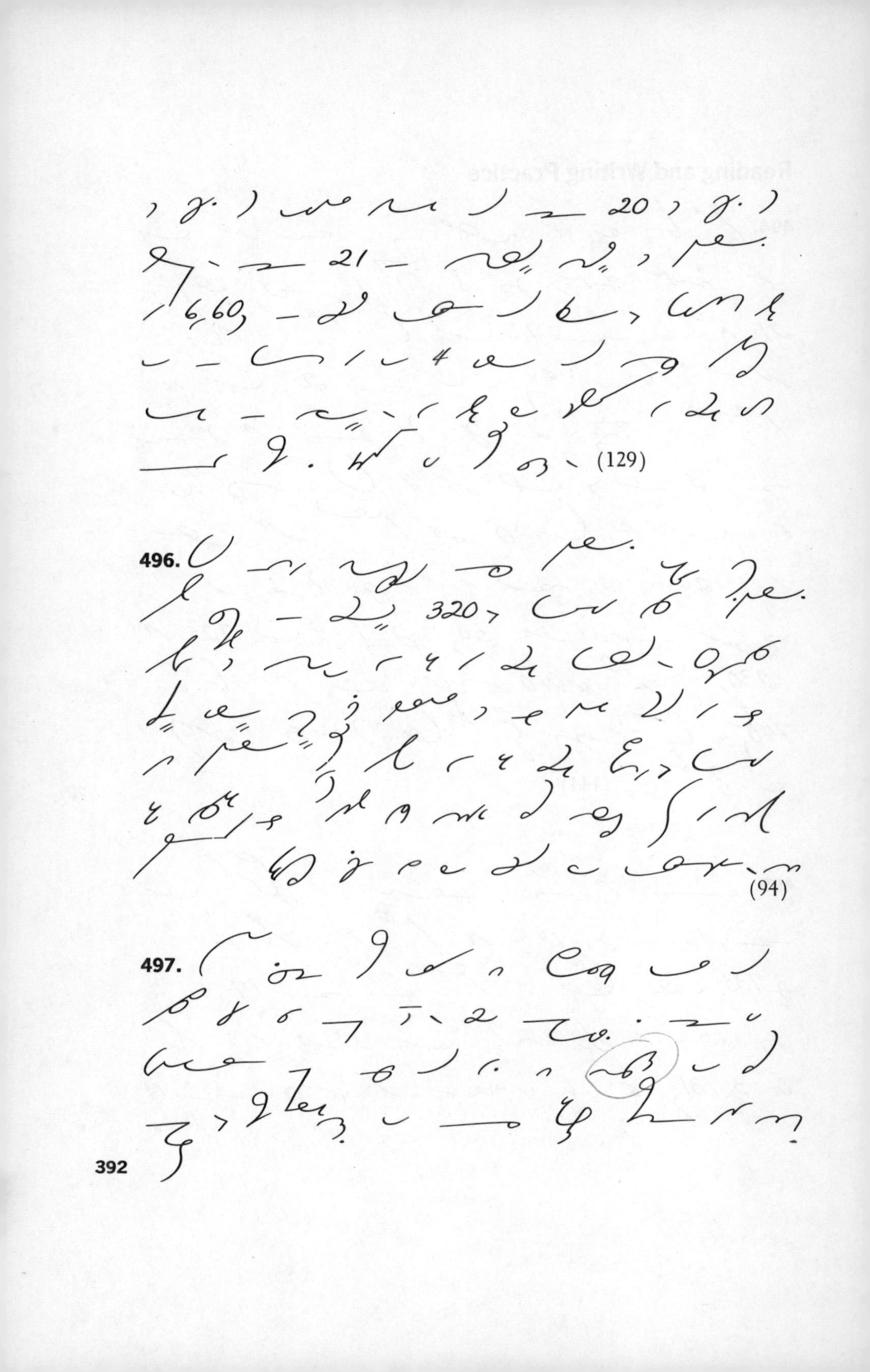

20

21

6.60

4

(129)

496.

320

(94)

497.

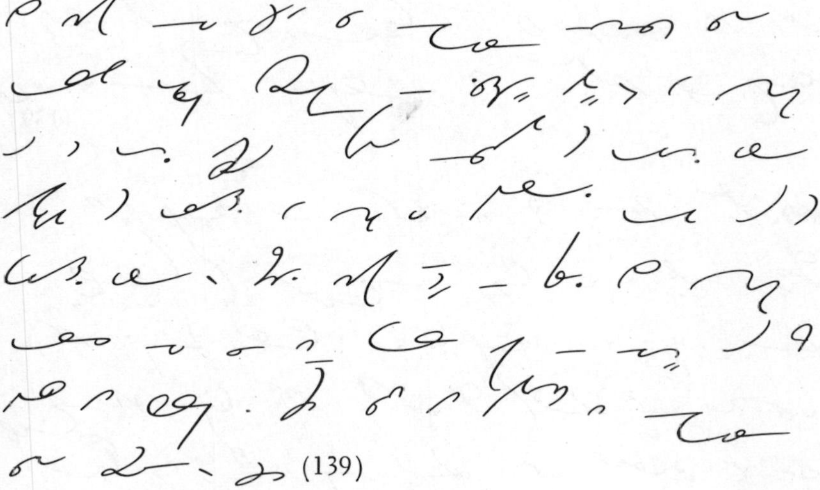

(139)

498.

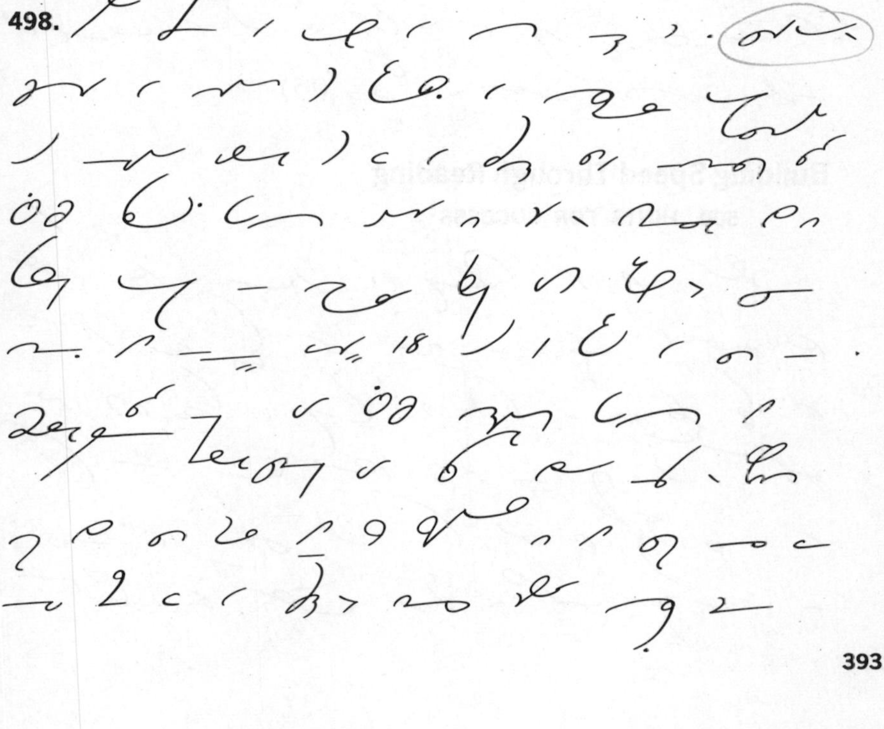

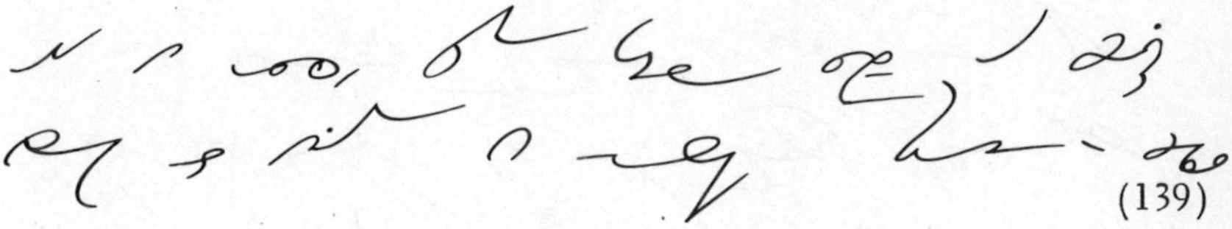

(139)

499. 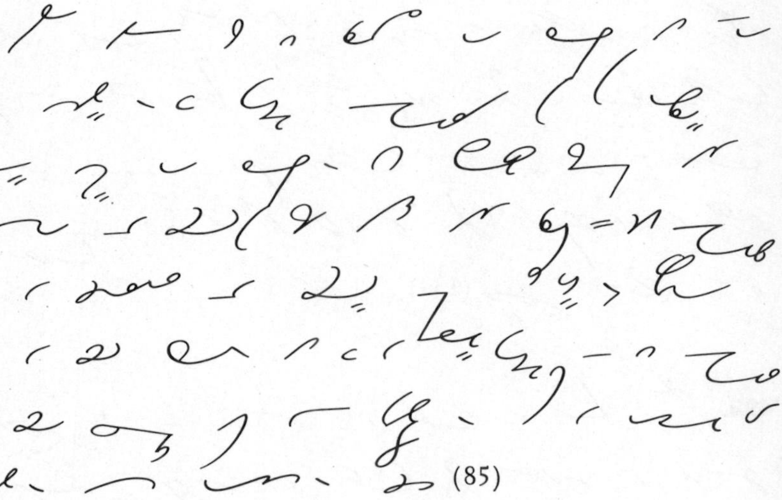

(85)

Building Speed Through Reading

500. HINTS FOR SUCCESS

(290)

Lesson 63

BUILDING PHRASING SKILL

One, Or

anyone else 

any one of our 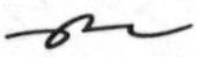

any one of the 

any one of them 

any one of these 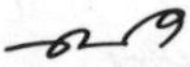

any one of those 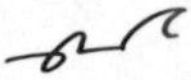

each one 

every one of the 

every one of them 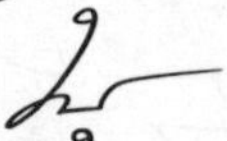

every one of those 

everyone else 

one of our 

one of the 

one of the best 

one of the most 

one of them 

one of these 

one of those 

one thing 

one time 

only one 

day or two 

day or two ago 

more or less 

once or twice 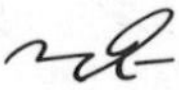

one or two 

two or three 

week or two 

Brief-Form and Phrase Letters

501.

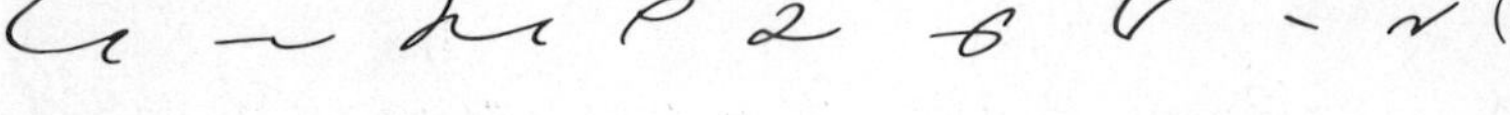 (221)

502. 

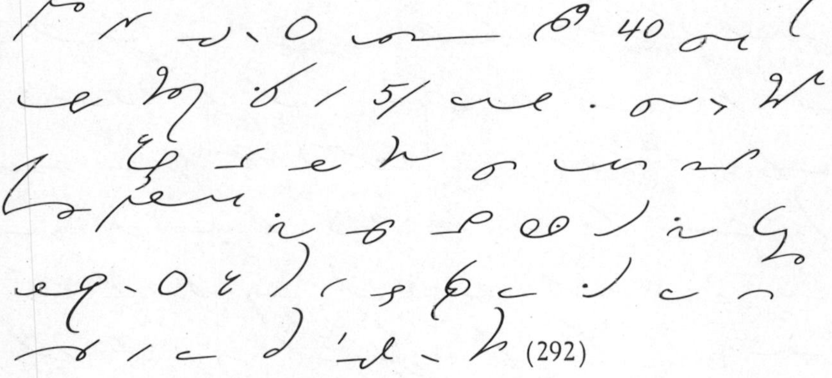

(292)

503.

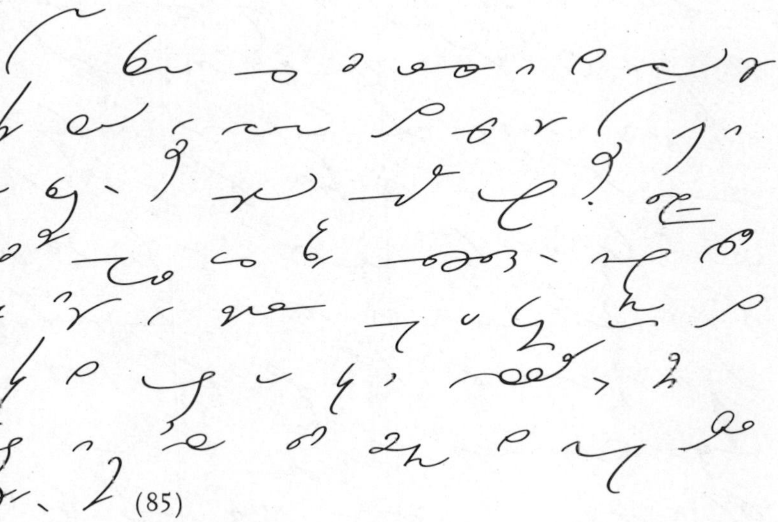

(85)

504. OIL IN A WOMAN'S WORLD

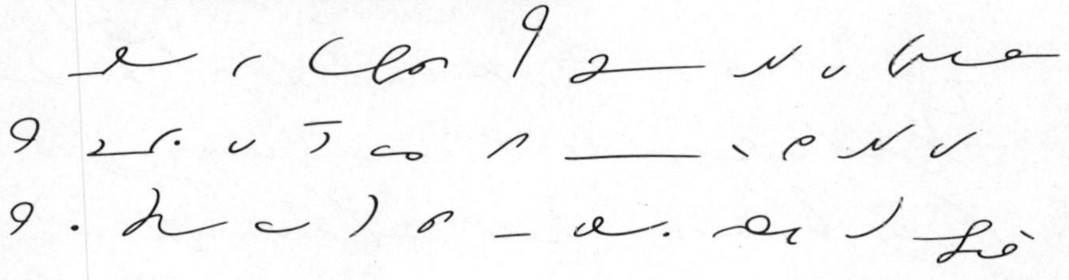

(359)

505. DISPATCHING BY REMOTE CONTROL

(93)

Lesson 64

PROGRESSIVE SPEED BUILDING

Half-Minute Progressive Speed Builder (120-145)

VOCABULARY PREVIEW

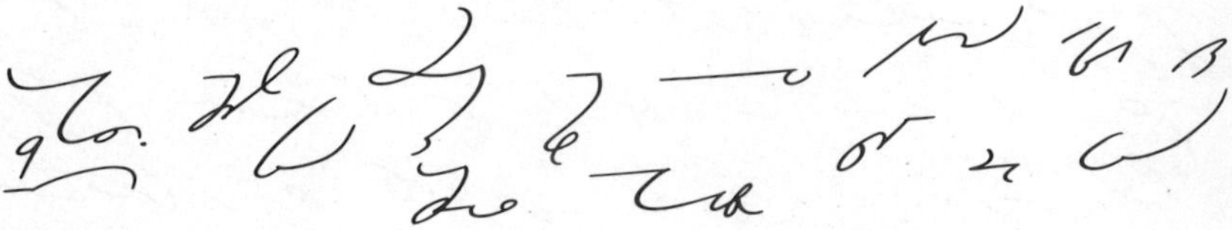

KEY

Lubricating, in a few days, valves, invoice, memo, discount, transportation, to us.

900 gallons, beyond, refinery, employees, out of town, as soon as, prompt.

(½ MINUTE AT 120)

506. Dear Mr. Nelson: We think that we can use all the No. 20 lubricating oil that you can ship during the months of August and September, but we are not so sure/ about the No. 30.

Therefore, please do not ship any 30's until you hear from us. We will make up an estimate of our needs in a few days. Yours truly,//

(½ MINUTE AT 130)

507. Gentlemen: On September 6 we purchased seven brass gate valves from you.

On your invoice No. 628 you charged us for freight as well as for the valves. As the valves are a stock item,/we think that a credit memo for this freight is proper.

On receipt of this credit memo, we will pass this invoice for payment and take our regular discount. Yours truly,//

(½ MINUTE AT 135)

508. Gentlemen: We received your invoice charging us $72 freight on delivery of Motor No. 528.

This motor ran only ten minutes before it failed. We shut/down the well at once and called you for another motor. The transportation charged to us is for the replacement of the motor.

Please forward a credit memo to this office. Yours truly,//

(½ MINUTE AT 140)

509. Dear Mr. Wood: On April 4 your agent, Mr. White, entered our order for approximately 900 gallons a month of your No. 1 grade of gasoline.

Conditions beyond your control/ have caused you to fall behind in your shipments. Now that the refinery employees have received an increased rate of pay, will it be possible for you to increase shipments? Yours sincerely,//

(½ MINUTE AT 145)

510. Dear Mr. Baker: This will acknowledge receipt of your letter to Mr. Warner about increasing our shipments of No. 1 grade gasoline.

Mr. Warner has been out of town for the last six weeks/but he is expected back next Monday or Tuesday.

As soon as he returns to the office, I shall call your letter to his attention. I am sure he will give you a prompt decision. Yours very truly,//

Minute Progressive Speed Builder (110-130)

VOCABULARY PREVIEW

KEY

Imperial, 6 cents, every gallon, a gallon, one of our, lobbyists, construed. Criticisms, to do, ourselves, months ago, merely, successful, degree.

(1 MINUTE AT 110)

511. Dear Gasoline Consumer: Your Imperial Oil dealers consider it important that you know what is happening to gasoline prices in your/state. As the tax situation stands at the present time, you are paying 6 cents tax on every gallon of gas you buy. Now pressures are being applied//for another increase of 1 cent a gallon. If this is allowed to happen, you will be paying 2 cents more tax a gallon of gas than any other///state in the country is paying.

I am sure that you will be glad to know that our company is fighting hard to prevent this tax increase. Very truly yours, (1)

(1 MINUTE AT 120)

512. Dear Mr. Joyce: I know that you have always been one of our most effective lobbyists in the state capital for the petroleum industry. My remarks are not/to be construed as criticisms of your past performance as our representative but merely as a way of asking you to work as hard as you can to prevent// the latest proposed increase in gasoline tax rate. You can see what another 1 cent a gallon tax is going to do to the industry.

We have just written a///letter to all of our credit-card holders informing them of the proposed increase and pledging ourselves to do whatever we can to prevent it. Yours very truly, (2)

(1 MINUTE AT 130)

513. Dear Gasoline Consumer: You may remember that we wrote you about three months ago that another tax increase on gasoline was being proposed at the rate of 1 cent a/gallon. This letter is merely a progress report on that situation.

Our lobbyists in the state capital have been working very hard to prevent the tax increase and were successful to a//large degree. The proposed tax increase was cut from 1 cent to ¼ cent a gallon. We had hoped to be able to prevent any increase, but the pressures were/// so great that we feel that a major victory was won in keeping the increase down to ¼ cent.

You can be sure we shall not relax our efforts to protect your interests. Yours truly, (3)

Reading and Writing Practice

514.

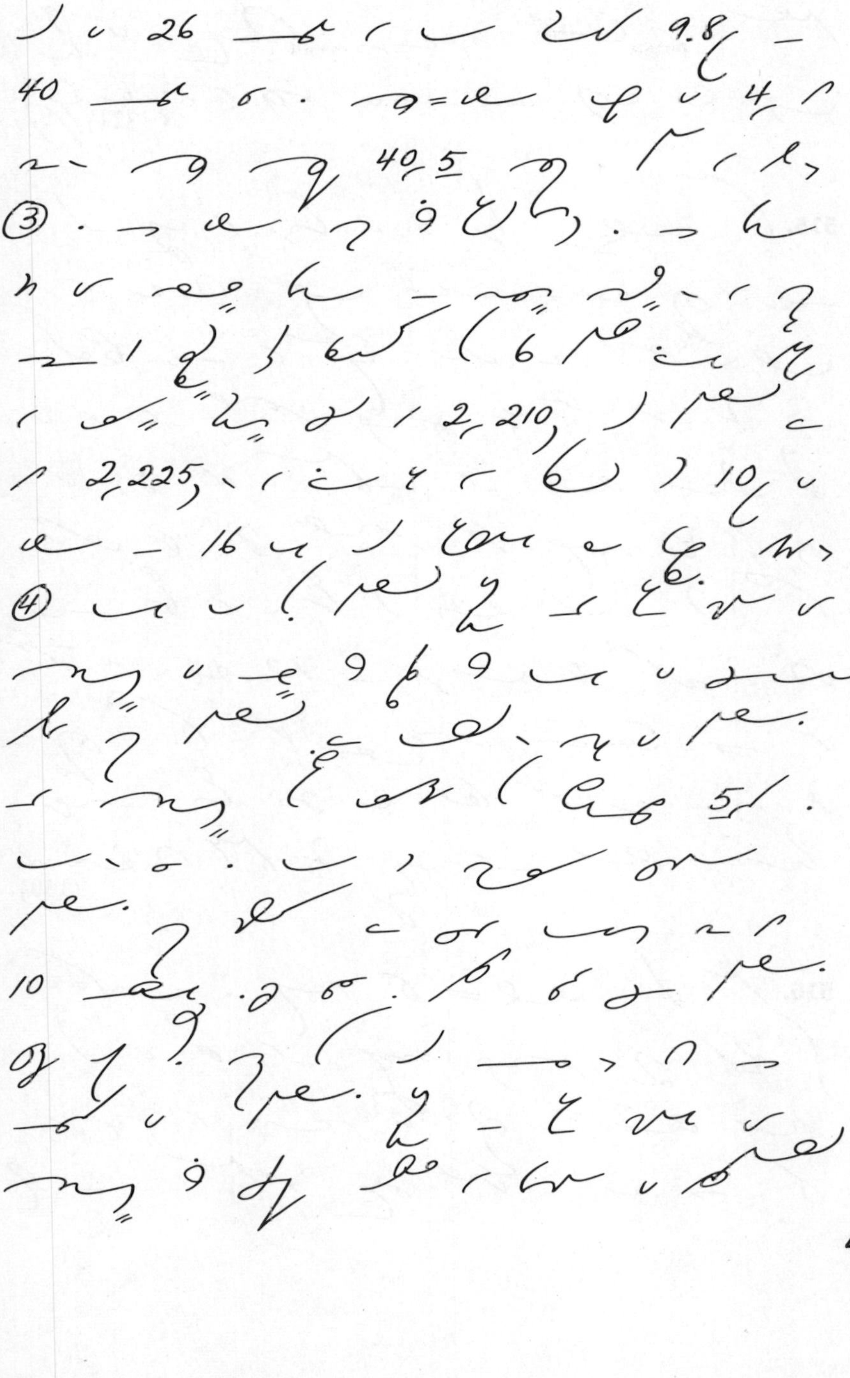

(324)

515. 

(130)

516. 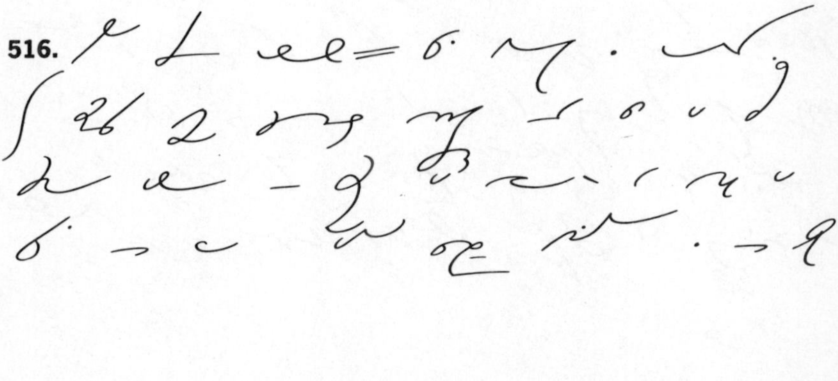

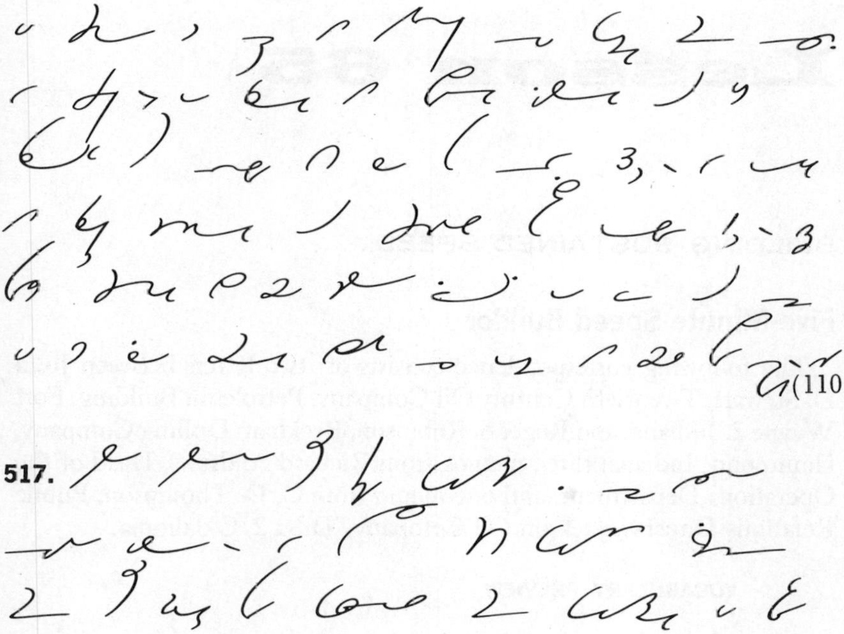

(110)

517.

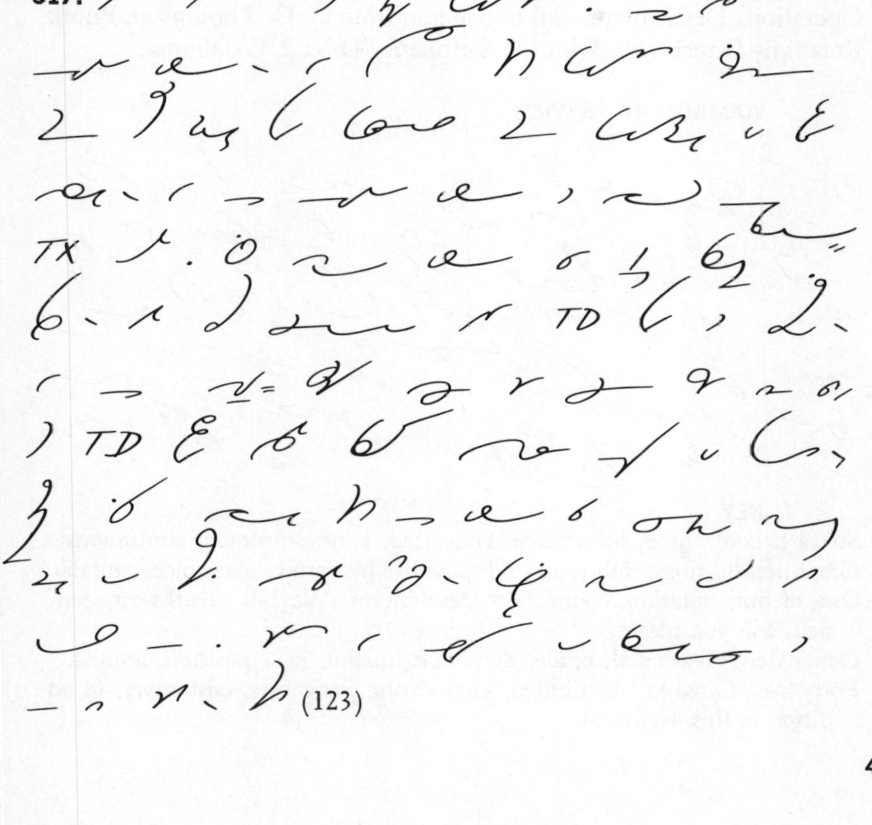

(123)

Lesson 65

BUILDING SUSTAINED SPEED

Five-Minute Speed Builder

The following correspondence consists of: two letters between John D. Stewart, Twentieth Century Oil Company, Petroleum Building, Fort Wayne 2, Indiana, and Roger S. Robinson, Beckham Drilling Company, Hammond, Indiana; three memos from Richard Andrews, Head of the Operations Department, and one memo from C. D. Thompson, Public Relations Director, Jackson Oil Company, Tulsa 2, Oklahoma.

VOCABULARY PREVIEW

KEY

Stewart, confronted, lubrication, converted, kilns, subjected, continuously.
Graphite, bearings, lubricant, 60 pounds, blueprint, assistance, suitable.
One of our, notation, connection, Accountant, Waybill, Southwest, certified, will you please.
Concluded, Associated, crude, dominant, inland, in a position, annual.
Forty-five thousand, distributed, engineering, repeating, customary, in addition to this, technical.

518. Dear Mr. Stewart: We are confronted out here with a problem in lubrication for a new unit we have[1] just installed. This unit is entirely different from former types, and its proper lubrication presents a[2] difficult problem.

As you know, our company mines an ore that is converted by an ore-roasting process. The[3] kilns for this purpose are similar to cement kilns. The feeding device consists of a screw about 10 feet long[4] made of cast steel, which revolves within a pipe for conveying the ore to the head end of the kiln. This screw is[5] subjected continuously to a temperature of between 700° and 800°F.[6]

We are at present using a cylinder oil and graphite, mixed together; but we find it[7] unsatisfactory, as the bearings last only a short while, and the lubricant must be applied under 60 pounds[8] of air pressure.

A blueprint of the unit is attached, and we shall be pleased to have your assistance in finding[9] an improved method of lubrication. Very truly yours,

519. Dear Mr. Robinson: We are glad that you wrote[10] us regarding your problem of finding a suitable lubricant for your new unit. We are sending one of[11] our men to visit your mine. He will bring with him samples of three of our oils and will test each one to see which one[12] will best solve your problem. You may expect him the early part of next week. Yours truly,

520. Memo to Mr. Lewis:[13] Please refer to my letter of August 10, to the Martin Freight Lines, Inc., Freight Bill No. 6349[14] attached, with the following notation: "Two rigs damaged."

We have received Invoice 7200 from[15] White's Machine Shop at Jackson, Mississippi, covering the repair of this damage. This invoice is covered by[16] Field Purchase Order GD-2485. The invoice calls for six hours of labor at $5 an hour plus[17] 65 cents state tax, making a total of $30.65.

This will be charged to expense in[18] connection with the repair of the rigs as received on the above-numbered freight bill.

521. Memo to the Chief Accountant:[19] I am attaching Martin Freight Lines, Inc., Waybill No. 6349, covering shipment[20] to ourselves at Jackson, Mississippi, from Southwest Rig Manufacturing Company. It bears this notation:[21] "Two rigs damaged." I am also attaching certified copy of the invoice from White's Machine Shop, covering[22] cost of repairs to this equipment.

This shipment consisted of two drilling rigs. Will you please file claim, crediting[23] Account No. 4271, Jackson Gasoline Plant.

522. Memo to Mr. Evans: We have successfully[24] concluded arrangements with the Harris & Green Associated Oil Company for supplying them with crude[25] oil.

As you know, the Harris & Green Associated Oil Company is a dominant factor in the[26] marketing of petroleum products in the New England states. They have water terminals and inland plants located[27] throughout the New England area and are in a position to render prompt and efficient service.

523 Memo[28] to Mr. Cook: This is the tenth year that we have offered copies of our annual report for use in college[29] classes. Forty-five thousand copies of last year's report were distributed to students in business and petroleum[30] engineering.

We are repeating our customary offer and are sending a sample copy of[31] this year's report to a selected list of schools. In addition to this service, we are offering to supply[32] students with copies of the report of our annual meeting. This report, we believe, contains technical and[33] financial data of value to majors in engineering and in finance. (674)

Reading and Writing Practice

524.

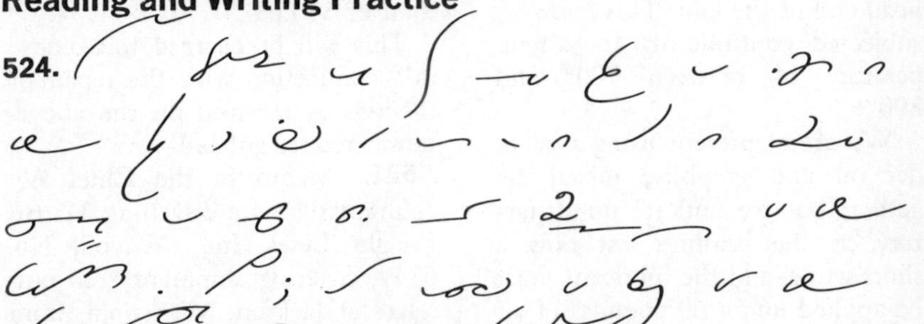

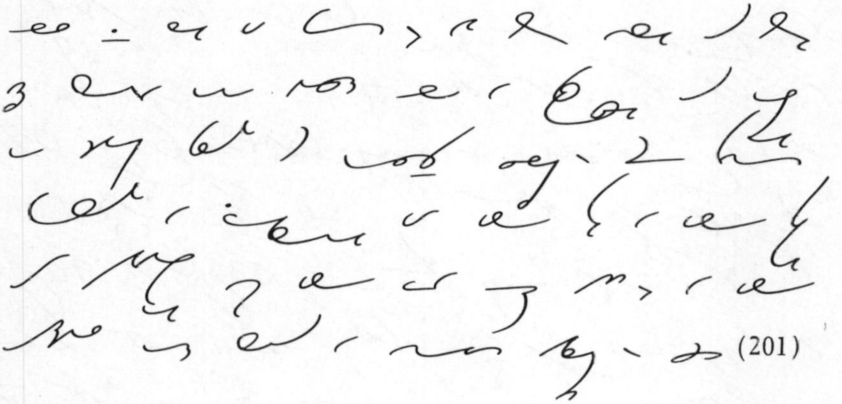 (201)

525. 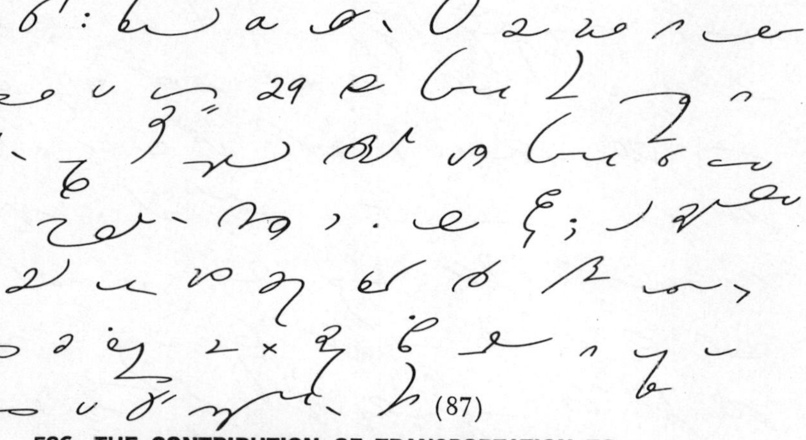 (87)

526. THE CONTRIBUTION OF TRANSPORTATION TO AMERICAN PROGRESS

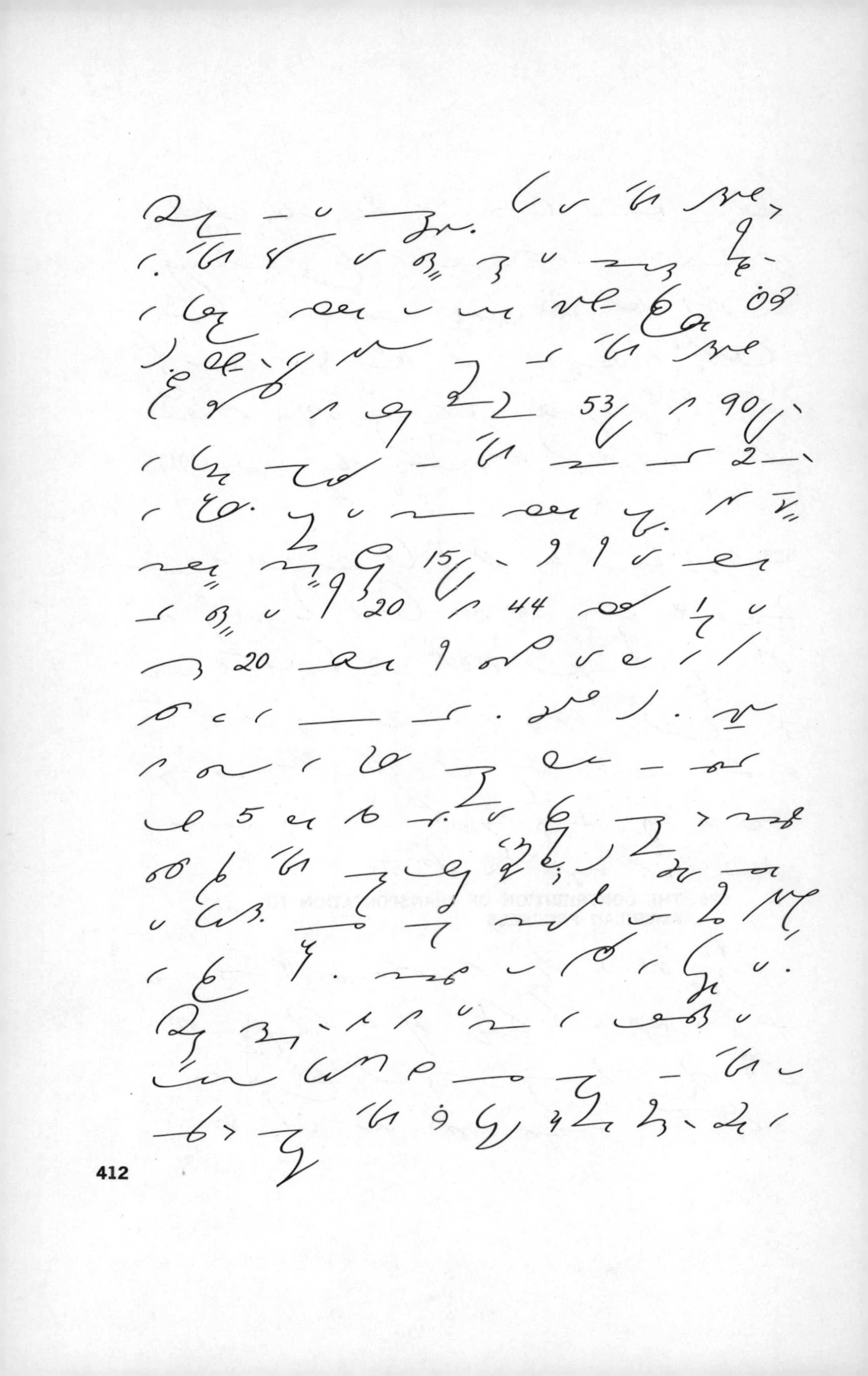

1865

1915

1940

(533)

14 Medicine

Word Study for Chapter 14

MEDICAL

Adenoid. Glandlike structure consisting of connective tissue supporting masses of small lymphocytes.

Ambulatory. Walking or able to walk.

Anesthetist. One who administers anesthetics.

Anorexia. Lack or loss of the appetite for food.

Anterior. Situated in front of or in the forward part.

Aphasia. Defect or loss of power of expression by speech.

Appendicitis. Inflammation of the appendix.

Asymptomatic. Showing no symptoms.

Atrophy. Wasting away of a cell, tissue, organ, or part.

Benign. Nonmalignant and favorable for recovery.

Bronchoscope. Instrument for inspecting interior of the bronchi.

Bursitis. Inflammation of a sac or pouch filled with fluid, located in tissue where friction might develop.

Cancer. A malignant tumor.

Carcinoma. A malignant tumor or cancer, originating in epithelial tissue.

Cerebral. Pertaining to the cerebrum, the main part of the brain.

Cholecyst. The gallbladder.

Convalescent. Returning to health after an illness. A patient who is in the stage of recovery.

Diastolic. Pertaining to the dilatation of the heart.

Dilatation. Enlargement of a part or an organ.

Dyspnea. Difficult or labored breathing.

Edema. Abnormal accumulation of fluid in the body tissues.

Electrocardiogram. A graphic tracing of the electric current produced by the contraction of the heart muscle.

Embolism. The sudden blocking of an artery by a clot of blood.

Epilepsy. A chronic functional disease characterized by brief convulsive seizures and loss of consciousness.

Fascia. A sheet of connective tissue that covers, supports, or binds together internal parts of the body.

Fracture. The breaking of a part, especially of a bone.

Gastrointestinal. Pertaining to the stomach and the intestines.

Hematocyte. Any blood cell.

Hemorrhage. Any copious discharge or flow of blood.

Hemostat. An instrument or a medicine for checking the flow of blood.

Hypertension. Abnormally high blood pressure.

Intercostal. Situated between the ribs.

Intravenously. In, into, or from within a vein.

Lesion. Reduction or alteration of the functional capacity, due to injury or disease.

Metabolism. The phenomena of synthesizing foodstuffs into living tissue and organized substance.

Mucosa. The mucous membrane, consisting of water, mucin, inorganic salts, with epthelial cells and leukocytes.

Neuritis. Inflammation of a nerve.

Palpation. Feeling with the hand, the application of the fingers with light pressure to determine the condition of a part or that of an underlying organ.

Palpitation. Unduly rapid action of the heart.

Penicillin. A strongly antibacterial nontoxic acid extracted from green mold.

Pericardium. Membranous sac that contains the heart.

Peritoneum. The colorless membrane that lines the abdominal walls.

Pharynx. The part of the alimentary canal between the cavity of the mouth and the esophagus.

Poliomyelitis. Inflammation of the grey substance of the spinal cord.

Posterior. Situated behind or toward the rear.

Prognosis. Forecast of the course of a disease or injury.

Psychoneurosis. Mental disorders of psychogenic origin, but presenting the essential symptoms of functional nervous disease.

Pulmonary. Pertaining to the lungs.

Radiology. The science of radioactive substances and X rays and its application, as in the diagnosis and cure of disease.

Respiration. The act by which air is drawn in and expelled from the lungs.

Rupture. Forcible tearing or breaking of a part.

Sanatory. Conducive to health.

Septum. A dividing wall or partition.

Spasm. A sudden, violent involuntary contraction of a muscle or a group of muscles.

Syndrome. A set of symptoms that occur together.

Tachycardia. Excessive rapidity in the action of the heart.

Thorax. The chest; the part of the body between the neck and the abdomen.

Tonsillectomy. Removal or excision of a tonsil.

Traumatic. Pertaining to, or caused by, a wound or injury.

X ray. Roentgen-ray photograph or shadowgram revealing the internal structure of objects opaque to ordinary light.

Lesson 66

BUILDING TRANSCRIPTION SKILL

Transcription English Pointers

HOW TO USE QUOTATION MARKS (CONCLUDED)

1. When a few words from a sentence are incorporated as a grammatical part of a sentence:

a. No comma precedes the quotation.

b. The first word is not capitalized (unless it is a proper noun or a proper adjective).

c. Only the exact words quoted are included within the quotation marks – any rearrangement of the original words is not included.

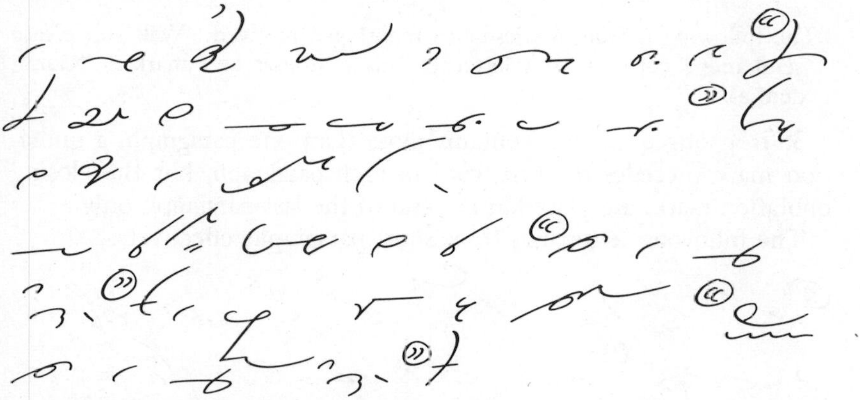

The correspondence supervisor warned us against using those "vague, general words that mean almost anything or nothing" because they waste the reader's time.

Mr. Edwards promised that he would "take the matter under consideration." (The original statement was doubtless, "*I will* take the matter under consideration.")

2. A quotation within a quotation is enclosed in single quotation marks (typed with the apostrophe key).

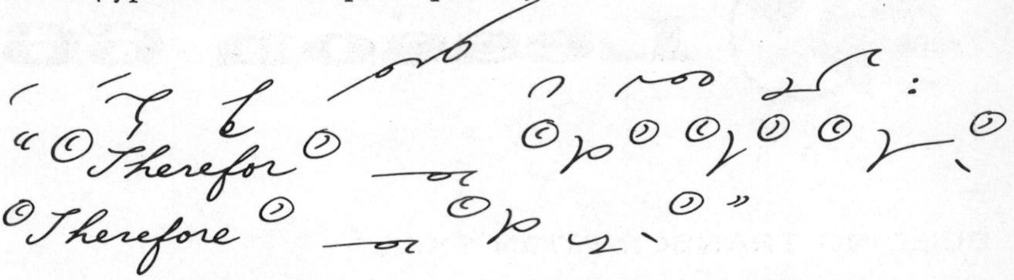

The transcription teacher dictated this tricky sentence: " 'Therefor' means 'for that,' 'for it,' 'for them.' 'Therefore' means 'for that reason.' "

Notice that the closing period comes within both quotation marks.

If another quotation occurs within the single-quoted matter, revert to double quotation marks for the inner matter.

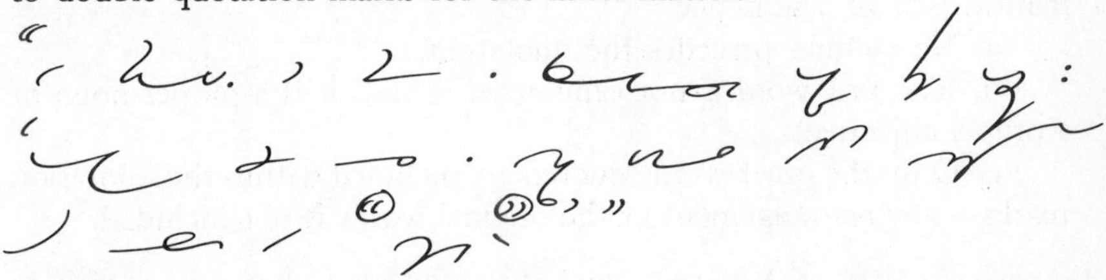

"The following is from a salesmen's report just received: 'Will you please send me a copy of your letter to this customer and mark it "Confidential." ' "

3. If a long quotation contains more than one paragraph, a quotation mark precedes the first word in each paragraph, but the closing quotation marks are placed at the end of the last paragraph only.

The following letter uses three short paragraphs effectively.

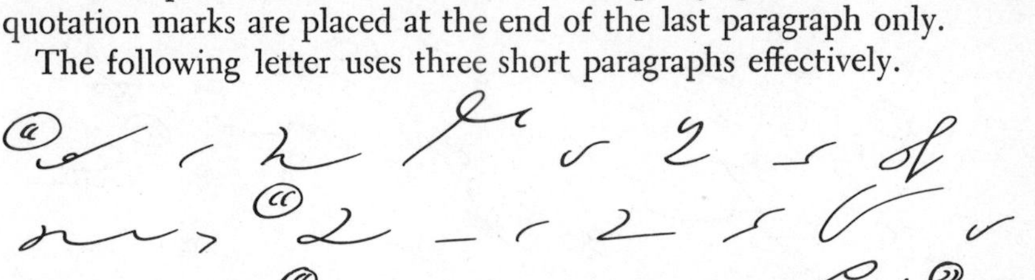

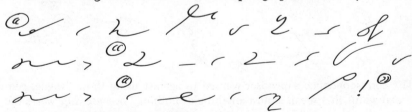

"Read the full details of the offer in the attached circular.
"Fill in the form at the bottom of the circular.
"Then mail the coupon today!"

Any quotation marks already in the extract must be changed to single quotation marks.

An alternative method for handling long quotations is to type them in single spacing, in a shorter line length than that used in the balance of the material. No quotation marks are then necessary, and any marks already within the extract may be left "as is."

Transcription Speed Builder

527.

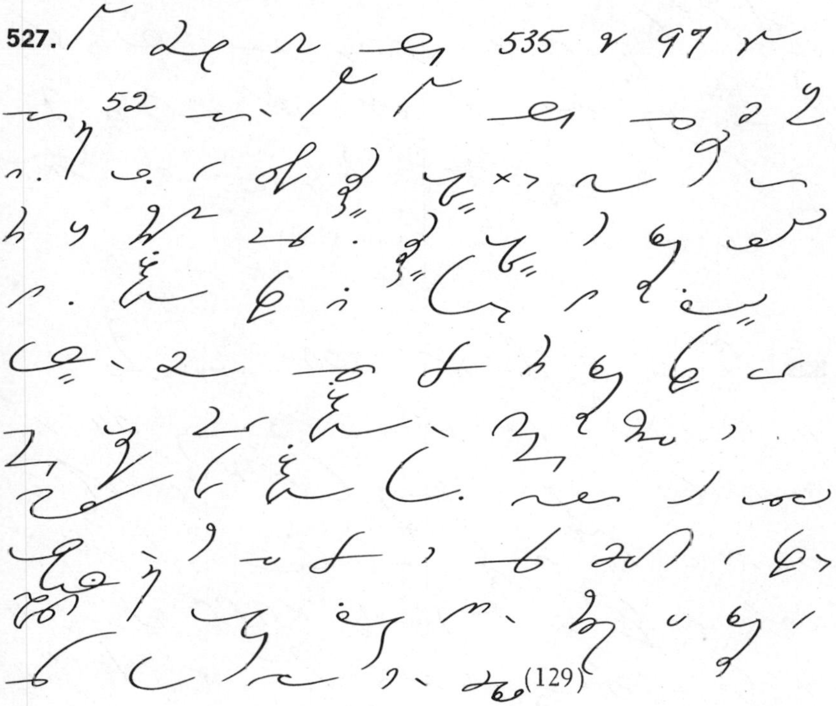

528.

(134)

529.

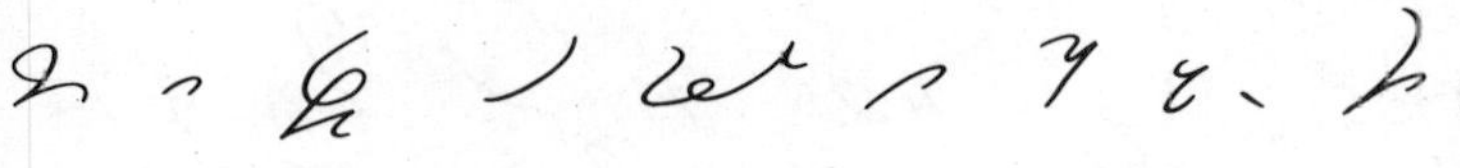
(133)

530.

(104)

531.
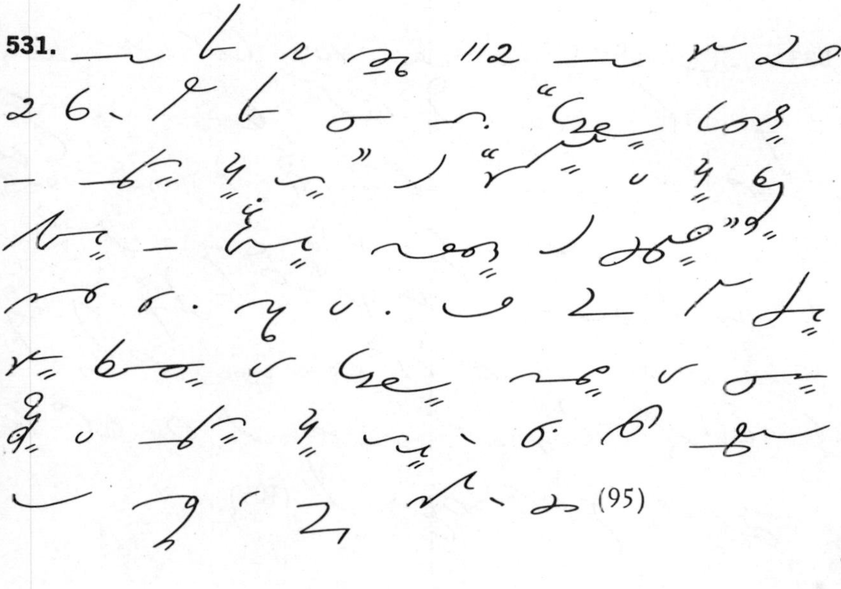
(95)

532.

(118)

533.

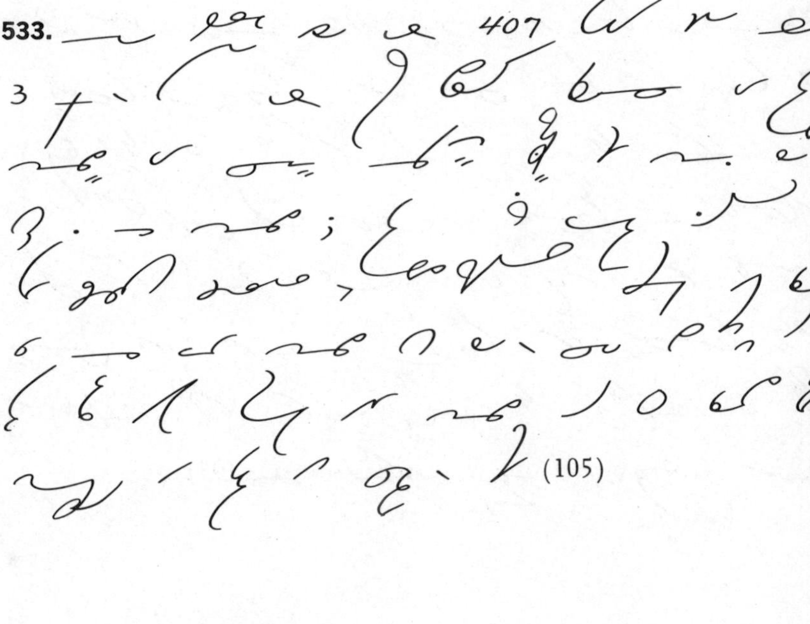

(105)

Lesson 67

MASTERING SHORTHAND THEORY

Word Endings

-ful

-gram

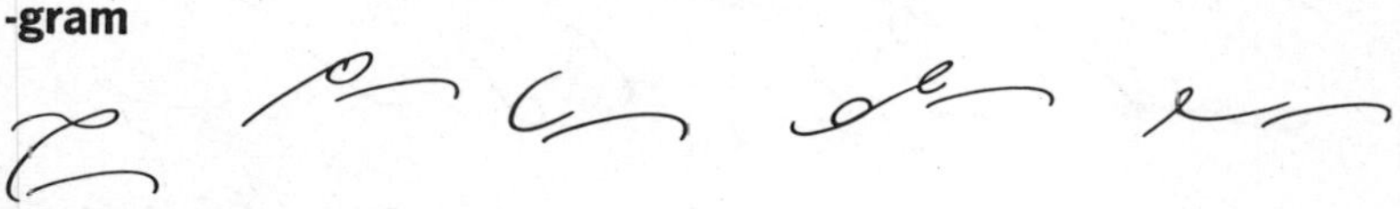

-hood, -ward

-rity

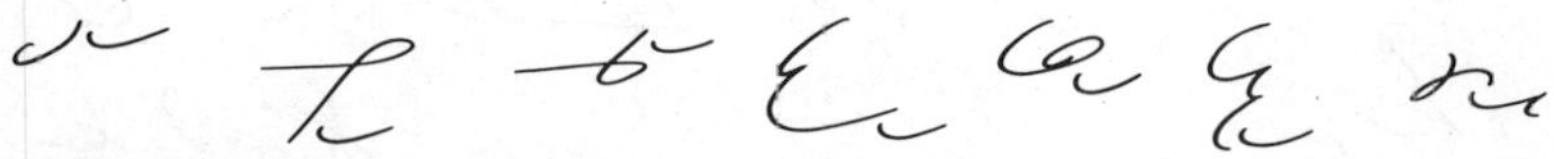

-self, -selves

KEY

Careful, cheerfully, doubtful, helpful, hopeful, powerful, successful, thoughtful, useful.

Cablegram, diagram, program, radiogram, telegram.

Boyhood, childhood, likelihood, afterwards, forward, rewarded, upward.

Authority, majority, maturity, popularity, priority, prosperity, securities.

Herself, himself, myself, yourself, ourselves, themselves, yourselves.

Reading and Writing Practice

534.

(173)

535. 5

"U.S.P."

25 30,

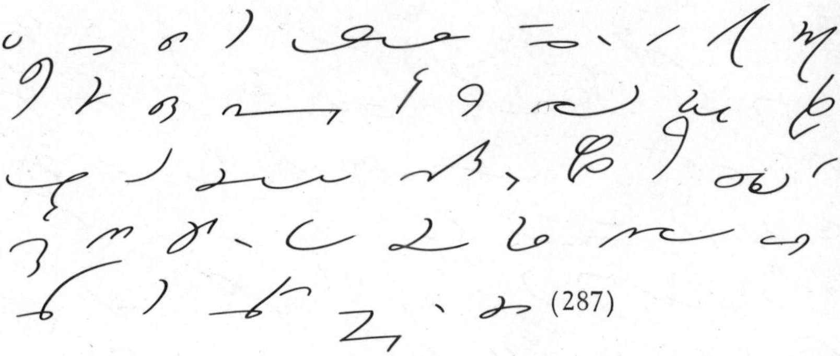

(287)

536.

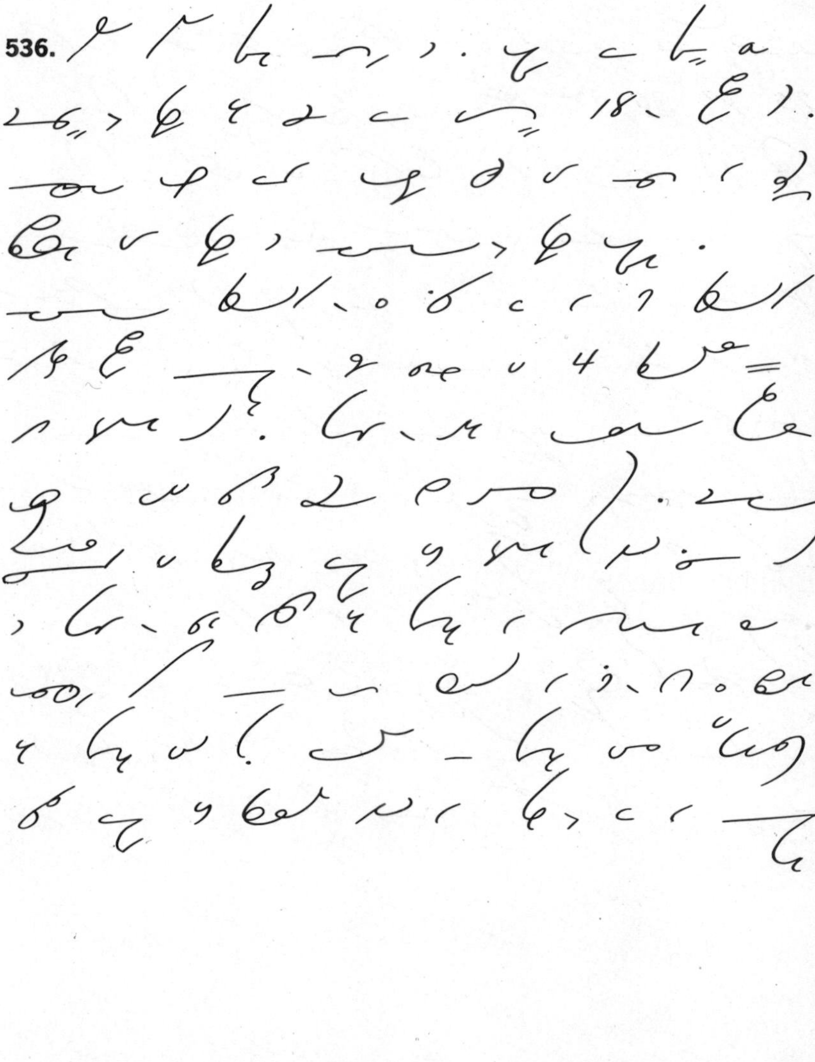

(304)

Building Speed Through Reading

537. HINTS FOR SUCCESS

(258)

Lesson 68

BUILDING PHRASING SKILL

Ago, Day, Yet

about ten days ago		any day	
day or two ago		for a few days	
few days ago		in a few days	
few minutes ago		next ten days	
few months ago		as yet	
long time ago		has not yet	
several days ago		has not yet been	
several months ago		have not yet	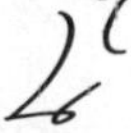
short time ago		have not yet been able	
so long ago	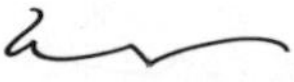	I have not yet	
some time ago		I have not yet been able	
some weeks ago		if you are not yet	
some years ago		they are not yet	
week or two ago		they have not yet	

Brief-Form and Phrase Letters

538.

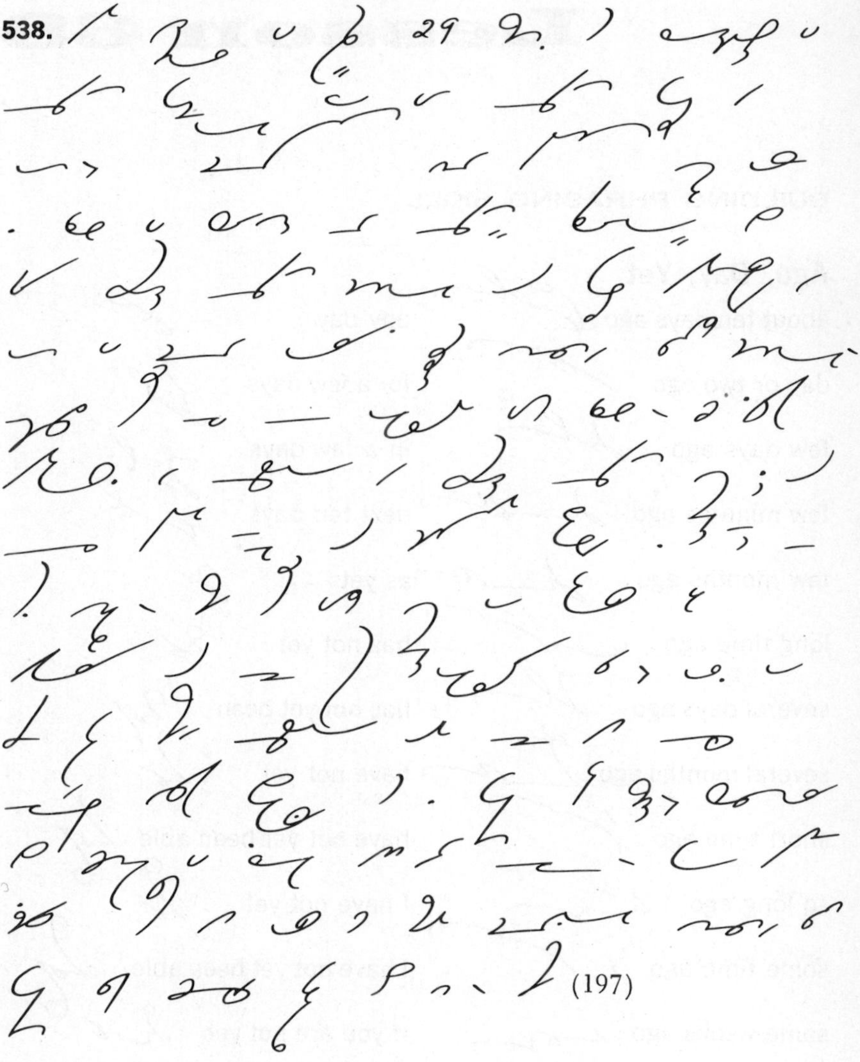

(197)

539.

(189)

540.

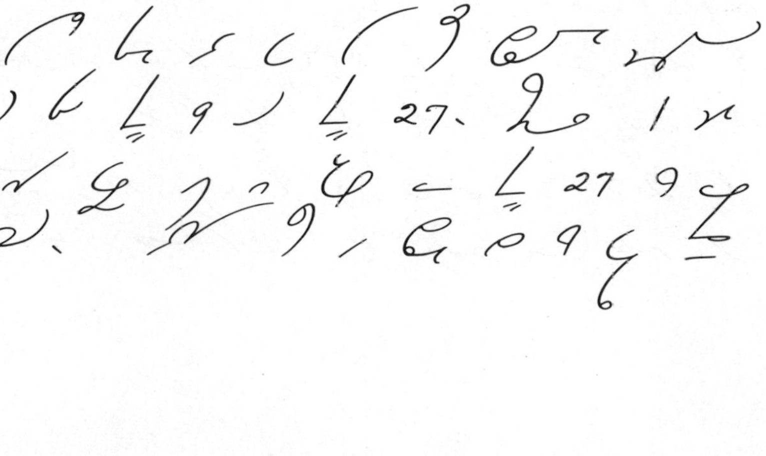

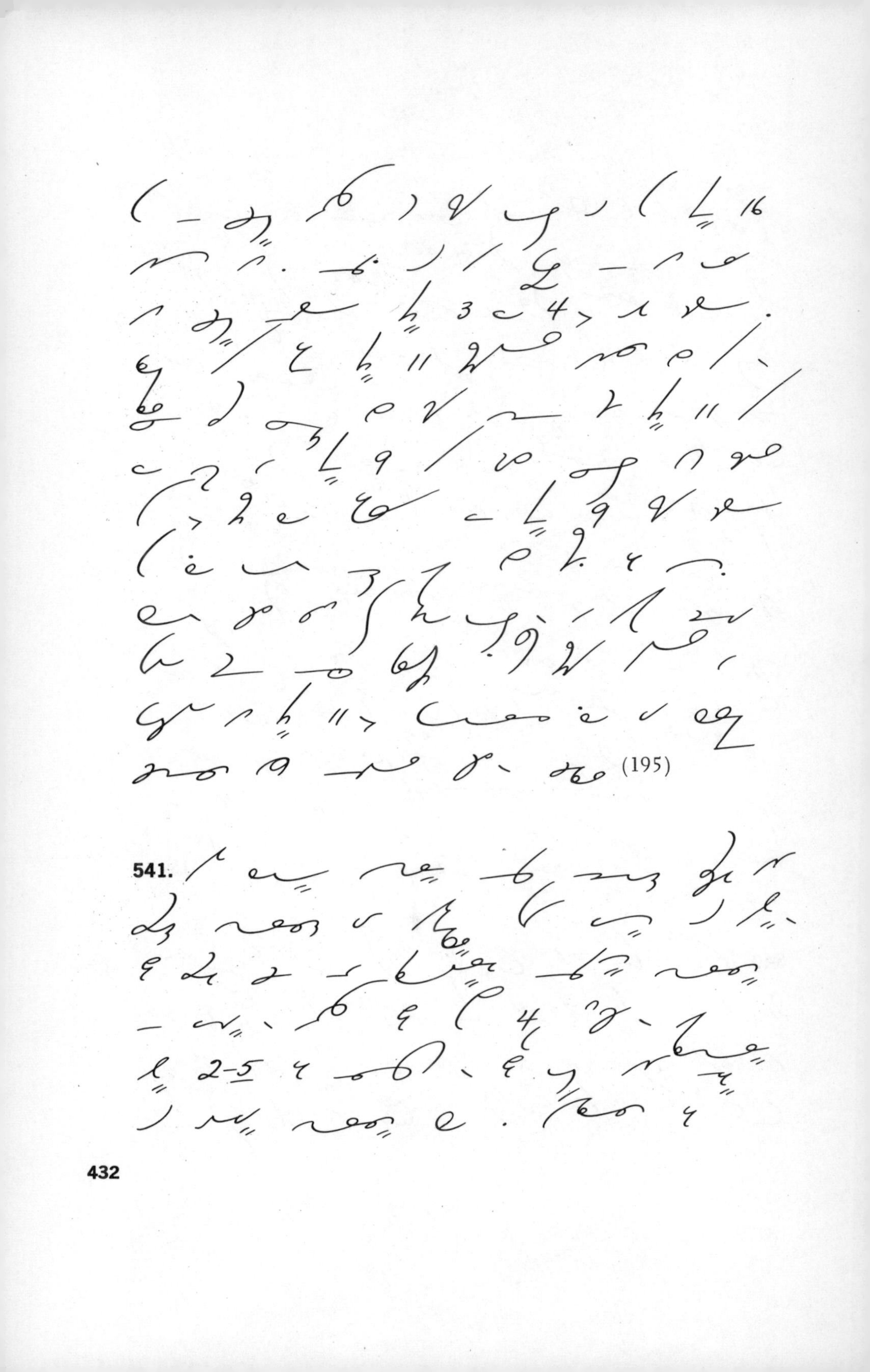

(195)

541.

(131)

542.

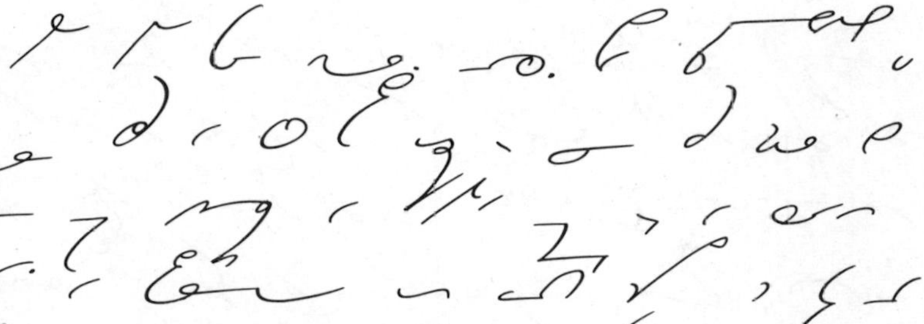

(157)

543.

(147)

544.

(47)

Lesson 69

PROGRESSIVE SPEED BUILDING

Half-Minute Progressive Speed Builder (120-145)

VOCABULARY PREVIEW

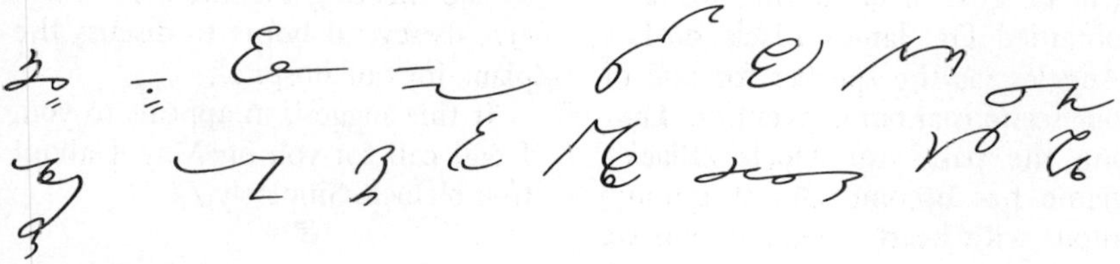

KEY

Sweeney, New Hamsphire, experiment, internal, attendance, I was not, discussion, I am sure.

Reservations, luncheon, thank you for your, speaker, during the past year, synonymous, fortunate, we hope to see.

(½ MINUTE AT 120)

545. Dear Doctor Sweeney: The New Hampshire Medical Association will have its convention May 5 through May 8. On the May 6 dinner program, Dr. William Burns will/speak on the Chicago experiment in internal medicine.

I am sure that we shall all find it most interesting. I hope you will be in attendance. Yours very truly,//

(½ MINUTE AT 130)

546. Gentlemen: I should like to reserve the extra room about which I wrote you on January 10. At that time I was not sure whether we would need four or five rooms for discussion/groups at the convention of the New Hampshire Medical Association.

Now I am sure that we shall need five; so I hope you can reserve the extra room for us. Very truly yours,//

(½ MINUTE AT 135)

547. Gentlemen: I now have the

final report on the number of reservations to be made for the luncheon and dinner meetings of the New Hampshire Medical Association convention/May 5 through May 8.

We shall have 130 persons at each of the luncheons and 90 at the dinner. Thank you for your help with the convention details. Very truly yours,//

(½ MINUTE AT 140)

548. Dear Doctor Alexander: You will be glad to know that we have obtained Dr. James Black, of Los Angeles, as the speaker for one of our sessions at our convention. During the past year Doctor/Black's name has become almost synonymous with heart medicine, and we feel very fortunate in being able to obtain him for our meeting on May 7.

We hope to see you there. Sincerely yours,//

(½ MINUTE AT 145)

549. Dear Doctor Smith: No doubt you are planning to attend the meeting of the New Hampshire Medical Association from May 5 through May 8. I, too, am planning to go; and the thought occurred to me that we/might drive to the meeting together. This will give us several hours to discuss the plans for our hospital.

If this suggestion appeals to you, I will call for you on May 4 about four o'clock. Sincerely,//

Minute Progressive Speed Builder (110-130)

VOCABULARY PREVIEW

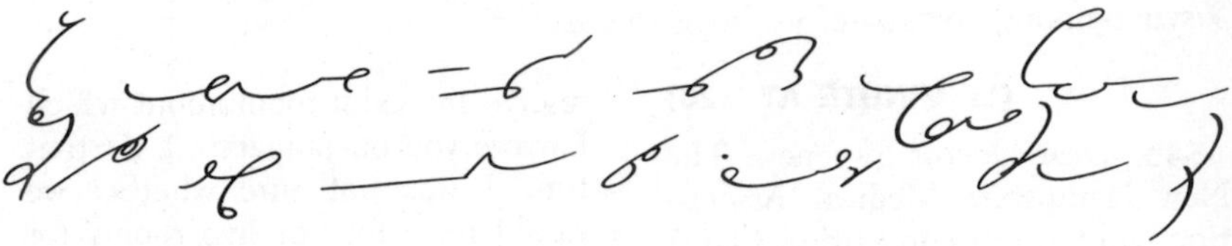

KEY

Observation, listlessness, intermittent, medications, laboratory, abnormality. Diet, therapy, mental, attitude, healthiest, vitality, vice versa.

(1 MINUTE AT 110)

550. Dear Doctor Black: I am sending you a patient, Mrs. Mary Foster, who has been under my observation for over two months. She came to me because/of a general feeling of listlessness, intermittent headaches, and a loss of weight.

As you will see by the enclosed chart, I have tried three different// medications with no success. I can find nothing in the laboratory tests that show abnormality.

I believe that she has an appointment///with you during the first part of next week. If I can help in any way, let me know, as I am very much interested in this case. Yours very truly, (1)

(1 MINUTE AT 120)

551. Dear Doctor Black: Thank you for writing to me about the condition of Mrs. Mary Foster. As I told you, I am very much interested in her case and/surely hope that the new program of diet and medication that you have proposed is helping her.

I agree with you that she needs confidence. I//recognized this early in my treatment of her. The therapy you proposed to bring about this confidence on her part sounds good.

I am sending you the results of some laboratory tests that///we made about two years ago when she was in with a different set of complaints. Perhaps a comparison with the present tests will help you. Yours very truly, (2)

(1 MINUTE AT 130)

552. Dear Doctor Black: Accept my congratulations for the fine job you did in restoring Mrs. Foster to health. She was in this morning; she looks very much better and her mental/attitude is the healthiest I have ever known her to have. She seemed to have more-than-average vitality. I don't know which came first – her change of mental attitude and her//improved health or vice versa, but you have done a fine job with her.

I am glad that I found the laboratory reports, especially as they seem to have helped you in your diagnosis.///If I had had those reports earlier and had noticed the change in blood count, perhaps I could have been more helpful.

I shall continue to see her periodically. Yours very truly, (3)

Reading and Writing Practice

553.

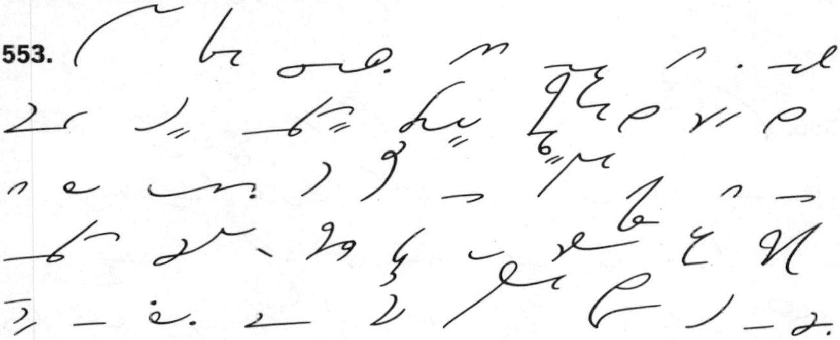

(77)

554.

(154)

555.

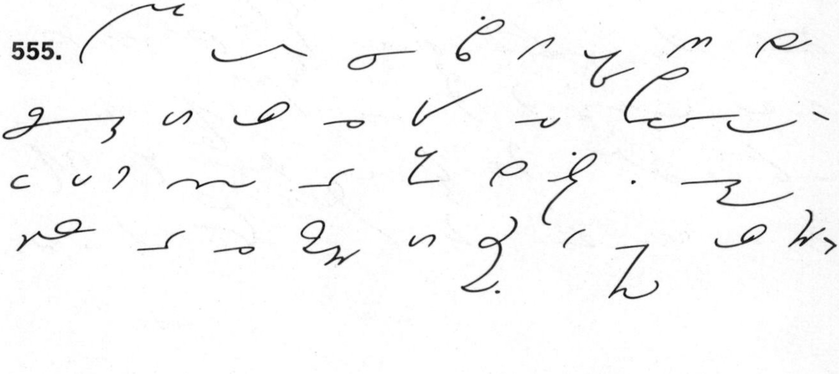

(141)

556.

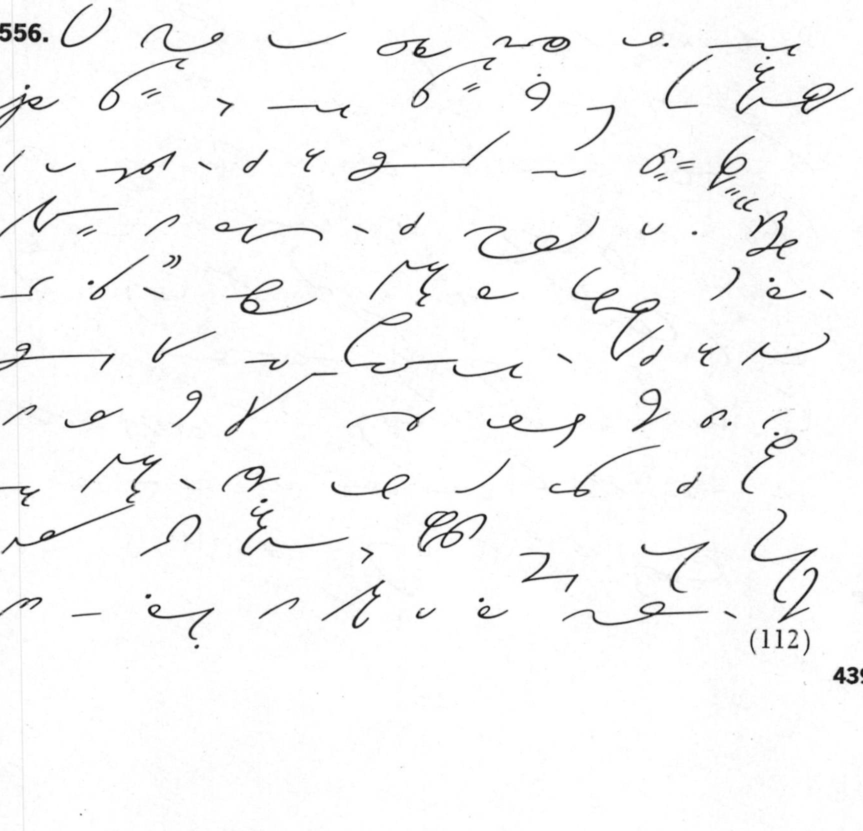

(112)

557.

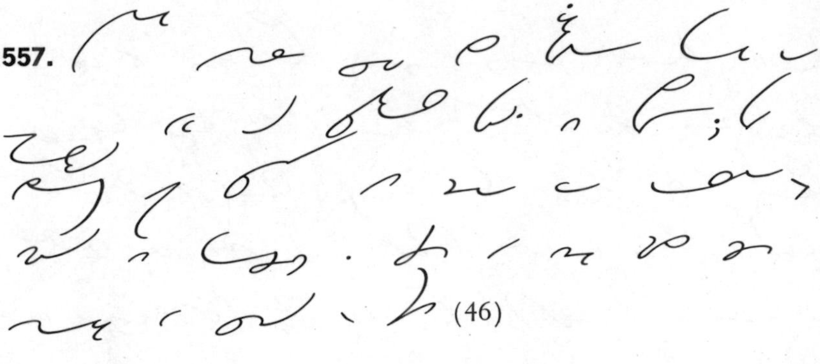

(46)

558.

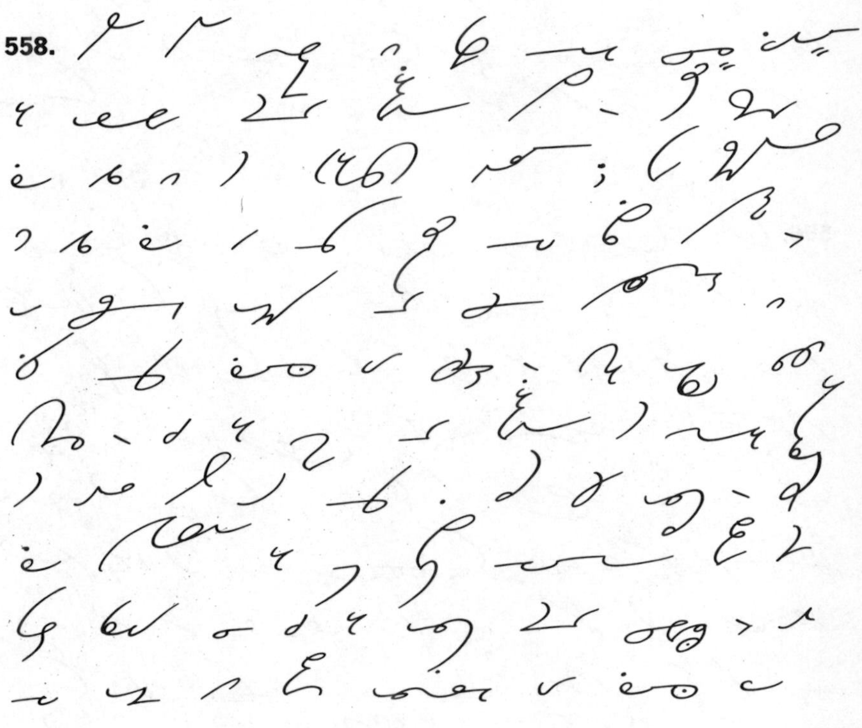

(141)

Lesson 70

BUILDING SUSTAINED SPEED

Five-Minute Speed Builder

The first two letters are written to Mrs. James S. Russell, 1211 West 18 Street, Amarillo, Texas. They were dictated by Mrs. Robert S. Young, Manager, General Optical Company, 147 Lynch Street, Fort Worth 7, Texas. The third letter is written to Dr. Horace J. Morgan, 1892 Defense Street, Des Moines 4, Iowa, and was dictated by Dr. John Skjelstad, 4281 Lawson Street, Roanoke, Virginia. The last letter is written by the Minnesota Health Plan. It is addressed to Imperial Plating Company, 140 South Street, St. Paul 4, Minnesota.

VOCABULARY PREVIEW

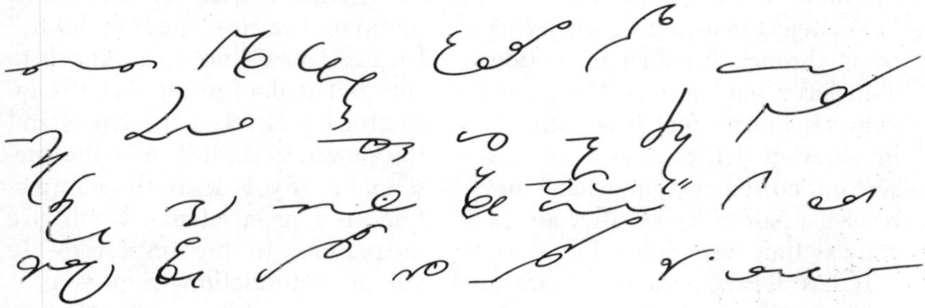

KEY

Neglect, during the past, prescriptions, splendidly, tendency, on the market.
Uncomfortable, virtually, minus, O.K., inspector, Jacobs, dilated.
Pupils, consistent, nuclear, opacities, intraocular, tension, irritation.
Astringent, expires, automatic, otherwise, undoubtedly, extending, re-enrollment.

559. Dear Mrs. Russell: Thank you for your letter of June 18 regarding our slow delivery service. Yes, we[1] know that delivery on our lenses has been slow recently. This is not due to any neglect on our part[2] but is due to a great increase in our sales during the past few months.

To meet this increase in our sales, we have put[3] on extra help in order to speed up deliveries; these new people, however, take a great deal of time to[4] train before we can let them work on prescriptions. They are coming along splendidly, however; and we are sure[5] that the service will be faster in the near future.

I appreciate your remarks about the Sight-Saver lenses[6] and assure you that we do not sacrifice quality for speed, as has been claimed by some of our competitors.[7]

We reject many lenses when they come through for final inspection. This has a tendency to slow down[8] delivery, but we feel it is better to be slow on deliveries and thus assure our customers that, when[9] they receive a pair of lenses, they are exactly as they were ordered.

It has always been our desire to do[10] everything possible to bring to you the best products on the market at the most reasonable prices.[11]

I hope that you will feel free to write to me any time you have any problems or any time you have suggestions[12] for improving our service or the quality of our lenses. Yours very truly,

560. Dear Mrs. Russell: I[13] have your letter regarding the quality of the lenses that were recently purchased from us. I have discussed[14] the matter of the sharp edges with our foreman and called his attention to the fact that sharp edges are very[15] uncomfortable. I know this because I fit these lenses virtually every day.

You say that the[16] prescription lens does not feel so good as the trial lens. You must realize that the trial lenses are made with a minimum[17] thickness over the entire surface. Your prescription lenses, on the other hand, are thicker in the center if[18] they are plus lenses and slightly thicker on the edges if minus lenses, although we do level them down.

In[19] regard to your questions about the matter of inspection stamp on the envelope, the "O.K." I realize, does[29] not mean much to you; but it does mean that the inspector has checked the lenses and the power, according to[21] the prescription. If you desire the information on your envelopes, I will give instructions to the inspector[22] to put this information on for you.

I hope that I have answered your questions satisfactorily.[23] Sincerely yours,

561. Dear Doctor Morgan: Mrs. Lee Jacobs was recently referred to me by her physician, Dr.[24] James Martin. She brought your report with her.

I dilated her pupils. The examination reveals changes[25] consistent with her age. Slit-lamp examination reveals nuclear opacities somewhat more advanced on the[26] right. With her present glasses, however, she can be brought up to 20/25 vision in the right eye and[27] 20/20 in the left. Glasses were not prescribed.

Her intraocular tension is 20 in the right eye[28] and 18 in the left eye. Because of some irritation of her eyes, astringent drops were prescribed. I believe[29] that no eye treatment is indicated at this time. I suggested that she return in six months for observation[30] and a check on the progress of further lens opacities.

If there is any further information I[31] can give you, please let me know. Sincerely yours,

562. Gentlemen: Your Health Plan Group contract is set up on a yearly basis[32] and expires on May 31. The contract provides for automatic renewal unless we should notify[33] you otherwise in writing at least thirty (30) days before this expiration date.

As you know, we try to assist[34] you in getting your annual enrollment before each renewal date of your contract. Our representative[35] has undoubtedly discussed this with you and is extending his help at this time. This annual enrollment[36] provides two important advantages:

1. For you, it permits your employees who do not already belong[37] to subscribe.

2. For us, it gives us the basic group enrollment requirements that are necessary for us to[38] continue this comprehensive Health Plan coverage.

According to our information, your annual re-enrollment[39] is not yet complete. As soon as this enrollment is successfully completed, we will officially[40] establish your contract renewal.

We hope that you will let us help you in every possible way. Very truly[41] yours, (821)

Reading and Writing Practice

563.

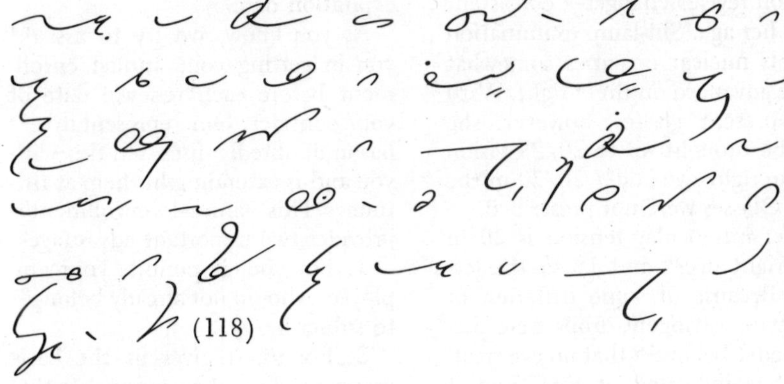

(118)

564.

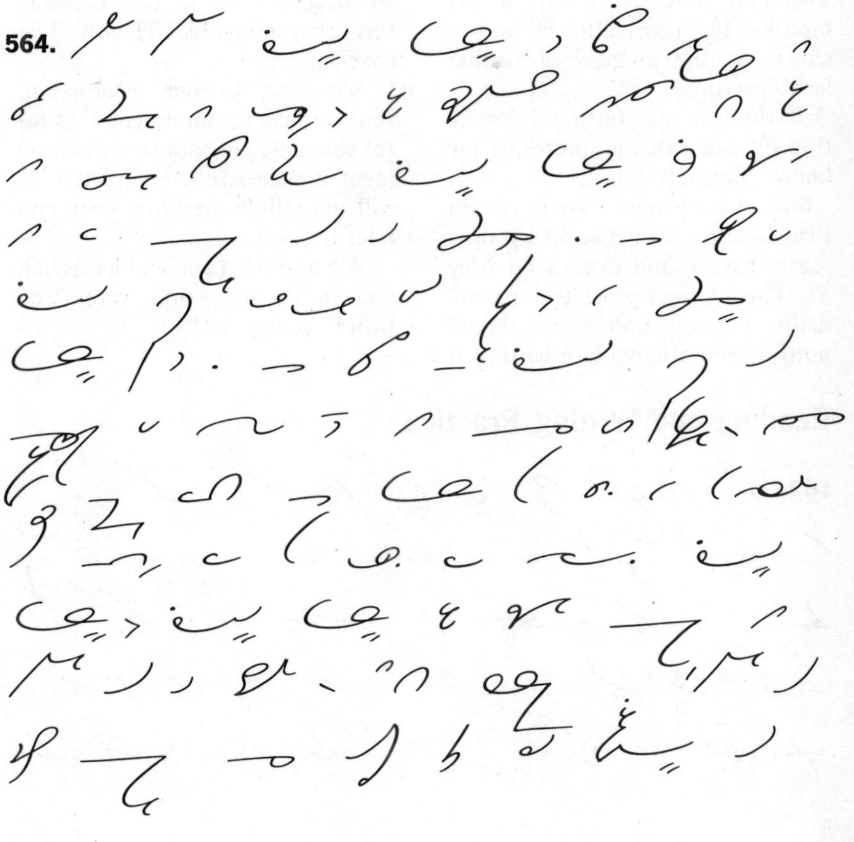

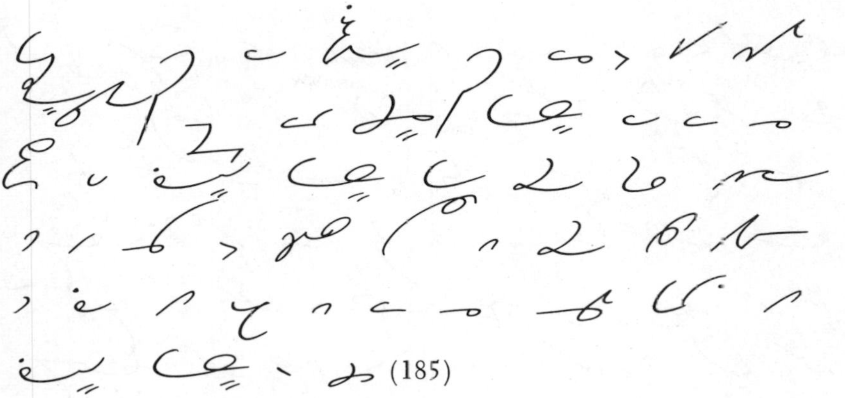

(185)

565. 

(104)

566. 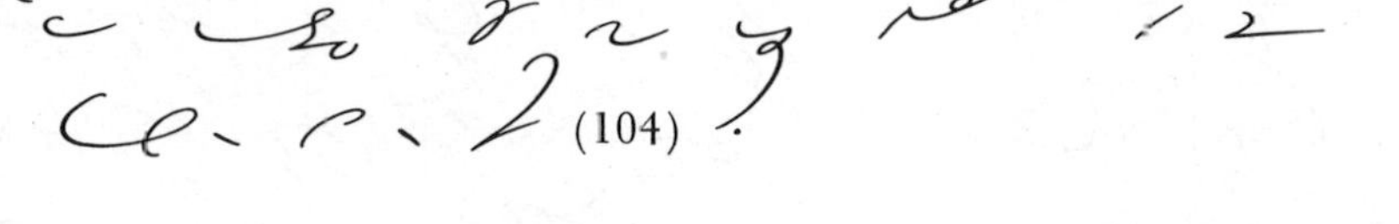

(112)

567.

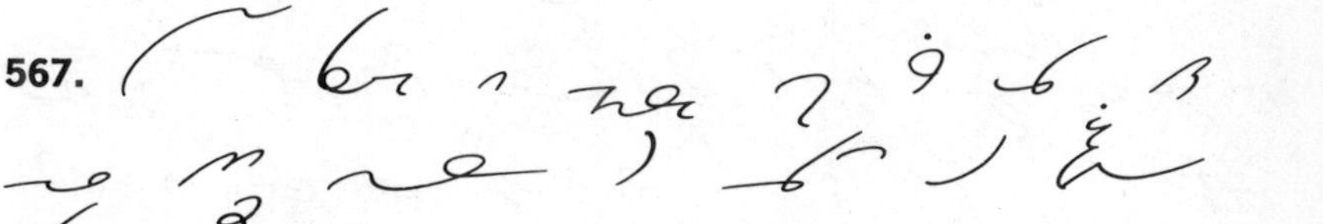

(111)

15

Utilities

Word Study for Chapter 15

UTILITIES

Alternating Current (AC). An electric current that reverses its direction of flow periodically as contrasted with direct current (DC).

Ampere. The unit of measurement of electric current.

Base Load. That part of the total load of electric current that is continuous, as distinguished from that which fluctuates widely as the total system load changes from hour to hour or seasonally.

Cable Miles. The total length of separately sheathed or pipe-type electric cables, expressed in miles.

Cable Terminal. A device connected to a cable to bring out pairs of wire and make them available for connection.

Carrier. High-frequency current superimposed on a voice circuit, on which can be modulated additional voice or signaling channels.

City Gate. The point or measuring station at which a distributing gas utility receives gas from a natural-gas pipeline company.

Conduit. A tube that is placed in the ground to form ducts through which cables can be passed.

Curb Cock. A shutoff valve in a gas service line, usually between the curb and the customer's property line.

Decibel. Unit measurement of sound used to measure transmission loss, gain, or relative level.

Dial. A calling device that can be wound up and released to transmit signals having different numbers of impulses.

Direct Current (DC). Electricity that flows continuously in one direction as contrasted with alternating current (AC).

Distribution Company. A gas utility company that obtains its major gas operating revenue from retail gas sales to ultimate customers.

Easement. A formal permission granted by landowners for laying and maintaining a gas pipeline.

Electric Energy. As commonly used in the electric utility industry, electric energy means kilowatt hours.

Exchange. One or more central offices, with associated plant and stations in a specified area.

Frequency. The rate in cycles per second at which a current alternates.

Generating Station. A station at which are located prime movers, electric generators, and auxiliary equipment for converting mechanical, chemical, and nuclear energy into electric energy.

Holiday. A break in the anticorrosion coating of a

pipeline, which leaves bare pipe exposed.

Hydro. A term used to identify the type of generating station, or power or energy output, in which the prime mover is driven by water power.

Insulator. A glass appliance mounted on a steel or a wooden pin to which line wires are tied.

Kilowatt. A unit of power equivalent to 1,000 watts.

Kilowatt-hour. The basic unit of electric energy equal to one kilowatt of power supplied to or taken from an electric circuit steadily for one hour.

Line Loss. Electric energy lost in transmission and distribution lines.

Load Factor. The ratio of the average volume of gas transported by a gas system during a specified time interval to the maximum volume transported during a comparable time interval.

Message Unit. One call within an exchange limit.

Meter Books. Books in which successive readings of utility customers' meters are recorded by meter readers. The difference between successive readings is the consumption for the period.

Modulation. Combination of one frequency with another in such a way that new frequencies are produced.

PAX. Private automatic exchange.

PBX. Private branch exchange.

Pole Miles. Miles of structures, poles, or towers carrying electric conductors.

Public Utility. A business organization performing some public service and hence subject to special government regulations.

Receiver. A device that transforms a varying electrical current into sound waves.

Service Cock. A small plug valve located just ahead of a gas meter and used to shut off the gas flow to the meter and the customer's piping.

Service Connection. The connecting piping between a gas main and the customer's meter.

Standby Service. Service that is not normally used but which is available, through a permanent connection, in lieu of, or as a supplement to, the usual source of supply.

Substation. An assemblage of equipment for switching and changing or regulating the voltage of electricity.

Therm. A quantity of heat equal to 100,000 B.T.U.

Transformer. An electromagnetic device for changing the voltage of alternating current electricity.

TWX. Teletypewriter exchange service.

Watt. The electrical unit of power. One horsepower equals 746 watts.

Lesson 71

BUILDING TRANSCRIPTION SKILL

Transcription English Pointers

HOW TO WRITE NUMBERS

In business, numbers are more frequently written in figures than in words. The following cases illustrate some of the major points to remember in handling numbers that are written in figures.

1. *Numbers.* The number 100 and numbers over 100 appearing individually in sentences are written in figures.

Carloadings for the week ended July 2 were 644,182.

a. In very large *round* numbers, the words *million* and *billion* follow a figure.

4 million new homes   a proposed $1 billion loan

This style, however, cannot be used when the number contains exact hundreds and thousands.

4,450,000 $1,300,000,000

b. All numbers occurring frequently, as in enumerations and statistical matter, are written in figures.

Over 100 agencies distribute our product in the East. Of these, 25 are located in New England, 34 in the New York City area, 25 in Pennsylvania, and 16 in the South.

2. *Time.* Clock time is expressed in *figures* when the exact time is given (*2:01*) and when *a.m., p.m.,* and *m.* are included (at *5 p.m.*).

Periods of time used in quoting discount terms or interest rates are usually written in figures.

We are willing to accept your 30-day note.

3. *Ages.* When a person's age includes years, months, and days, figures are used. No comma separates the parts of such expressions, as the expression is considered a unit.

The policyholder's age on May 1 will be 55 years 3 months 10 days.

4. *Money.* In business, amounts of money, large or small, domestic or foreign, are written in figures.

$10   10 cents   £10   10 pesos

a. When amounts of cents appear individually in a sentence, they should be written in figures and followed preferably by the word *cents.*

This gadget was made to retail for 10 cents.

b. In technical matter containing many items below $1, the symbol ¢ is often used.

Rates for service on regular checking accounts are: each check paid, 6¢; each deposit ticket, 6¢; each check deposited, 3¢; each debit and credit memo, 6¢; monthly maintenance, 50¢.

5. *Decimals.* Decimals are always expressed in figures.

2.5   0.56

The cipher before the decimal point in the second illustration indicates that the writer has not overlooked the fact that this amount is less than one whole number.

6. *Percentages.* Percentages should always be expressed in figures.

2 per cent   1.5 per cent

Fractional percentages are usually written as common fractions.

3½ per cent   66⅔ per cent

But, in very accurate or technical work, decimal fractions are preferred.

3.5 per cent   66.66 per cent

7. *Ratios and Proportions.* Ratios and proportions are expressed in figures. In general matter, the word *to* in such expressions is usually written out, but in technical matter a colon represents the word *to.*

The chances are 3 to 1 that she will recover.
There must be some mistake—the ratio of 1:500 is impossible!

(Concluded on page 483)

Transcription Speed Builder

568.

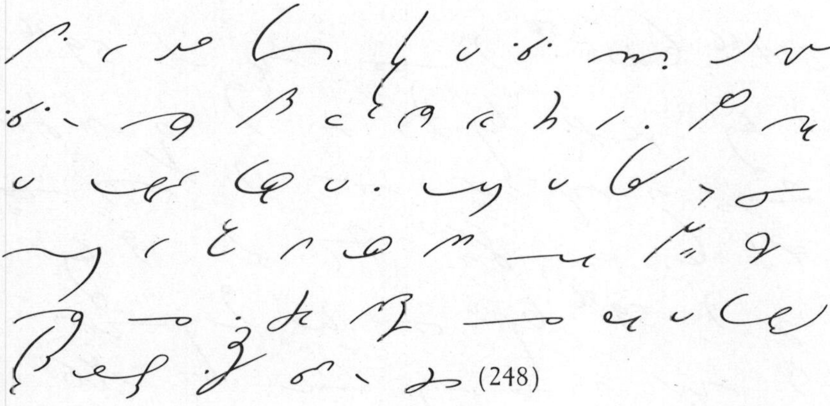

(248)

569.

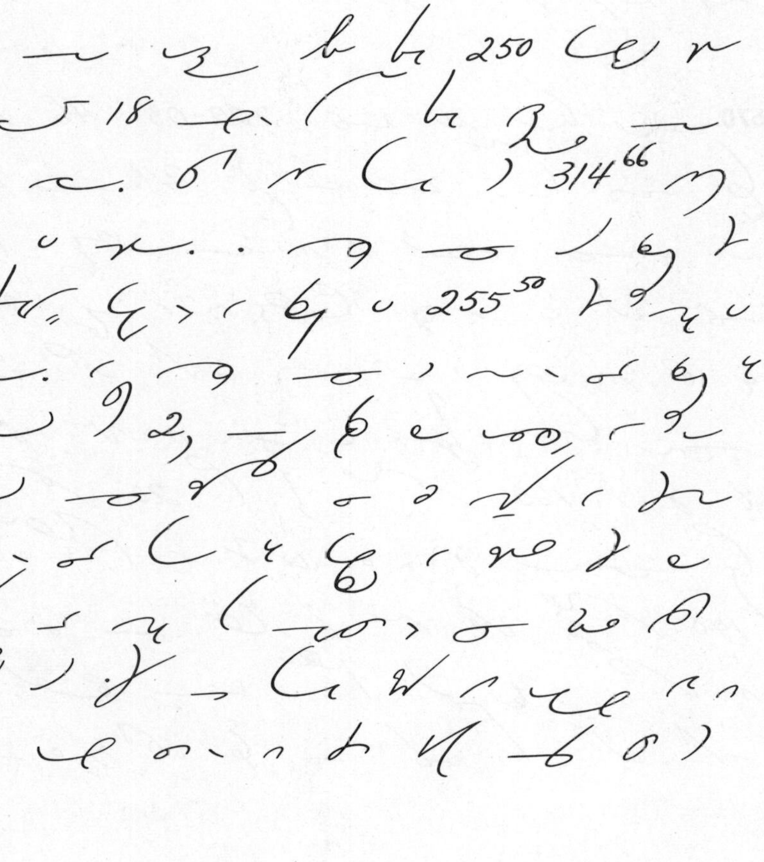

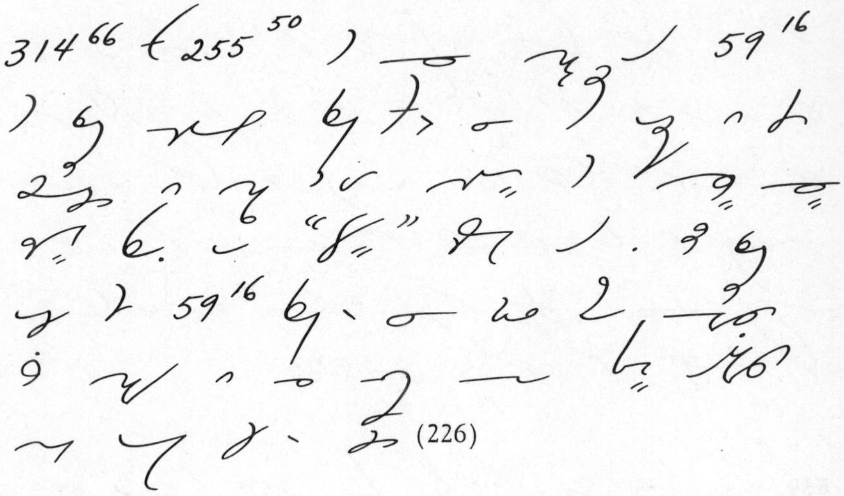

(226)

570.

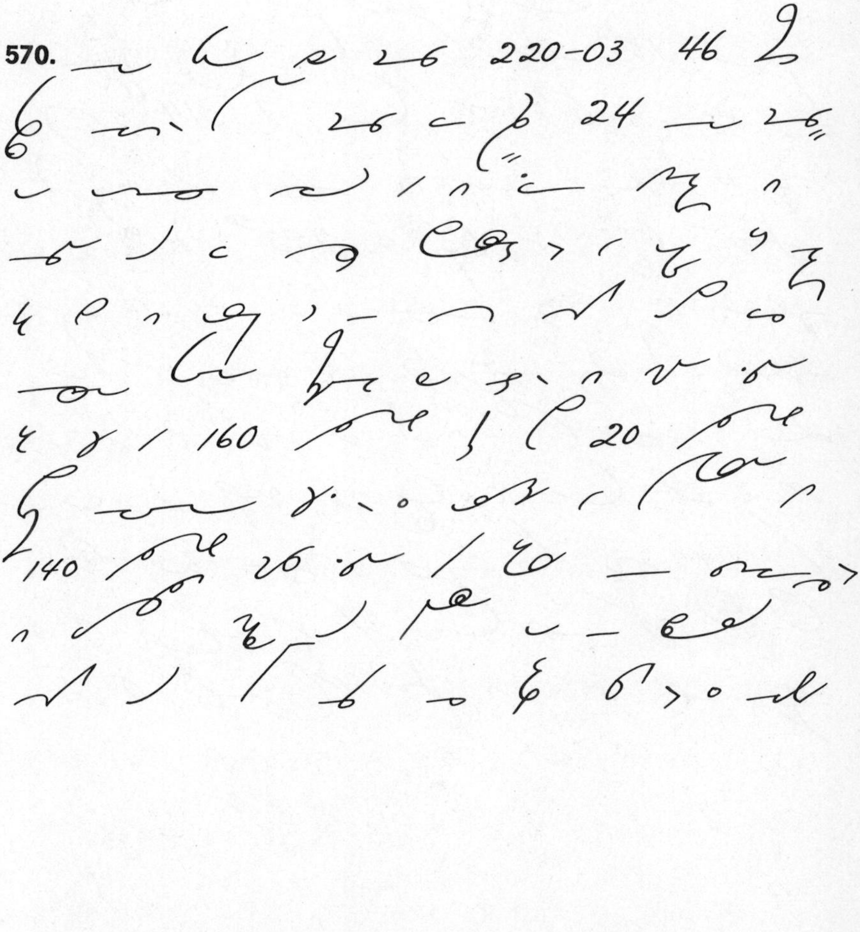

(254)

571.

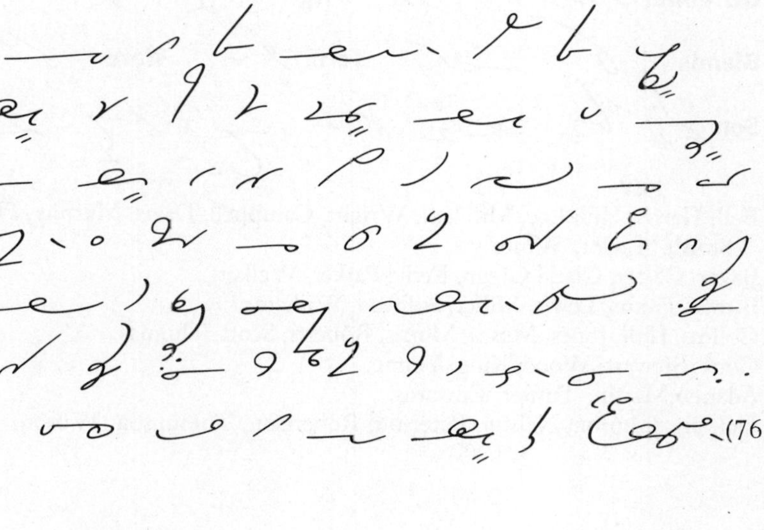

(76)

Lesson 72

MASTERING SHORTHAND THEORY

Fifty Frequently Used Surnames

Inside Curves, Outside Angles 

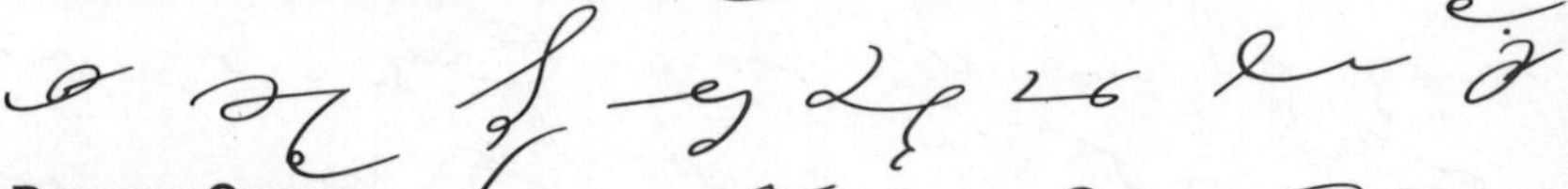

Reverse Curves 

Omission of Vowels 

O Vowel 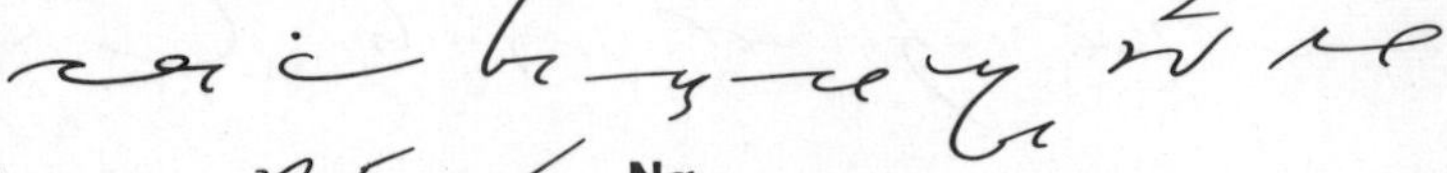

OO Vowel  **Ng** 

Blends 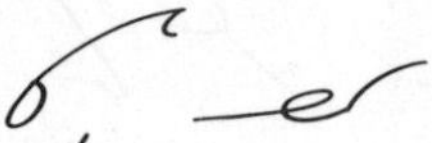 **Tern**  **Ward** 

Son 

KEY

Bell, Harris, Hill, Lee, Mitchell, Wright, Campbell, Davis, Murphy, Philips, Smith, Taylor, White.
Baker, Carter, Clark, Green, Kelly, Parker, Walker.
Brown, Evans, Lewis, Miller, Sullivan, Williams.
Collins, Hall, Jones, Moses, Morris, Roberts, Scott, Thomas.
Cook, Stewart, Wood; King, Young.
Adams, Martin; Turner; Edwards.
Jackson, Johnson, Nelson, Peterson, Robertson, Thompson, Wilson.

Reading and Writing Practice

572.

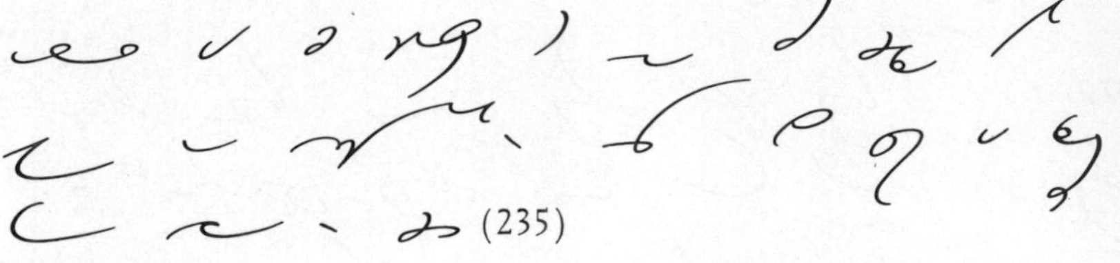

(235)

573.

(111)

574.

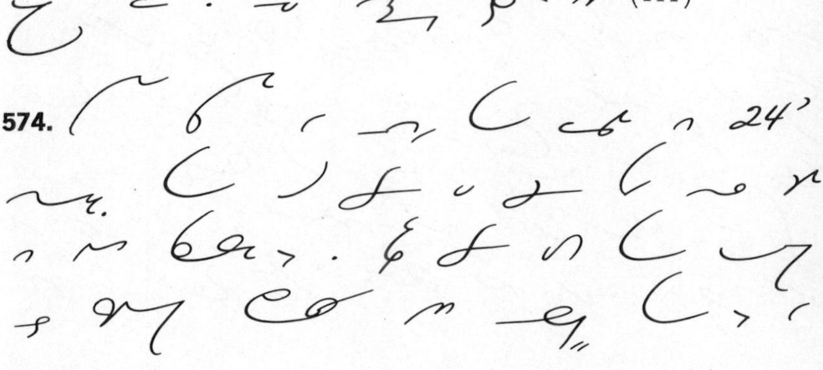

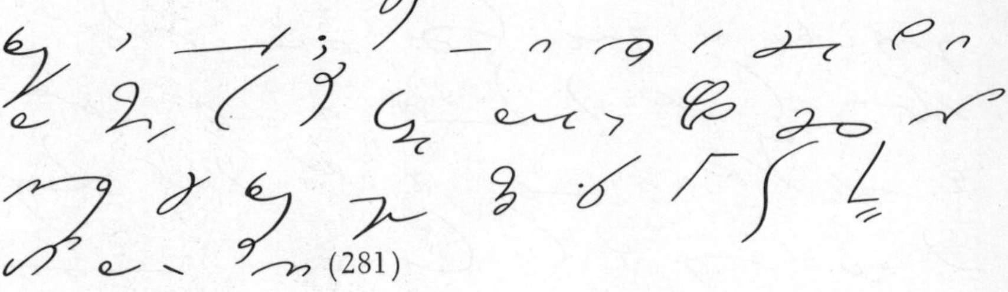

(281)

575.

(110)

Building Speed Through Reading

576. HINTS FOR SUCCESS

(231)

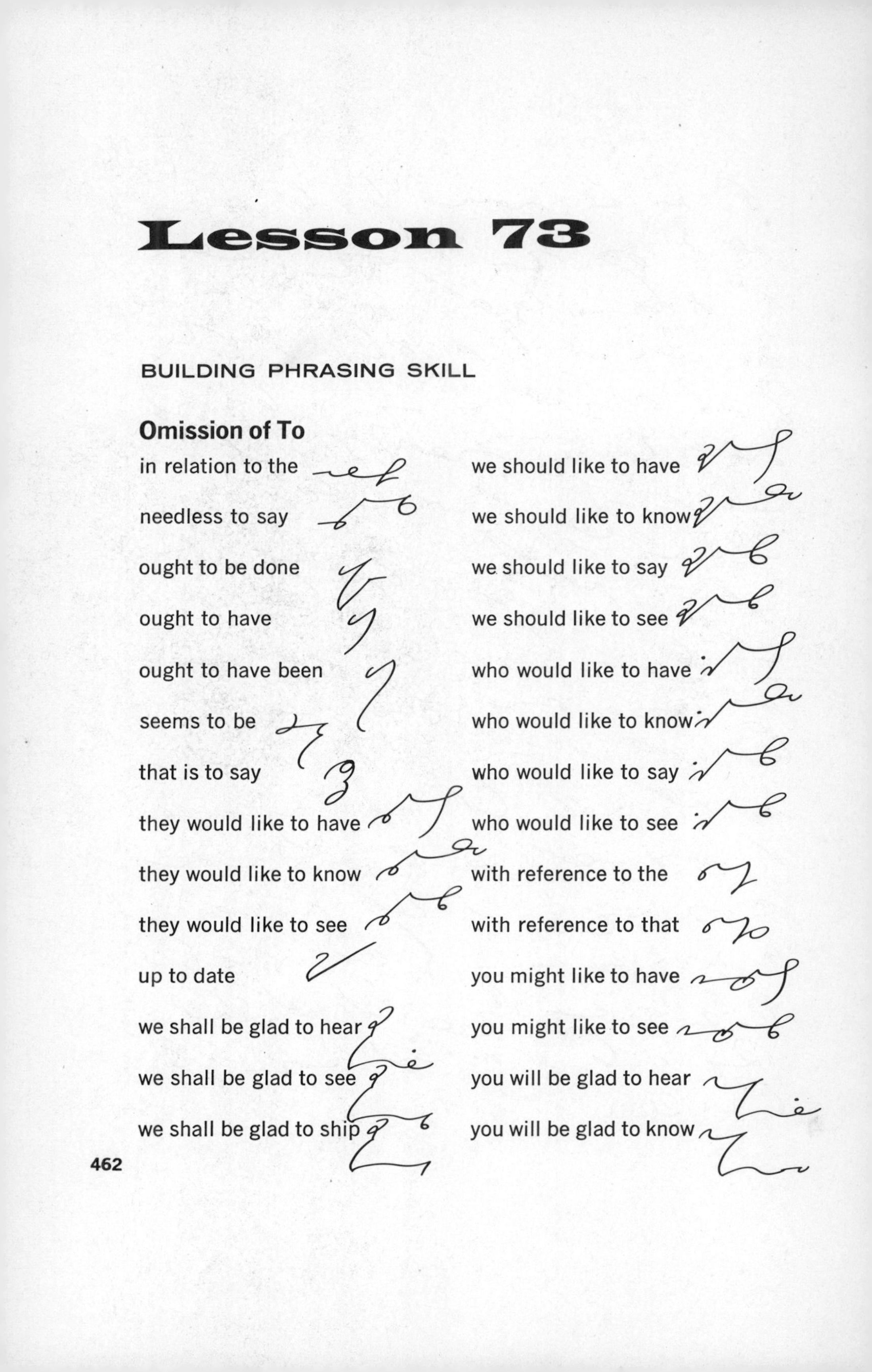

Lesson 73

BUILDING PHRASING SKILL

Omission of To

in relation to the

needless to say

ought to be done

ought to have

ought to have been

seems to be

that is to say

they would like to have

they would like to know

they would like to see

up to date

we shall be glad to hear

we shall be glad to see

we shall be glad to ship

we should like to have

we should like to know

we should like to say

we should like to see

who would like to have

who would like to know

who would like to say

who would like to see

with reference to the

with reference to that

you might like to have

you might like to see

you will be glad to hear

you will be glad to know

Brief-Form and Phrase Letters

577.

(186)

578.

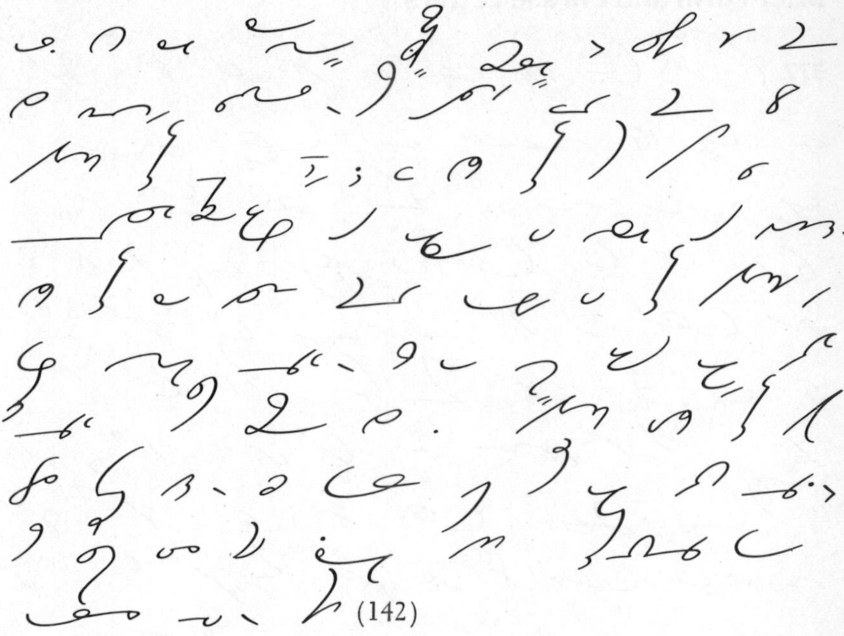

(142)

579.

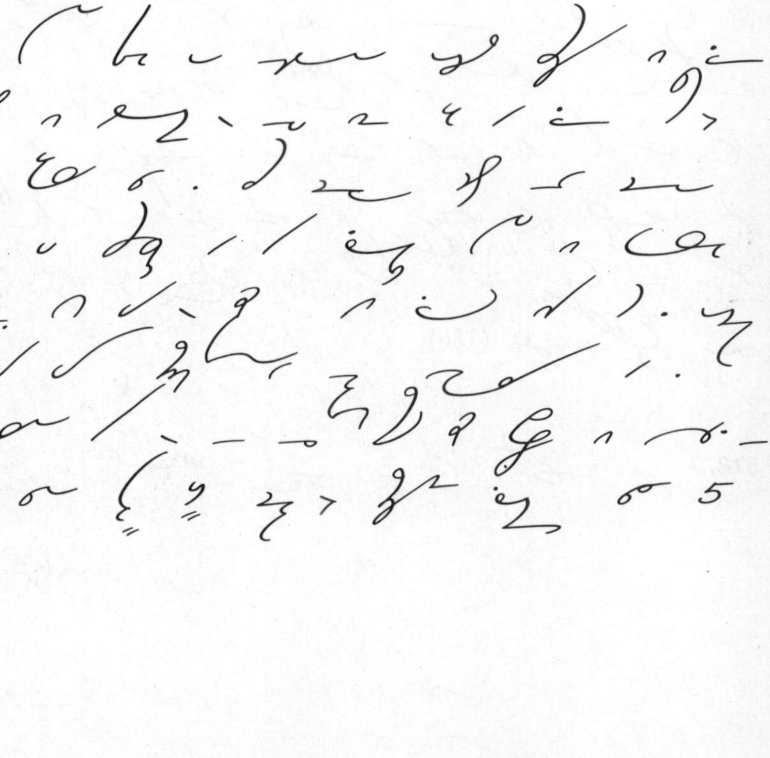

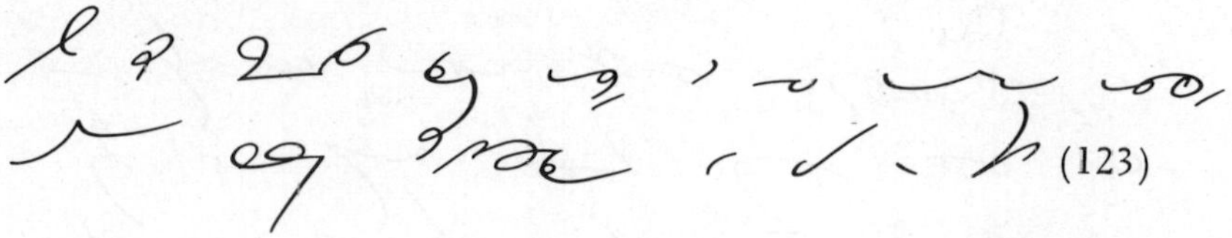 (123)

580. 

(134)

581. 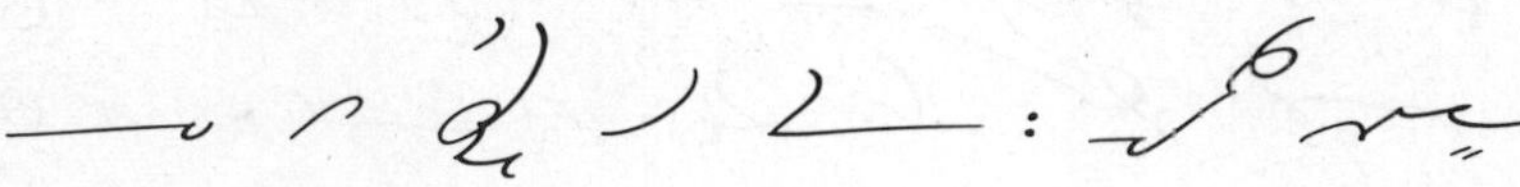

(119)

582.

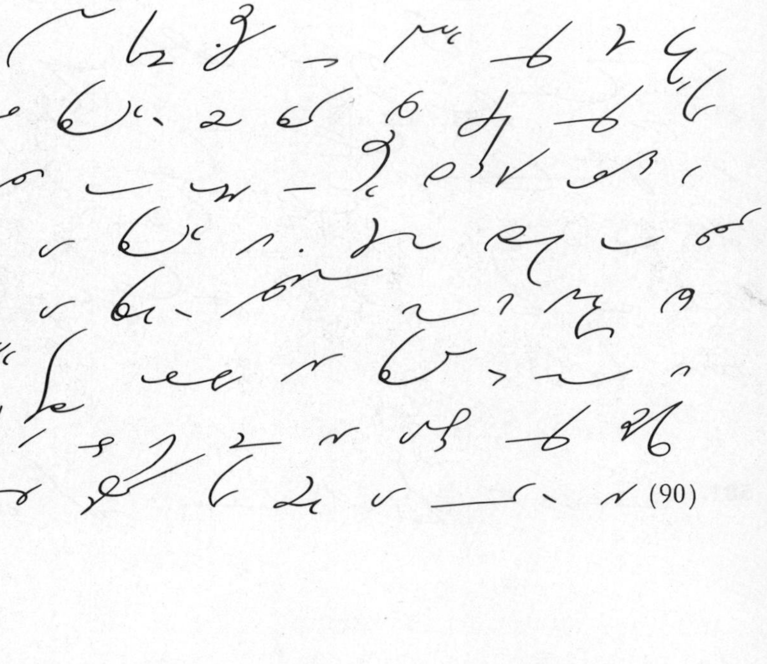

(90)

583.

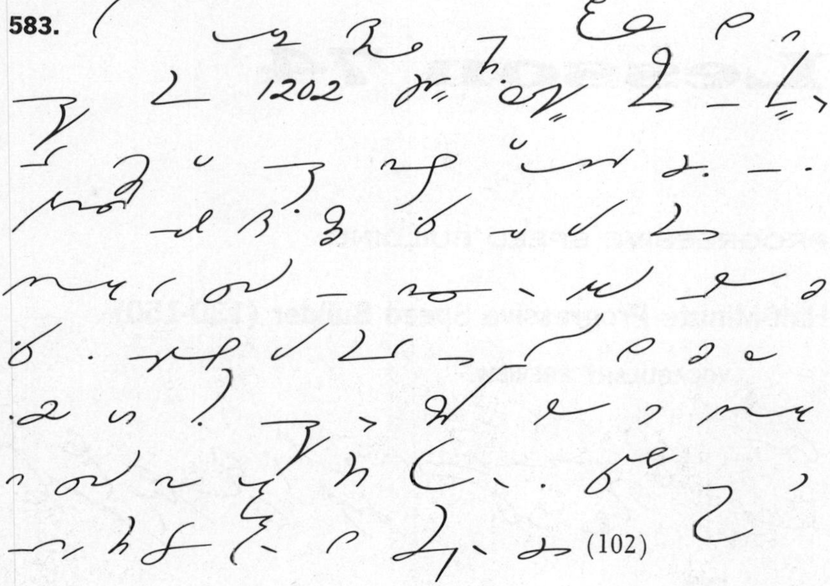

(102)

584.

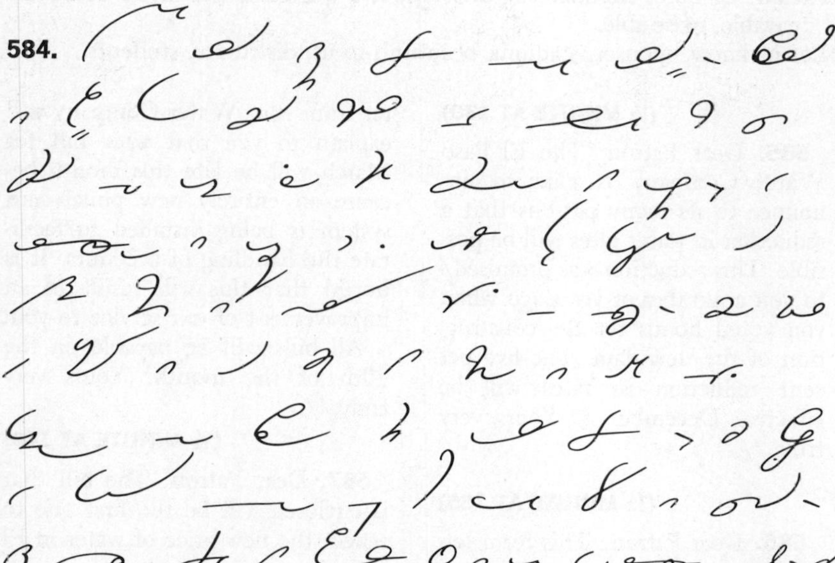

(106)

Lesson 74

PROGRESSIVE SPEED BUILDING

Half-Minute Progressive Speed Builder (130-150)

VOCABULARY PREVIEW

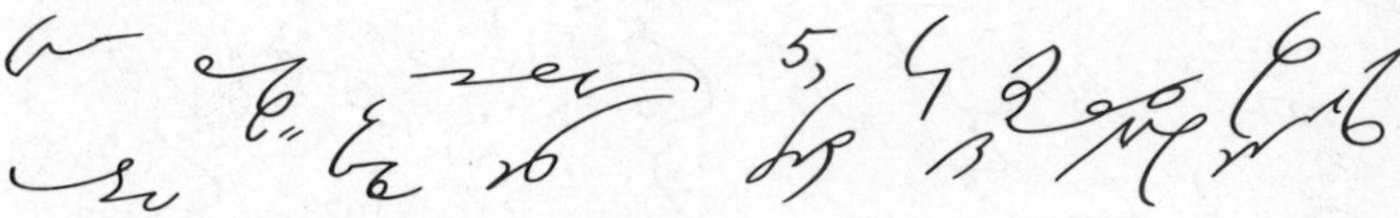

KEY

Patron, El Paso, number of years ago, five per cent, punch, to facilitate, payable, to be able.

Let us know, sponsor, stadium, beautiful, to us, distribute, students.

(½ MINUTE AT 130)

585. Dear Patron: The El Paso Water Company is glad to announce to its many patrons that a reduction in water rates will be possible. This reduction was promised/ to you a number of years ago when you voted bonds for the construction of the new dam. The five per cent reduction in rates will be effective December 1. Yours very truly,//

(½ MINUTE AT 135)

586. Dear Patron: This form letter from your Water Company will explain to you that your bill for March will be late this month because an entirely new punch-card system is being installed to/facilitate the handling of accounts. It is hoped that this will result in an improvement of our service to you.

All bills will be payable on the 20th of the month. Yours very truly,//

(½ MINUTE AT 140)

587. Dear Patron: The bill that is enclosed will be the first one to reflect the new price of water in El

Paso. We are pleased to be able to pass this saving on to you and hope that we may continue/to offer you improved services at lower rates.

If there should ever be a time when you are not pleased with our service, we hope you will let us know immediately. Sincerely yours,//

(½ MINUTE AT 145)

588. Dear Patron: In connection with the state fair to be held in Dallas next month, the El Paso Water Company, in co-operation with other water companies throughout the state, will sponsor a/water show each evening in the outdoor stadium. The show will feature the beautiful dancing waters that have become so popular in the East.

We hope you plan to attend the fair. Yours very truly,//

(½ MINUTE AT 150)

589. Dear Miss Gray: The El Paso Water Company has just issued an interesting booklet describing the services that we offer. It occurs to us that you might like to distribute this booklet to the/students in your class in business training. We shall be glad to supply you with as many copies as you have students.

To make it easy for you to request copies, we are enclosing a self-addressed postal card. Yours truly,//

Minute Progressive Speed Builder (120-140)

VOCABULARY PREVIEW

KEY

Extended, Oklahoma City, 30 per cent, directory, enthusiasm, project, activity, absorb.

Authorized, thanks, substantial, during the last year, standard, necessitated, adequate, faithful.

(1 MINUTE AT 120)

590. Dear Customer: Beginning July 1, your telephone company is offering another extension of its many services. This new service will make it/possible for you to enjoy your telephone even more than before. On that date, extended service dialing from Oklahoma City will go into effect, and you//will be able to dial direct any place within thirty miles of the city limits. This will increase by 30 per cent the number of places that you can call toll///

free. We are proud of this new achievement and hope that it will add to your pleasure as much as we think it will. Yours truly,

P.S. We are also sending you the new directory, (1)

(1 MINUTE AT 130)

591. Dear Customer: Have you enjoyed your new extended dialing service that the telephone company made available to you July 1? We are proud of this achievement and hope/you share in our enthusiasm.

Like any other new project, a number of troubles arose in connection with this service.

Now, we have to ask your help. The cost of new//lines, the increased activity in our controls, and other factors have added to our expenses to such an extent that we can no longer absorb them without a rate increase. We///have been authorized to increase telephone rates by 2 per cent.

I am sure that you will understand why this is necessary and will co-operate with us as you always have. Sincerely yours, (2)

(1 MINUTE AT 140)

592. Dear Customer: Thanks to you, we are now able to offer you better telephone service. Although we tried to keep instances of substandard service at a minimum, we know there were times/during the last year when it was necessary for us to give you less than our standard service. This was necessitated by our sincere effort to try to stay within the rates that had been in effect//for eight years.

Now the 2 per cent increase in rates is in effect, and we are able again to hire an adequate staff for serving you. If there are any extra telephone services that you///desire, be sure to call on us now and give us a chance to show you that we really wish to be your most faithful public servant.

By the way, have you seen the kitchen extension phone yet? Sincerely yours, (3)

Reading and Writing Practice

593.

(87)

594.

(301)

595.

(181)

596.

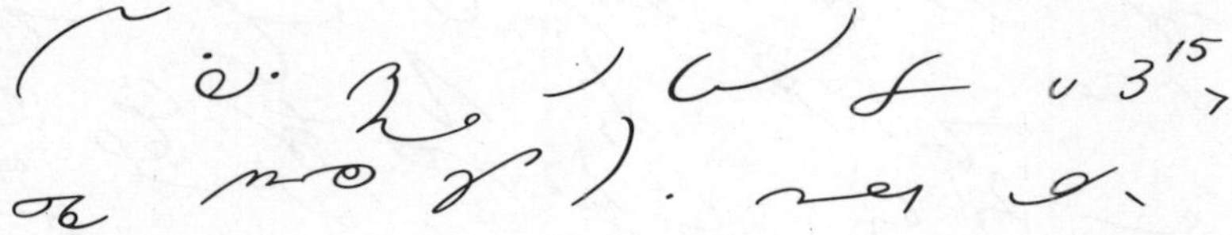

(113)

Lesson 75

BUILDING SUSTAINED SPEED

Five-Minute Speed Builder

The first letter is written to Mr. Samuel R. Roberts, 9248 Elm Street, Ames, Iowa. This letter and all the succeeding form letters were written by the Midwest Telephone Company.

VOCABULARY PREVIEW

KEY

Customer, deceased, facilities, thoroughly understand, burden, liberty, will you please.

Directory, sympathy, dial, Jacksonville, digit, nationwide, preparation, prefix.

Underhill, effective, serviceman, provided, demand, central, announce.

Thank you for your, trouble, prevented, however, your order, necessity, refund, as soon as possible, to connect.

597. Dear Mr. Roberts: It has been brought to our attention that our good customer, Mrs. Jane Roberts, 1417[1] Oak Street, Ames, Iowa, is now deceased.

We wish to offer our assistance in enabling the present[2] user of the service to dispose properly of the telephone facilities.

We thoroughly understand[3] that business matters are a burden at times like these, but we should very much appreciate your co-operation[4] in telling us what arrangements you desire.

We have taken the liberty of enclosing a form that, when[5] signed and returned to our office, will place the telephone in the name of the person wishing to continue the[6] service. Will you please sign the form in the manner in which you wish the service listed in our directory and[7] return it in the enclosed envelope.

May we offer our sincere sympathy in your time of sorrow; and, if[8] we may be of any further help, please call our Business Office. Yours very truly,

598. Dear Customer: We are pleased[9] to tell you that the new dial telephone office for the Mason Village area of the Jacksonville exchange[10] will be placed in service next March. At that time all Jacksonville telephone numbers beginning with the digit 7[11] will be changed in order to conform to the nationwide numbering plan. This change is being made in preparation[12] for Direct Distance Dialing, which is soon to come to your area.

The new dial telephone numbers for[13] your community will have the prefix UNderhill 7- and four other digits. The new numbers will appear[14] in a special directory, which is to be delivered shortly before the new numbers become effective.[15] Between now and that time a serviceman will call to make the necessary changes in the telephone. Also,[16] you will be furnished your new telephone number, with instructions as to when it is to be used.

This advance[17] notice is provided to give you general information about our plans. You will receive more detailed[18] information as the time for these changes draws nearer. Yours very truly,

599. Dear Customer: To take care of the increased[19] demand for telephone service, a new central office with the most modern equipment has been opened. A[20] group of FOrest and MAin numbers, including yours, will be changed and transferred to this new office in May.

A short time[21] before the date of change you will receive a special folder with your new telephone number and the exact date[22] on which it is to be used. After this change takes place, calls placed to your old number will be referred, for a limited[23] time, to your new number. The June Omaha Directory, to be delivered at the same time as the number[24] change, will contain the new telephone numbers.

We announce changes of this sort as far in advance as possible,[25] so that you may keep them in mind when making plans for the future. Thank you for your continued co-operation.[26] Yours very truly,

600. Dear Customer: This is to

acknowledge your letter regarding your telephone service.[27]

We are sorry to hear of the trouble you have had with your party line. We should like very much to furnish all[28] our customers with the type of service they desire and also to comply with their requests for changes to[29] another line when difficulty arises with the other party, but we are prevented from doing so because[30] of the lack of sufficient facilities.

We shall be glad, however, to talk with our other customer[31] on your line in an effort to obtain his co-operation in the use of the service, and we sincerely[32] hope that our efforts will result in a more pleasant condition for you. Yours very truly,

601. Dear Customer:[33] Completion of your order for telephone service has been delayed because of the necessity of installing[34] additional facilities.

We are sorry we cannot install your telephone service immediately,[35] but we assure you that everything possible is being done to provide the necessary service at the[36] earliest possible date.

Because of this delay in completing your order, we are returning the amount[37] of the payment you made at the time you applied for service. This refund will not have any bearing on our efforts[38] to provide you with service as soon as possible.

We will let you know just as soon as the facilities[39] are available to connect your telephone. Yours very truly, (793)

Reading and Writing Practice

602.

(100)

603.

(113)

604.

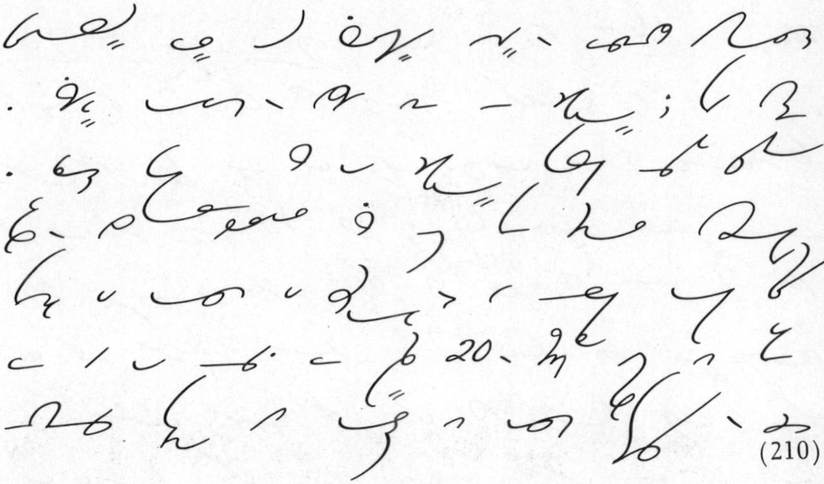

(210)

605.

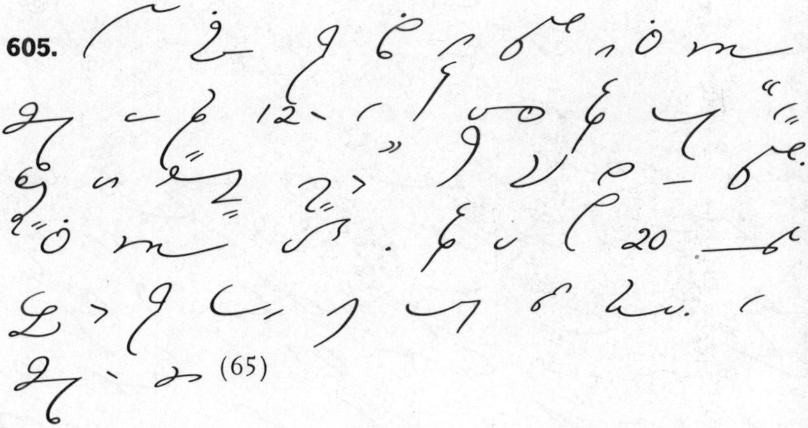

(65)

606.

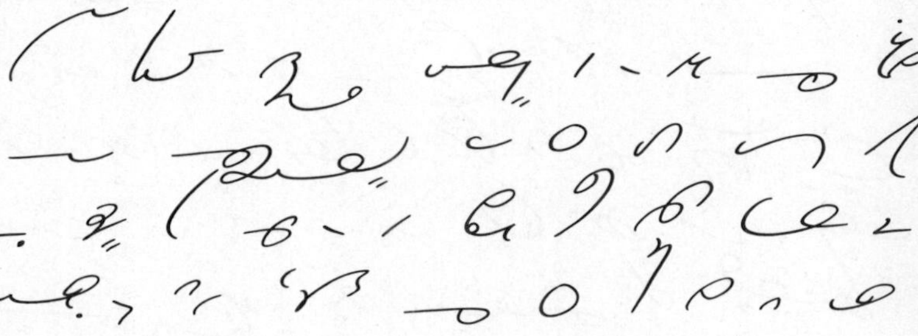

(210)

607.

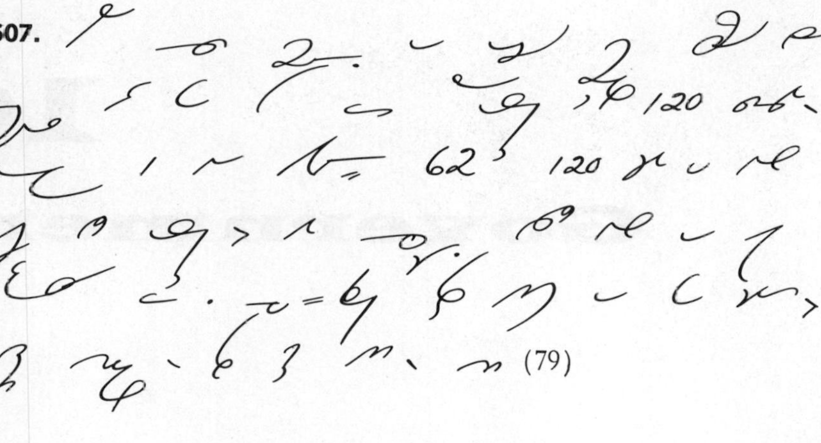

(79)

16

Government

Word Study for Chapter 16

GOVERNMENT

Note: Because of the frequency with which some of the expressions in the following list occur in government dictation, shortcuts are provided for them. Additional shortcuts will also be provided in the previews for Lessons 79 and 80. Learn these shortcuts well; they will be of great help to you in taking government dictation, especially Congressional Record dictation.

Administration. The persons collectively to whom are entrusted the execution of laws and the superintendence of public affairs.

Ambassador. An official representative of the highest rank accredited to a foreign government as the official representative of his own government.

Amendment. Any alteration made or proposed to be made in a bill or motion by addition, change, or omission.

Appropriation. Money that is, by formal action, set aside for a specific use.

Arbitration. The act of hearing and determining a cause between parties in controversy by a person or persons chosen by the parties, or appointed according to statutory authority.

Attorney General. The chief law officer of the state or of the Federal Government.

Bureau. A government department or office.

Bureaucrats. Members of a government system that has become narrow, rigid, and formal and that lacks initiative.

Candidate. A person who offers himself, or is put forward by others, as a contestant for an office.

Capital. The city in which government activities are concentrated.

Capitol. The building in which governmental bodies carry on their work.

Census. An official enumeration of the population of a country or of an administrative district of the country.

Civil Service. All branches of the public administrative service that are not military or naval.

Congressional. Pertaining to the Congress of the United States.

Constituent. Any citizen or resident of a district represented in a legislative body, considered with reference to the representative.

Consul. An official appointed by a government to reside in a foreign country, to care for the commercial interests of the citizens of the government making the appointment, and to protect its seamen.

Democrat. One who is a

member of the Democratic Party.

Diplomacy. The art and practice of conducting negotiations between nations.

Export (n). A commodity that is conveyed from one country to another in the way of traffic.

Immigration. The act of going into a country for the purpose of becoming a permanent resident.

Import (n). A commodity that is brought in by one country from another by way of traffic.

Inauguration. The act of inducting a person into office by appropriate ceremonies.

Joint Resolution. A resolution that is adopted jointly by the two branches of a legislative body.

Jurisdiction. The authority of a sovereign power to govern or legislate; also, the power or right to exercise authority.

Legislature. The body of persons in a state invested with the power to make, alter, or repeal laws.

Municipality. A town, city, or other district that has powers of local self-government.

Negotiation. Act or process of treating with another with a view to coming to terms, as negotiations for a treaty.

Nomination. Act of designating someone for an office or a duty.

Parliamentary. In accordance with, or permitted by, the rules and usages of Parliament, originally of Great Britain, but adopted by other governments.

Patriotic. Characterized or moved by love of one's country.

Politician. One actively engaged in politics.

Politics. The theory or the practice of managing or directing the affairs of public policy.

Ratification. The act of confirming or making legally operative.

Representative. A person who represents the people in a district in the House of Representatives. The term of office is two years.

Republican. One who is a member of the Republican Party.

Senator. A person who represents the people of a state in the Senate. Two senators are elected from each state and serve a period of six years.

Statute. A law enacted by the supreme legislative branch of a government.

Subcommittee. A part or a division of a committee.

Subsidy. A grant of funds or property from a government to assist in the establishment or support of an enterprise that is considered to be advantageous to the public.

Tariff. A duty imposed by a government on imported goods.

Lesson 76

BUILDING TRANSCRIPTION SKILL

Transcription English Pointers

HOW TO WRITE NUMBERS (CONCLUDED)

In dealing with numbers there are several important points to be remembered, regardless of whether the numbers are written as words or as figures. These points are illustrated below.

1. *Dates.* Dates are always important and must be unmistakably clear no matter how they are written.

a. The following forms are preferred in *business correspondence:*

August 15, 1958 (*not* Aug. 15, nor Aug. 15th, nor August fifteenth)
Monday, September 1 (*not* Mon. nor Sept.); either: the 10th of June or the tenth of June (that is, when the day precedes the month)
June, 1949, will be remembered as the record dry month. (Comma follows the year in a sentence.)

Notes: (1) When the signs of the ordinals *(th, st, d)* are used, *d* is preferred to *nd* or *rd* (as in *2d, 3d*), and no period follows the ordinal sign.

(2) In Army and Navy correspondence, as well as in letters from foreign countries, this form is often used: *12 September 1958.*

(3) The styles *5/10/58* and *5-10-58* are not to be recommended even for informal notations, for they are easily misunderstood. The reader of the foregoing date, for example, may hesitate and wonder whether May 10 or October 5 was intended.

b. In *social correspondence and formal documents,* these forms are common:

the thirtieth of June
the thirtieth day of June
June the thirtieth

nineteen hundred fifty-eight (in legal documents: one thousand nine hundred and fifty-eight)

2. *Money*. When amounts of dollars and cents are to be written, it is likewise extremely important that they be absolutely clear and accurately written.

a. When an amount consists of dollars alone – when no cents are given – no ciphers and no decimal point is needed; as, *$84* (not *$84.* nor *$84.00*).

In tabulations, however, if any amount in a column contains cents, ciphers should appear with amounts that do not, in order to even up the columns.

Note that in tabulations the dollar sign should be at the margin of the widest figure.

$ 25.00
150.50
5.05

b. In a series of amounts in sentences, the dollar sign should be used with each amount.

Articles on this table: $10 to $15 (not $10 to 15).

c. Amounts of cents are preceded by a dollar sign and a decimal point if the amounts of cents occur in a series of other amounts consisting of dollars and cents.

Please limit your purchases not to exceed $8 for a blouse, $5.50 for a hat, and $.75 for rubbers.

d. Care is necessary in placing a decimal point in the correct place in amounts in cents; *.25 cents* means 25/100ths of a cent, or ¼ cent.

3. *Percentages*. The following points are important to remember when you are dealing with percentages.

a. The words *per cent* (two words are preferred by Webster, but the single word *percent* is also correct) are used when the percentages do not occur too frequently.

I would say that 99 per cent of business letters are typewritten.

b. In accounting, statistical, technical, or other work where percentages occur frequently, the % sign is used.

The legal rate of interest in New York State is 6%, in California 7%, and in Michigan 5%.

The eyewash prescribed comes in both a 0.25% and a 1% solution.

Transcription Speed Builder

608.

(164)

609.

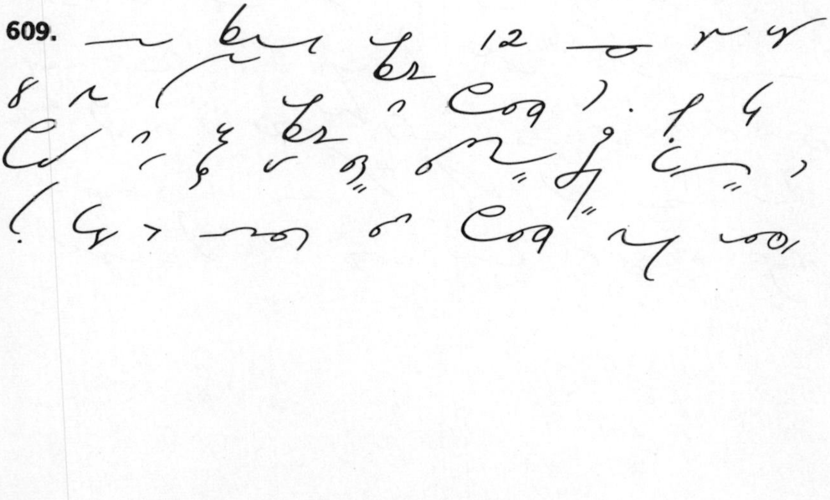

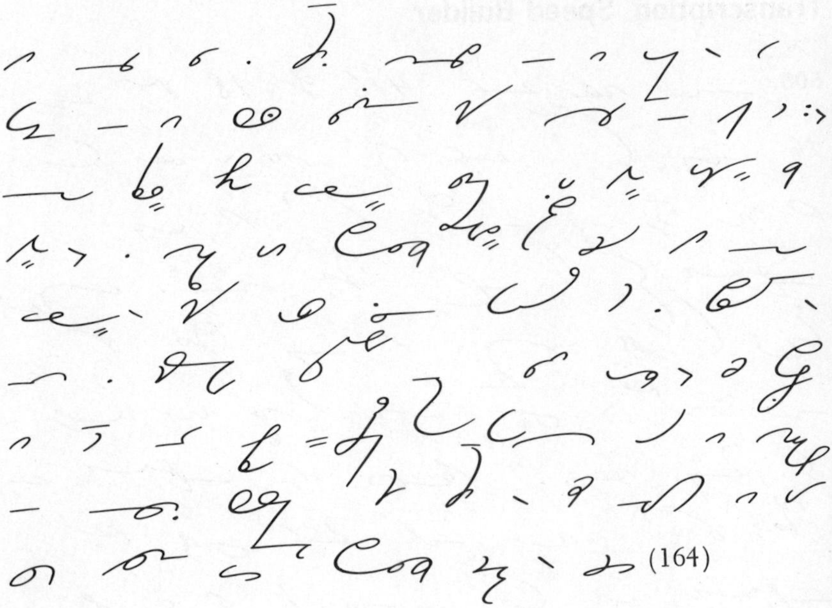

(164)

610.

(299)

611.

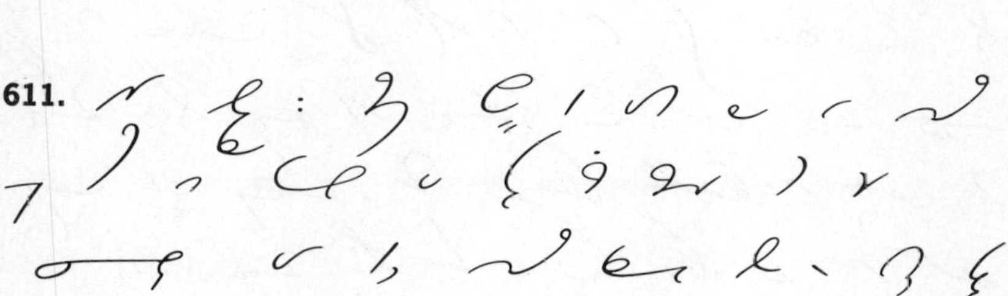

Lesson 77

MASTERING SHORTHAND THEORY

Numerals

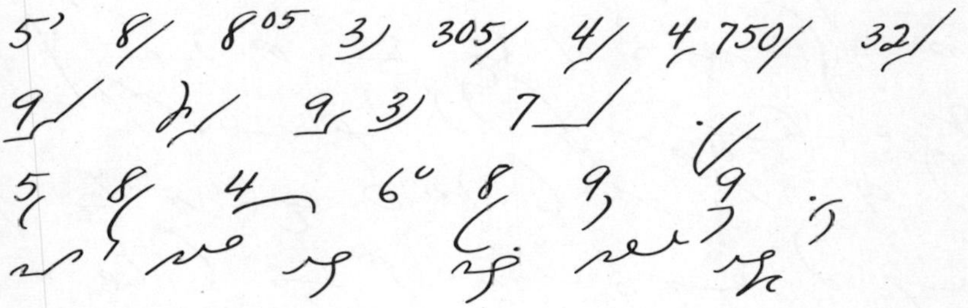

KEY

5 cents, $8, $8.05, $300, $305, $4,000, $4,750, $32,000.
$900,000, few thousand dollars, $900,300, $7,000,000, a billion dollars.
5 pounds, 8 bushels, 4 gallons, 6 o'clock, 8 barrels, 9 feet, 900 feet, a thousand feet.
One or two, two or three, three or four, one-half, two-thirds, three-fourths.

Reading and Writing Practice

612.

(70)

613.

(133)

614.

1956-57

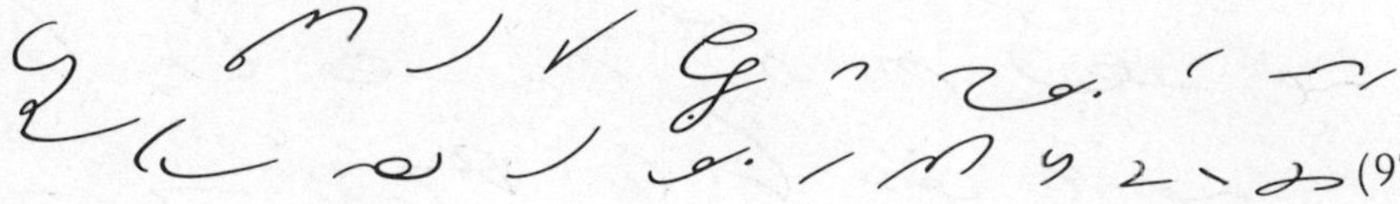
(97)

615.

(112)

616.

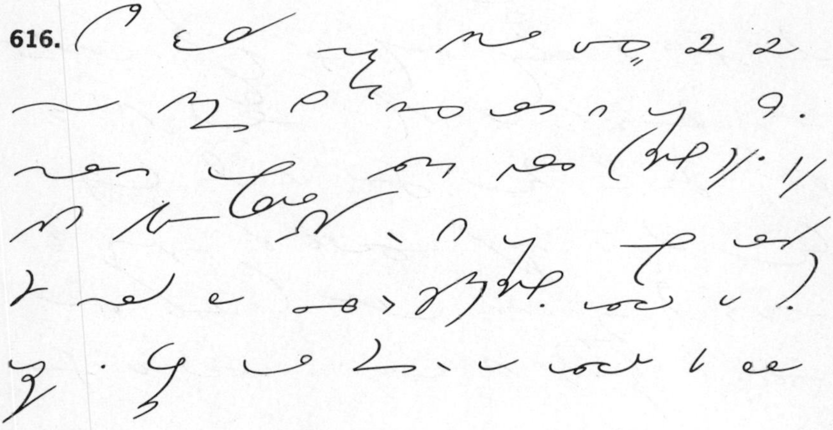

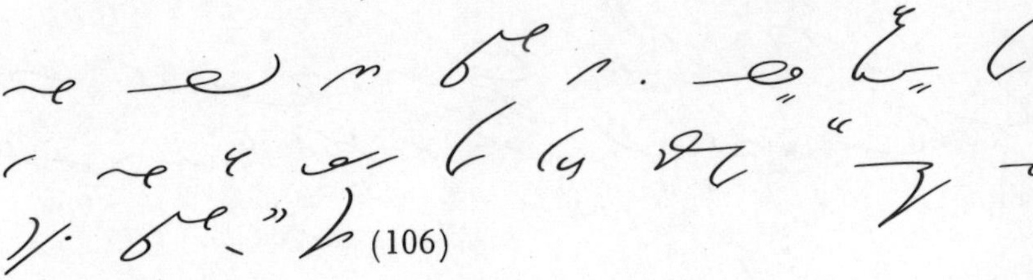
(106)

617. 

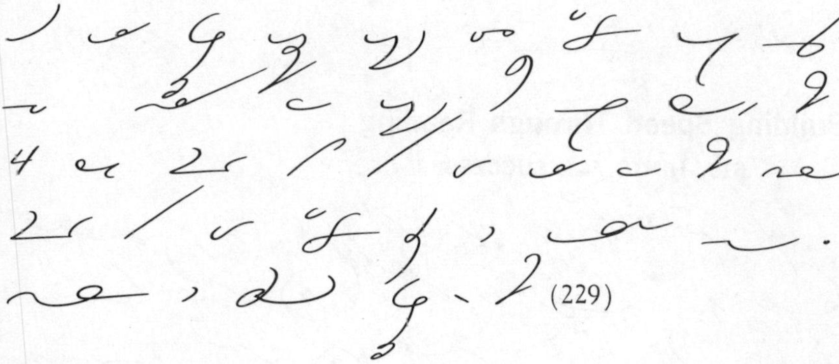

(229)

618.

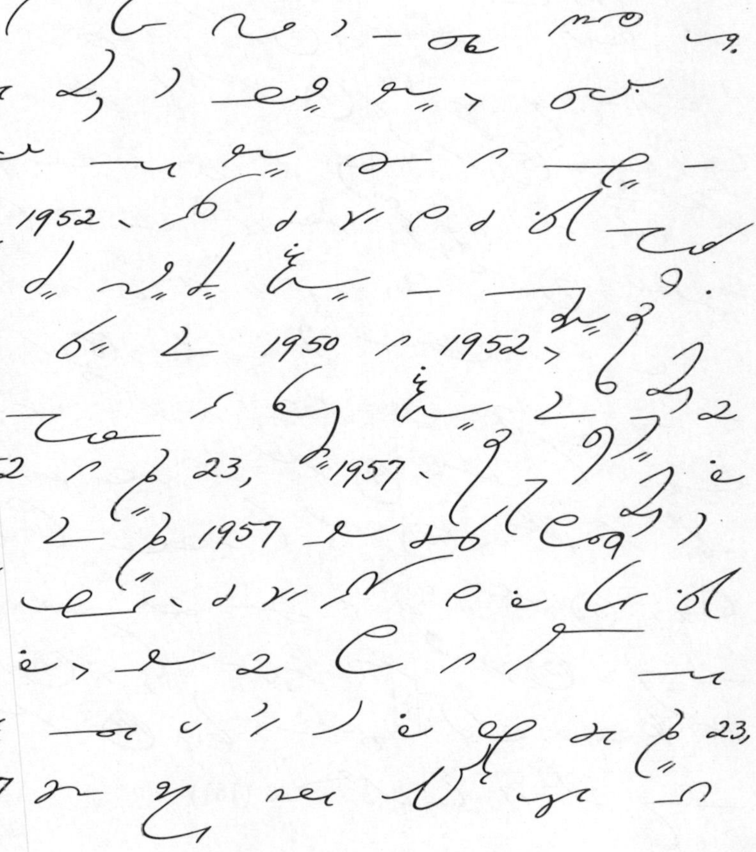

(195)

Building Speed Through Reading

619. HINTS FOR SUCCESS

(181)

Lesson 78

BUILDING PHRASING SKILL

And, Any, and If

and hope that	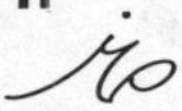	if any	
and I am		if anything	
and I am sure		if it isn't	
and I will		if it was	
and I will be		if that	
and let us		if these	
and that the		if they are	
and was		if they cannot	
and which		if they would	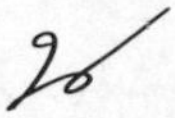
any more than		if you are sure	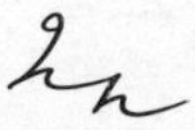
any one of our		if you decide	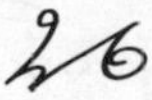
any one of these		if you know	
any others		if you think	
any way		if you want	

Reading and Writing Practice

SHORTCUT PREVIEW

KEY

Mr. President, amendments, appropriations, appropriated, committee, Senate, bureau, Secretary of the Treasury.

620.

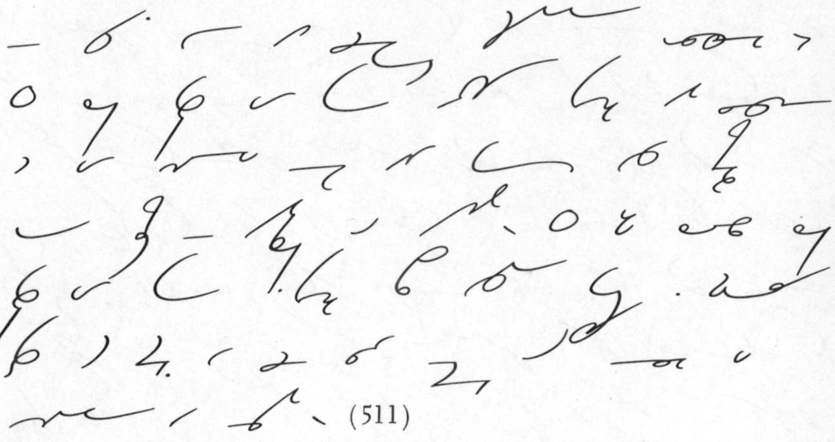

(511)

SHORTCUT PREVIEW

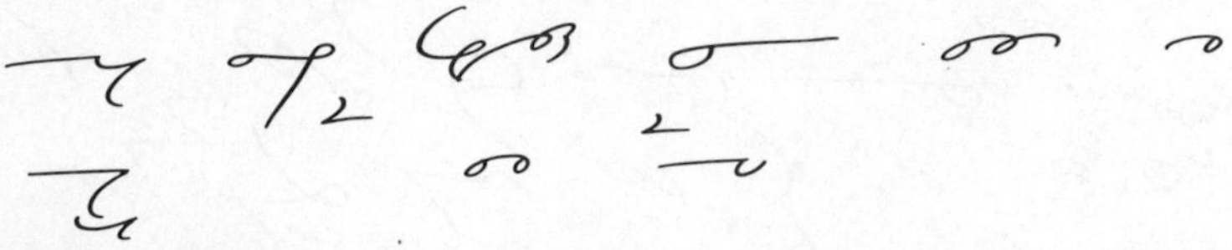

KEY

Mr. President, emergency, President of the United States, amendment, economic, committee, employers, Senator, economy, Senator from Missouri.

621.

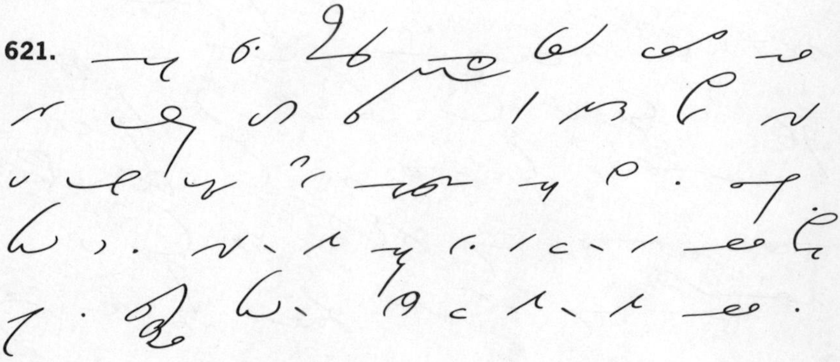

(531)

Lesson 79

PROGRESSIVE SPEED BUILDING

Half-Minute Progressive Speed Builder (130-150)

VOCABULARY PREVIEW

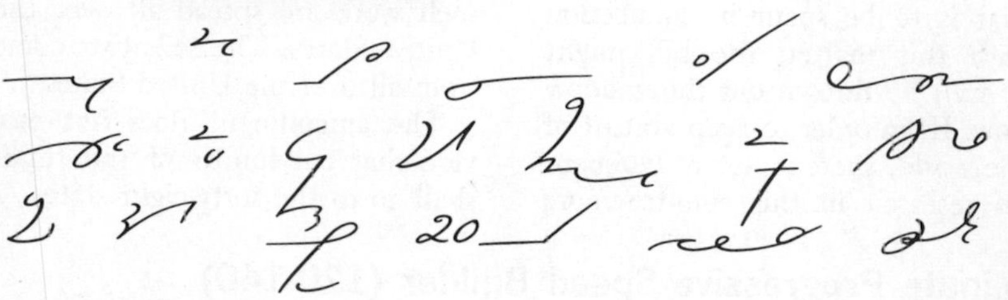

KEY

Mr. President, Senators, unduly, amendment, included, argument.
Gatherings, Senator from Ohio, projects, Foundation, everyone else, Senator from New Jersey, disagree.
Offered, substantial, majority; $20,000,000; correlate, scientists.

(½ MINUTE AT 130)

622. Mr. President, it seems to me that Senators are becoming unduly excited about the amendment. A similar provision was included in the bill last year./On the question involved, the argument that has just been heard has been proceeding for two years in conferences, in meetings where witnesses were heard, and in many public gatherings.//

(½ MINUTE AT 135)

What the Senator from Ohio said is true, or it might be true if the major projects could be left entirely in the hands of the Foundation.

I may say that, after two years of/discussion with Senators and everyone else, this is about the first time the Senator from New Jersey and I seem to disagree. At least, we have not yet come to an agreement.//

(½ MINUTE AT 140)

Why the provision was not placed

in the bill again this year I do not know, because last year there was agreement on the amendment as offered by the Senator from Maine. The Senate agreed by a/substantial majority.

If there were to be only these major projects, and if only $20,000,-000 were to be spent, the argument by the Senator might be well taken.//

(½ MINUTE AT 145)

But, Mr. President, if that is all that is to be spent in connection with this matter, the bill might as well be thrown out the window now. If, in order to keep abreast of the world, there is not to be/spent on research in this country more than $20,000,000 a year, then we had better quit now. Although there will be great projects, the real purpose of the bill is to correlate all types and forms of research.//

(½ MINUTE AT 150)

As certain scientists who were in the gallery yesterday and who may be in attendance today will tell you, Mr. President, these projects were not developed entirely at any one place. The scientists/engaged in such work are spread all over the United States. The scientists come from all over the United States.

The amendment does not provide that one-fourth of the funds shall go to the forty-eight states.//

Minute Progressive Speed Builder (120-140)

VOCABULARY PREVIEW

KEY

Mr. President, amendment, modifies, clarify, allocations.

Distribute, President of the United States, Senator from Alabama, conceive, quantity, commitments, survival.

Atmosphere, included, legislation, accomplish, America.

(1 MINUTE AT 120)

623. Mr. President, I spoke at some length on this amendment when it was offered on August 15. Since that date, I have added a section to the amendment, which in/no way takes away from or modifies its original purpose, but which may serve to clarify the conditions by which the President shall be required to put allocations/into effect.

It was thought by some that, if the President took this action, it would be necessary to distribute through normal channels of trade the//balance of the supply, even though there might be some complaints from the trade. The amendment would leave it entirely up to the President of the United States at that time.(1)

(1 MINUTE AT 130)

I think it is a good amendment, and it was suggested by the Senator from Alabama. I do not think I could conceive of its being applied unless there was a definite/need. This makes it perfectly clear.

Mr. President, we all know it is certain that the President will move immediately into the application of agreements for/the distribution of these materials.

We also know that a sufficient quantity of these materials must be assured to all who need them.

This amendment deals only/// with the distribution of available supply after prior commitments have been made. It deals particularly with the survival of small business in such distribution.(2)

(1 MINUTE AT 140)

The pending bill pays a great deal of lip service to small business. In it are several references to creating a desirable atmosphere for small business. Such thinking in behalf of/small business has been included in previous legislation, some of which is still in effect; but I can assure the Senate that nothing has been done to help small business.

Mr. President,/there is no provision in this bill that assures to small business a fair position in the distribution of scarce materials.

To accomplish this purpose, the amendment provides that any//allocation covered by this bill must utilize the normal channels of trade.

America has become great as a result of the independence of action afforded the small business.(3)

Reading and Writing Practice

SHORTCUT PREVIEW

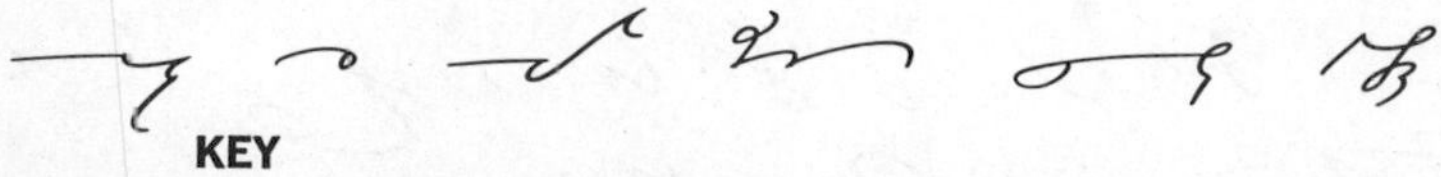

KEY

Mr. Speaker, Committee, millions of dollars, session of Congress, administration, Treasury of the United States.

624.

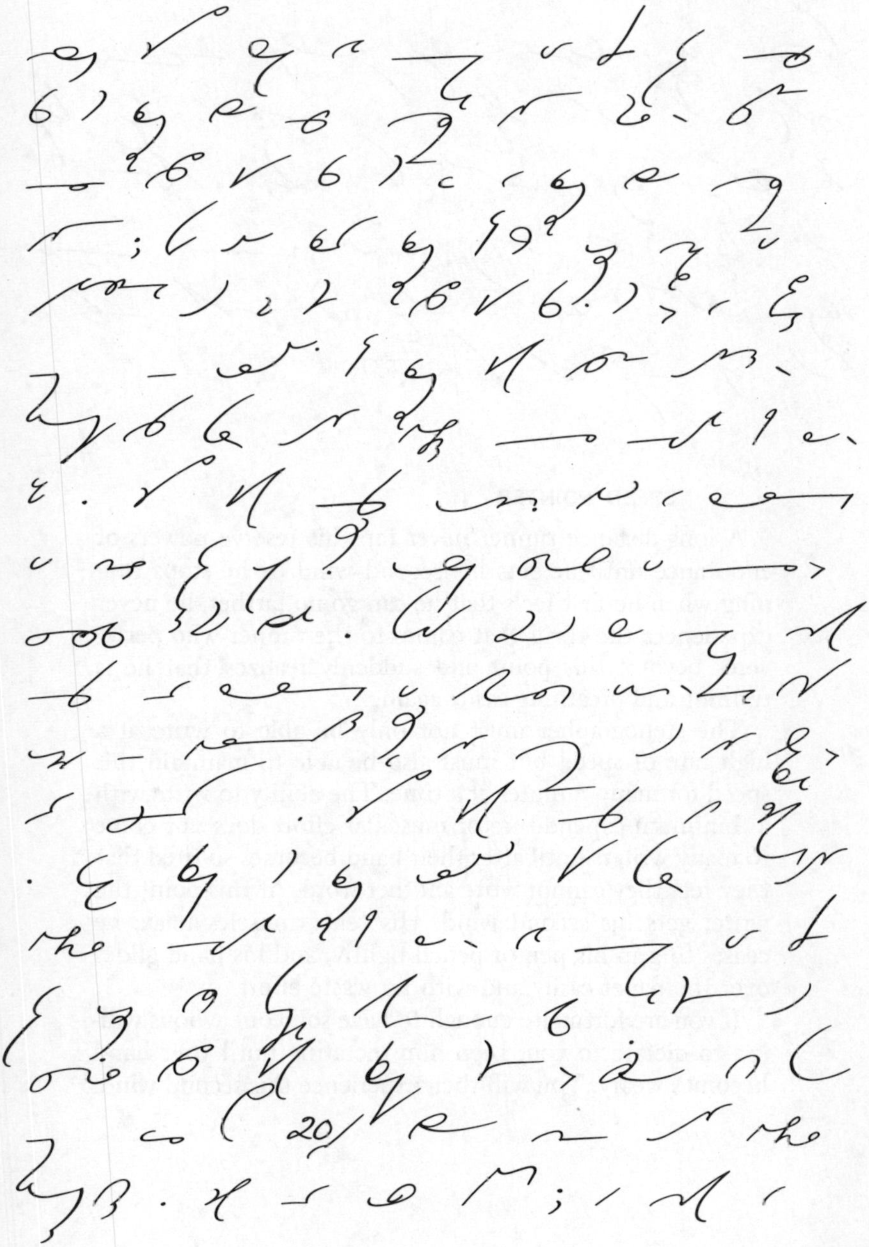

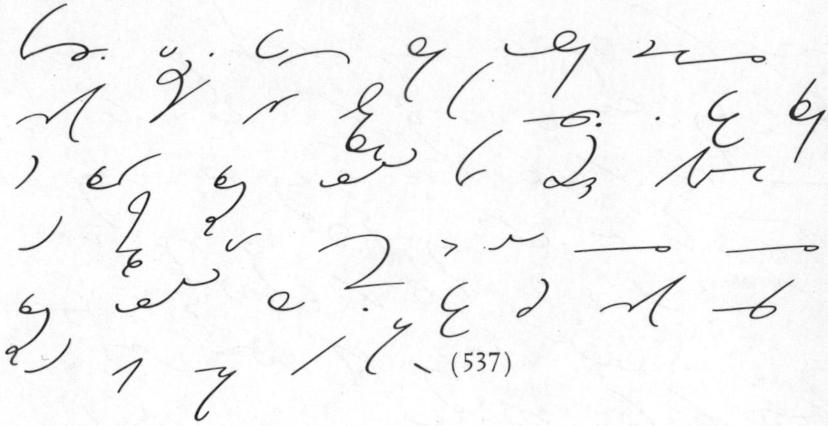

(537)

SPEED POINTER

A long-distance runner never taps his reserve powers of endurance until he gets his second wind. If he stops running when he first feels that he can go no farther, he never experiences the thrill that comes to the runner who perseveres beyond this point and suddenly realizes that he is running and breathing easily again.

The stenographer must not only be able to write at a high rate of speed but must also be able to maintain this speed for many minutes at a time. The ability to write with a minimum expenditure of muscular effort does not come to many writers until after their hand becomes so tired that they feel they cannot write another word. At this point the writer gets his second wind. His tense muscles relax; he ceases to grip his pen or pencil tightly; and his hand glides over the paper easily and with no waste effort.

If you are fortunate enough to have someone who is willing to dictate to you, keep him dictating until your hand becomes weary. You will then experience this second wind.

Lesson 80

BUILDING SUSTAINED SPEED

Five-Minute Speed Builder

VOCABULARY PREVIEW

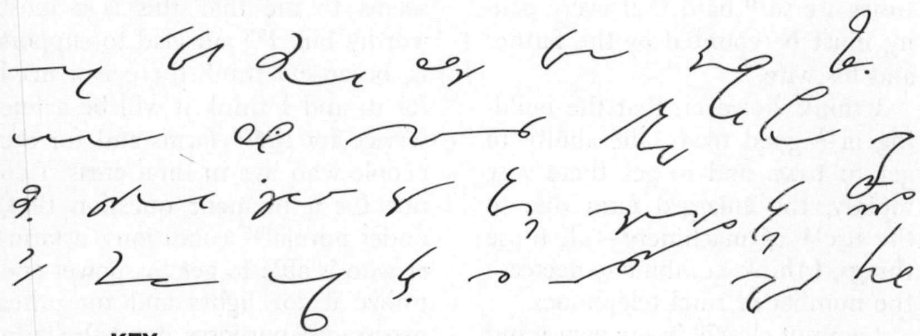

KEY

Mr. President, transportation, facilities, earliest, partner, subscribers, adjoining.

Rural, areas, great many of the, dispensed, ability, combine.

Existing, utilities, whether or not, sustain, speculation, constructed, population, worthy.

Support, for a moment, will be able, possessing, committee, undoubtedly, competent, jurisdiction.

625. Mr. President, I think what has been said has much to do with the question. The roads, too, have been greatly improved,[1] transportation facilities are better, and a farmer can go to town by automobile in ten or fifteen[2] minutes from almost any part of a county.

One of the earliest business ventures in which I engaged[3] was the establishment and operation, along with a partner, of a small telephone system in a small[4] town. We had a number of subscribers scattered throughout the county and even in an adjoining county. With[5] the coming of the depression years, which came early in our section, the telephone subscribers in the rural[6] areas rapidly dropped off. Whereas we had something over 100 or 150 telephones[7] at one time in the rural areas, at the first sign of a depression, a great many of the subscribers[8] discontinued the service. Then a few years later there was a further dropping off, because the telephone, while[9] vitally necessary and highly useful in the rural areas, can be dispensed with when times are so[10] hard that every penny must be counted by the farmer and his wife.

I think, however, that the building of[11] good roads, the ability to get to town and to get there very rapidly, the enlarged farm due to the use[12] of machinery – all those things, I think, combine to decrease the number of rural telephones.

I am not clear[13] in my own mind whether the existing small system, which is a purely private enterprise in my state, would be[14] affected by the provision we are considering. We have a utilities commission that would pass on the[15] question of whether or not the service was needed. I am not at all sure that the small companies would have[16] a right of recourse, because under our system the judgments reached are final. It is not possible to get around[17] them if there is a bit of evidence to sustain the findings.

It, therefore, would be most proper, it seems to[18] me, if it were said that the findings may be questioned in the proper court. That would take the matter out of the realm[19] of speculation and would, in my judgment, improve the bill.

I do not think there is any lack of need for[20] telephone service in the rural areas. As lines are constructed in the rural areas, and there is a[21] tendency to rebuild the farm homes and perhaps to increase the rural population, there is a very great[22] need for rural telephone service. Properly safeguarded, it seems to me that this is a most worthy bill. I[23] am glad to support it, because I think there is a need for it; and I think it will be a fine service for the[24] farms and for the people who live in rural areas. I do not for a moment question that, under normal[25] conditions, a farmer who is able to get his power and utilize it for lights and for other necessary[26] purposes about the farm will be able to take care of his telephone bills. There has been a very great change[27] in the rural life in America in my section of the country. This is one of the things that would add to the[28] comfort and convenience of the people and give assurance to the farm population residing in the rural[29] areas of possessing the necessary conveniences and facilities to enable them to[30] protect themselves and their families. The bill would enable them to get medical attention quickly and to[31] obtain broken parts for their farm machinery without delay, and it would aid them in many other ways. While[32] the committee undoubtedly believes that the administrators' findings of fact would not be final, I express[33] the view that they may become final. It could be easily provided in the bill that they might be reviewed[34] in any competent court having jurisdiction of the subject matter. (694)

Reading and Writing Practice

SHORTCUT PREVIEW

KEY

Senator from Wyoming, parliamentary, legislation, chairman of the committee, emergency.

626.

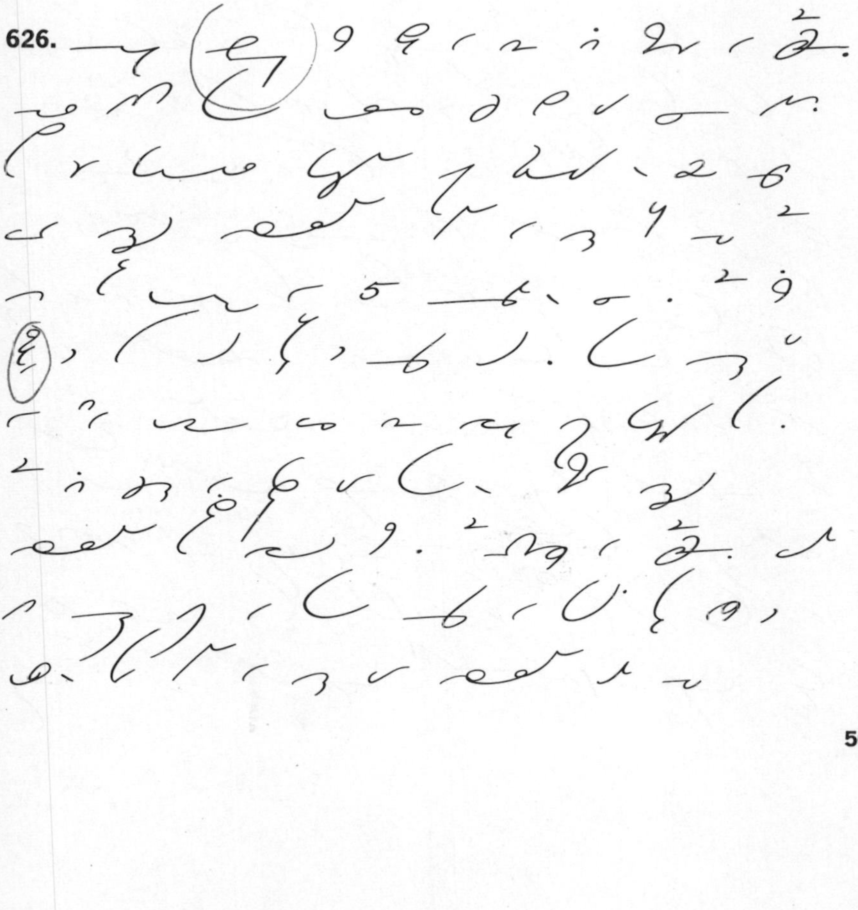

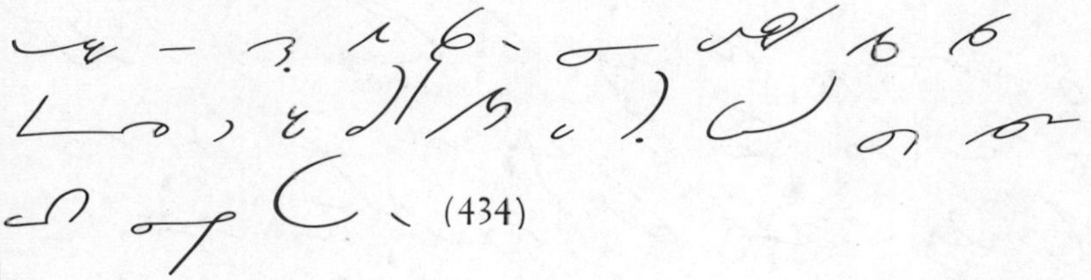 (434)

SHORTCUT PREVIEW

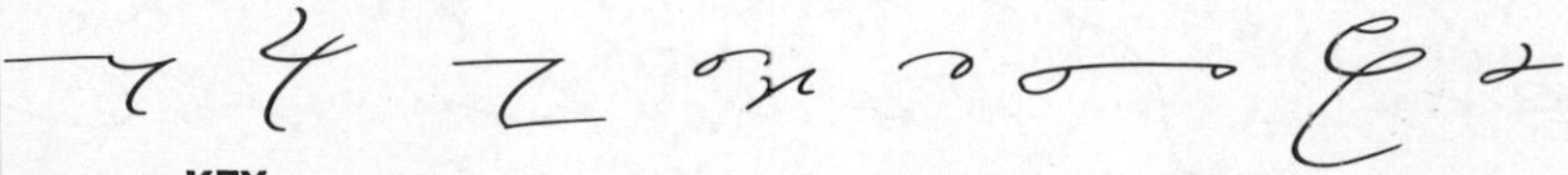

KEY

Mr. President, Federal Reserve Board, employment, economists, committee, amount of money, appropriation bill, Senate.

627.

(381)